ISSUES IN CONTEMPORARY ISLAMIC THOUGHT

SHAYKH TAHA JABIR AL-ALWANI

on

Issues in Contemporary Islamic Thought

•

COMPILED FROM
THE AMERICAN JOURNAL OF
ISLAMIC SOCIAL SCIENCES

THE INTERNATIONAL INSTITUTE OF ISLAMIC THOUGHT
LONDON • WASHINGTON

THE INTERNATIONAL INSTITUTE OF ISLAMIC THOUGHT
P.O. BOX 669, HERNDON, VA 22070, USA

LONDON OFFICE
P.O. BOX 126, RICHMOND, SURREY TW9 2UD, UK

ISBN 1-56564-414-X paperback
ISBN 1-56564-415-8 hardback

Cover Design by Shiraz Khan
Typesetting by Jay Willoughby

Printed in the United Kingdom
by Biddles Limited, King's Lynn

CONTENTS

FOREWORD i

INTRODUCTION iii

PART I: ISLAMIC THOUGHT 1

SOME REMARKS ON THE ISLAMIC AND THE SECULAR PARADIGMS OF KNOWLEDGE 3
- Introduction 3
- *Tawḥīd* 5
- Revelation 5
- Purifying Methodology from Negative Elements 7

TOWARD AN ISLAMIC ALTERNATIVE IN THOUGHT AND KNOWLEDGE 9
- Introduction 9
- The Present State of Thought 9
- The Present State of Knowledge 10
- The Present State of Muslim Education 11
- The Present Civilizational State of the Ummah 12
- Toward an Islamic Alternative 13
- Toward a Strategy for Knowledge 15

THE RECONSTRUCTION OF THE MUSLIM MIND: THE ISLAMIZATION OF KNOWLEDGE 21

THE ISLAMIZATION OF KNOWLEDGE: YESTERDAY AND TODAY 26
- Introduction 26
- The Reality and Importance of the Islamization of Knowledge 30
- The Six Discourses 35
- The Islamization of Knowledge Undertaking 42

THE ISLAMIZATION OF THE METHODOLOGY OF THE BEHAVIORAL SCIENCES 49
- The Shariʿah Sciences 55

PART II: ISSUES IN ISLAMIC JURISPRUDENCE 63

THE CRISIS OF THOUGHT AND IJTIHAD 65
- Introduction 65
- What Do We Mean by Ijtihad? 66
- Ijtihad: The Ally of Jihad 66
- Right or Wrong, the *Mujtahid* Is Rewarded 67
- The Lexical and Technical Meanings of Ijtihad 68
- How Can the Problems of *Taqlīd* and Dependency Be Overcome? 68

Taqlīd and the Stagnation of the Muslim Mind .70
The Origins and Beginnings of *Taqlīd* .70
Taqlīd and the Ummah's Crisis .71
Taqlīd: A Natural (Original) Condition or a Deviation? .71
Taqlīd: For Muslims or Non-Muslims? .73
Sources of Knowledge .74
How Did Muslims Sink to the Level of *Taqlīd*? .76
The Consequences of *Taqlīd* .77
Conclusion .80

Taqlīd and Ijtihad (Part One) .82
The Polemics of Ijtihad .82
The Dynamism of Ijtihad in Restructuring Islamic Methodology *(al-Minhāj)* .83
A Panoramic Assessment of Ijtihad's Progression .85
The Traditional Role of the *Faqīh* .89
Unresolved Issues of Ijtihad .90

Taqlīd and Ijtihad (Part Two) .97
The Lexical and Technical Meanings of *Taqlīd* .97
The Legal Ruling on *Taqlīd*: The Companions and *Taqlīd* .98
The Imams and *Taqlīd* .100
The Forms of *Taqlīd* as Defined by the *Fuqahā'* .102

The Crisis in *Fiqh* and the Methodology of Ijtihad .108
Introduction .108
The Decline of Ijtihad .110
Figh and Intellectual Freedom .112
Figh in the Ottoman Empire .114
Significant Features of the Ottoman Period .114
The Crisis of Figh .115
A Methodological Perspective: Is the Door of Ijtihad Closed? .120
Conclusion .123

The Role of Islamic Ijtihad in the Regulation and Correction of Capital Markets .129
Ijtihad .132
Economics and the Capital Market .138
Conclusion .156

PART III: HUMAN RIGHTS .159

The Testimony of Women in Islamic Law .161
The Evidence of the Sunnah .170

Naturalization and the Rights of Citizens .187

The Rights of the Accused in Islam (Part One) .196
Introduction .196
Historical Development of the Judiciary .197
Judicial Organization and Its Sources .201
The Accused .202
Principles That Must Be Considered .205

The Rights of the Accused in Islam (Part Two) 212
The Right to a Defense 212
The Accused's Seeking Legal Defense from a Lawyer 213
The Accused's Right To Remain Silent and To Be Heard 215
Statements Made under Duress 215
Confessions Obtained by Deceit 220
The Accused's Free Confession and Right to Retract 221
The Accused's Right to Compensation for Mistakes in Adjudication 222
Conclusion 223

PART IV: POLITICAL THOUGHT 227

Political Science in the Legacy of Classical Islamic Literature 229
Challenges Facing Muslim Scholars 230
Steps along the Way 231

Missing Dimensions in Contemporary Islamic Movements 235
Introduction 235
The Contemporary Islamic Discourse: Missing Dimensions 236
Testimony and Responsible Witnessing (236) • Missing Dimensions: A Discovery Procedure (237) • Toward a Comprehensive Awareness (238) • Universal Crisis, Universal Solution (238) • The Tendency To Compromise or Reject: Its Origins (239) • The Need for Methodology (240) • The Acquisition of Power: Is It a Solution? (240) • Constituents of Well-Being in the Past (241) • Wrong Analogy (242)
The Ummah's Decline: Underlying Causes 242
Secularism vs. Reform (242)
Toward a Comprehensive View of the Revelation and the World 245
New Logic (245) • Methodological Understanding and the Combined Reading of the Qur'an and the Universe (246) • Impasses of Contemporary Muslim Action (250) • Collective Ijtihad and Collective Action (251) • Going It Alone: The Pitfall of Exclusiveness (252) • The Genesis of Exclusive Thought (255)
Summary 256
Toward a Resolution of the Crisis 258
Comprehensiveness (258) • The General Approach to Humanity, Time, and Place (259) • Purposefulness (259) • Universality (260) • Obstacles on the Way to Islamic Universality (261) • Islamic Universality vs. Western Universalism (262) • Contemporary Western Civilization: Background and Distinguishing Features (263) • The Logic of Entering into the Peace of Islam (266) • Determinants of the Crisis in the Western Mind (268)
Course of Action 270
Determinants of the Crisis in the Muslim Mind (271)
Concluding Remarks 275

Authority: Divine or Qur'anic? 280

INDEX 295

Foreword

The International Institute of Islamic Thought (IIIT) takes great pleasure in presenting this collection of articles and essays originally published in the *American Journal of Islamic Social Sciences* and the London Office's Occasional Papers series by a prominent scholar well-versed in the issues under consideration, Dr. Taha Jabir al-Alwani. Collectively, they offer the author's valuable insights and observations gained from long experience in dealing with these issues and the process of regaining the civilizational and intellectual role of the Ummah.

Dr. al-Alwani, is a graduate of al-Azhar University and a leading figure in promoting a comprehensive approach to knowledge that combines the two readings of the Revelation and the real-existential, as well as a holistic and disciplined inquiry into contemporary issues challenging Islamic thought. The book will be of interest to scholars, researchers, and all those interested in understanding the intellectual crisis facing the Muslim world.

The IIIT, established in 1981, has served as a major center to facilitate sincere and serious scholarly efforts based on the vision, values, and principles of Islam. Its programs of research, seminars, and conferences during the last twenty-four years have resulted in the publication of more than 250 titles in English and Arabic, many of which have been translated into other languages.

We would like to express our thanks to Jay Willoughby for all of his efforts in producing this book for publication, and for working closely with the editorial team at the IIIT London Office in incorporating their comments and suggestions for completion of the work. May God reward them and the author for all their endeavors.

Rabi` II 1426
June 2005

Dr. Anas S. al Shaikh-Ali
Academic Advisor
IIIT London Office, UK

Introduction

In this book, we present the reader with a collection of studies, all of which deal with reform-oriented and goal-oriented Islamic intellectual issues and belong to the same intellectual approach: The Islamization of Knowledge, which has been active since the 1950s, promotes knowledge and thought, as well as their accompanying elements and philosophy, dedicated to achieving a culture that widens one's intellectual horizons and expands the opportunities for cultured and civilized interaction between cultures and civilizations.

First established in a Muslim environment, its engaged Muslim intellectuals and scholars focused on rethinking, critiquing, and analyzing the most pressing Islamic intellectual issues. Success in this endeavor will enable them to take an active role in laying the foundations for an Islamic revival that will empower all Muslims to engage with their times; share with all people their vision and efforts to solve global crises; achieve peace and security; strengthen the effort to protect human rights, the environment, and minorities; support freedom and resist the elements of terrorism and criminality; improve interfaith relations through dialogue, cooperation, and joint efforts to rebuild the values that allow people to maintain their humanity; and gradually achieve cooperation among all members of humanity: "O people, We have created you from a male and a female and made you into peoples and tribes so that you may know one another. Verily, the most honorable among you is the most pious among you. Verily, God is All-Knowing and All-Wise" (49:13).

Indeed, both the "religion and path of Abraham" can convince all people of their common origin from one father and one mother, and that their external differences exist for a great reason, which is understood by those who posses knowledge. Earth is a vast abode for humanity, and differences in location do not change this fact. Rather, dispersal encourages people to cooperate and exchange benefits so that everyone will receive his or her share of the bounties and blessings of this collective house.

The Islamization of Knowledge has successfully raised educated Muslims' awareness of the need to review the many issues related to their heritage and to rebuilding Islamic education in order to produce a Muslim personality that can reform Muslim concepts, ideas, and practices. These reformed concepts, ideas, and practices can then fulfill the expectations of a community whose values and civilization enable it to play an important role in improving human relations and building shared foundations of scholarship among all people.

The reader will find a variety of articles dealing with the crises and intellectual problems that the Muslim Ummah must solve before it can move forward. One chapter analyzes ijtihad's role and history, since our intellectual problems cannot be solved without the scholars' use of independent reasoning and creativity. Another chapter discusses imitation (*taqlīd*). Here, the author calls upon Muslim scholars and intellectuals to abandon imitation and to stop favoring the past over the present when trying to solve modern problems. There is also a chapter on human rights that focuses on cases in which the individual is weak and helpless, such as when he or she is accused of some crime in a court of law.

Another chapter addresses the testimony of women and points out that many of the issues concerning Muslim women must be removed from the habits and practices that arose during the development of Islamic jurisprudence. This chapter also provides a model for understanding the Qur'an, one that differs from the legalistic and *fiqhī* mentality that interprets everything in terms of what is permitted and what is prohibited, and what is subject to legislative rules and foundations. In addition to such legalities, the Qur'an actually encompasses social and individual advice and guidance, as well as a system of ethics that shows people how to interact with each other properly.

This chapter also raises the issue of how to interpret the controversial verse 2:282, which deals with the large difference between a woman's leadership (over the community) and her testimony (authority over a limited individual matter). The author considers her testimony within the context of all of the issues raised in the verse and reveals the lack of any evidence differentiating a woman's testimony from that of a man's. Her testimony is not a titular honor as much as it is an attempt to help the legal system understand events as they truly are. Any testimony that gives the judge a better understanding of the case being heard is valuable.

These chapters represent a vision that urges the Muslim Ummah to review its heritage and reformulate many of its aspects, as well as to establish a critical and curious mindset among its members. When taken together, these chapters present a reformist project calling upon Muslim intellectuals and scholars everywhere to comprehend the vast breadth and depth of the crisis in Muslim thought today. In addition, they point out the necessity of solving this crisis so that the Ummah may experience a revival and fulfill its role among the nations of the world.

We pray that this rich set of studies will be useful and beneficial to the reader.

IIIT

Part I:

Islamic Thought

Some Remarks on the Islamic and the Secular Paradigms of Knowledge

INTRODUCTION

By the time secularist thought had succeeded, at an intellectual level, in challenging the authority of the Catholic church, its roots had already taken firm hold in western soil. Later, when western political and economic systems began to prevail throughout the world, it was only natural that secularism, as the driving force behind these systems, should gain ascendency worldwide. In time, and with varying degrees of success, the paradigm of positivism gradually displaced traditional and religious modes of thinking, with the result that generations of Third World thinkers grew up convinced that the only way to make "progress" and reform their societies was to follow the way of the secular West. Moreover, since the West had begun to progress politically, economically, and intellectually only after the Catholic church's influence had been marginalized, people in the colonies believed that they would have to marginalize the influence of their particular religions in order to achieve a similar degree of progress.

Under the terms of the new paradigm, turning to religion for solutions to contemporary issues is an absurdity, for religion is viewed as something left over from humanity's formative years, from a "dark" age of superstition and myth whose time has now passed. As such, religion has no relevance to the present, and all attempts to revive it are doomed to failure and are a waste of time.

Many people have supposed that it is possible to accept the western model of a secular paradigm while maintaining their religious practices and beliefs. They reason that such an acceptance has no negative

This "reflections" article first appeared in the *American Journal of Islamic Social Sciences* 12, no. 4 (Winter 1995): 539-44, and was translated by Yusuf Talal DeLorenzo. It has been slightly edited.

impact upon their daily lives, so long as it does not destroy their places of worship or curtail their right to religious freedom. Thus, almost every contemporary community has fallen under the sway of this paradigm. Moreover, this paradigm has had the greatest influence on how different peoples perceive life, the universe, and the role of humanity. In addition, it can provide them with an alternative set of beliefs (if needed) and suggest answers to the ultimate questions.

Throughout this twentieth century and most of the last, Muslims have taken it upon themselves to reconcile the western vision of life, humanity, and the universe with their own, or to reconcile the Islamic vision of the same with the precepts of the western vision. As a result, many practicing Muslims have inclined toward rationalizing whatever appears to challenge their constructs or contradict their concepts of the universal nature of positivism and the secular paradigm. For example, we have seen some Muslims equating jinns with microbes, angels with electrons, or prophets with geniuses! To such apologists, Islam touches only the "spiritual" life of its followers and thus may be considered another link in the rusty chain of "religions." For such "thinkers," the concepts of *shūrā* (consultation) and *khilāfah* (vicegerency, stewardship) correspond with western ideals of democracy and republicanism, while socialism and social justice are represented by zakah!

In short, the crisis of the Muslim mind and the absence of intellectual creativity or an ijtihad (deduction)-based mentality have stymied the development of a contemporary Islamic paradigm of knowledge. In fact, the entire matter has been ignored, with the result that the distinguishing features of such a paradigm have yet to be identified. Moreover, in the Muslim world there are two streams of education. The first stream, which produces the Muslim world's technical experts, scientists, social scientists, intellectuals, and public opinion makers, is based on and functions completely within the secular positivist paradigm. The second stream, perhaps more akin to a backwater, is the religious education stream. However, the sources of this stream owe more to tradition than to any understanding of the parameters of a truly Islamic paradigm of knowledge. For centuries, this stream of education has been able to do no more than repeat itself, by offering the same commentary on the same texts in the same disciplines of fiqh (Islamic jurisprudence), *uṣūl* (the sources of Islamic jurisprudence), Hadith (the Prophet's (ṢAAS)[1] actions and sayings), and *tafsīr* (Qur'anic commentary).

The Islamization of Knowledge undertaking seeks to develop an Islamic paradigm of knowledge that will serve as an alternative to the secular positivist paradigm that presently dominates the arts and sciences. Such an alternative combines Islamic and universalistic perspectives; addresses the intellectual and conceptual problems of all humanity, not just of Muslims; and includes a *tawḥīd*-based[2] reconstruction of the concepts of life, humanity, and the universe. What, then, is this Islamic paradigm of knowledge, and what are its basic components?

TAWḤĪD

The Islamic view of knowledge takes as its starting point the concept of *tawḥīd* (unicity, unity) in God's (ṢWT)[3] divinity and attributes. In fact, the entire edifice of the Islamic paradigm of knowledge stands on the foundation of *tawḥīd*. The epistemological aspects of *tawḥīd* are manifested via God's attribute of absolute knowledge and His teaching humanity that which it did not know. Moreover, God created within humanity the capacity to learn, teaching Adam "the names" of things, endowing human beings with the aptitude to read and write, and instilling within them a natural sense of curiosity about themselves and their surroundings. He also sent messengers to present His revelation and explain, by means of scripture, all matters connected to the Unseen. In other words, He made it possible for human beings to expend their energies on making sense of the physical world, harnessing its power for the common good, uncovering its laws and mysteries, and developing methodologies for dealing with revelation.

REVELATION

Both the Qur'an and the Sunnah represent sources of revealed knowledge that complement the natural universe. In addition, revelation may be taken as a creative source of belief, thought, worldview, and conceptualization. Revelation also gives the necessary order to establish human concepts; clarifies the relationships between God, humanity, and the universe; and then regulates these in such a way as to develop an integrated *tawḥīd*-based society. The Sunnah clarifies and elaborates on the Qur'anic epistemic methodology by linking the Prophet's example and the Qur'an's values so that these may be applied to the actuality of changing circumstances. By means of this methodology, humanity may transcend the dilemma of the relative and the absolute, and of the real and the ideal.

In addition to revelation, there are other sources and means of knowledge, such as reason, the senses, intelligence, intuition, and experience (including experimentation and observation). The Islamic paradigm of knowledge augments its sources with several principles and fundaments that are essential to its comprehensive and encompassing nature. Among these are *khilāfah* and *amānah* (responsibility for society) as the guiding factors in determining the meaning of life for humanity, a worldview that regards this world and the next as a single continuum, and a belief that intellectual activity is a religious and social responsibility for which the individual may be rewarded or punished. A very close relationship exists between knowledge and values, which lends the attribute of purposefulness to knowledge and, in turn, makes individuals responsible for distinguishing between useful and useless knowledge. At the same time, the Islamic paradigm of knowledge lends itself to academic activity at various levels. The Prophet, for example, once said: "Be a scholar or a student, but beware of the third category [ignorance], for that leads to destruction." In this way, the spread of knowledge was assured, because no individual or class could claim a monopoly over it.

The Islamic paradigm enjoys a harmonious relationship with human nature (*fiṭrah*), which enables human beings to erect certain intellectual standards. It is with this context in mind that we can understand the saying: "Question your own heart [and rely on what it tells you], even if the so-called authorities tell you something else." This paradigm also includes many fundamental characteristics that can help bring about a truly global and universalistic human outlook. Among these are humanity, utility, harmony, positivity, stability, globality, universality, methodology, intermediacy, comprehensiveness, guidance, spirituality, expansiveness, and openness.

Owing to the linkage that exists in the fine relationship between God and humanity, between this world and the next, and between the religious and the worldly life, this paradigm is not subject to closure. This explains how the Islamic paradigm can be simultaneously selective and comprehensive, and how it can adapt itself to whatever is positive and avoid whatever is negative in knowledge. Ultimately, all of this will result in the establishment of an intellectual criteria that will link knowledge with values, higher purposes, and universal principles.

The positivistic secular paradigm boasts of its analytical proficiency, which is quite impressive. However, analysis and deconstruction are not to be undertaken merely for their own sake, but rather in order to comprehend what has been analyzed and to correct what has gone wrong. Although the secular paradigm has made its analysis and deconstructed its subjects, it has proven to be extremely limited in its utility, because it has not produced a program of successful reconstruction. While it has been effective in explaining situations, the explanation is only as good as the intellectual goals that it serves. Thus, when the goals are limited or restricted to certain parameters of inquiry, the resulting benefits must necessarily be limited as well.

The oneness of humanity enables the Islamic paradigm of knowledge to effect constructs. God states in the Qur'an: "O people! Verily, We have created you from a male and a female, and have made you into nations and tribes, so that you might come to know one another. Verily, the noblest of you in God's sight is the one who is most heedful among you" (49:13); "He has created you out of a single soul, and from it He fashioned its mate" (39:6); and "Nor have We sent you (O Prophet) save as [an evidence of Our] grace toward all the worlds" (21:107). Moreover, the Islamic perspective on the essential oneness of the universe further enables its paradigm to develop constructs.

PURIFYING METHODOLOGY FROM NEGATIVE ELEMENTS

The Islamic paradigm of knowledge protects methodology from speculation and whim. As a result, the Islamic creed can serve as a protection from all such elements, for it leaves no scope for accepting anything that originates outside the ecclesiastically established sources. This is important, for even up until our own time humanity has been unable to rid itself or move beyond speculation, whim, caprice, and the like.

According to the Islamic paradigm of knowledge, human knowledge is enriched by knowledge of the divine, so that people are always aware of God's assistance and never have the sense of being left entirely to their own devices. Therefore, the attitude so haughtily touted by the secular paradigm, that the Unseen has no epistemological value, is rejected by the Islamic paradigm. Instead, Muslims are fortified by the confidence coming from their reliance on the two most important sources of knowledge: revelation and the universe.

The Muslims' association with prophecy and its revelational legacy adds a dimension of universality, humanity, and ethics to their intellectual orientation. In addition, *tawḥīd* and the acceptance of the divine as a source of knowledge prevent Muslims from placing undue dependence upon the self (with its vain and overweening tendencies) and from seeking to hide knowledge from others. A further benefit of *tawḥīd* is that it purifies espistemological issues through the constant scrutiny and revision demanded by the dynamic of ijtihad and the *tawḥīdī* rejection of any ultimate other than God. Thus, whatever is considered final by an individual or an entire generation of Muslims will not necessarily remain the final word for another individual or a following generation; others will always have the right to open or reopen any issue for further consideration, refinement, or rejection.

Tawḥīd also averts the misuse of knowledge as power, for the paradigm includes the concept of a participatory and sharing community of knowledge that, by its very nature, precludes any such monopolization and elitism. The fundamental sources of knowledge are available to everyone, as are the methodological steps necessary for dealing with them. Furthermore, the connection between knowledge and values precludes any notion of a need to adhere to established epistemological norms, and thus opens the door to continued examination and analysis. All of this, in turn, ensures that people will not live under the impression that they have found all of the answers, when, in fact, they possess knowledge of little more than the outward aspects of the life of this world.

The paradigm's religious aspect also ensures that knowledge is linked with every aspect of human life, be it past, present, future, or in the Hereafter, and that it can contemplate eternal truths and endow them with a greater, purer, and more comprehensive relevance. It is this aspect that ensures that knowledge remains elevated and never succumbs to the baser inclinations, artistic or otherwise. All of this springs from humanity's role as *khalīfah* (steward), and from its natural dignity, humanness, trust, and responsibility for improving society.

The above should be viewed as no more than brief preliminary remarks intended to explain the differences between the Islamic and the secular positivistic paradigms of knowledge. It should be possible, however, to base more intensive, comprehensive, and detailed studies on what has been outlined here.

NOTES

1. ṢAAS (*Ṣallā Allāhu ʿalayhi wa Sallam*): May the peace and blessings of Allah be upon him. Said whenever the Prophet's name is mentioned.
2. *Tawḥīd* (adj. *tawḥīdī*): Attesting to Allah's unity and uniqueness, and affirming that Allah is the One, the absolute, transcendent Creator, the Lord and Master of all that is. Traditionally and simply expressed, *tawḥīd* is the conviction and witnessing that "there is no god but Allah" – the essence of Islam that gives Islamic civilization its identity, binds its constituent parts together, and thus makes of them the integral, organic body that we call civilization.
3. ṢWT (*Ṣubḥānahu wa Taʿālā*): May He be praised and may His transcendence be affirmed. Said when referring to Allah.

Toward an Islamic Alternative in Thought and Knowledge

INTRODUCTION

Current developments and the many acute problems facing the Muslim Ummah, especially at the intellectual level, present a serious challenge to Islam. Given this reality, an attempt to outline an intellectual Islamic alternative in thought and knowledge has never been so urgent and imperative. This undertaking will help formulate a clear and coordinated policy with regard to cultural transformation, one based on firm principles and a sound strategy. It is also hoped that this policy will lead to scientific findings.

By way of introduction, I will give a brief description of the state of knowledge and thought, as well as of the educational and cultural systems, in the contemporary Arab and Muslim worlds.

THE PRESENT STATE OF THOUGHT

When examining the present state of thought among Muslims, three basic approaches can be identified:

- The "authentic" or "traditionalist" approach, which, by and large, considers the Ummah's "traditional" thought to be self-sufficient and capable of being presented with very little or no alteration. This approach suggests that the Ummah's contemporary intellectual life can be formed and organized, and that its civilization's structure can be built on this basis.
- The "modernistic" approach, which considers contemporary western thought and its worldview (e.g., its concepts of existence, life, and humanity) to be universal and without which a modern culture and civ-

This article first appeared in the *American Journal of Islamic Social Sciences* 6, no. 1 (September 1989): 1-12. It has been slightly edited.

ilization cannot be built. This tendency maintains that western thought must be adopted *in toto*, and that any consequent negative aspects are the price that must be paid for establishing a modern culture and civilization.

- The "eclectic" approach, which contends that one must select from traditional thought that which is most sound and from modern contemporary thought that which one considers and proves to be correct. These two then must be welded together to form an intellectual structure that will provide a guaranteed basis for achieving what is required.

However, the traditional approach, in the manner it was presented and applied, did not prevent the Ummah from falling into a state of decline and failure, from which it is still suffering. Likewise, western thought, as it was presented and applied, cannot protect the Ummah from its inherent adverse, harmful, and even disastrous effects. The advocates of the eclectic (selective) approach have presented no details of this proposed blend; nor have they tried to put it into effect. All of this is conducive to a wide-ranging question: Is the Ummah going through a serious intellectual crisis, and, if so, how can it find its way out?

THE PRESENT STATE OF KNOWLEDGE

To answer the above question, a brief look at the contemporary state of knowledge is necessary. At present, our students are taught two types of knowledge. First, there are the contemporary social, technical, and applied sciences that control the organization and functioning of all aspects of modern life. They comprise – regardless of the Muslim contributions to many of their bases – a body of knowledge whose principles, rules, objectives, and methods were formed by the western mentality through its religious and intellectual framework, philosophy, and background. Every aspect of this knowledge is closely bound to the western form of civilization.

Second, there is the knowledge that Muslims describe as *sharʿī* (relating to the Shariʿah [Islamic Law]) or *aṣlī* (relating to the bases of Islam). This knowledge can be further subdivided into the knowledge of objectives and the knowledge of means. Experts on classification and cataloging include both under the heading of *al-ʿulūm al-naqliyyah* (transmitted knowledge).

Most of this knowledge was produced to deal with the issues that arose during the third Islamic century, a period when the Islamic sciences had been established, and in response to the Ummah's historical reality at that time. The books and reference works current among its students were prepared after the door of ijtihad had been closed and *taqlīd* (imitation of the works of previous scholars) had become widespread. The authors of these works used to prepare them with the utmost care, paying great attention to linguistic details and artistic style in order to display the depth of their knowledge to their students, colleagues, and rivals. They are more like monologues than teaching books.

The methods and contents of such material supported the concept of *taqlīd* and encouraged people to adhere to it. The intention was to prevent people from exercising any form of ijtihad other than that needed to understand the books themselves, and, in the process, to make people despise ijtihad. This type of knowledge could not equip anyone to face life's realities. Rather, it strenuously promoted blind following and imitation, and ended intellectual activity and creativity. People seeking knowledge were thus caught between following alien contemporary thought or sticking to old traditional ways of thinking. Neither type of knowledge enabled them to achieve an operative ijtihad that help them face current problems in a sound and appropriate way.

THE PRESENT STATE OF MUSLIM EDUCATION

Turning to the educational systems throughout the Muslim world, we notice the prevalence of a dual system. The first system, the traditional "Islamic system," offers students a program consisting of the Shariʿah sciences (viz., those sciences pertaining to Islamic law). This system is confined to preparing and enabling graduates to deal with personal affairs, meet some educational needs, and lead the prayers in mosques. For the most part, this system remains a private affair that has limited access to public funds. The necessary funds come from the residue of charitable endowments, not the state's budget. Where public funds are made available, demands of secularization are imposed in the name of modernism.

The second, and by far the more widespread, is the secular system, which presents all kinds of contemporary knowledge and science during the student's educational career. It advocates un-Islamic orientations and has assumed tremendous proportions, elbowing out the Islamic system. Since the Islamic system's graduates are isolated from the reality of contemporary life and its challenges, they usually present no competition to the secular system's graduates. Consequently, the un-Islamic secular system produces the

Ummah's intellectual, political, and social leaders, as well as the managers of its services and means of production.

This dichotomy in educational systems soon became a means of dividing the Ummah and draining its energy. In reality, education should be a means of bringing Muslims together and providing them with a unified cultural perspective, of directing them toward progress and construction. It should create harmony and provide a common purpose, thus directing all efforts toward developing the righteous Muslim individual, whose mind and soul, culture and behavior, and powers of individual initiative and reasoning are strong and productive.

Much of the division and fragmentation – even the tragic conflict afflicting many parts of the Arab and Muslim worlds – bears traces of this dichotomy's negative aspects. In addition, the negative effects of other branches of education (e.g., military, private, and foreign) are reflected in the graduates' attitudes and cultural visions.

THE PRESENT CIVILIZATIONAL STATE OF THE UMMAH

Today, the Ummah's territory is the world's most strategically important and richest area. Its lands contain the most important raw materials for western industry, as well as tremendous human resources. The Muslim world also has a magnificent legacy and possess the best sources of guidance: the Divine Revelation (*waḥy*), namely, the inimitable Qur'an (including its interpretation and application), and the Prophet's Sunnah. Despite this, however, the Muslim world is plagued by inner strife and division, turbulence and self-contradiction, war and threats to world peace, extravagant wealth and excessive poverty, and famine and epidemics.

The Ummah is divided against itself, torn up and fragmented into nearly fifty nation-states separated by artificial boundaries designed to create and ensure continued tension and confrontation, especially among neighboring states. None of these states has had the chance to attain the outright freedom and stability, or social integration, that would enable it to concentrate its energies on construction and development. Sectarianism, factionalism, and nationalism, all of which cause disharmony, have dominanted affairs to such an extent that they have led to a continual state of instability, which foreign powers can easily manipulate at a time of their choosing. Such a situation only leads to more turmoil and anarchy. The lack of individual freedom prevents the people from pursuing their own intellectual and cultural growth, to say nothing of their natural psychological development. Muslims continue to live under the shadow of poverty, oppression, and terror, either from those who were specifically prepared to impose western forms of thought and culture on the Ummah, or from military dictators who seize power and impose their own frivolous, arbitrary, and whimsical policies through force, torture, and intimidation. In such dictatorships, the role of political and administrative bodies and institutions is completely eclipsed, a disaster that destroys all of the people's qualities and cultural potential.

The overwhelming majority of the Ummah is illiterate. The people's needs far outweigh the goods, materials, and services that they can provide for themselves. Even in the important and vital necessities of life, almost no Muslim state is self-sufficient. This deficiency is usually made up by imports, which only increases dependency on foreign powers. What makes the situation even more intolerable is that raw materials are bought from Muslim states at the lowest prices, or even taken for nothing, and are returned to them as manufactured goods at the highest prices. Many of these states are living at the level of starvation, while the rest could be reduced almost immediately to such a level if the exporters and foreign powers so wished.

The few Muslim states that have followed the path of industrialization have not attained complete self-sufficiency, because they still depend on foreign sources for most of the equipment needed to develop their industries. As a result, these foreign sources can control the nascent industries and direct them according to their own political and economic interests.

In most cases, "Muslim industry" was not designed to meet the Muslim world's desperate, immediate, and vital needs, but to meet only its inhabitants' tangential and secondary needs and to satisfy and cater to the consumeristic desires and habits planted in the Muslims for the benefit of others.

Unfortunately, the Muslim world has developed the habit of consuming the products of a contemporary non-Islamic civilization and has adopted many of its outer aspects, such as "modern" roads, buildings, and places of entertainment in its capitals. It has also established some political and economic institutions based on the western model. But these measures have failed to bring about the desired transformation and have not even set the Ummah on the road to achieving that transformation. How can this situation be rectified?

TOWARD AN ISLAMIC ALTERNATIVE

In order to present the Islamic alternative to the Ummah, we must reform Muslim thought as a whole and reassess its methodologies. We must understand the position of regional and nationalistic thought, as well as western thought, both Marxist and liberal. Furthermore, we must realize how influential western thought has become in the Muslim world. This will enable us to become aware of the enormous and stupendous challenge we are facing, and the pressure that history and the present are exerting on the Muslim mind.

Several important conditions must exist for such a reformation of thought: It should be comprehensive and free of all psychological pressures, whether historical or contemporary; and, it should be carried out for the purpose of correction and self-criticism, as a serious quest for scientific alternatives governed by theoretical and intellectual principles.

Such a revision should examine the controversial issues that have occupied the Muslim mind and prevented it from being positive, effective and influential: causality, the alleged conflict between revelation and reason, the blind imitation of previous scholars and its crippling effects, the dignity of humanity, and so on. It should reinterpret these issues in a sound and objective fashion, and seek to free the Muslim mind from the negative effects and shackles that these issues have had on its psychology, mentality, education, and way of life.

We must revise and correct the Ummah's inherited historical and cultural structure and rid it of the weakness, dichotomy, and lack of reality that hamper its efficiency and effectiveness. We must reexamine all of the prevalent concepts and work to achieve the correct perspectives on life, the universe, humanity, and all other related issues. In addition, we must agree on these perspectives' sources and design Islamic systems and institutions that can define a role for each of them. In this way, these systems and institutions may achieve Islam's goals, even if they do not exactly match its historical reality in form and structure. This design should lead to an Islamic concept of civilization that will enable Muslims to rebuild the Ummah and achieve its goals and objectives. We should seek to transform all of the above – according to a defined method – into a coordinated cultural system that will acculturate and educate the entire Ummah so that it may become a thriving operational system.

A sound intellectual basis, which is the starting point for building a civilizational system, must have three characteristics: 1) infallible sources that are free of error and destructive deviation, so that thinking will not degenerate into imagination and meandering meditation; 2) that are acceptable in both rational and logical terms, so that ideas presented to the Muslim mind will not be quickly discarded; and 3) that are realistic, so that Muslims will be able to interact with reality in order to change and influence it positively.

TOWARD A STRATEGY FOR KNOWLEDGE

Nowadays, scientific knowledge is defined according to the following maxim: "Every piece of knowledge is subject to tangible experiment." This definition, which has been around for centuries and has been adopted by the United Nations Educational, Scientific, and Cultural Organization (UNESCO), is used to decide what type of knowledge is "scientific." Due to the adoption of and the widespread reliance on this concept, revelation was rejected as a source of knowledge, culture, and civilization. In addition, all knowledge based on it was excluded from scientific knowledge, regardless of whether it dealt with the tangible or the intangible world. All such knowledge was considered "fables" or "unscientific," and of no benefit.

As a result, only the empirical method was considered capable of producing scientific knowledge. Humanity was regarded as being no more than a mass of biological substances, and the social sciences and humanities were subjected to the laws of natural science. Experiments were carried out on animals in an attempt to identify those laws that could be applied to humanity and to human behavior, reaction, influence, obedience, refusal, and ways of meeting material and other needs.

Muslims also accepted this approach, with the result that the contemporary western social sciences and humanities, not to mention their underlying philosophy, became the basic sources of their education, mentality, and attitudes toward the values of truth and goodness. Likewise, the arts based on this philosophy formed their psychology and defined their tastes and attitudes toward aesthetic values. The teaching methods and curricula in universities, educational institutes, and schools were subjected to this concept, and thus the students' westernization and alienation from Islam deepened. Consequently, the matters dealt with by revelation were classified as fables. A strong link was established between the West's power, productivity, and ability on the one hand, and western thoughts, beliefs and concepts of God, the universe, humanity, religion, life, nature, time, history, matter, men and women, the soul, science, knowledge, and various other matters on the other.

In light of the above, the first step toward formulating an Islamic cultural strategy is to redefine knowledge in terms of an Islamic epistemology and in a way that will be acceptable to Muslims everywhere. In this context, we need to emphasize that all knowledge is derived from revelation, reason, perception, or experiment. The contemporary theory of knowledge affirms that the sole source of scientific knowledge is the tangible universe. The Islamic theory of scientific knowledge, on the other hand, stresses that knowledge has two sources: revelation and the tangible universe. Revelation is the source of absolute facts and truth about which there is no doubt and no concept of relativity. Revelation is contained in the Qur'an, which Allah revealed to Prophet Muhammad. Allah has challenged humanity to produce a surah (chapter) that can match even the shortest one of the Qur'an: "And if you are in doubt as to what We have revealed to Our Servant, then produce a surah like thereunto" (2:23).

Reciting the Qur'an is, in itself, a form of worship. The Qur'an opens with *Sūrat al-Fātiḥah* and closes with *Sūrat al-Nās*. The second source of revelation is the legally binding elaborations upon the Qur'an that are contained in the Prophet's Sunnah. This consists of his reported actions and decisions (i.e., all that he said, did, approved of, or condemned, provided that the particular narration has been proven to be authentic).

The Islamic theory of knowledge considers the means of gaining knowledge to be reason, perception, and experiment. The Qur'an says: "And Allah has brought you forth from your mothers' wombs knowing nothing – but He has endowed you with hearing, sight, and minds so that you might have cause to be grateful [to Him]" (16:78).

According to Islam, no piece of knowledge can be considered as true or worthy of acceptance without corroborating evidence from revelation or the tangible universe. Knowledge of the tangible universe has to be derived by one of the three means mentioned above: reason, perception, or experiment. The Qur'an challenges people to "produce evidence for what you are claiming, if what you say is true" (2:111). As for those who affirm unsubstantiated beliefs, it asks: "Have you any [certain] knowledge that you could offer to us? You follow only conjectures and do nothing but guess" (6:148). And it categorically affirms: "Never can surmise take the place of truth" (53:28).

Humanity should have some knowledge and understanding of two fields: the "unseen world" (*ʿālam al-ghayb*) that is beyond the reach of a created being's perception, and the "seen world" (*ʿālam al-shahādah*) that can be witnessed by a created being's senses or mind. The primary source of knowledge about the unseen world is revelation, from which humanity derives evidence about it. The basic source of knowledge about the seen world is the tangible universe. Experiments and perception provide evidence about the seen world through a variety of means that may support one another. If we lay a firm foundation for the theory of Islamic knowledge and present it as an alternative to the contemporary western theory of knowledge, we will have established the second basis of the proposed cultural strategy.

This strategy must be based on the realization that every nation has a main issue of concern, a belief, or a basic goal that provides it with a motivation, inspiration, and impetus in all of its activities related to knowledge and labor. Usually, each nation seeks to plant this belief or goal in the consciousness of its youths through all possible means, especially during childhood. The nation then continues to nurture and strengthen this belief throughout the individual's development.

The Muslim world's current system of education has failed to instill any such belief, sound vision, standards, or motives. As a result, the goal of education for Muslims is to obtain decent employment with a decent income. Materialism has become widespread among the educated classes, which have lost any sense of a clear purpose in life. Academic syllabi have failed to establish a sound purpose in the Muslim conscience. The only way to achieve this goal is to establish a strong Islamic belief (*ʿaqīdah*) and instill an Islamic vision in the hearts and minds of Muslim youths. We must use all available means and resources to nurture and develop this belief and vision in order to achieve a sense of belonging to the Muslim Ummah. We must make this belief the motivation and the inspiration for our thoughts and feelings.

Secondary schools in the West, despite its secularism, teach students about western heritage, cultural history, and traditions in an integrated and comprehensive manner. This gives the students a sense of belonging and instills in them their nation's basic goals and strategy. They grow up with this feeling and carry their nation's vision and concepts of life, the universe, humanity, other cultures, as well as other aspects of its worldview.

Our proposed cultural strategy must firmly establish Islam and its vision not through limited classes on "religion," but throughout the entire education system. Every syllabus and program must seek to form and establish this belief. We must rid every syllabus of anything that contradicts or opposes belief by reorganizing the education system in all Muslim countries and by discarding the negative influences of the division between religious, secular, civil, and military education. This division has created, and continues to perpetuate, divisions among our people, with the result that graduates of religious schools and universities have ideas, opinions, and concepts that differ sharply from those who graduate from secular or military schools and universities. We do not want to abolish variety and specialization; what we want to end division.

This could be achieved by integrating existing systems and creating a single system based on Islam's teachings, spirit, and vision. The new education system, its syllabi and methods, and those responsible for it, should all be infused with Islam's principles and goals. It should abandon the tradition and the educational programs, content, and methods of other nations that were adopted without considering our Ummah's particular needs and aspirations. It should generate a sense of mission, whereby professional achievement and material success may be regarded as bonuses, not as the purpose and objective of education. The proposed education system must unify ideas, concepts, and feelings on all major issues. If, at this stage, there is some diversification into various specializations, students and scholars would feel no sense of isolation or alienation.

If this unification is carried out properly, it will help to provide all educated members of the Ummah with a good share of Islamic knowledge that deals with Islamic beliefs, values and goals, and morals and behavior. In addition, this unification will help familiarize the Muslims with Islamic legislation, history, and civilization, as well as with what is necessary and essential to contemporary modern knowledge.

While developing an Islamic alternative in thought and knowledge, special attention must be paid to the study of Islamic civilization. Such a study, when undertaken according to a proper methodological syllabus (to which a number of selected Islamic thinkers, educationists, and psychologists have contributed), is considered one of the most important means of creating and crystallizing the individual's feeling of belonging to the Ummah, and enabling him or her to understand the spirit that motivated our ancestors to make their great achievements to art and science, as well as political, social, and economic thought. At the same time, individual Muslims will become aware of the pain and suffering of earlier generations, what they failed to achieve, and how and why they failed. Such insight will help them develop self-awareness and the ability to compare themselves with other peoples and civilizations. In addition, studying Islamic civilization will help create and develop an awareness of its legacy, the spirit that produced and animated it, and what distinguishes it from other civilizations; develop the ability to plan for and look forward to the future; and help protect Muslims from being swept away by the conflicting currents of civilization that are seeking to dominate them. Certainly, no one can escape unscathed from this conflict unless he or she belongs to one of the contending civilizations that can be a real alternative when the other civilizations decline and fail.

Our new educational strategy must include a course of study that explains the bases, values, sources, and goals of Islam as a source of thought, culture, and civilization. This four-year course should be studied in the first stages of university education by all students, regardless of their specialization. It would deal with Islam's history, the historical achievements of Islamic civilization, and the basic features of Islamic culture.

Following on from the above, we need to present the humanities, social sciences, and arts from an Islamic perspective. We must appreciate that the methods and theories of the modern humanities, social sciences, and arts were formed in a way that reflects western thought, as well as its beliefs, strategies, and goals in life. The issues they deal with stem from western theories of knowledge. But with regard to all of these sciences, people in the West have begun to sense their shortcomings and inability to meet even their own needs. These sciences are now encountering many serious problems in their methods, theories, and application, and their adherents in the West are trying to correct them.

The Muslims desperately need to have their own humanities, social sciences, and arts, ones based on their beliefs and the theory of knowledge derived from the sources of those beliefs. If this is achieved, it will not be only the Muslims who attain their goal by gaining knowledge of the Islamic humanities and social sciences that are connected to moral values. Such values will, indeed, contribute to humanity's general welfare.

This objective could be achieved through studying the directives of the Qur'an and the Sunnah on all social and human matters, and then classifying them according to the issues of these sciences so that they could provide guidelines and principles for our societies. This work should be carried out by groups of researchers composed of specialists in the humanities, social sciences, the Arabic language, and the sciences of the Qur'an and the Sunnah.

In addition, the Islamic legacy must be studied and all available material must be classified according to the issues of these sciences. This classification should be precise, so that the knowledge contained in the Islamic legacy is readily available to researchers and specialists in a convenient and authentic form. Computers and information technology are invaluable tools for any such project. A critical study of contemporary thought must be undertaken in order to select its best elements according to strictly defined standards.

Finally, plans need to be drawn up to use and benefit from all of this material. Colleges, institute, and school textbooks need to be rewritten so that they will reflect the Islamic vision of contemporary reality and needs.

Moreover, they need to be written and designed in a way that makes them attractive and convenient to use.

All Arab and Islamic universities must cooperate to realize these goals. The International Institute of Islamic Thought has detailed plans for all of these matters, and is willing and eager to share its expertise with the Islamic Educational, Scientific, and Cultural Organization (ISESCO), as well as with anyone who seriously wishes to cooperate in these matters.

In closing, I would like to express my appreciation and thanks to ISESCO for bringing together Muslim scholars from all over the world to discuss and propose a concept for a cultural and civilizational Islamic system. Such a system is long overdue and is urgently needed. May Allah (SWT) grant us success and help us achieve that which will please Him.

The Reconstruction of the Muslim Mind: The Islamization of Knowledge

The Islamization of Knowledge may be understood as a cultural and intellectual project aspiring to correct the processes of thinking within the Muslim mind so that it can produce Islamic, social, and humanistic knowledge based on the two sources Muslims accept as the established sources for knowing the truth: *waḥy* (Divine revelation) and *wujūd* (existence). In this endeavor, we shall use reason and the senses to help us acquire such knowledge. Therefore, we reject any approach or source of knowledge that cannot be established on revelation and existence.

The Islamization of Knowledge is an effort, a process, to restructure the Muslim mind so that it can once again engage in ijtihad and return to its own unique track. Once there, it can operate in all of its historically recognizable genius in order to clarify to itself, and then to humanity, the purpose and the aims of the Shariʿah and revelation, and then ascertain how they may be projected forward and applied in current situations.

We do not regard this project as being relevant only to the Islamic Ummah. On the contrary, we view it as seeking the salvation of humanity – the way to show the world how to reestablish the relationship between knowledge and values. Indeed, ever since the moment the division between knowledge and values became pronounced, civilization has steadily declined.

The Islamization of Knowledge may also be understood as the attempt of Islamic culture and thought to open channels of meaningful communication and cultural exchange so that it can offer humanity the divine truths

This keynote address first appeared in the *American Journal of Islamic Social Sciences* 7, no. 3 (December 1990): 453-57, and was translated by Dr. Jamal Barzinji and Yusuf Talal DeLorenzo. It has been slightly edited.

for which it has thirsted so long. In the words of Roger Garaudy, the French Muslim philosopher, it is a means and an approach in the dialogue of civilization.

We have called this project the "Islamization of Knowledge" in order to address the seeds of faith residing in Muslim hearts, to awaken within Muslim minds a real appreciation of the Muslim world's contemporary situation as well as its total absence as an influencing factor in present-day civilization. The emergence of a consciously felt need for an Islamization of Knowledge can be viewed as the opening gambit of a culture that is struggling to break out of and transcend the limiting bonds of its historical experience so that it may reconcile itself with a dominant culture that is completely alien in terms of its constitution, philosophy, belief, and objectives.

The Islamization of Knowledge may also be seen as a conscious attempt to provide humanity with a way to discover and then act on rational, workable, and realistic solutions to resolve its ills. Indeed, many of today's pressing social, political, economic, and behavioral problems lend themselves to Islamic solutions. These solutions, which reflect the divine nature of their origin, also serve a second purpose: to spread Islam among Muslims and non-Muslims by showing them that it has something relevant to say about current problems and can offer solutions that work. We must further the cause of *daʿwah* (propagation of Islam) by providing concrete examples of Islamic teachings in action, not just in the abstract. When such solutions succeed, their source will be respected, admired, and appreciated. In this manner, people will gradually embrace Islam.

I should now like to explain the challenge confronting the educated Muslims of today. Essentially, Muslims find themselves in a peculiar and contradictory situation. On the one hand, there are Islam's eternal truths, truths considered to be the source of all that is good. On the other hand, Muslims live in a world that has little or no use for those truths, a world that seems to be based on the very opposites of those truths. Due to the inherent difficulties of functioning within such an unnatural situation, there is an apparent, but temporary, weakening of the Islamic consciousness among some Muslims when they are confronted with the realities of the world around them. At other times, their resolve will seem to grow, and their vision will become clear enough so that they attempt to reconcile their situation with the truth of Islam. To do this successfully, however, a study of the systemic causes underlying the reasons for the Muslim Ummah's decline is essential.

Contemporary Muslim thought has produced some good results in political science, economics, the social sciences, and culture. Moreover, it has contributed to international discussions of such issues as war and peace, justice, human rights, the right of peoples to self-determination, relations between societies, ethics, and many others. But still the question remains: When will Muslims come forward with a plan for a global civilization bearing the distinct imprint of its Islamic origin and nature, one that draws from the wellspring of its Islamic way of life, and for the Ummah of Islam? Will Muslims ever again be the bearers of guidance and light to humanity?

Today's Muslims, after nearly two centuries of repeated but ultimately futile attempts to overcome their backwardness and reinject their original vitality into the Ummah, find this goal as far as ever from realization. In fact, they remain enmeshed in social, political, and economic upheaval; blind acceptance of alien thought and transplanted values that were opposed by individual and Ummah-wide efforts; and controlled by military cliques, or by cultural, ethnic, factional, or creedal elites.

As a result, Muslims are forced to adopt any means that seem to protect their identity, beliefs, and the fundamentals of the Islamic character. If, however, the means fail and Muslims cannot extract themselves from the resulting enveloping crisis, the usual reaction is to blame either one's self or others and then adopt another course of action. This is the background against which an explanation of the multiplicity and division seen throughout the Muslim world may come into clearer focus.

In our estimation, the Islamization of Knowledge, in its wider perspective, provides Muslims with the intellectual underpinnings for a complete civilizational transformation. Essentially, this may be effected by reforming thought and removing traditional and historical obstacles that hobble the Muslim mind, such as the question of the relationship between the imam and *shūrā*, the issue of human choice and accountability in the light of *qaḍā'* (a juridical decision or court ruling) and *qadr* (fate, destiny) the difference between theory and application, the question of a Muslim's relationship to worldly life and the individual's role within it, as well as issues of reason and revelation, *taqlīd* (imitation) and ijtihad, mutual understanding, and many others.

Regardless of whatever misgivings others may have about our attempt to restore the Muslim Ummah to its former position of global centricity and its status as a witness and exemplar for humanity (misgivings based on the perception that these could only be attained at the expense of others), the fact is that this revival is in the interest of the entire world community. Recent international developments and the frightening destructive capabilities of the major technological powers should be enough to make this assertion apparent to all. Doubtless, dialogue between nations, as well as their exchange of ideas and appreciation for one another's cultures, promote the kind of understanding presently required. The Islamization of Knowledge will contribute positively to this dialogue.

The Islamization of Knowledge is a project for the entire Ummah. Unless all of the Ummah's resources are tapped, its success will remain in doubt. This project is not a *farḍ kifāyah*, for it does not relieve the Ummah of its responsibility by allowing a small group to undertake it on its behalf. On the contrary, this project is a *farḍ ʿayn*, for each individual is responsible for doing his or her part. Thus, such organizations as the International Institute of Islamic Thought (IIIT), the Association of Muslim Social Scientists (AMSS), and the Association of Muslim Scientists and Engineers (AMSE) need to play pioneering roles.

Certainly, such a project requires resources far greater than those at the disposal of any single organization. Each has its own part to play. In order for an organization to fulfill its responsibility in a befitting manner, two things are necessary:

- It must receive our individual and collective support, so that its course of action is well-planned and its programs are advocated and sustained.
- All studies and research undertaken by scholars must be directed toward this end. In the case of applied science and technology, efforts should be concentrated on redressing underdevelopment. This priority must guide professors, professional researchers, and even graduate students, so that no opportunity to harness the available human resources is lost. In the case of the social sciences, all efforts must be directed toward dealing with issues of Islamic thought, knowledge, culture, and civilization.

In the world today, many of the poorest, least-developed, and most disadvantaged nations belong to the Muslim Ummah, from Mali and Chad to Bangladesh. On the lists of such countries, we read the names of dozens of Muslim countries before coming to a single non-Muslim country. It is regrettable that nearly all Muslim countries suffer from poverty, ignorance, and disease. Thus, the challenge is clear. Answers must be found to such problems as the encroachment of deserts on arable land, drought, the lack of modern agricultural expertise, the absence of heavy industry and modern management techniques, and so on.

Furthermore, we must solve the problems that stand in the way of allowing these countries to become self-sufficient in the production of indigenous Muslim scholars and experts so that they no longer need to rely on experts imposed from the outside, so that they no longer need to risk losing their best students by sending them abroad for higher education.

Certainly, our Muslim social scientists can direct their attention toward solving the problems of contemporary Muslim and Muslim-minority societies – problems such as sectarianism, the unequal distribution of wealth, drugs, the wasting of natural resources, and so on. Under such circumstances, responsible Muslim scholars should only undertake research that has immediate relevance for the Ummah.

Yet, by way of example and despite the efforts expended by Muslim scholars in economics, we are still unable to produce an integrated and methodologically sound textbook on the subject. Nor, for that matter, has any of our economics experts produced a coherent theory of Islamic economics. And, this is in spite of the impressive growth of literature on all aspects of economics! Quite simply, the reason for this inability is that such matters require not hundreds, but thousands of research efforts on the part of specialists in the field, each building on the work of both contemporaries and predecessors. This same situation is found in education, psychology, sociology, and so many other disciplines, with the result that we are faced with gaping lacunae in our Islamically oriented scholarship.

Thus, the challenges before contemporary Muslim scholars are legion. More than ever before, Muslim thinkers need to meet those challenges with all of the acumen at their command. These are the circumstances under which this organization, and organizations like IIIT and others, have raised the banner of Islamization aloft and proclaimed the beginning of a new direction. We await the results of both our efforts and yours. May Allah guide all of us to that which earns us His pleasure.

The Islamization of Knowledge: Yesterday and Today

INTRODUCTION

Within the Islamization of Knowledge approach, the idea of Islamizing knowledge has always been understood as an intellectual and methodological outlook rather than as an academic field, a specialization, an ideology, or a new sect. Thus, it has sought to view issues of knowledge and methodology from the perspectives of reform, inquiry, and self-discovery without any preconceptions, doctrinal or temporal constraints, or limitations on its intellectual horizons. Furthermore, it is keenly aware of the workings of time on ideas as they pass from stage to stage and mature and, therefore, is the first to say that this project is not to be understood as a set of axioms, a rigid ideology, or a religious movement. Rather, in order to comprehend the term's full meaning, it must be viewed as designating a methodology for dealing with knowledge and its sources, or as an intellectual outlook in its beginning stages.

An ongoing critique and the attempt to derive particulars from the general are essential to development. The initial articulation of this undertaking and the work plan was, therefore, produced in general terms. At that early stage, the focus was on criticizing both traditional Muslim and western methodologies and then introducing the Islamization of Knowledge and explaining its significance. The first edition of the Islamization of Knowledge pointed out those principles that are essential to fashioning an Islamic paradigm of knowledge based on the Islamic worldview and its unique constitutive concepts and factors. It also addressed, briefly, the project's intellectual

This "reflections" article first appeared in the *American Journal of Islamic Social Sciences* 12, no. 1 (spring 1995): 81-101, and was translated by Yusuf Talal DeLorenzo. It has been slightly edited.

aspect. The main focus, however, was on how to produce textbooks for teaching the social sciences, as this was considered the first priority at a time when the Muslim world was losing its best minds to the West and the western cultural and intellectual invasion. Accordingly, twelve steps were identified as the basis from which the preparation of introductory social science texts might proceed.

The work plan and the principles elaborated in the first edition of *The Islamization of Knowledge* were met with a great deal of enthusiasm, as these represented a novel intellectual endeavor. There was wide acceptance for the new ideas, and many scholars were quick to endorse them. The project's popularity and appeal were so great that several academic institutions immediately attempted to give practical form to its concepts. Some people, however, were unable to discern its essential methodological issues, perhaps due to the pragmatic manner in which Islamization was first articulated. As a result, they considered it little more than a naïve attempt to replace knowledge with knowledge that had somehow been Islamized. In addition to such critics, others sought to ridicule the effort and still others wanted to interpret everything they read in terms of their own preconceived notions. Some people went so far as to view the undertaking as an attempt by Islamic fundamentalists to somehow transform culture and the world of ideas into tools that would enable them to attain political power. Undoubtedly, this last view led some people to consider the Islamization of Knowledge as an ideological, as opposed to an epistemological or a methodological, discourse.

Likewise, those captivated by contemporary western knowledge and its supposed generation of scientifically objective and universally applicable products assumed that the Islamization of Knowledge was symptomatic of a state of conscious or unconscious denial of the "other." To them, this undertaking reflected an attitude of self-affirmation through the attempted characterization of everything of significance as Islamic. Some saw it as a manifestation of the Islamists' desire to control everything in the state and society, including secular knowledge or the social sciences and humanities in particular, by making scholarship and academics their exclusive domain. They also saw it as attempt to strip from the Marxists, leftists, and secularists in the Arab and the Islamic worlds their right to practice their scholarship or, at the very least, to speak with authority on anything having to do with Islam or Muslim society. In reality, however, such ideas never occurred to any of those involved in the beginning of this undertaking.[1] In fact, this approach's literature has never mentioned any of these matters.

The Islamization of Knowledge approach is not blind to the fact that it may take decades before the methodological and epistemological issues involved in this proposition are clarified in a definitive manner. Indeed, such matters cannot be outlined in a declaration of principles, a press release, or a party manifesto. Instead, they should be understood as landmarks on the road to the type of learning that will help reform the Muslim mind so that the Muslim world can address its own crisis of thought and actively participate in the attempt to deal with the crises of thought affecting the rest of the world.

Moreover, those involved in the Islamization of Knowledge realize that intellectual undertakings, especially at this level, represent the most difficult and complex activity of any society, and that their fruits may not be seen for decades or even generations. Even then, they rarely come to an end, for knowledge is limitless and Allah's creation is greater ... and for every learned person there is one who is more learned. As the essence of knowledge and its foundation is method, in the general sense of the term, the message of Islam is said to be a complete way of life rather than a specific set of guidelines, except for those very few fundamentals that are unchanging and unaffected by the differences of time and place.[2]

The scholars of the Islamization of Knowledge do not seek to provide a strictly inclusive and exclusive definition in the classical manner when they speak of this particular approach. Rather, this process is spoken of in general terms only and, in fact, should be understood as a loose designation calculated to convey the undertaking's general sense and priorities. Take, for example, the definition proposed by ʿImād al-Dīn Khalīl:

> The Islamization of Knowledge means involvement in intellectual pursuits, by examination, summarization, correlation, and publication, from the perspective of an Islamic outlook on life, humanity, and the universe.[3]

Or that of Abū al-Qāsim Ḥajj Ḥammād:

> The Islamization of Knowledge is the breaking of the connection between the scientific achievements of human civilization and the transmutations of postulative philosophy, so that science may be employed by means of a methodological order that is religious rather than speculative in nature.[4]

He defined the Islamization of Knowledge as

> ... the Islamization of applied science and of scientific principles as well. This may be accomplished through an understanding of the similarities

> between the principles of the natural sciences and those of nature itself. This, in fact, is the foundation upon which all religious values are based. Therefore, the philosophical references in scientific theories may become "Islamized" when they negate the postulative aspect of those theories and recast them in terms of the natural or the universal, which carries with it the notion of a divine purpose to all existence and movement.[5]

Thus, Abū al-Qāsim, like all of the other scholars involved in this undertaking, asserts that the Islamization of Knowledge is not a cosmetic addition of religious terminology and sentiment to studies in the social sciences and humanities or the grafting of relevant Qur'anic verses onto the sciences or disciplines intended for Islamization. On the contrary, the Islamization of Knowledge may be viewed as a methodological and epistemological rearrangement of the sciences and their principles. Moreover, it is not to be understood as a blanket extension of personal conviction to all of the disciplines in an attempt to lend a sort of religious legitimacy to the accomplishments of human civilization. Nor should it be understood as a negation of those achievements by the logic of empty semantics.

Rather, these definitions have been proposed to clarify the issue and describe its characteristics and distinguishing traits. These were never intended to be precise delineations in the classical mold. In fact, we prefer that the Islamization of Knowledge not be limited to the confines of a hard and fast definition. After all, it is the foundation of the *tawḥīdī* episteme, which holds that the universe has a Creator who is One and Unique, the Originator of all things and their Provider, Observing yet Unobserved, Subtle and All-knowing, Unfathomable and beyond human comprehension. He has charged humanity with His stewardship and taught it what it knew not. He made revelation and the natural world the principle sources of knowledge, so studying them within a framework of pure *tawḥīd* would produce proper, discerning, and purposeful knowledge.

Therefore, when we present our ideas and attempt to formulate principles, we do so by the logic that our proposals are no more than landmarks or indicators for the benefit of scholars interested in producing academic work from an Islamization of Knowledge perspective. These first steps are the result of a variety of experiences in dealing with the project's practical and theoretical aspects. Undoubtedly, as researchers continue to work with these indicators, or with any of the six discourses explained later in this paper, they will clarify the issue further, postulate its principles, and test its intellectual and academic efficacy.

THE REALITY AND IMPORTANCE OF THE ISLAMIZATION OF KNOWLEDGE

The Islamization of Knowledge represents the intellectual and epistemological side of Islam that began with the Patriarch, Abraham (Ibrāhīm), and was completed by the Seal of the Prophets, Muhammad. Indeed, the final Revelation began with the words: "Read ..." and ended with the verse: "Today I have completed your religion for you ..." Islam's epistemological aspect was first evinced in the following verses:

> Read! In the name of your Lord who created, created humans from a clot. Read! For your Lord is Most Bountiful, He who taught by the pen, taught humans what they did not know. (96:1-5)

It was continued in the revelation of the opening verses of *Sūrat al-Qalam*: "*Nūn.* By the pen and what they write ..." (68:1-2), and in the opening verses of *Sūrat al-Raḥmān*: "The All-Merciful [Who] taught the Qur'an, created humanity, and taught it expression ..." (55:1-3).

From the above verses, it may be deduced that humanity has been commanded to undertake two different kinds of readings and to understand its situation in the universe by understanding how the two readings complement one another. The first reading is the book of Allah's Revelation (the Qur'an), in which all matters of religious significance are explained;[6] the second is the book of His creation (the natural universe), from which nothing has been omitted.[7] To undertake a reading of either without reference to the other will neither benefit humanity nor lead it to the sort of comprehensive knowledge necessary for building and maintaining a civilized society or to knowledge worthy of preservation and further development or exchange. In fact, such a one-sided reading will never enable humanity to fulfill its role as the steward of Allah (*istikhlāf*) or the keeper of His trust (*amānah*). If this destiny remains unfulfilled, humanity will never be united in faith or guided, and the divine purpose behind creation will never be realized. Earth will never be united in worshipping Allah, and the stars will never join the rest of creation in bowing to His will and praising Him: "There is not a thing but celebrates His praise: And yet you do not understand how they declare His glory" (17:44).

Any disruption in any aspect of human life indicates an imbalance in how the readings were undertaken. Perhaps only one reading was done, or the two were not done together, or there was a preponderance in the scales by which matters are measured. It could also be possible that the wrong methods were used: "To each among you have We prescribed a law and a way" (5:48).

Under such circumstances, nothing will begin to go right unless and until equilibrium has been reestablished through a balanced and complementary reading of the two books. Clearly, each reading must be considered an epistemological fundament and a creative source that may not be ignored. A discerning and sound society cannot exist without joining these two readings and integrating them in a comprehensive manner, for a society that ignores the first reading in favor of the second will lose sight of its relationship to God and its responsibilities of stewardship, trust, and accountability to a higher authority. The result is a self-centered and overweening society that comes to believe that it is independent and free of the Unseen. Such a society inevitably spins for itself a web of speculative philosophy that, ultimately, blocks it from attaining true knowledge. On the contrary, such knowledge will lead its people, under the best of circumstances, to become like "those who know only the outer aspects of worldly life, but who, in regard to the afterlife, are very negligent" (30:8).

The philosophies produced by such societies cannot answer the ultimate questions and generally dismiss everything beyond their sensory perceptions as supernatural. Such philosophies are also prone to suggesting utterly baseless replies to these questions, leaving people to wander and stray. Even in regard to God, people nourished on such philosophies think of Him as just another element of the supernatural. If He actually created the universe, so their reading goes, He did so all at once and then forgot or ignored His creation and left it to act and react mechanically according to previously established natural laws. This type of reading, even if undertaken by people who consider themselves religious, cannot, on its own, lead to true and accurate knowledge of God. Rather, if such people believe at all, they believe in a deity who is the way they want it to be, often equating it with the powers of nature itself. Such faith, generally speaking, jumbles doctrines of incarnation with *shirk* (associating others with God) and idolatry, and often leads to theories that deny the existence of any creator (e.g., dialectical materialism) or to those that are unacceptable and inadequate alternatives to belief in God (e.g., natural selection and evolution).

Within the framework of such a one-sided reading of the natural universe, the world may assume the form of mutually opposed powers. Based on the resulting distorted reading, individuals may suppose themselves divine and answerable to no one but themselves. Supposing, with their limited knowledge and understanding, that they control their surroundings, they will worship themselves, make their desires their guides, and attempt to derive their values from nature. For them, religion becomes no more than something to be used when the need arises, to fill a psychological gap, or to fulfill a subliminal desire: "Nay, but humanity transgresses all bounds when it looks upon itself as self-sufficient" (96:7).

When humanity becomes so presumptuous, it becomes so overbearing and tyrannical that it destroys the environment by polluting the land, sea, and air. When the natural order is disrupted, Earth is inundated with diseases of excess and perversion. Entire continents are enveloped by hunger, destitution, pestilence, and destruction, and the majority of people are forced to live in misery: "Those who turn from remembering Me shall live lives of misery" (20:124).

The second reading, that of the real-existential, may be ignored by those undertaking the first reading (the Revelation). When this happens, great imbalances result, such as developing an aversion to the world and worldly pursuits that will encourage people to become ascetics and shun participating in and contributing to society. As a result, individuals will fail to undertake their responsibilities as stewards and keepers of God's trust. In other instances, such a loss of equilibrium will prevent people from engaging in independent and creative thought. When people begin to believe that human beings are not really capable of independent actions, they no longer value their own deeds and, ultimately, conclude that there is no meaning to their existence. Such ideas contradict the teachings of the Qur'an and Sunnah.

To neglect the reading of the natural universe or to fail to balance and complement it with the reading of revelation often leads to confusion over important issues of faith. Often, those who read only the book of Revelation suppose that eliminating anthropomorphic elements from the concept of deity requires negating the value of human actions, rejecting belief in free will, and formulating a mystical denial of God's positive role for humanity. Anyone who reads the writings of such people, Muslims and non-Muslims alike, finds that they are thoroughly confused about what constitutes human, as opposed to divine, deeds, the meanings of free will and predetermination, and issues of cause and effect, among others.

In conclusion, the two readings must be combined, for if they are not allowed to complement one another, the result will be an unbalanced understanding of reality. This is why the Islamization of Knowledge is such an epistemological and civilizational necessity, not only for Muslims but for humanity in general, and why it may be considered a solution to the global crisis of contemporary thought. After adopting rationalism as the basis for thought, western civilization found itself confronted with the problem of defining methodologies in ways based on its own scientific progress. For example, Marxism sought to fashion a western scientific methodology based on dialectical materialism. Clearly, however, neither Marxism nor any other liberal, positivistic, or secular western schools of thought have provided answers to the issues besetting western society and the rest of the world.

The crisis is especially vexatious for Muslims. By virtue of our submission to western intellectual, cultural, and institutional influences and the impact that these have had on our lives, we are now full partners in the worldwide crisis. Our relationship with the West is no longer marginal, as some continue to believe. We and the rest of the world have accepted its methodology, worldview, and perspectives on history, science, knowledge, culture, progress, and so on.

What, then, is this Islamization of Knowledge proposal? What solutions does it offer to the crises of thought that presently plague the world, and how can these solutions be realized?

As indicated earlier, the Islamization of Knowledge may be brought about through combined readings of the two books and, based upon their similarity and complementarity, the establishment of a methodology for research and discovery. The Qur'an, like the natural universe, bespeaks and directs toward the other: The Qur'an is a guide to the real-existential, and the real-existential is a guide to the Qur'an. Moreover, true knowledge is attained only through a complementary reading – a "combining" – of these two sources.

One reading is that of the Unseen, in which revelation is accompanied by interpretation and the attempt to discover its universals and how they manifest themselves in nature, while the other reading is an objective reading of the real-existential in light of the universals expounded in the verses of revelation. The reason for revelation, then, is to settle from the general to the particular and to link the absolute to the specific, to the extent that relative human rational abilities allow.

The other reading, that of the categorical real-existent, represents an ascent from the specific and the particular toward the general and the absolute, also to the extent that relative human rational abilities allow. In this way, the supposed differences between revelation's teachings and the natural universe's objective truths may be seen as nonexistent, as emphasized in *Sūrat al-ʿAlaq:* "Read! In the name of your Lord who created, created humans from a clot. Read! For your Lord is Most Bountiful, He who taught by the pen, taught humans what they did not know" (96:1-5).

When these two readings are undertaken separately, the results may be perilous. Those who rely solely upon revelation, thereby ignoring knowledge of the real world, transform religion into something mystical that accords no value to humanity or nature, rejects cause and effect, and ignores the uses of society, history, psychology, and economics. Ultimately, thought becomes rigid and inflexible, and ignores the elements of time and history. Quite often, this approach is thought to be religious; in fact, it has nothing to do with religion.

Those who undertake only the second reading are actually rejecting – or ignoring – the unseen presence of the Creator and Manager of the natural universe. As a result, they gradually arrive at a positivistic understanding of knowledge that negatively influences the makeup of society, as we see in contemporary western civilization: All notions of anything being sacred have been stripped away, and everything has been deconstructed and reduced to its minimum. This is why western society, from its vantage point on the verge of extinction, often views existence itself as a worthless commodity. This further explains the West's preoccupation with "ends": the end of history, civilization, progress, modernity, or humanity itself.

Thus, humanity is divided between mysticism and positivism, even though the first verses of the Qur'an clearly refute the mystical, in the western sense of the term, as being a part of the Unseen. In fact, the first verses clarify the link between the Unseen and the second (objective) reading of the real-existential, which is recorded by means of the pen. These same verses, by linking the real-existential to revelation, reject the speculative ends that result from a one-sided reading of the real-existential. Thus, the balanced "reader" is the individual whose faith in, and understanding of, revelation on the one hand, and understanding of the real-existent and the principles that determine and govern categorical real-existents on the other, qualify him/her for the responsibilities of stewardship.

It is impossible to estimate, in terms of human suffering, the damage caused to modern society by the rift between science and religion seen in its educational institutions and curriculum. Yet, even so, humanity has shown little interest in producing students who are grounded in both. Obviously, this is because modern society has adopted the western attitude of separating the two, so that students of theology attend seminaries and students of science attend colleges of engineering. In the Muslim world, where western influence is all-pervasive, the same rift exists between schools and colleges of Shariᶜah studies and theology and colleges of practical and applied sciences, or social sciences and the humanities.

This attitude of separation is responsible for the rift between religious values and contemporary knowledge. For us, as Muslims, this attitude is perilous because it drives a wedge between the Shariᶜah sciences and the social sciences, which have been developed largely in accordance with a one-sided reading of the real-existential. The Shariᶜah sciences, for their part, have contented themselves with descriptive and lexical studies of the Qur'an and the Sunnah and have largely ignored the real-existents of societal phenomena and their spatial and temporal effects.

The dominant western cultural paradigm has cast the social sciences and humanities in a positivistic mold that excludes revelation's axiological verities. This narrow paradigm is responsible for humanity's debate over the conflicting dualities of mysticism and positivism, which inflates the self's place at the expense of religious and ethical values. This has led to the spread of individual liberalism and the ensuing social and communal turmoil.

The Islamization of Knowledge is primarily a methodological issue designed to identify and articulate the relationship between revelation and the real-existential. In its essence, that relationship is one of integration and permeation that clarifies the comprehensive manner in which the Qur'an deals with the real-existential and its governing and regulating natural laws (*sunan*) and principles. Indeed, knowledge of those *sunan* is invaluable to understanding the principles of Qur'anic methodology.

To summarize, then, the Islamization of Knowledge undertaking may be pursued only by those endowed with a vast knowledge of the Qur'an and a firm grounding in the social sciences and humanities.

THE SIX DISCOURSES

A brief description of each discourse forming the present focus of attention for the Islamization of Knowledge undertaking is given below.

The First Discourse: Articulating the Islamic Paradigm of Knowledge. This discourse, which is concerned with identifying and erecting a *tawḥīd*-based system of knowledge (a *tawḥīdī* episteme), is based on two fundaments. The first one is the conceptual activation of the articles of faith and their transformation into a creative and dynamic intellectual power capable of presenting adequate replies to what are known as ultimate questions. This may take place through a perceptive understanding of theology and the elements of its methodology. For example, what is the benefit, at an epistemological level, of faith in Allah; in His angels, books, and prophets; or in the Day of Judgment? What is the methodological significance of these articles of faith?

All ideas, not to mention all sciences and civilizations, are based on a particular worldview or understanding of its beginnings, ends, and principal elements, whether seen or unseen. Thus, rejecting a Creator, adopting a position of neutrality on whether or not a Creator exists, or rejecting any article of faith presupposes a worldview that is entirely different from that of the believer. The Muslim mind is generally content to view the articles of faith as matters of personal conviction that do not reflect on or influence anything related to methodological or intellectual issues. However, the Islamization of Knowledge outlook, in keeping with the higher purposes of the Shari^c^ah and the character of Islamic teachings, is based on the idea that these represent the foundations of the societal and epistemological paradigm sought by Islam. At the same time, it should be clear that no society or reformation of society can take place without an epistemological and methodological basis. Indeed, whatever Islam has accomplished has been based on its unique vision of such elements as the Unseen, the universe, life, and the rest of the belief system located at the base of that worldview.

The second fundament of the Islamic (or *tawḥīdī*) episteme is elaborating the paradigms of knowledge that guided historical Islam and its legal, philosophical, and other schools of thought. This must be done in order to link those with the intellectual output of the past and to evaluate the extent to which they contributed to the dynamism and comprehensiveness of that output. Such an elaboration will also help define the relationship between those paradigms and the various intellectual trends and crises faced by the Muslim world at different periods in its history. A further benefit is determining the extent to which those paradigms influenced the development or decline of thought in those periods. In addition, an effort must be made to discover and clarify how limited or partial epistemic systems drew from the comprehensive *tawḥīdī* episteme mentioned above. This process will serve as an introduction to the feasibility of developing partial systems for the various social and applied sciences based on *tawḥīd* and a complementary reading of the two books while, at the same time, borrowing from the paradigms that were prevalent in earlier stages of Islamic history and those developed by western and contemporary thought.

The Second Discourse: Developing a Qur'anic Methodology. The methodological shortcomings besetting the Muslim mind make its reconstruction via the development of a new methodology an absolute necessity. While a Qur'anic methodology may spring from the *tawḥīdī* episteme and be based on its premises and principles, its prolonged disuse makes the effort required for its activation more akin to discovery than recovery. A Qur'anic methodology will enable the Muslim mind to deal effectively with its historical and contemporary problems, for it is a means to attain truth and to understand and analyze phenomena.

In addition to its link to methodology, a paradigm's base will include what Maḥmūd Muḥammad Shākir called the "premethodological." According to him, this involves such matters as culture, language, and psychological and intellectual disposition. This methodology also includes philosophy and tools. The philosophical element springs from the epistemic, theological, and cultural paradigms, and the same is true in regard to methodological tools. In spite of al-Suyūṭī's legal maxim – that which may not be forgiven if it were an end may be forgiven as a means – the means for dealing with phenomena or the tools used for research, which at first may not appear to be subject to cultural or religious considerations, in reality are never completely free of those considerations. Therefore, the advancement of Islamic methodology will proceed through its search to establish its own philosophical foundations and its discovery of appropriate methodological tools that accord with those foundations. Certainly, the landmarks of such a methodology will be derived from the *tawḥīdī* episteme's religious and cultural premises.

The structure of Islamic methodology in general, or what may be termed the foundations of that methodology, must be grounded in authentic scholarship, rather than in the attempt to be different simply by opposing contemporary western methodology. The purpose behind developing an Islamic methodology should be to achieve harmony among the elements of the Islamic paradigm of knowledge, regardless of any notions of rapprochement, comparison, confrontation, imitation, or whatever. In addition, such an undertaking should strive to enable the Muslim mind, through an integrative methodology, to practice ijtihad and be intellectually creative. Constructing this methodology should be considered a major priority and an essential precondition to the four following discourses, just as the previous discourse should be considered an essential precondition to this discourse.

The Third Discourse: A Methodology for Dealing with the Qur'an. This element may be considered the Islamization of Knowledge's third pillar. Developing such a methodology may require a review and reorganization of the Qur'anic sciences, even to the extent of discarding some traditional areas of study that played a role in the past. The Arab individual of the past understood the Qur'an from within the special characteristics of his/her simple and limited social and intellectual natures. Clearly, these stand in stark contrast to the nature of contemporary civilization. When the revelational sciences (those that mainly revolved around the Qur'an and the Hadith) were first formalized, the dominant mentality among Muslim scholars was descriptive in nature. As a result, they concentrated on analyzing the texts primarily from lexical and rhetorical perspectives. Thus, at that period in Muslim intellectual history, the Qur'an was understood in terms of interpretive discourse (*tafsīr*).

At the present time, however, the dominant mentality is the methodological understanding of issues through disciplined research, employing criticism and analysis, into topics of significance for society and their various relationships. This requires Muslims to reconsider the disciplined means by which they are to interpret the texts of revelation and read the books of revelation and the real-existential. Furthermore, the Qur'an needs to be liberated from the sort of interpretation that neglects the dimensions of its absoluteness, as well as of its verification and safeguarding of previous revelations. Such interpretations have been susceptible to the relative, either in the form of *isrā'īlīyyāt* (stories and narratives based in the Jewish or Talmudic tradition and then adapted to fit Qur'anic situations) or as *asbāb al-nuzūl* (narrations concerning the specific events occasioning the revelation of Qur'anic verses).

This link to the relative did not stop at qualifying general terms by means of specific occasions, but extended even to linking the Qur'anic revelation to a specific spatial and temporal framework. The end results were clearly contrary to Islam's universality, the finality of the Prophet's mission, and the Qur'an's sovereignty, all of which require the Qur'anic text to be absolute and unqualified in its appeal to the Muslim mind of every time and place. Indeed, the Qur'an will remain forever rich in content, its wonders will never cease, its recitation will remain fresh forever, and it will continue to exceed the ability of humanity, regardless of time and place, to comprehend it completely.

The Qur'an, as the explanation of all things and a guidance, mercy, and good tiding for the Muslims (16:89), is the only originating source in Islam, whereas the Sunnah is an explanatory source that provides further elaboration on its meaning. God has pledged to preserve the Qur'anic revelation and to clarify its meanings: "Verily, We shall bring it together and recite it. Then, when We recite it, follow its recitation. Thereafter, shall We be responsible for its explanation" (75:17-19). No other source of knowledge, culture, or civilization is protected by God or surrounded by so many divine pledges. As the Qur'anic text is guaranteed against alteration and distortion, its authority is complete and its sovereignty is absolute: "Whatever matter you differ over, its ultimate disposition is with Allah" (5:49).

This is why reconstructing a methodology for dealing with the Qur'an as a methodological source of knowledge for the natural and social sciences will empower those sciences to contribute effectively to human life and the crises now confronting it. Such an undertaking is certain to return values to the balance of these sciences and link them to the higher purposes for which creation was intended by its Creator.

The Fourth Discourse: A Methodology for Dealing with the Sunnah. As the major source for clarifiying and explaining the Qur'anic text, the Sunnah's nature and role must be thoroughly understood. Without the Sunnah, it would be impossible to elaborate on the methods or the lore required for making significant contributions to human society or to apply Qur'anic values to real-existent situations. The period of prophethood and the time of the Companions represented a time during which direct contact with the Messenger was possible. The Muslims of that time could know and emulate whatever he said or did. For example, he said: "Take the rites of hajj from me ..."[8] and "Perform salah (prayer) as you see me perform it...."

Emulation and compliance depend upon practical action, and when such action is present, no difficulties will arise in application. Thus, the Prophet's deeds and words narrowed the distance between the hidden wisdom of the Qur'anic way and the existential, although they did so in terms of the particular mental, linguistic, and intellectual abilities of the people he addressed. The hadith narrators, whose only concern was to preserve the Prophet's every word and deed, transmitted this information to the best of their ability, for it represented the methodology by which disputed issues could be solved via revelation. This explains the Sunnah's incredible magnitude, which allows us to follow the Prophet in his daily actions, whether at home or away, at war or at peace, as teacher or judge, and as leader or a simple human being. The Sunnah also enables us to witness and interpret how he dealt with and combined the Qur'an and the real-existential.

In addition, the Sunnah reveals the characteristics of the reality with which the Prophet had to deal. Obviously, that reality differs considerably from the reality confronting us today. This realization leads us to construct a methodology based on how he applied the teachings of revelation to real situations, rather than ones based on imitation springing from deference or *taqlīd.* In other words, the way of true emulation is quite distinct from the way of *taqlīd.*

The Sunnah represents the embodiment of a methodology for applying the Qur'an to the real-existential. It is difficult to comprehend many of the issues brought up by the Sunnah if one does not understand the prevailing circumstances at the time and place of the Prophet's mission. This is also true when one seeks to follow the Sunnah or emulate the Prophet's example, in terms of its particulars, without first constructing a methodology for emulation that can systematize the Sunnah in an objective manner by placing its particulars within a methodological framework.

For example, even though the Prophet prohibited sculpture and the graphic representation of the human form and characterized portrait artists as the most severely punished on the Day of Judgment, this should not be taken as the basis of a position toward the entire realm of aesthetics. Such a position would clash outright with the Qur'anic teachings about how prophet Sulayman (Solomon) understood the matter: The Qur'an records that he recruited the jinn to produce all manner of sculpture for him. Contemporary debates on the subject will never be resolved through recourse to historical particulars, nor will such recourse answer those who maintain that they feel no inclination to worship pictures and question why, then, there should be a prohibition on representing the human form. Certainly, particularized fatwas (legal responses) that permit one sort of picture and prohibit another will solve nothing. Rather, a methodology that considers such elements as the Prophet's saying, made several times: "Had your tribe not been only recently involved in idolatry, I might have done... [this or that]" is needed.[9] At that particular time, the Prophet was seeking to abolish idolatry among a people for whom it had become a way of life and to replace it with the simplest and purest form of *tawḥīd.*

Clearly, a systematic methodology capable of regulating these issues and reading them in a disciplined manner is required. Using such a tool, Muslims will be able to deal with the Sunnah in a methodical manner and not merely as a collection of particularized responses to specific questions and circumstances that, all too often, are transformed by the litigious into conflicting statements, much as if they were legal opinions voiced by different imams.

During the period of Qur'anic revelation, the Arabs embraced the concept of emulation and took the Prophet as their exemplar and as the one who embodied for them a certain way, in accordance with their conditions and spatial and temporal circumstances. Within this particular framework, the concepts of *ma'thūr* (reported) and *manqūl* (transmitted) originated. Over time, the narration of hadiths continued without reference to the circumstances or situations that occasioned the events recounted or to other elements that would contribute to a comprehensive understanding of their true import. In general, hadiths were treated in the same way as the Qur'anic text was treated: Lexical considerations were given the greatest priority. In an attempt to diminish the effects of this approach and escape the confines of the strictly *ma'thūr*, some took recourse in esoteric or symbolic interpretations. These undertakings, however, only exacerbated and confused the situation further, for what was needed was the construction of a systematic methodology for dealing with the texts of the Qur'an and the Sunnah. Only such a methodology could consider the particulars of those texts from a comprehensive methodological perspective and in the light of Islam's higher aims and purposes.

The intellectual mentality constantly searches for a scientific ordering of issues and attempts to construct a methodology for dealing with all of their aspects. Within such a methodological framework, the processes of analysis, criticism, and interpretation assume a more comprehensive and penetrating role in dealing with universal and particularized phenomena. Such a methodology, while allowing for consideration of the Qur'an's higher purposes, will liberate research from the confines of *taqlīd*, esotericism, and attempts to graft historical applications onto present-day situations. Old solutions in new guises are still old solutions and will never engender the needed reform or serve the higher purposes of Islam's universal message.

The Fifth Discourse: Reexamining the Islamic Intellectual Heritage. Renewed attention must be given to the Islamic intellectual heritage. This treasure must be understood critically, analytically, and in a way that delivers us from the three spheres that usually influence our dealings with it: total rejection, total acceptance, and piecemeal grafting. These three spheres represent obstacles not only in the present, but for the future as well. A critical and methodologically sound reexamination of this heritage should overcome these three spheres and establish a system in which the Islamic paradigm and its methodology can deal effectively with issues that, although not the focus of study, may shed light on how the Muslim mind has dealt with social and other phenomena in the past and, therefore, on how it may deal with contemporary phenomena.

As Islam's intellectual heritage is the product of the human mind, it is subject to the relative considerations of the "when, where, and who" of its origins. Even so, its links to revelation, itself above all relative considerations, make this intellectual heritage closer to the truth than those intellectual traditions that do not spring from revelation. Finally, however, it is necessary to understand our intellectual heritage as ideas, treatments, and interpretations of a historical reality that differs significantly from our own. In our reexamination, we must discern what objectives the heritage sought to serve and then evaluate the methods used, if not the solutions suggested, for their utility in our own time and place.

The Sixth Discourse: Dealing with the Western Intellectual Heritage. If the Muslim mind is to liberate itself from the dominant paradigm and how it deals with that paradigm, it must construct a methodology for dealing with western thought, both past and present. Outright rejection or wholesale acceptance, as well as the cosmetic grafting of elements without reference to a systematic methodology or to sociocultural differences, will not benefit the Muslims.

THE ISLAMIZATION OF KNOWLEDGE UNDERTAKING

These are the steps or, more specifically, the six discourses from which the concept of the Islamization of Knowledge may proceed. At present, we find ourselves confronted by a ubiquitous positivism that, in the name of scientific research and progress, promotes the idea that science may be served by breaking the relationship between the created and the Creator. This is accomplished, in part, by proposing ideas about existence that seem to conflict with much of our Islamic thinking. In fact, these ideas may or may not actually be inconsistent with Islamic teachings or principles.

Here, the issue is not that we should search our religious teachings for matters that seem to agree with such ideas, solely for the purpose of being able to say "we already knew about that" or to reject summarily such ideas as unbelief (*kufr*). In principle, the project's position toward the natural sciences is anything but ecclesiastical or an attempt to follow the examples of others. In fact, their experience with knowledge and progress differs considerably from our own. Were the Qur'an to be considered theology and no more, then only one reading – the first one – would be permitted. That this is not the case is made clear by the fact that God has commanded us to undertake two readings. This is why we are not interested in disputing science, for we realize that the revelational truths in the Qur'anic verses (*āyāt*) are the same truths found in the signs (*āyāt*) of God's creation. If misconceptions, supposedly based on scientific principles, should appear, our duty is to reexamine or exonerate those principles.

This task is, in fact, the basis of the concept of the two readings. When religion was challenged by purely rational and positivistic thought, it never sought to defend itself through the practical and applied sciences and the theoretical schools that supported them. Thus Muslims, as a nation charged with guiding humanity, must reexamine science in order to deliver it from the clutches and influences of mistaken theories so that science may be used and regulated by the logic of the two readings.

The undertaking that we, as Muslim social scientists, advocate is a noble undertaking, even if some believe that it falls within the specific geographical and religious framework of Islam. In today's world, we are a part of the reaction against the invasion of the experimental and applied sciences in much the same way as our predecessors of the last two centuries reacted against the cultural invasion of the West and its emphasis on pure reason. Today's confrontation, however, is with an experimental and positivistic mentality that has rearranged the natural and social sciences. Our options are therefore limited: We may either adopt feeble dogmatic positions or positions based on the Islamization of Knowledge, which seeks to orient and direct the natural sciences in accordance with a comprehensive Qur'anic outlook on the natural universe and, at the same time, to reconstruct the natural and social sciences in consonance with that outlook. In fact, most of the approaches found in the experimental sciences continue to be qualified by the particular rather than characterized by dimensions of the universal. The universal dimension, however, is one that is embodied by the Qur'anic revelation:

> Verily, those who dispute over the signs of Allah without His vouchsafing them authority, those are the ones whose breasts are filled with naught but pride; and never will they attain what they wish. So seek refuge in Allah, the All-Hearing and All-Knowing. Verily, the creation of the heavens and Earth was greater than the creation of humanity. Yet, most of humanity does not know. (40:65)

The Islamization of Knowledge undertaking is both universal and Qur'anic. In the face of impetuous religiosity and the failure of modern civilization, the Qur'an stands out as the sole source qualified to direct a comprehensive methodological and intellectual undertaking that can make a continued contribution to knowledge and society. The present battle of civilizations represents a trial for us in our understanding of the Qur'anic methodology and our ability to safeguard society by means of applying it to the social sciences. It is our position that, via the complementarity of the two readings, the element of balance may be restored to science, the social sciences, and society. At the present time, science has reached a stage in which phenomena may be reduced to infinitesimally minute or galactically expansive proportions. Phenomena may no longer be understood in the same way they were understood by our predecessors. Phenomena are commonly regarded as what used to be visible before the technological revolution opened up the worlds of microscopic and electronic sensing devices. Whereas earlier generations visualized the atomic level in terms of grains of sand, the atomic and subatomic levels of today are purely microscopic: "So I do call to witness what you see and what you see not" (69:38-39).

Furthermore, whereas our predecessors understood time as a progression, today we understand it in terms of qualitative and classifiable – not merely quantitative – change. This essential difference is at the core of the difference between objective and rational causation, as it was understood in the past, and the scientific causation of the present.

Therefore, the Islamization of Knowledge must not be understood as idle theorization, but as an undertaking that has come to restore balance to knowledge through the two readings and to liberate human thought from the enervating clutches of ecclesiasticism and mysticism on the one hand, and from the positivisitic framework for scientific thought, which seeks to separate the created from the Creator on the other. Each extreme has had dreadful consequences for human life and society. The Islamization of Knowledge may be understood as a methodological and paradigmatic introduction to a worldwide societal alternative that seeks to deliver both Muslims and non-Muslims from their present crisis. Such an undertaking requires a great deal of outstanding study and research, beginning with studies of the Qur'an, and has to be carried out in the light of new understanding and perspectives. This responsibility falls to the Islamization of Knowledge undertaking and to the generations required to bring it to fruition.

Without a methodological understanding of the Qur'an (within the framework of its complete and integrative structure) to equal our methodological understanding of natural phenomena and their movement (within the framework of their particular structure), the Islamization of Knowledge will remain an impossibility. Moreover, as we attempt to explain the issue to the world, we should expect to be beset by many difficulties, one of them being that the present-day intellectual mentality is ill-disposed toward writs claiming the status of "revelation." In some instances, these may be tolerated by intellectuals, but only to a point. For the most part, however, the sacred and the transcendental have been relegated to the domain of personal conviction, which renders anything stemming from such literature scientifically unacceptable. Thus, contemporary knowledge considers the unseen beings referred to in these books, as well is their accounts of the past, as contrary to positivistic history and an objective scientific understanding of the world.

However, such an understanding is the result of an incomplete grasp of the two readings, which seek to comprehend natural and real-existent phenomena guided by revelation's higher truths, and not through a reading of these phenomena on their own. Such a one-sided reading leaves us in the realm of positivism and its deconstructed and relativistic ideas about existence, and leads to fragmented and partial, as opposed to holistic, thinking. When the two readings are allowed to complement one another, a natural progression occurs from the part to the whole – from the qualified to the absolute. Thus every rejection of the "metaphysical" or the "transcendental" is, in fact, a rejection of the first reading (revelation), which considers the transcendental to be a fundamental element in its method, not only as a matter of faith but also as an indicator of a greater universal existence. This, in turn, is indicated by the second reading (the real-existent).

If the world is to emerge from its current crisis of thought and civilization, it needs to comprehend both the natural and the metaphysical dimensions of existence in their entirety. The Islamization of Knowledge undertaking is responsible for bringing about this awareness. Such an undertaking is as considerable as it is ambitious. Beginning with the two readings, its goal is no less than Islamizing human knowledge so that truth may prevail and guidance may become widespread. This, in summary, represents the Islamization of Knowledge's *raison d'être*, and its overall goals may be summarized, as follows:

The First Goal: Restoring the link between knowledge and values or, more precisely, returning knowledge to the realm of values, from which it was expelled by positivism. It is now clear that separating knowledge and values was a serious mistake. Any observer of how contemporary knowledge developed will notice that the intellectual output of Europe and the United States has begun to show signs of concern, in nearly every discipline, with topics related to knowledge and values. Indeed, certain postmodernist trends represent this concern, particularly in view of modernism's complete failure and uncompromising partition of knowledge and values. The Islamization of Knowledge undertaking seeks to make this issue one of universal concern by laying out its philosophical and strategic frameworks, providing the means necessary to achieve it, and establishing the guidelines required to connect scholars with truth rather than speculation. Therefore, efforts expended on theorizing will not be wasted on the attempt to separate knowledge from values or the self from the subject, but on distinguishing between truth and reality as well as between suspicion and supposition. This rule may be derived from the following Qur'anic verse: "And let not your dislike of a people lead you to be unjust. Be just. Surely, that is closer to heeding God" (5:2).

The Second Goal: Bringing about an interplay and exchange between the reading of revelation and the reading of the real-existential. This is to be done in such a way that the end result will be harmony between humanity and all other elements of creation, all of whom are governed by the same natural laws (*sunan*) and strive toward the same end, namely, to worship their Creator and recite His praise. This means that the social and natural sciences will be linked, but not in the way envisioned by the so-called logic of positivism, which holds that if the social sciences are to be considered true sciences, they must be based on the same methodology as the natural sciences.

Rather, the Islamization of Knowledge approach is to return both of these fields to a single philosophy, one that fuses and interacts with the reading of revelation while, at the same time, strives to discern the general principles regulating both sciences. This philosophy, moreover, engenders a sound understanding and respect for nature that, in turn, leads to good treatment and overall benefit, rather than to the environmental destruction and natural resource squandering caused by the beliefs that nature must be conquered and the wilderness tamed. On the contrary, the Islamization of Knowledge encourages humanity's interaction with nature, for the latter was created to serve the former and, in its role as a trust, is an important factor in humanity's stewardship.

The Third Goal: Solving the problem of ends posited by the static philosophies in which contemporary western scholarship is mired. These philosophies speak constantly of the end of history, liberalism, and the world.[10] This is done in order to avoid answering those questions that all human philosophies, because of their refusal to consider revelation, have failed to answer, such as "What is the purpose of the universe?" and "Where will it end?"

Marxism sought to delimit an imaginary end that was to occur when true communism would spread over the world and each individual would work according to his/her abilities and be recompensed according to his/her needs. Liberal capitalism, however, views its own success as the end of history. The Islamization of Knowledge and its proposed systems and paradigms are not concerned with such theatrical ends or imaginary scenarios for the continued existence of humanity and its civilization. On the contrary, the undertaking completely negates the idea of ends as an intellectual problem, preferring instead to widen its horizons, as the problem of ends is wide open and limitless. The Prophet said: "When the Last Hour comes and one of you has a seed in his hand, then go ahead and plant it, if you can."[11] Evidently, he meant to emphasize that no one, regardless of the signs and indications, should suppose that the end has come or seek to limit human life and society.

This is the Islamization of Knowledge as we understand it, in its present state of development. It is a call for a global Islamic cultural and intellectual mobilization to rethink the foundations of human society and then rebuild it. The end result of this process is the realization of felicity now and in the Hereafter, and the rescuing of humanity from a future in which destruction looms large.

NOTES

1. The Islamization of Knowledge, as understood by the International Institute of Islamic Thought, is a systematic methodological concept that the institute, as well as its branches and representatives, are attempting to develop and realize in practical terms. However, it appears that the concept, in general, has appealed to several different quarters and that these, in turn, have produced various publications in its name (or in similar names they have chosen either with or without care). The institute does not consider itself responsible for the work or views of such groups. In fact, their work so far fails to express the issue in terms of the methodology and comprehensiveness that characterize the institute's concern with it, as evinced through its literature and publications.
2. These include such matters as the pillars of faith, the prescribed duties, the acts of worship, the prohibited acts and substances, or the things referred to by certain scholars as being "known to be an essential part of Islam."
3. ʿImād al-Dīn Khalīl, *Madkhal ilā Islāmīyat al-Maʿrifah* (Herndon, VA: IIIT, 1991).

4. Abū al-Qāsim Ḥajj Ḥammād, *Al-ʿĀlamiyyah al-Islāmiyyah al-Insāniyyah* (Beirut: Dār al-Masīrah, 1980).
5. Ibid.
6. See Qur'an 12:111.
7. See Qur'an 6:38.
8. This was related by Imām Aḥmad ibn Ḥanbal in his *Musnad*, 3:218, on the authority of Jābir ibn ʿAbd Allāh.
9. This was related by al-Nasā'ī in his *Sunan*, "Book of Zakah," hadith no. 900, on the authority of ʿĀ'ishah.
10. Once such an "end" is seen to have reached its end, the terminology changes to "post-." In either case, however, the emphasis remains the same. [Trans.]
11. Imām Aḥmad ibn Ḥanbal related this hadith in his *Musnad*, 3:184, on the authority of Anas ibn Mālik.

The Islamization of the Methodology of the Behavioral Sciences

Many years ago, and after numerous conferences and exhaustive studies and consultations on our Ummah's present situation, as well as an extensive analysis of our past and future aspirations, an idea crystallized in the minds of a group of young committed Muslims: The Ummah's crisis, in both its essence and its reality, is an intellectual crisis, because everything else in the Ummah is sound, except for thought. The Ummah still possesses all of the fundamentals that had once made it "the best of peoples evolved for humanity" (3:110); all that is missing is the soundness of its thought and the ability to develop, utilize, and strengthen it. As far as the rest is concerned, if the Ummah is no better than it was, at least is no worse off. Therefore, the various phenomena of corruption in the Ummah are, in our opinion, only a reflection and embodiment of the crisis of its thought.

Thought is the fruit of all sources of knowledge, education, experience, ability, and social concepts and trends. For Muslims, it is formulated by revelation as well as humanity's inherent intellectual capacity, cultural developments and knowledge, and experience, in addition to one's *fiṭrah* (inherent nature) and potential, which Allah has bestowed upon every person. Thought is like a tree, for it needs healthy and strong roots to survive. Hence, if the roots and sources of knowledge are sound, the methodology correct, and the aims worthy, then both its situation and that of it supporters will improve. However, if there are mistakes or deliberate alterations and distortions in these sources, then thought will be corrupted and all aspects of life disrupted. Consequently, people will become short-sighted and narrow-minded, begin to neglect the basics and essentials because of their concentration on minor and irrelevant issues, ignore the long-term

Presented at the Fourth International Conference on Islamization of Knowledge. It first appeared in the *American Journal of Islamic Social Sciences* 6, no. 2 (December 1989), 227-38. It has been slightly edited.

aims and objectives, and focus on ritualistic details. In addition, they will either ignore the relationship between effects and their causes, or attribute effects to the wrong causes and thus fall victim to superstitions and fail to identify their priorities.

When a society reaches such a stage, its social equilibrium crumbles and collapses, and conflict among members of the group (or Ummah) will come to dominate all political, intellectual, and social aspects of life. Security will disappear, and distrust and corruption will prevail. Odd ideas and principles will predominate and create serious divisions and schisms. People will be hesitant and afraid to participate in or contribute to collective and public work, endeavors, and activities. Lacking both in trust and confidence, they will tend to isolate themselves from society. Positive, disciplined, and fair attitudes will disappear, only to be replaced with whimsical, frivolous, and erratic ones. Objective thinking will be lost, only to give way to Machiavellian and precautionary ideas and thought and to mixing up different issues and means. The members of the Ummah will have nothing in common. Killing, torturing, and the repressive silencing of all opposition will become the only way of communication between the rulers and the people. As a result, the Ummah will lose its ability to understand its own situation and fail to plan for the future; its efforts and activities will be limited to combating non-issues that are the product of selfishness and greed. All of these systems serve as clear indicators of nothing more or less than a crippling intellectual crisis.

If a nation's thought is distorted and suffers such a crisis, its situation cannot be rectified or improved, so that it may develop, without reforming its thought. Any attempted reform undertaken before resolving the crisis of thought is doomed to fail and lead to more confusion and corruption. Undoubtedly, all means of reform will become ineffective if they are influenced to any extent by corrupted and distorted thought. The positive results, if any, of such attempts will be short-lived and may even be used as a means of repression and destruction. Indeed, there are many striking examples of this in our own history.

Allah has ordered us to believe in *qadar* (i.e., His assignment of ends to all processes of life and existence on Earth). Belief in *qadar* is considered one of the most important pillars of *īmān* (i.e., the conviction that Allah is the One and only God and that Muhammad is His last Prophet). Anybody who does not believe in it cannot be considered a *mu'min* (a believer). Belief in *qadar* encourages Muslims to achieve great things, releases people from all kinds of desires and fears, and frees them from all sorts of pressures and evil influences. It gives them self-respect and enables them, in accordance with the will of Allah, to explore the universe, utilize it for their own benefit, and study its natural laws and the interrelationships among them so that they can build civilizations and establish truth, goodness, and beauty.

When the Ummah's first generation, namely, that of the Ṣaḥābah (the Companions) and the Tābiʿūn (the following generation), combined this driving force with enlightened thought and were able to understand it within this framework, no obstacle could hamper them and no difficulty could prevent them from achieving their aims and goals. But when this pillar of *īmān* (belief) is combined with disturbed and distorted thought, it leads to laziness, indifference, and apathy.

If we study the relationship between causality and divine power, we find that the first generation of Muslims understood it in a comprehensive and clear manner. Each of them would use what they had and, if successful, would thank and praise Allah, Who had created and made available such means and brought about the desired result. However, if they failed, they would go back and carefully reexamine the means to find out where they had gone wrong in order to rectify the mistake. After this, they would do their best again, within the Allah-given *sunan* (laws), to achieve the desired results. At the same time, they believed that Allah has complete power to do whatever He wills and "has power over all things" (2:20).

The first generation of Muslims knew that complete divine power did not prevent them from using the available and appropriate means to bring about the required result. All believers, they rightly felt, must do everything possible in the most proficient, accurate, and sincere manner, and then leave it to Allah to bring about a result in accordance with His *sunan* and *qadar*. Allah has the right to test His servants, but they do not have the right to test Him by neglecting the necessary means and causes to see whether or not the same result would occur. The first generation always sought the appropriate means in any matter. None of them felt that this detracted from the sincerity of their *īmān* or the reality of *tawakkul* (reliance on Allah). The Prophet summed up this matter in a single sentence. When an upset and surprised Bedouin, who had left his camel untied outside the mosque and later on learned that it had run away, complained to the Prophet that he had relied on Allah to take care of his camel, the Prophet said: "Tie the camel up (*ʿiqil*), then rely on Allah (*wa tawakkal*)."

However, the thought of the contemporary crisis-stricken generations has dramatically changed this simple, clear matter into an insoluble problem. The scholastic theologians (*kalāmīyūn*) have spoken and written a great deal on the reality and the nature of the cause and the relationship between causes and effects. They have raised such questions as: "Is the effect necessarily brought about by the cause?" and "When is it necessary, and when is it not, to mention and explain causes?" Such questions and consequent arguments confounded, bewildered, and confused the Muslim mind. Sometimes Muslims were told that resorting to means is a sign of weak *īmān* and *yaqīn* (apodictic certainty of the truth of Islam and its claim); other times they were told that adopting and resorting to means is a requirement of faith.

In all cases, this had a tremendous shattering effect on the Muslim mind and conscience. The Ummah now needs to make a great educational and intellectual effort to rid itself of these debilitating and paralyzing effects. The deviation of thought caused by the principle of causality is responsible, to a great extent, for the spread of superstition, indifference, lack of objectivity, and apathy. These negative effects have been exacerbated by the exponents of superlative fiqh and cryptic issues. An example would be those who seek to block the punishment of a woman who, pregnant through adultery, claimed that a jinn had impregnated her, thereby rendering her guilt "doubtful."

For the first generation of Muslims, the relationship between the intellectual capacity of *ʿaql* (reason) and *naql* (revelation, transmitted knowledge) was complementary. No narration indicates that any member of that generation felt that there was any dichotomy between the two. Whenever there was a revelation concerning *ghayb* (hidden, invisible, unseen, that which is beyond perception), they would submit to it, with no *iʿtirād* (objection), *jidāl* (argument), *taʿtīl* (delay), *tashbīh* (doubt), or *taʿwīl* (interpretation); with no argument or objections; and without trying to find an explanation. In other words, they had no need for such procedures because their intellect had already played its role in determining whether or not the Prophet was speaking the truth, and they had already pondered, argued, discussed, and asked for evidence (the miracle) before they had embraced Islam.

As long as they believed that the Prophet was the Messenger of Allah and was telling the truth, and that the Qur'an was the Book of Allah in which "no falsehood can approach from before or behind it" (41:42), they could easily accept whatever the Prophet told them about such matters. They were genuinely convinced that some things can be known only through revelation, and that the Revelation had been proven correct and authentic by miracles. Therefore, there was no need to waste precious intellectual energy or time on these matters. Rather, it is far better to devote ourselves to the study of the tangible universe and to use it as creatively as possible.

The relationship between the intellectual capacity of reason and revelation was severely affected by this crisis, which damaged scholastic theology and philosophy. This led to a great deal of distortion, confusion, and sterile arguments about fate, free will, cause and effect, people's deeds, humanity's role, and the value and importance of life and its goal. All of this affected the Muslims' way of thinking, outlook, education, behavior, attitudes, and reactions. In fact, they transformed Muslims into weak-willed, short-sighted, negative, indifferent, and fatalistic beings who blindly imitate others and are totally occupied and exhausted by trivialities. Such Muslims are like worthless flotsam, for no harmony whatsoever exists between them and their surroundings.

If the wonderful harmony between intellectual capacity and revelation had continued, and if Muslims had continued to study the universe and its laws and find ways to harness it for the benefit of humanity in order establish truth and justice, we would not find ourselves in this situation. It would not be possible for the reins of civilization to be in alien hands, nor for Muslims to be worthless flotsam. If Muslims had remained industrious, worshipping and meditating upon Allah with their mind and intellect, as well as with their actions and deeds, would this present intellectual lethargy, laziness, and inertia be arresting and paralyzing their intellectual capacity?

Moreover, if Islamic thought had continued to ascribe the appropriate importance to the *sunan* of cause and effect and establish the relationship between results and their causes, could superstition still dominate the Muslim mind? If it were not for the blind imitation of others, which has made Muslims behave like a lost herd, would we now find our Ummah being driven headlong into destruction and ruin as millions of Muslims are killed (most of them by other Muslims)? The situation is so chaotic that the killers do not know why they kill, and the dead do not know why they are dead. If it were not for the widespread confusion caused by this intellectual crisis, would it be possible for thousands of Muslims to die of diseases caused by overeating and other features of imported alien cultures while millions of others die of starvation and a lack of shelter?

This Ummah has been in existence for fourteen centuries. Although it is difficult to determine exactly when its crisis actually began, the split between the political leadership and the *ʿulamāʾ* and *fuqahāʾ*, which appeared after the era of the four rightly guided caliphs (632-61), can be considered a starting point. This split continued to grow and develop, leading eventually to the formulation of policies that, unlike those of the rightly guided caliphs, bore no relationship to the goals of Islam. These policies, which have had the worst effect on the Ummah and its thought, heralded the spread of those wrong ideas and concepts that brought about intellectual corruption.

Undoubtedly, the field of knowledge, along with its sources and methodologies, and the field of education, which is based on such knowledge, have been seriously affected and damaged by the current ongoing intellectual crisis. The human personality is formed from an intellect and a psyche, two features that distinguish people from animals by enabling them to think, analyze, and decide. The human intellect is formed by education and knowledge, plus the experiences and experiments of life. The psyche is formed by the arts, literature, and attitudes. So, any distortion in education is necessarily reflected in the intellect, and any disturbance or change in the arts and literature is reflected in the psyche.

The social sciences and humanities (e.g., psychology, sociology, education, economics, politics, and media) form the intellect of modern people (whatever their religion) in accordance with their orientation and educational influence. All of these subject areas are the product of the western mind, which formed them in accordance with its own philosophy and complicated outlook on the universe, life, and humanity, and then molded them to suit their own needs and without any regard for the needs of other peoples. The Soviets often describe the standards and methods of these sciences as being *capitalist.* I wonder what term Muslims will ascribe to them after their thought is reformed and their will is freed from their shackles and fetters.

The methodologies of these sciences, as well as their subject matter, results, aims, behavior, and outlook on life and the universe, are all in sharp conflict with our beliefs, concepts, and aims in life. They have succeeded in dividing educated Muslims into several groups, each adhering to one of its various philosophies and schools of thought. Some of them are described as "logical and positivist," others as "existentialist," and still others as "materialist."

Shortly after its formation, Israel established a committee for the social sciences and entrusted it with conducting research in those fields and calculating the extent of the threat they posed to Jewish and Zionist thought. The committee was required to devise a way to rid these fields of any negative effects to the Jewish mentality, because Israel's leaders and thinkers were well aware of the negative and destructive effects that these sciences could have on life. The fact that many of the main exponents of these philosophies and schools of thought were Jews has not prevented Israel from seeking to neutralize their effect on the Jewish people, both inside and outside of Israel.

Tragically, however, Muslim youths are being greatly influenced and affected by all of these alien ideas and concepts. They accept and propagate the positive and negative elements without thinking; they become absorbed in daydreams. Their excuse for accepting such cultural and intellectual colonialism is that the West took the foundation of its culture and civilization from the Islamic legacy. In the whole Islamic world, there is no single center for the critical study of these sciences from an Islamic viewpoint, let alone centers that could provide an Islamic alternative.

The time has come for our universities to turn away from their role of producing clerks and officials and to begin producing educated scholars: not merely graduates with general knowledge, but educated Muslims who are aware of their duties, well-versed in their fields, and understand and are committed to the Islamic concepts of the universe, life, and humanity. This cannot be achieved unless educated Muslims resume their proper role in life: conveying the message of Islam and reformulating their own legacy, as well as humanity's cultural and scientific heritage, by giving an Islamic character to its methodologies, principles, results, and aims. Thus, all fields and methods of knowledge, both in the arts and the sciences, will begin and end with Islamic concepts. However, this cannot be achieved without Islamizing knowledge.

THE SHARI^cAH SCIENCES

Our knowledge suffered a split very early in its existence. The origins of this split may be traced to the second to fourth Islamic centuries, the age of translation, classification, compilation, and recording. As a result, knowledge was divided into two separate areas: Shari^cah knowledge and "other" knowledge. This division still prevails. When the West colonized the Islamic world, it reinforced this division and gave it a new impetus. Western strategists took advantage of the dual system of education to completely isolate Islam from life and confine it to mere theoretical issues that served little practical purpose and had no great effect on everyday life. In each Islamic country they colonized, they established a secular system of education that enforced the westernization of the Muslim mind.

Consequently and tragically, Muslims began to believe in western values and adhere to western methodologies in all aspects of life and knowledge. The colonialists enabled this secular educational system to influence society and provided it with all the means to do so. In order to kill any serious opposition, they allowed some religious schools to remain. In most countries, these schools were attached to mosques; in others, they were kept independent. They taught the legacy of fiqh, *kalām,* and *uṣūl,* as well as Arabic sciences, using books written and ideas formulated after the gates of ijtihad had been closed.

This dual system of education caused the split of the Ummah's educated members into two groups: the westernized group that tries to establish all kinds of connections and rapport with the West, thinking that this will improve the Ummah's situation, and an opposing group that strongly resists this, not through sound thought but through the thought and mentality formulated during the period of decline, when the bases of such studies and education were formed. This conflict, which continues to waste the Ummah's energy and destroy its unity, is a major reason for its backwardness.

Given the above, we can clearly realize the urgent necessity for what we call the Islamization of Knowledge, which, in addition to the goals mentioned above, seeks to abolish this dual system of education in order to rid the Muslim mind of this dichotomy of knowledge. This goal, once achieved, would produce a united education system and a methodological syllabus capable of providing the Ummah with Muslim specialists in every practical area as well as in the social sciences and the humanities. These specialists would understand the general *aḥkām al-Sharīʿah* (rules of the Shariʿah) in addition to the rules of their field, so that they would know what to accept and what to reject. This would enable them to align their own activities with the general goals of Islam and its conception of the universe, life, and humanity.

Those studies known as "Shariʿah studies" need to be completely revised with regard to the books used, the tutors involved, the subject matter studied and researched, and the teaching methods followed. A great deal needs to be added, and the syllabus needs to be changed. Both the humanities and the social sciences, as well as the study of human nature and natural laws, should be added to the syllabus so that the *fuqahā'* can understand human nature and instinct, both individual and social, and life's various aspects. Equipped with such knowledge, they can interact effectively with these realities and, by becoming aware of its problems and values, play an active part in society.

This Ummah must establish academic institutions for research and study that deal with and specialize in the areas mentioned above in order to utilize its potential to hold meetings, invite scholars to research and write, adopt the most intelligent young people, and prepare them to devise the methodologies, programs, steps, plans, and conditions necessary for reforming its thought and Islamizing knowledge. Moreover, such institutions would strive to make this undertaking the main concern of educated Muslims, thereby establishing a trend that will lead the Ummah to a real, solid renaissance; carry the message of Islam from a comprehensive, civilized viewpoint and perspective; and put its basic issues into action. This will lead the Ummah toward a life of goodness in this world and a great reward in the Hereafter.

The First International Conference on the Islamization of Knowledge was held in Europe in July 1977. A decison was taken to establish an institute that would work toward reviving Islamic thought and its methodology. Thus, IIIT was established in Washington, DC, in 1981 by some Muslims who volunteered to shoulder this responsibility and duty and devote themselves to fulfilling the institute's objectives and securing its independence. The Second International Conference on Islamization was held in Islamabad, Pakistan, in 1982, as a joint effort between IIIT and the International Islamic University of Pakistan. As a result of the participants' research and discussions, a plan for Islamizing knowledge was crystallized and published as *The Islamization of Knowledge: General Principles and Work Plan.*

One result of this conference was that the Islamic trend in Pakistan was not confined to knowledge. The Pakistani president himself participated in the conference and instructed his advisers and the nation's leading figures to take part in the research and discussions. Since then, Pakistan has taken wide-ranging steps toward Islamization in many fields. Civil and criminal laws have been reviewed and replaced with Islamic alternatives. A system of zakah was announced and is being enacted. The study of Islamic civilization and Islamic thought has been included in the syllabi of all universities, and specialist research centers have been established in many branches of knowledge in the universities to study how to Islamize those subjects. Many Pakistanis see a direct connection between that conference and the Islamic changes that followed it.

The Third International Conference on the Islamization of Knowledge was held in Kuala Lumpur, Malaysia, in cooperation with the International Islamic University of Malaysia. The prime minister, as well as other officials, party members, and many prominent Malaysian scientists and scholars, participated. This had far-reaching effects on the wide-ranging steps that Malaysia has taken toward Islamizing many fields. Useful alterations have been made to most syllabi, and an international Islamic university and an Islamic bank have been established in Kuala Lumpur. One is delighted to hear that Malaysia's non-Muslim minority has welcomed the call for Islamization and the various moves in that direction. This proves beyond any doubt that if Islam is presented to people in a correct and positive way, and as a solution to their problems, a cure for their ills, an answer to their questions, and a just and practical way of dealing with matters, then they will rush to embrace it. But if Islam is presented in a negative way, merely as empty words and slogans and strict actions, then it will be rejected and resisted.

Today, the institute is holding its Fourth International Conference in cooperation with the University of Khartoum. We hope that this conference will produce a comprehensive view of the Islamic methodology and a practical conception that will enable the Islamization of the behavioral sciences, which form the basis of the social sciences. These should be presented to the teachers of those sciences so that they can give examples and evidence of the Muslim mind's ability to structure and develop knowledge, and reintroduce these sciences to their students from an Islamic angle by adopting from the Qur'an and the Sunnah their ideas of the human soul and human nature, the rules of individual and social *fiṭrah*, the purpose of creation, and the divine laws governing the universe, humanity, and life.

At the same time, they should seek to use all of the sound means and methods of scientific research that Allah has bestowed upon His servants so that these sciences can help produce strong new Muslims that can fulfill their role as Allah's vicegerent on Earth. Therefore, humanity's *raison d'être*, which is to serve of Allah, involves building civilizations and utilizing all of the energies and potentials – both apparent and hidden – that Allah has provided so that humanity can fulfill its role.

The institute hopes that Sudan will carry out this trust, especially since its government is led by an important Muslim thinker who has contributed a great deal to many Islamic causes and issues. We also hope that the prime minister will include this message in his suggestions to the Islamic Summit Conference and ask Muslim leaders to give due and appropriate attention to reforming the methodology and Islamizing knowledge.

As we pointed out earlier, three western behavioral sciences (viz., psychology, sociology, and anthropology) are considered the basis and the starting point for all western humanities and social sciences. Their assumptions, rules, and theories define the understanding of humanity and its nature, aims, motives, and reactions, as well as the significance of people's activities, relationships, and interactions with others. One could almost say that the other social sciences consist merely of applying the assumptions and rules of these sciences to education, politics, economics, administration, media, law, and so forth. However, the western thought found in these sciences has many negative features and serious shortcomings, the most important of which are listed below:

- *Limitation of the Sources of Knowledge:* As the West confines the sources of its knowledge to human intellect alone, it has deprived itself of the most important source of knowledge, namely, Divine revelation, which provides comprehensive and detailed knowledge.
- *Limitation of the Means of Examining the Knowledge Produced by the Human Intellect:* As the West limits these means to experiments alone, it has made this the only proof of soundness in any branch of knowledge. Hence, westerners think that experiments are the only means of verification and therefore are suitable for every field of knowledge. But this is not the case.
- *Application of Deduction Regardless of Wide Differences:* The West subjected the behavioral and social sciences to the rules and methodologies of the natural and applied sciences. The motive for doing so was its great achievements in the applied and natural sciences

At this point, I hope you will permit me to pause briefly in memory of two great martyrs of the institute: Professor Ismāʿīl Rājī al-Fārūqī and his wife Lois Lamyā' al-Fārūqī (may mercy fall on them).

Ismāʿīl Rājī al-Fārūqī was an exponent and a leader of this cause. He traveled throughout the world, advocating it in his books and lectures. Like his ancestor ʿUmar ibn al-Khaṭṭāb al-Fārūq, al-Fārūqī distinguished between truth and falsehood. Like him, he also compensated as a committed and devoted Muslim for all of the time and energy he had wasted in earlier gatherings, meetings, and activities. The cause of reforming the methodology of thought and the Islamization of Knowledge ignited his *īmān*, which until then had lain dormant, shrouded in the fog of philosophy, both ancient and modern, western and eastern. This cause stirred up strong emotions that had been scattered among many causes. Suddenly, he became devoted to this one cause: the Islamization of Knowledge. It dominated his life and activities as he pondered, discussed, and planned with his fellow Muslims how to realize it and how to mobilize enough people and resources for it.

Al-Fārūqī always expressed himself sincerely and clearly, and presented his arguments in the best possible manner. He was aware of the faults of Christianity and Judaism, having studied and mastered both, in addition to being well-versed in the history of religions. As an expert in western philosophy, he had identified its limits and was cognizant of the Shariʿah's advantages. He enjoyed an international reputation, and there was hardly a conference in any field of the humanities and social sciences at which he was not one of the main speakers or did not captivate the minds of his audience.

Always by his side was his wife, the *shahīdah* (martyr) Lois Lamyā' al-Fārūqī. She had been his partner in life since his arrival in the United States. A distinguished scholar in the field of arts and civilization, she combined her energies with his. For many years, she devoted her efforts to tracing the roots of and establishing a theory for "Islamic arts." She took it upon herself to Islamize the arts and succeeded in doing, with the utmost humility and modesty, that which hundreds of Muslim women, raised in Muslim homes, have failed to do. The whole family was the enemy's target, and so Lamyā' was killed by the same Rambo knife as her husband. She died minutes before him. The killer tried to finish off their pregnant daughter, whom he repeatedly stabbed with his knife, stopping only when he thought she was dead.

This is the institute's first conference since the martyrdom of the al-Fārūqīs. We want to ensure that the flag will be kept flying, that the institute will continue spreading its message, and that the brothers and sisters of al-Fārūqīs will carry on their mission regardless of all challenges, obstacles, and hindrances.

In conclusion, we ask Allah to enable us to complete our task and achieve our aims; grant us all resolution and sincerity; bless this conference, from which we shall be able to take on that which will benefit our Ummah and help to spread progress; and make our efforts and those of all sincere Muslims successful. Indeed, He is the only One we can ask for success, and the only One who can grant it.

Part II:

Issues in Islamic Jurisprudence

The Crisis of Thought and Ijtihad

INTRODUCTION

The Muslim mind experienced a crisis of thought when, during the early centuries of the Islamic era, ijtihad (independent judgment in juridical matters) began to be viewed as limited to legal matters, rather than as a methodology for dealing with all aspects of life. This limited understanding engendered a malaise that allowed *taqlīd* (imitation) to attain such prominence and respectability that its cancerous, constricting, and irrelevant fiqh (jurisprudence) spread throughout Muslim life. Had ijtihad retained more of its lexical meaning and creativity, and had fiqh been considered only one of its uses, perhaps Muslims would have overcome many of the problems that confronted them. However, this particularization of ijtihad confined the Muslim mind, and *taqlīd* eventually paralyzed its creative abilities.

Had ijtihad remained a way of life for Muslims, as Allah commanded, they would not have fallen behind in establishing the Islamic sciences necessary for their society and civilization. They also would not have had to watch the reins of leadership pass to the West, whose most important qualification was its ability to engage in creative and scientific reasoning. Although its intellectual tradition was tainted with pagan Greek influences, the West achieved world leadership. Had Muslims taken up those sciences and laid the foundations of their society on the basis of *tawḥīd* (unity), Earth would be different today and the state of civilization itself would be far more felicitous than it is at present.

Before ijtihad was confined to the purely legalistic framework of fiqh, the Muslim mind was enlightened, eager to deal with all manner of thought, able to meet challenges, generate solutions, and achieve its goals. Had it not been for *taqlīd* and its subduing of the Muslim mind, that mind would have

This "reflections" article first appeared in the *American Journal of Islamic Social Sciences* 10, no. 2 (Summer 1993): 234-37, and was translated by Yusuf DeLorenzo. It has been slightly edited.

achieved great things. Certainly, a mind with its beginnings in the verse "Read! in the name of your Lord Who created ..." (96:1) should be more than able to renew the Ummah's mentality, continually adjust to changing circumstances, and initiate the sciences of civilization at a time when the West was still overrun by wild forest tribes.

WHAT DO WE MEAN BY IJTIHAD?

For the reasons indicated above, we are calling for a new type of ijtihad. Rather than the ijtihad specified by the scholars of *uṣūl,* we speak of an ijtihad that is more of a methodology for thought. Such an understanding would allow the Muslim mind to participate in an intellectual jihad, a jihad launched to generate ideas and build a new Muslim identity, mentality, and personality. This jihad would apply to all fields of knowledge, seek to make the Ummah qualified to shoulder its responsibilities as regards vicegerency (*khilāfah*), and enable it to serve as a median nation (*wasaṭiyyah*). While such an ijtihad would apply to legalistic, juridical, and jurisprudential fiqh, it would also apply to such new forms of fiqh as the fiqh of religiosity (*fiqh al-tadayyun*) and dialogue (*daʿwah*), as well as to all fields requiring the Ummah's attention and creative thinking.

IJTIHAD: THE ALLY OF JIHAD

Both ijtihad and jihad are derived from the lexical root, *j-h-d,* and both seek the same goal: to release all beings from devotion to the created so that they may be free to practice devotion to the Creator, to take them from the injustice of religious deviation and superstition to the justice of Islam, and to take them from the restrictions of the physical world and limited thinking to the wide horizons of Islam and the Qur'an. For this reason, ijtihad is counted among the pillars of Islam in the same way that jihad is. Without jihad there would be no Ummah, and without ijtihad the Ummah would have no vitality. Thus, both may be considered as essential and continual responsibilities.

Once *taqlīd* in matters of fiqh established itself as a pervasive intellectual attitude, all that remained of ijtihad was its extremely rare use – maybe once in a century – by individual Muslim thinkers and scholars. Their role was of inestimable importance and was, in some ways, just as important as that of modem parliamentary and democratic institutions.

Ijtihad was the methodological means that allowed Muslims to confront ignorance, oppression, and deviation. But when the Muslims themselves abandoned it, all manner of trouble beset them. By closing the door of ijtihad, Muslims believed that they were solving their legislative problems. In reality, however, they only succeeded in crippling their own intellectual powers. Although the call to revive ijtihad was never entirely silenced, such calls were never enough to extract the Ummah from the intellectual crisis in which it had become mired. As a result, ijtihad was left mainly to heretics and deceivers, and, finally, to Orientalists. If a true Muslim were to articulate ideas to which people were unaccustomed or to announce his/her readiness to practice ijtihad, he/she would become an immediate target of ridicule and abuse by the supporters of *taqlīd.*

The Ummah must understand that ijtihad provides it with the fundamental means to recover its identity and reestablish its place in world civilization. Without ijtihad the Muslim mind will never rise to the levels envisioned for it by Islam, and the Ummah will not take its rightful place in the world. Unless the call to ijtihad becomes a widespread intellectual trend, there is little hope that the Ummah will make any useful contribution to world civilization or correct its direction, build its own culture or reform its society. To liberate the Muslim mind, the Ummah needs ijtihad in every aspect of its life. If it is to play its preordained role, it must undertake a new reading of the Qur'an and the Sunnah, study its past, analyze its present and, by means of these, ensure its future.

RIGHT OR WRONG, THE *MUJTAHID* IS REWARDED

No mere call, announcement, or advertisement will result in ijtihad or produce a *mujtahid.* Such developments depend upon the preparation of needed intellectual and cultural atmospheres, for a *mujtahid* is one of the Ummah's most gifted and accomplished scholars. When the Prophet spoke of ijtihad and how one who performed it correctly received a double reward, and how one who made a mistake received one reward, he was addressing an Ummah that understood that only a few people could undertake it. The resulting responsibility was so great that even those few individuals who dared to undertake it did not always announce their opinions if they seemed contrary to those of majority or the rulers.

Clearly, any mention of ijtihad and its importance should be accompanied by serious efforts to bring about the right sort of intellectual and cultural atmosphere. The first step toward this goal is to create an environment of complete freedom of thought and expression. If people lack the courage to perform jihad, they find it even harder to perform ijtihad and accept the consequent responsibilities. How many intellectual positions are harder to defend than military positions?

In the present straightened circumstances, no one who can generate sound ideas or perform even partial ijtihad should hesitate to announce the results of his/her ijtihad. No one who is aware that there is a reward even for those whose ijtihad is incorrect has an excuse to refrain from playing a role or from giving the Ummah the benefit of his/her ideas and creativity. After all, those ideas might become the foundations of a new cultural and intellectual order within the Ummah. Nor should anyone continue to listen to those who warn of the dangers inherent in allowing ijtihad. The Ummah has heard all of their arguments, and nothing they say has been of any help.

THE LEXICAL AND TECHNICAL MEANINGS OF IJTIHAD

In the Arabic dictionary, the root *j-h-d* is defined as "the exertion of effort on a matter that requires it." In all of its different applications, the term denotes the expenditure of mental and intellectual effort. A *mujtahid*, therefore, is a scholar who researches and studies all of the sources, information, statistics, and available material about a subject until he/she is satisfied that he/she has done everything to learn about the subject in question. After expending all of that effort, it may reasonably be assumed that his/her opinion is reliable. This is why al-Ghazālī defined ijtihad as "the expending, on the part of a *mujtahid*, of all what he/she is capable of in order to seek knowledge of the Shariʿah's injunctions." In a further clarification of this definition, he then wrote: "Complete ijtihad happens when the *mujtahid* expends all of his/her energies in seeking, to a point where he/she is satisfied that no more can be done." This definition refers to ijtihad in the field of law and indicates that the effort expended must be exhaustive and emanate from those who are qualified. If an unqualified person undertakes these same efforts, one cannot say that ijtihad has been performed.

HOW CAN THE PROBLEMS OF *TAQLĪD* AND DEPENDENCY BE OVERCOME?

In order to extract ourselves from the clutches of *taqlīd* so that we can create the circumstances under which ijtihad can flourish, we must define our intellectual premises carefully. In doing so, however, we must avoid the modern western paradigm that, for too many reasons to list, has become the center of every academic circle and the starting place for the majority of modern thinkers. One major reason for doing so is that the western paradigm is based on secular materialism, an outlook that rejects revelation outright. It views only that which can be measured or quantified as a suitable subject for serious study. Those who have come under the West's influence define knowledge as information acquired either through the senses or experimentation. All of the contemporary social sciences and humanities, as well as the natural sciences, are founded on this premise. This is why modern theories of politics, society, economics, and ethics have their roots in the same definition. Secularism, therefore, has become the basis for all intellectual and academic research, analysis, and synthesis. Thinkers and scholars the world over have now accepted the secular paradigm of knowledge.

The acceptance of this western model has only served to increase the Ummah's intellectual dependency. At the same time, it has helped to eradicate whatever traits distinguished non-western cultures and civilizations from their western counterparts, and perhaps has had a role in the latter's outright plundering of the former. Unless the mentality of dependency is overcome, there can be no ijtihad or intellectual ingenuity.

Taqlīd and the Stagnation of the Muslim Mind

THE ORIGINS AND BEGINNINGS OF *TAQLĪD*

Allah Most High chose the Muslims to be the Ummah of mission (*risālah*), exemplary good (*khayriyyah*), the golden mean (*wasaṭiyyah*), and witnessing (*shahādah*) to humanity. Along with these responsibilities came the capacity for renewal, ijtihad, and interpreting the Shariʿah correctly. As a result, there is a certain inseparable mutuality between the Ummah's roles as a median community cum civilizational witness for humanity and its other role as a moral and ethical exemplar, and between its capability for ijtihad and effecting reform. In order to facilitate these roles, Allah endowed the Qur'an and the Sunnah with the necessary flexibility in every aspect of Islam: its belief system, methodology, the Shariʿah, and organization.

Thus, it was only natural for the early generations of Muslims, both on an individual and a community level, to offer a unique picture to the world: the complete liberation of the human mind from all forms of mental slavery and idolatry. Further protection against falling from this exalted position was the provision made for avoiding mistakes, deviations, and misinterpretations: Only those statements that could be proven by acceptable, or supported by valid, testimony were to be believed. A look at the Companions' ijtihad, whether they were learned *qurrā'* (Qur'anic reciters) or common people, will suffice to illustrate the amazing transformation that Islam achieved.

Why do we not see this situation today? What has happened to the penetrating and enlightened mind, inspired by Islam, that freed our ancestors from their idols and the obstacles blocking their progress? How did such a mind return to its former prison and fetters, robbed of any chance to renew

This "reflections" article first appeared in the *American Journal of Islamic Social Sciences* 8, no. 3 (December 1991): 513-24. It has been slightly edited.

and reform the Ummah through ijtihad? In a word, the answer is *taqlīd*, an illness that entered the Muslim mind and fed on it until it returned to its prison. This paper is a study of *taqlīd*, one designed to reveal why it has overtaken the Ummah.

TAQLĪD AND THE UMMAH'S CRISIS

Muslims and non-Muslims alike are amazed that one of history's most advanced civilizations could fall into such a state of overwhelming wretchedness, ignorance, backwardness, and decline. Why are there so many crises in the Ummah's thought? Why, when the Ummah possesses sufficient natural, human, spiritual, and civilizational resources, does its vision remain cloudy and its list of priorities confused? The answer(s) to such questions has not been found, despite the innumerable studies dealing with the overall problem by means of different methodologies and despite the fact that their results and conclusions about the causes have been identified, published, and analyzed.

But the amazement and frustrations remain. A civilization that placed such emphasis upon literacy and knowledge remains largely illiterate. An Ummah that received such clear divine guidance remains mired in a morass of misunderstanding, misinterpretation, and outright confusion.

Other questions are waiting to be answered: How did the Ummah of unity and *tawḥīd* become divided into so many sects and subsects? Why does the Ummah, blessed with all of the means and resources necessary for economic prosperity, continue to suffer from abject poverty? Why does the Ummah, blessed with all the means of dominance and invincibility, remain subjected to continuing political and military humiliation? Why does the thought of it people, to whom all the sources of guidance were revealed, remain awash in fallacy and delusion?

Unfortunately, our situation is even worse, for we see parts of our Ummah trying to defend these aberrations by presenting them as wholesome, ascribing them to others, trying to find scapegoats, or even attempting to downplay their importance by explaining that such things are natural and common.

TAQLĪD: A NATURAL (ORIGINAL) CONDITION OR A DEVIATION?

Allah has blessed this Ummah with an ʿ*aqīdah* (creed), a Shariʿah, and a *minhāj* (method). This ʿ*aqīdah* gives Muslims a clear perception of life and the universe based on the principle of pure *tawḥīd* in harmony with the *fiṭrah* (the pattern on which Allah has made humanity[1]), in balance with all that exists and in explanation of all civilization's elements: *istikhlāf,*[2] *ibtilā',*[3] *tamkīn,*[4] *tadāfuʿ,*[5] *taskhīr,*[6] *takrīm,*[7] *amānah,*[8] *ʿibādah,*[9] and *shuhūd.*[10]

The Shariʿah is a blessing because of its universality, comprehensiveness, perfection, effectiveness in preserving all of the necessities of existence, and provision of what is needed to build a civilization and its identity. The Shariʿah, moreover, comprehends all of the elements that give Islamic life its particular color and taste, and also contributes to achieving Islam's higher objectives. As such, the Ummah will achieve success and felicity in this life and in the Hereafter, and the Muslims will fulfill their role as Allah's vicegerent, only if the Shariʿah's objectives, purposes, and principles are clearly understood and appreciated.

The *minhāj* of Islam is a blessing, for the Prophet said: "It is the shining path whose night is as clear as its day." Thus, one who uses his/her reason and senses cannot go astray, for following the *minhāj* leads an individual to felicity, society to the common good, and the Ummah to its goals of *wasaṭiyyah* and *shahādah.*

Islam's *ʿaqīdah*, Shariʿah, and *minhāj* can be applied only by a mind illuminated with sure knowledge of and faith in Allah, able to understand its purposes and principles, conscious of Islam's premises so that they may be connected intelligently, and capable of achieving the highest degree of discernment. This is why Islam is so determined to free the human mind from its previous and present fetters. The Qur'an even states that if this is not accomplished at the outset, His Ummah will fail to perform ijtihad, carry out reform, give guidance, or follow in the prophets' footsteps: "Those were the ones who received Allah's guidance; so emulate the guidance they received" (6:90). Thus, we can say that the Muslim mind's present state is unnatural, for it has accepted, without proof, many concepts and practices that have led to reason's arrest and petrifaction.

For the Ummah, *taqlīd* represents a blameworthy innovation (*bidʿah*) as well as a deviation (*ḍalālah*) from the straight path. No researcher or scholar has ever found a valid text from either the Qur'an or the Hadith, or even an argument based on pure reason, to support Islam's approval of *taqlīd*, for the very idea is alien to Islam's view of humanity. Islamic teachings clearly state that all assertions must be supported by verifiable evidence or proof. If these elements are absent, the statement must be rejected. This applies to all statements (a fact has to be verifiable), a claim (it also to be verifiable), a ruling (it must have either valid testimony or evidence), or a command or a prohibition (they must have an issuing authority based either in revelation or existence and thus subject to empirical validity). If such conditions are not met, the assertion has to be rejected. These are the basic landmarks in the methodology of the Muslim mind.

TAQLĪD: FOR MUSLIMS OR NON-MUSLIMS?

A Muslim, or one who has been liberated from all shackles and fetters by the grace of Allah, has a free mind and a clear conscience. Thus, he/she will accept only the truth – that which is supported by proper evidence. Non-Muslims, those who have remained chained to and enslaved by their continuous idolatry (*shirk*), have been and remain easy prey for any sort of falsity. Of them, Allah has stated:

> When it is said to them: "Follow what Allah has revealed," they say: "On the contrary, we shall follow the ways of our fathers." What? Even though their fathers were devoid of wisdom and guidance? (2:170)

and:

> In the same way, We never sent a warner before you to any people except that the wealthy ones among them said: "We found our fathers following a certain religion; and certainly we shall follow in their footsteps." (43:23)

And they said:

> O Lord! We obeyed our chiefs and our great ones, and they led us astray from the right path. (33:67)

Sometimes an overbearing person will deceive others so as to influence them and, in the name of religion, gain control of their thinking. This is usually done by claiming one of the uniquely divine attributes, like that of legislation. Calling those who follow such people deluded, Allah has said: "They take their priests and anchorites to be their lords, in derogation of Allah" (9:31).

Commenting on this verse, Hudhayfah related a hadith in which ʿAdī ibn Ḥātim (a convert from Christianity) said to the Prophet: "But we didn't actually worship them, O Messenger of Allah." The Prophet replied: "But did they not make what was *ḥarām* for you *ḥalāl* and what was *ḥalāl* for you *ḥarām*? And did you not follow what they told you?" ʿAdī replied: "Yes," to which the Prophet said: "This is how you worshipped them."[11]

Such evidence has caused Muslim scholars to agree that *taqlīd* is wrong and must be avoided. Counter-arguments that these verses were directed toward only the non-Muslims' use of *taqlīd* are rejected on the grounds that any similarity between a *muqallid* (one who follows blindly) in matters of *kufr* (unbelief) and a *muqallid* in anything else is not *kufr*, but only following the customs of deceased Muslims that may or may not have conformed with the Shariʿah.

In addition, Muslim scholars are generally agreed on the blameworthiness of *taqlīd* in general, even if they differ on its degree and various forms. Obviously, one who follows an unbeliever is not the same as one who follows a sinner. Likewise, one who follows an ignorant person on a question of daily life is not the same as one who follows an ignorant person on a matter of religion. Still, a Muslim should not be involved in any sort of *taqlīd*, as Allah has explained to humanity what may protect and preserve it from this: "Allah will not mislead a people after He has guided them, in order to make clear to them what they are to avoid" (9:115).

A Muslim must never accept anything without proof or believe anything without evidence of its validity. Allah has emphasized this by linking a Muslim's legal competence with his/her ability to use reason. Thus, if he/she becomes incapable of reasoning according to Islamic norms and values, his/her competence is invalidated.

Any supposition unsupported by sound evidence (*ẓann*) is subject to certain rules, for there are some matters in which it, in the absence of anything better, is acceptable. Generally speaking, however, any supposition is to be rejected, for a Muslim is expected to actively seek out what is certain and not to rest until he/she is satisfied that the evidence is conclusive. Among the early Muslims this was a self-evident fact, and none of them ever accepted, used, cited, or fell back on *taqlīd*.

SOURCES OF KNOWLEDGE

Allah has divided the sources of knowledge into two basic categories: a) revelation (*waḥy*), as He has said in the Qur'an: "He revealed to you the Book (the Qur'an) and *ḥikmah* (the Sunnah), and He taught you that which you did not know"(4:113); "He taught Adam the names of all things" (2:31); and "Recite in the name of your Lord Who created, created humanity from a blood clot! Recite, for Your Lord is the Most Noble, the One Who taught by means of the eternal pen (of revelation); Who taught humanity what it did not know" (96:1-5); and b) the universe (*al-kawn*), for He has told us that:

> Verily in the creation of the heavens and Earth, in the alternation of night and day, in the ships that glide through the ocean with what benefits humanity, in the water Allah sends down from the sky to revive the earth after it was dead and to scatter throughout it every manner of beast, in the changing of the winds, in the clouds made subservient between the heavens and Earth, are signs for a people who reason. (2:164)

Allah has even informed humanity how it can attain knowledge from these two sources: "Allah brought you forth from you mothers' wombs when you knew nothing; and then He gave you hearing and sight and intelligence" (16:78); "It is not given to any human that Allah should speak to him/her except through revelation, or from behind a screen, or by sending a messenger who reveals, by His leave, what He wills. Surely He is Most Sublime, Most Wise" (42:51); and "Likewise, We have revealed to you a spirit by Our command, when before you did not know what the Book was nor what faith was" (42:52).

However, one can benefit from these means only if his/her mind is enlightened and capable of digesting and then developing from this information the theories and conclusions necessary for living in an Islamic manner. Apparently, it is not unusual for the mind to gain no benefit from the information that the senses provide, for Allah has said: "And they must have passed the town on which was rained a shower of evil; did they not see it?" (25:40); "Deaf, dumb, and blind, they are void of wisdom" (2:171); and "Many are the jinn and men We have made for Hell. They have hearts that do not understand, eyes that do not see, and ears that do not hear. They are like cattle – nay, even more misguided. Indeed, such people, they are the heedless ones" (7:179).

We notice that *taqlīd* is not presented as a third source of knowledge. In other words, it is not an alternative to either revelation or science. Thus, its use is unacceptable even if, in a rare instance, it leads to what is right or correct. Instead, individuals are asked to discover the truth through the faculties that Allah gave them so that they could explore, observe, and contemplate His creation. Allah has taught humanity to seek proof and search for evidence. In order to emphasize this and inform humanity that it should not give up this quest even in matters having to do with Him, He has said: "... so that humanity, after the coming of the prophets, should have no proof against Allah" (4:165). It is as if Allah wanted to explain to humanity that it must make every effort to find the necessary evidence to support its position(s). Thus, if Allah expects this sort of verification from humanity in its dealings with Him, what of its dealings on an individual level?

HOW DID MUSLIMS SINK TO THE LEVEL OF *TAQLĪD?*

The Ummah did not suddenly plunge to the depths of *taqlīd.* On the contrary, we can trace the beginning of its gradual fall to the Tābiʿūn's era and as taking place in three phases: a gradual strengthening of the people's reliance upon the learned scholars' opinions, a deemphasis among the people on learning and scholarly pursuits, and a general hardening of hearts.

The major factor initiating the first phase was the individual Muslim's lack of interest in acquiring true learning and hard evidence. Instead, they grew more dependent on the scholars' reputations in the belief that such trust could replace his/her duty to seek evidence and proof for what the scholars taught.

Of course, the *qurrā'* and *fuqahā'* with which the early generations of the Muslims were blessed were greatly respected for their learning and piety, and deservedly so. However, the average Muslim soon forgot how these people used to ask the Prophet if he had spoken on his own authority (which could be disputed) or on that of revelation (which would immediately end all controversy). When the Prophet gave his own opinion, he would often encourage his Companions to help him make the correct decision. Sometimes he would even do what they suggested. Many hadiths report that he said: "Come on, people. Tell me what to do." A similar case is found in his telling ʿUmar and ʿAmīr: "Use ijtihad." Indeed, this encouragement motivated the *uṣūlī* scholars to debate whether the Prophet's ijtihad was subject to error or not, for he taught them never to accept anything he said or did until they were certain that it was based on revelation. *Taqlīd* could not exist in such an environment. As a matter of fact, the Muslims of that time considered it to be a trait of hypocrites and non-Muslims.

This state prevailed from the hijrah until around the last Companion's death in 99 AH. After this, deviation began to creep in as some Muslims seeking *fatāwā* began to feel somewhat awed in the presence of such great *ʿulamā'* and *mujtahidūn* as ʿUmar ibn ʿAbd al-ʿAzīz (101 AH), al-Ḥasan al-Baṣrī (110 AH), and Ibn Sīrīn (110 AH). Their vast knowledge, when joined with the gap between the generation of the Companions and that of the Tabīʿūn, gradually caused them to seem somewhat larger than life. This awe instilled within the common people a certain reluctance, born of admiration, esteem, and perhaps not a little awe, to ask them for evidence corroborating their legal rulings and opinions. At this stage, however, the majority of questioners still demanded proof, a practice that the scholars knew was their duty to provide and therefore did not resent.

But by the time of the third generation, learning and scholarly pursuits were no longer priorities for most Muslims, as they were more occupied with making a living. Thus, very few people attended the scholars' sessions to discuss knowledge or study and reflect on the textual evidence presented. Instead, when they had questions they would satisfy themselves with an answer (minus the requisite proof) from the scholars. This new practice permeated the intellectual environment and laid the groundwork for *taqlīd*.

The third stage was characterized by the Muslim masses accustoming themselves to accepting legal opinions without listening to either arguments or evidence, and by the legal scholars becoming comfortable with making pronouncements and providing no justification for doing so. In such an atmosphere, the following questions began to be asked: Is *taqlīd* permissible for an individual who is not a Shariʿah scholar? Who is a scholar? Who is required to seek evidence? Who cannot search for evidence on his/her own? Such questions divided the scholars of this period (circa 128 AH).

One group of scholars maintained that scholars still had to explain their evidence and that it was the questioner's duty, as stated in the Shariʿah, to demand this evidence. This group also claimed that it was *ḥarām* for scholars not to explain their proof, for doing so would seriously hinder the questioner's ability to make up his/her own mind. Another group of people, however, held that it was permissible for a non-scholar to follow a scholar: in other words, that *taqlīd* was *ḥalāl*. This opinion led to the widespread saying: "An *ʿāmmī* has no *madhhab* of his own; his *madhhab* is the *madhhab* of his mufti."

Thus, *taqlīd* was given a certain amount of legitimacy, even though, at least in theory, the *ʿulamā'* agreed that it was blameworthy and prohibited. Despite this, however, its popularity continued to spread, a development that would have very serious consequences for the Muslims' psychological disposition and mentality. At this point, *taqlīd* began to create a serious gap in the Muslim mind, for its acceptance led to generations of Muslims relying on unsubstantiated opinions and resulted in the creation of a mentality and a proclivity for slavish imitation.

THE CONSEQUENCES OF *TAQLĪD*

Realizing that the Ummah needed to change course, some people have sought a cure. Among those suggested were codifying a certain *madhhab*, giving it government support, and then requiring all citizens to follow it; and supporting only those *madhāhib* followed by a significant number of Muslims.

Several factors led the *ʿulamā'* to such ideas. One was the split between the Ummah's intellectual and political leadership that accompanied the deepening crisis of thought. Those in charge of the Muslims' affairs (*ulu al-amr*) were divided into two mutually opposed parties: the rulers (who had the power) and the *ʿulamā'* (who had the legal proofs and arguments).[12] This polarization shattered the two group's former complementarity and replaced it with a ruinous conflict over legitimacy and earning the Ummah's allegiance and support.

Under such circumstances, the rulers began to think of codifying the legal texts and declaring a state *madhhab*. The Abbasid ruler al-Manṣūr (d. 158 AH/755 AC) considered forcing his subjects to follow Mālik's *Al-Muwaṭṭa'*. Fearing that people would no longer deal directly with the Qur'an and the Sunnah if this policy were implemented, and that one solution might not be applicable to all locations, Mālik discouraged the idea. Several rulers attempted to lend state support to a particular legal school, but in each case the scholars opposed the idea because they feared that it might lead to *taqlīd*.

Another factor that led to *taqlīd's* increasing influence was the growing belief in fatalism (*jabr*). This attitude helped *taqlīd* gain even more adherents, and it became increasingly common for political leaders to justify their mistakes and aberrations by citing this doctrine. Quite simply, if their actions and decisions had been determined beforehand, they could not be held accountable for them and their subjects had no justification to revolt. In effect, it gave rulers *carte blanche* to rule the Ummah as they saw fit. As *taqlīd* was to their advantage, many rulers and court-supported scholars favored it despite the traditional *ʿulamā's* opposition.

Thus, *taqlīd* cleared the way for fatalism, which prepared the ground for tyranny, injustice, and despotism. The "great ones," to use the Qur'anic expression, accustomed themselves to giving orders, and the "lowly ones," by the same logic, learned to submit. This result, which should clarify for the Ummah once and for all the vital and inseparable relationship between *taqlīd* and despotism, is even mentioned in the Qur'an: "Thus did he (Firʿawn) make fools of his people, and they obeyed him" (43:54) and "Firʿawn said: 'I only show you that which I see myself, and I only guide you to the path of [what is] right'" (40:29).

In conclusion, both the Qur'an and history show us that those who engage in *taqlīd* soon lose sight of the truth of what they are following and do not think of the consequences. Through this voluntary cessation of independent thought, such people hand over their destiny to whoever is able to establish control over them, even if this new leader leads them and the entire Ummah to destruction.

* * *

Among *taqlīd's* most obvious consequences are the following:

First: The spread of indifference and the will to follow. *Taqlīd* has created within the Muslim's psychological makeup feelings of his/her inability to accept responsibility. As the Shariʿah's essence is the acceptance of personal and communal responsibility, we can understand the extent of *taqlīd's* negative effect upon the Ummah.

Second: Taqlīd and partisanship for a specific legal school have led to the spread of public debates on theological and legal topics. This, in turn, has led to further polarization and increasing disunity. The end result has been the emergence of popular factions and heretical sects dedicated to destroying Islam and the Ummah. An even more dangerous result was that this *taqlīd*-based mentality and fiqh-based partisanship gradually replaced the mentality of free inquiry that the Qur'an had instilled in the early Muslims.

Third: This *taqlīd*-based mentality has also manifested itself among the previous generations of Muslims in their uncertainty regarding any legal decision for which there was no clear ruling. It has filled contemporary Muslims with doubts about how to conduct themselves in different spheres of Islamic activity without an opinion from the classical scholars. Amazingly enough, the most important thing today is that the opinion cited should be old; the writer's reputation or the work's value does not matter.

Muslims who have grown up in such an intellectual void can hardly be expected to engage in any serious analysis of Islamic subjects, whether they agree with the content or not. Instead, the Ummah has defaulted on this duty and has left it to the Orientalists, despite the latter's obvious biases and preferences, and to their clones among Muslim students.

All of this has contributed to the creation of a very significant gap in our thought, which I call the "vacuum of ijtihad." Out of fear of making an error, it seems that Muslims have declared ijtihad out of bounds for themselves, in effect leaving it to either non-Muslims or westernized/secularized Muslims who no longer understand or practice Islam's fundamental tenets. In short, it is wide open to the depredations of well-meaning but unqualified people, as well as those who are hostile to Islam.

Fourth: The negative environment engendered by *taqlīd* led to a consumptive syndrome, for Muslims began to retreat into their historical intellectual legacy in order to consume all that it had to offer. When the European awakening began, Muslims looked in all directions for a path that would lead them to the place that they felt they deserved. However, when the legacy's keepers were unable to provide direction, several groups decided to imitate the West, based on the belief that such a step would meet with success. However, they met with an identity crisis of such proportions that committed Muslims set out to find their historical identity while westernized Muslims searched for a geographical or cultural identity. Such a development was only possible after *taqlīd* had caused the Ummah's personality to melt away by laying the foundations for its backwardness and introducing into it a state of civilizational absence despite its former civilizational preeminence.

Fifth: The Ummah's *taqlīd*-based mentality resulted in a worldview dominated by expedience. This, in turn, actually made *taqlīd* a method for avoiding innovation (*bidᶜah*). As it was generally felt that ijtihad would lead to error or one's adherence to the unacceptable, *taqlīd* became attractive as a prudent alternative.

Sixth: Among *taqlīd's* more disastrous side effects is its quasi-sanctification of the status quo, regardless of whether or not it adheres to the Shariᶜah. As *taqlīd* is the consort of custom, the *muqallidūn* who become more accustomed to certain social conditions tend to block any movement for change or reform. Thus, *taqlīd* impedes social reform and represents a mentality that must either be significantly altered or destroyed before meaningful change can occur.

CONCLUSION

The curse of *taqlīd* continues to obstruct the Ummah's attempts at self-revival and self-reform. *Taqlīd's* negative and crippling effects cannot be overcome by changing the methods by which it is practiced or the people whom it venerates. Nor can we expect to accomplish anything by transforming issues of *taqlīd* into institutions that make a virtue of abandoning creative thought for the principle of following others and designating certain people as custodians of backwardness in the sacred name of *taqlīd.*

NOTES

1. See Qur'an 30:30.
2. *Istikhlāf*: Allah's appointment of humanity as His *khalīfah* (vicegerent) on Earth. See Qur'an 2:30; 10:14; 27:26; 35:39.
3. *Ibtilā'*: trial by affliction or through abundance. See Qur'an 3:186; 21:35; 89:15-16.
4. *Tamkīn*: Allah's aid in establishing people in the world, be it politically, financially, professionally, or otherwise. This concept carries with it the responsibility of the individual and his/her society to reciprocate by establishing prayer and doing good deeds. See Qur'an 22:41; 6:6; 7:10.
5. *Dafʿ* and *tadāfuʿ*: checking and balancing one group of people, or individual, checking another. See Qur'an 22:40; 2:251.
6. *Taskhīr*: Allah's subjection of nature and its laws to humanity for its benefit. For this favor, it is essential that humanity shows its gratitude (*shukr*). See Qur'an 22:36-37; 14:32; 16:12, 14; 22:65; 35:13.
7. *Takrīm*: the honor and favor bestowed on humanity by Allah. See Qur'an 17:70.
8. *Amānah*: the trust that Allah gave to humanity; the innate ability to choose between good and evil. This trust sets humanity at the pinnacle of Allah's creation. See Qur'an 33:72.
9. The purpose of humanity's creation is *ʿibādah*. See Qur'an 51:56.
10. *Shuhūd*: the concept or civilizational witnessing that Allah has made obligatory on His Ummah. See Qur'an 2:143; 3:140; 4:135, 5:8; 22:78.
11. This hadith was related by several Qur'anic commentators. The original hadith is found in al-Tirmidhī's collection.
12. In his commentary on the Qur'an, *Al-Manār* (4:203-4), Rashīd Riḍā wrote: "It is well-known that the *mufassirūn* give two interpretations to the term *ulu al-amr:* one is that they are the rulers or the governmental authorities, and the second is that they are the scholars, in particular the *fuqahā'* or the legal authorities. It is equally well-known that there were no governmental authorities in the time of the Prophet and no group of people called *fuqahā'*. So the intended meaning of *ulu al-amr*, as in the verse: 'When an issue of public security or agitation comes to them, they spread it abroad. But if they would refer it to the Prophet or to the authorities among them, those who derive meaning from it would come to know of it' (4:83), is the people of wisdom and importance in the Ummah who have the Ummah's interests at heart, who are capable of protecting those interests, and whose opinions are widely accepted by the Ummah at large."

Taqlīd and Ijtihad

(Part One)

THE POLEMICS OF IJTIHAD

From the second Islamic century until the present day, the reality, essence, rules, conditions, premises, means, and scope of ijtihad have remained a source of debate engaging some of the Islamic world's greatest theologians, scholars of *uṣūl*, and *fuqahā'*. This debate has also been enriched by proponents of the view that the door of ijtihad was closed and that the fiqh left by the Four Sunnī Imams (viz., Ibn Ḥanbal, Mālik, al-Shāfiʿī, and Abū Ḥanīfah) obviated the need for any further ijtihad, as well as by those who claimed that this door was still open and that the existing fiqh was not sufficient to guide the contemporary Muslim world.

In our own times, attention is focused on the Shariʿah's suitability as an order and a way of life. This new topic of debate, before unknown among Muslims, emerged after the crushing defeats experienced by the Muslim Ummah after the First World War, such as the dismantling of the *khilāfah* and the creation of artificial states ruled by Europe. Many Muslims blamed Islam and its institutions for their defeat, and soon began to emulate their conquerors. Others, however, had a quite different view: The Muslim Ummah experienced these disasters because it had become alienated from the eternal truths of Islam. Thus, what was required was a return to the true Islam, rather than its wholesale rejection in favor of alien institutions and ideologies. One fundamental part of this return would have to be the use of ijtihad, for how else could Muslims incorporate Islamic principles into situations with which they had never had to deal?

This article first appeared in the *American Journal of Islamic Social Sciences* 8, no. 1 (March 1991): 129-42. It has been slightly edited.

Muslims who hold the latter view know that they must meet their opponents in the realm of ideas, for that is where the Ummah's future course will be decided. To be successful, great energy will have to be expended in scholarship and conceptual thinking, in seeking to understand humanity's place in the divine scheme of existence and what is expected of it, and how this knowledge might be applied by Muslims as they struggle to make themselves and their societies conform with the will of Allah. Without a complete civilizational design, by means of which the Ummah may by restored to its former median position and fulfill its role as being a "witness unto nations," it will never regain its former position or even make a new beginning.[1]

Today, the Muslim Ummah is in a deplorable state. No longer can it present itself as having a unique culture, system of values, personality, or anything else that makes a civilization distinct from all others, for large-scale borrowing from the West has undermined and distorted all of its inimitable features. It is now a travesty of its former self, and can only perpetuate itself by producing religious specialists whose academic background is limited to the personal laws of Islam alone.

However, there are some signs that change is in the air. This has taken the form of an attempt at revival (*ṣaḥwah*), which is striving to raise the Ummah's consciousness, outline the features of its character, and bring together its past and present so that it can intelligently chart its future course by studying its cultural personality and civilizational components as reflected in its thought, methodology, sciences, disciplines, aesthetics, and so on.

However, none of this activity will be of any use if the end result is something other than a recognition of the fact that the Ummah's existing crisis of thought can be solved only by restructuring its cultural mold and reordering its priorities. The only way for even the first steps to be taken involves a coming together of those enlightened and capable Muslims who can see what has to be done. Ijtihad is indispensable, for it can be shown historically that the Muslim Ummah only entered its current crisis after ijtihad fell into disuse and was gradually replaced by *taqlīd*.

THE DYNAMISM OF IJTIHAD IN RESTRUCTURING ISLAMIC METHODOLOGY *(AL-MINHĀJ)*

The study of ijtihad and its principles is one of the pillars of the Islamization of Knowledge, and, as such, comes within the framework of studying a distinct Islamic methodology. If applied, this methodology will produce a comprehensive and uniquely Islamic understanding of sociological phenomena, their agents, essential elements, and relationships, along with an appreciation of their governing laws and principles. Such a development is now impossible, for the current methodological foundations are all creations of the West and, as a result, inherently hostile toward Islam and its concepts.

What is needed is the erection of an Islamic methodology that can replace its western counterpart. This is no easy undertaking, for it involves establishing a unique framework of knowledge, defining the sources of knowledge and the rules that govern their use, and initiating a critical review of all facets of both the western and the Islamic methodologies so that the suitable elements are retained and the unsuitable ones are either transformed and accepted or rejected outright.

In addition to dealing with characteristics of the western model, which will influence how Muslims deal with the Islamic model, there is an additional problem: the use of western terminology. It is next to impossible to free oneself from the categorizations and concepts upheld by western scholarship, or from their influences, when dealing with studies of any other civilizational model. Thus, most of

> ... the scientific methodologies in the West are incapable of looking at Islam, or Islamic society and its social strata, its economics, its political order. And this is what strips such West-oriented studies of their academic integrity, so that they appear little more than presumptuous deductions based on superficial similarities. This is because it is impossible to understand Islam from the perspective of what Western scholarship presupposes in regard to organized religion. In the same way, it is unrealistic to suppose that the Islamic model of society could be understood through the categories propositioned by the Western model as a result of its own historical experience.[2]

However, Muslims are fortunate in that they do not have to start this undertaking from the beginning, for a great deal of material in the classical Islamic legacy can be used. This same legacy also provides contemporary Muslim scholars with a framework for organizing the rules relevant to the Islamic epistemological sources and delineating the relationships between them. Thus, one may state that the level of scholarship attained by previous Muslim scholars using the methodology developed by the early *mujtahidūn* was extremely mature.[3]

As we consider the Islamization of Knowledge to be one of Islam's higher purposes, as well as a living and civilizational necessity, the need for ijtihad becomes obvious. Not only is it required for creating an Islamic methodology, but it also plays a pivotal role in a Muslim's daily life as well as in forming a spiritually, mentally, and intellectually balanced Muslim personality that can assume the role of Allah's vicegerent and pursue the Ummah's best interests. Thus its correct exercise, in conformity to the specified conditions, is extremely important.

This illustrates a fundamental difference between the two types of Muslims we see today. One group accepts the viewpoint outlined above, while the other rejects it and calls for the wholesale adoption of western knowledge. This latter group, frequently referred to as "reformers," has yet to acquire an appreciation for the differences between Islam and the West, differences that sometimes reach the point of outright contradiction.[4]

As we noted earlier, the role of ijtihad in freeing the Muslim Ummah from its bondage to the West is primary. Only through ijtihad will Muslims be able to construct a new methodological infrastructure that can replace the current western one and enable Muslim scholars to once again base their knowledge and epistemological paradigms upon Islam's original sources. The degree to which we can accomplish this task is directly related to the amount of success we will have in freeing ourselves of western domination.[5] No efforts will be wasted, for all of them are investments in Islam's future and may eventually solve the apparent contradictions that bedevil us today: traditionalism versus modernism, classical thought versus contemporary thought, the material world versus the afterlife, science versus religion, and others.

Many of the current theories dealing with Islamic thought need definition, perspective, and proper points of departure, for the lack of a proper methodology and a clear overview make them appear to be the result of muddled and opaque thinking. The resulting theories are repeated and restated, discussed again and debated, and, finally, are treated to solutions either imported from abroad or inherited from the past. Thus, nothing gets settled, solved, or agreed upon, which is certainly an intolerable situation. For Muslims, ijtihad provides the way out of this morass.

A PANORAMIC ASSESSMENT OF IJTIHAD'S PROGRESSION

In this study, we would like to evaluate previous studies and extract what is useful. Also, we would like to discuss ijtihad from being the preserve of the few to one suited to the needs of all qualified scholars and thinkers in the Ummah. Hopefully, this may be the catalyst needed to help the Ummah break through the barriers blocking its own cultural, scientific, and epistemological frameworks and then regain its former position in the world community.

In classifying previous studies of *taqlīd* and ijtihad, we may say that they fall into two general categories: specialized *uṣūl* studies and non-specialized studies.

The first category can be subdivided into two additional categories. The first one consists of comprehensive works on *uṣūl al-fiqh* in general, meaning those works dealing with source evidence and how legal rulings are derived from it, as well as with the status of the *mujtahid* or *muqallid* who derives such rulings. Regardless of the author's *madhhab* or whether he/she wrote in the style of a *mutakallim* or a *faqīh*, or in a combination of both, these works have changed little over the centuries. Nearly every work contains a book, a chapter, or a subchapter on ijtihad and *taqlīd*. The topics discussed nearly always include the reality (*ḥaqīqah*) and different kinds of ijtihad, the ijtihad of the Prophet, whether or not every *mujtahid* is right, and similar complicated technical matters concerning its principles and how they are applied to obtain legal rulings.

The second one consists of books written specifically on ijtihad. In classical times, this kind of study closely resembled the type of studies found in the first category. The main difference, however, is that where the comprehensive *uṣūl al-fiqh* works only treated this subject briefly, these works explained at length the points that the comprehensive works only summarized, provided instances and examples, and even added such new topics as "Closing the Door of Ijtihad," "Partial Ijtihad," "Ijtihad within a *Madhhab*."

Nonetheless, the two categories are alike in presenting ijtihad in a purely descriptive perspective.[6] This makes it a complex, specialized exercise that is limited and qualified by its means, methods, and conditions.[7] Thus, it is no longer a creative and contemplative endeavor, but rather a technical one limited in its methodology and means, as well as restricted in the scope of its concern. On the other hand, non-specialized studies deal with ijtihad as an expression of a human intellectual and creative activity seeking to understand humanity, life, the universe, and creation. As such, it views *taqlīd* as a rigid and negative force.

These non-specialized sources may be described as generalized social studies, for they deal with matters of concern to the entire Ummah, such as its mental and intellectual state, the history of its culture and thought, its inertia and backwardness, and its failure to contribute anything new to the contemporary world. Thus, this group is clearly distinguished from the former one by its understanding of ijtihad not in the strict terminological sense, but rather in the wider lexical sense of expending intellectual effort, in the sense of a uniquely creative mental state diametrically opposed to the prevailing intellectual rigidity found among Muslims.

These studies often speak of closing the door of ijtihad and thereby opening the way for *taqlīd*, and then attempt to project this as symptomatic of the entire Ummah's mentality. But they are often surprised by others who claim that this door was never closed and that the final rulings have not been made. At this point in the discussion the larger focus usually gets lost, for participants then begin the endless debate over the exact status of ijtihad, who can or cannot practice it or close the door, and other ancillary matters. Regardless of all of the arguments presented by both sides, regular ijtihad has not been practiced for centuries, despite its very rare use by individual *fuqahā'*, and the Ummah's intellectual and cultural conditions have not been very conducive to its use.

These non-specialized studies may also be further subdivided into two categories: secular and non-secular. The first group consists of works by Muslim secularists, writing in Arabic, that present revival and modernity, in the western sense of those terms, as cures. Many of their arguments come from the European Age of Enlightenment, a time of intense anti-church feeling. Their use of such arguments has caused them to view Islam and Christianity, mosque and church, as well as *faqīh* and cleric, as one and the same. This leads to their further assumption that Muslims need a Renaissance to free themselves from these shackles so that they can follow the Christians down the road of progress, which, of course, includes secularism. They regard ijtihad as tailor-made for this endeavor, for once it has been stripped of its lexical and juridical meanings and made synonymous with one's personal opinions and inclinations, the path of the West can be followed quite easily.

However, those very people who stretched the meaning of ijtihad to the breaking point in order to justify their dream of modernization and westernization now find themselves hard-pressed to conceal the shallowness of their thought or the crisis of their identities. As a result, they have started to use other means and terminologies, both contemporary and classical, to accomplish their goal. Such writings are unmistakable for the kind of symbolism they employ and the folly they espouse.[8]

The second group consists of works by Muslims who believe that the Ummah is passing through a period of intellectual crisis that can only be ended by recovering its pristine character, reforming its inner life, reshaping its mentality, and building up its individuality. In their opinion, the Ummah reached its present deplorable state only after its members had stopped making relevant and intelligent contributions to its daily life.

This group also eventually comes around to the same discussion engaging the first group of writers, but only after passing through the following steps: the rationalists (*ahl al-ra'ī*) versus the traditionists (*ahl al-ḥadīth*), the codification of fiqh-oriented ijtihad, and the history of the call to end further ijtihad and accept the legal authority of the Four Sunnī Imams or *taqlīd* – a truly barren landmark in the Ummah's intellectual life, as well as the starting point of its present intellectual crisis and cultural decay.

Then the discussion about opening and closing the door of ijtihad begins. Some participants, however, fail to realize that the Ummah's overall intellectual and cultural climate is one matter, while the discussion of ijtihad's lack of movement in one limited field of knowledge (i.e., fiqh) is an entirely different matter. Thus, discussion becomes controversial among those who argue whether ijtihad is still allowed or not.

In my opinion, the majority of those who claim that the door of ijtihad is closed are, in reality, pointing to the fact that the Ummah's intellectual contribution to the social sciences has ended, whereas the second group is saying that the collected corpus of *fiqhī* literature can still address current problems, regardless of whether legal decisions are issued or not. Nonetheless, *fiqhī* questions are essentially questions about details. Thus, if one scholar refuses to or cannot make a legal decision, another one will do so on the basis of earlier fatwas, through the application of basic principles and in consonance with the Shariʿah's higher purposes, or on the basis of analogy (*qiyās*). But this is not the matter of contention. Rather, the crisis is in regard to absolute and unrestricted ijtihad, to open minds, structured thought, and comprehensive vision – all matters without which the Ummah cannot build a viable society or serve as a "witness among nations."

Regardless of its apparent current abeyance, in its strictly legal sense (i.e., ijtihad being the knowledge of juridical source methodology, the rules for deriving legal rulings, and the ways of indicating legal preference) the practice of ijtihad never ended. Even in our own time, fatwas dealing with legal problems are issued. However, this does not balance out the occurrence, from a very early date, of an unhealthy intellectual and psychological state of mind, one that did not come about through a sultan's decree, government legislation, or the lethargy of one or more scholars. On the contrary, this situation is the result of several factors, and as the crisis worsened its ill effects spread to every aspect of life, including the *fiqhī* aspect. As the *muj-*

tahid played an essential role in Islamic civilization and may be regarded as the Muslim version of what the West would call a "Renaissance Man," the Ummah's scrutiny of the role of fiqh and of the *fuqahā'* are perfectly legitimate and understandable.

THE TRADITIONAL ROLE OF THE *FAQĪH*

Historically, the *fuqahā'* formed a major pillar of Islamic society. Trained as scholars of the Qur'an and the Sunnah so that they could use ijtihad when dealing with religious and temporal problems, such people were the Ummah's fundamental guarantee that its leaders would not lead it astray. In a sense, they were the equivalent of such major contemporary American institutions as the House of Representatives and the Senate, and performed the check and balance function of a federal judiciary system vis-à-vis the government's executive and legislative wings. Moreover, their voice was always a moral force for enjoining good and forbidding evil.

A traditional scholar never waited for someone to come along and "award" him a degree that qualified him to exercise ijtihad. On the contrary, this status was achieved by dint of personal study, travel, instruction, and by keeping the company of the learned. When he judged himself ready, he would choose a pillar in the mosque, face the public, and begin his discourses. His resulting success or failure depended upon his ability to answer the questions of other scholars and his students, use his knowledge and ability in ijtihad, solve new problems, and whether his published works and decisions were accepted or rejected by his peers and society at large. If his views were accepted, what he viewed as correct would gradually become part and parcel of the general public's mentality and psyche, while what he viewed as incorrect would be rejected.

The Role of the Faqīh *in the Judiciary System.* Muslim scholars supervised the judiciary system (*al-qaḍā'*) and protected the Ummah's rights vis-à-vis its rulers. Not only were they entrusted with ensuring that the rulers did not transgress their proper bounds, but they were also expected to force those rulers who did go astray to mend their behavior. Thus, Muslims have always seen scholars as protectors of the Ummah and its rights. And so when it seems that the scholars have stopped fulfilling these functions, thus bringing many problems and disasters upon the Ummah, it is only logical for the average Muslim to blame all of the ensuing misfortunes on them. They do not consider it unreasonable to assume that the scholars' inability to perform ijtihad lies at the root of the Ummah's current backwardness, lack of contribution to humanity, and muddled methodology.

The Faqīh *as a Social Scientist.* The time has now come for the Ummah to realize that the *faqīh* is essentially another of those social scientists that the Ummah needs so badly. While he cannot replace other social scientists, they cannot replace him. Moreover, the *faqīh's* traditional role can now be undertaken only by institutions that deal with educational, research, public management, supervisory, or moral-advisory matters. Clearly, the Ummah needs such institutions to give order to its life, direct its movements, oversee its policies and directions, and watch over the education and psychological well-being of all Muslims. Life today is so complex that it is entirely unrealistic to expect one *faqīh* to master all of the knowledge needed to deal with it. In reality, academic committees and academies that combine the various disciplines, including the *fiqhī* disciplines, must be established.

UNRESOLVED ISSUES OF IJTIHAD

I have gone through nearly 160 studies, research papers, and articles dealing with *taqlīd* and ijtihad, in addition to numerous chapters dealing with these subjects in books of fiqh, *al-uṣūl,* and the history of Islamic law. Despite this, I have noticed that almost all of these studies follow the same path laid down in the fourth and fifth Islamic centuries by the authors of the classical *uṣūl al-fiqh* compendiums. Moreover, these studies confine themselves to the same issues tackled by classical scholars: the meaning of ijtihad and *taqlīd,* the categories of ijtihad and how they are divided, the relation of ijtihad and *taqlīd* to certain related concepts, the essential conditions for exercising ijtihad, how there are no *mujtahidūn* today, how ijtihad has become fragmented, correct and incorrect ijtihad, and so on. At most, some of these studies may differ in their inclusion of other topics, possibly because of their author's viewpoint or because they include different and varied examples of ijtihad.

Thus, the majority of these studies proceed along nearly the same lines, differing only in unessential matters. For example, one might elaborate on what others merely indicate or arrange the subjects in a different way. In addition, I have noticed that many important subjects have been either entirely ignored or mentioned only in passing. Among the most relevant of these subjects are the following:

a) *The historical background of ijtihad and* taqlīd. This background is essential for understanding many of the issues related to these two questions,[9] such as the division between intellectual and political authority in the history of Islam and its positive and negative effects on ijtihad and *taqlīd*; the advent of sects and doctrinal divisions (i.e., the Jabrites, the Qadarites, and the Muᶜtazilites) and their positive and negative effects on ijtihad and *taqlīd*; the growth of a Muslim public character incorporating feelings of alienation and a slave mentality due to a distorted understanding of religion, the world, humanity, *shūrā*, authority, the head of state, relations between authority and citizenry, internal strife, the appearance of heretical thought and politics, and the effects of all this on ijtihad and *taqlīd*; and the lack of those institutions necessary for establishing the requisite methodological consciousness, which caused the consequent reliance on individual undertakings.

b) *The connection between ijtihad and the Shariᶜah's higher objectives* (maqāṣid al-Sharīᶜah). Many of these studies fail to illustrate either the affinity between ijtihad and the *maqāṣid* or the antipathy between *taqlīd* and the *maqāṣid*. The only exceptions have been works dealing exclusively with the question of the *maqāṣid* in an attempt to focus on the essential connection between ijtihad in its general sense and ijtihad as related to the *maqāṣid*.[10]

c) *The effect of multiple trends in ijtihad, how this effects the understanding of the "Oneness of Truth, Reality, and What is Correct," as well as the clarification of the true parameters of the controversy regarding this issue and its important intellectual, psychological, and educational consequences on the Muslim mind.* Moreover, this subject requires minute attention, for it deals with the most important factors leading to the realization of actual multiplicity in ïijtihad, clarifying the truth behind differences of opinion (*ikhtilāf*), and distinguishing between two different kinds of *ikhtilāf* (i.e., differences of diversity and differences of contradiction, or, in other words, praiseworthy and permitted differences, and blameworthy and prohibited differences). Likewise, most studies dealing with ijtihad and *taqlīd* do not pay enough attention to the "Oneness of the Truth" and differences among scholars as to exactly what this means and entails. Also missing is any concern for the potentially dangerous effects of not placing this issue in its proper perspective in order to spare the Ummah any damaging negative thinking.

d) *None of these books have presented a realistic and practical solution to the present crisis of ijtihad or dealt with the possibilities of "group"* ijtihad *or establishing research institutions and academic organizations to support such an undertaking.* The absence of any solution has left the field wide open for those who wish to create and then impose man-made legislation derived from their own understanding, which may or may not include the relevant *fiqhī* literature.

e) *The issue of* fiqh al-wāqiʿ (*real-world* fiqh), *its contributory factors, and the necessity of linking it with ijtihad has been ignored.* As *fiqh al-aḥkām* (rulings derived from linguistic and lexical studies) was, therefore, not dealt with in a satisfactory manner, the circumstances surrounding the formation of the ruling in question (i.e., the occurrence itself, the time, the place, and the human element) were overlooked. This resulted in many scholars understanding the entire process of ijtihad in only a partial manner. As a result, they placed it under *fiqh al-aḥkām* rather than *fiqh al-wāqiʿ* where it belongs, and did not properly reference the one to whom the judgment would apply (the *maḥkūm ʿalayhi*). Thus, they lost one of the most important elements in the overall process of ijtihad.

f) *Many of these studies have not gone into the details of* taqlīd *as regards to the individual or explained how ijtihad relates to the individual in question.* Is the relationship completely negative, as the majority of studies would suggest, or is there some scope for a positive role? If so, what would be the nature of that role, not to mention the role itself? Studying such details is part of studying the *maḥkūm ʿalayhi* as an element in the process of ijtihad, for surely the individual is one of its aspects. Moreover, the individual is an invaluable source of information for acquiring a proper understanding of *fiqh al-wāqiʿ* and its constituent elements, not to mention a representation of where the resulting rulings are to be applied. Thus, we can see the importance of regularizing and defining the individual's role vis-à-vis ijtihad.

g) *The element of continuous self-renewal through meeting and adjusting to changing circumstances based upon rulings conducted within the framework of ijtihad is missing in many of these works.* This might be due to the view of ijtihad as a purely legalistic and legislative function, which severely limits its traditional and intended role. Without this element, and without a real understanding of the ties that bind the sources of Islamic thought and culture to the dynamics of ijtihad and the realities currently facing it, the Ummah is destined to remain where it is, mired in hopelessness and stagnation.[11]

h) *The necessity of clarifying concepts.* Ijtihad is one of several fundamental Islamic concepts that Muslims have either misused or misunderstood.

At present, there are essentially two interpretations of the term: It is either a technical and limited *fiqhī* exercise for the qualified few to the exclusion of everybody else, or it is represented by all new thoughts and ideas, regardless of whether their holders are qualified to exercise ijtihad or not.

It seems that neither the strict nor the liberal interpretations of ijtihad have given us this term's true meaning. Also, might there not be other interpretations, such as the one represented by those who believe that the Four Sunnī Imams have already done this duty, thereby obviating it for the Ummah at large? Or what about those who say that the entire *fiqhī* legacy must be discarded and replaced by a new one that is not necessarily based on traditional principles and guidelines, or those who believe that the Ummah's decline is the reason for the gulf that has opened up between it and the reality of Islam? This latter group, while well aware of what needs to be done to restore the Ummah to its former position in the world community, unfortunately does not have the necessary resources and numbers needed for actually changing the course of events. In addition, the Ummah's existing condition is so far removed from the purity of its original sources, and consequently distorted by secularism, westernization, and the process of cultural change, that no one group alone can do the job.

Given all of the above, are there any specific courses of action that will actually contribute to opening the door of ijtihad? Upon reflection, it seems that there are two: considering all of the guidelines, rules, and preconditions for the process of ijtihad, along with its higher purposes (i.e., so entrenching ijtihad in the Muslim mind that it becomes the regulator of the Ummah's every move); and accepting the option advocated by the secularists and non-religious Muslims: fling open the door of ijtihad as wide as possible and then interpret ijtihad in such a way that it can be used to justify the results, regardless of whether the rulings were based on traditional *fiqhī* criteria or not. Currently, it seems that this latter group has the upper hand, for it has found many unqualified people willing to issue the desired rulings. Also, some contemporary *fuqahā'* are more than willing to issue the rulings "requested" by those in authority. Moreover, those *fuqahā'* who have, for whatever reason, chosen to remain aloof and uninvolved have, in effect, left all self-proclaimed scholars free to issue their rulings.

A final factor is the failure of many contemporary *fuqahā'* to provide workable solutions to problems, due to their incomplete understanding of the issues or their inability to fully realize the significance of their premises and predicates. Thus, many of their rulings seem to be more applicable to an earlier age, a development that only discredits the entire endeavor and the people involved.

Given all of the above, this study will focus on several of the previously ignored issues connected with ijtihad. The study's main goals are to place these issues within the overall context of the ijtihad process, explain why they must be studied, establish their validity and relevance, and define them. By doing this, establishing a contemporary Islamic methodology based on the classical discipline of juridical source methodology and fiqh may proceed apace by using its methodological resources to treat those issues that must be dealt with if the goals are to be realized.

Among these issues are the following:

- Presenting the Islamic theory of knowledge and its most important elements, means, and devices, as well as the role of each.
- Formulating an exact and precise definition of the relationship between revelation (*waḥy*) and reason. This will help Muslims solve many of the problems arising from the relationship of knowledge to religion and of knowledge to practice. It will also help us understand ijtihad from the perspective of reality, experience, and practice.
- Developing an agreed-upon system of argument and dialogue, respect and acceptance for differing opinions and results, and an understanding as to why this is essential if scholars are to guide the Ummah's footsteps aright.

Therefore, this article is presented in the spirit of being the first in a series designed to clarify the source methodology of fiqh and the methodology of ijtihad for those social scientists who are interested in applying what has been discussed here to the effort to Islamize knowledge in general, and its methodology in particular. Hopefully, this methodology will benefit from the resulting definitions, clarifications, and organization of a discipline so that it can one day stand on a solid methodological foundation. Only if this present dream becomes a reality will Muslim social scientists be able to study social phenomena, with all their attendant diversity and complexity, within an Islamic framework and an epistemological paradigm. Then, they will begin to rebuild Islamic civilization on the basis of its own understanding of the social sciences. This deconstruction and subsequent reconstruction must be achieved if the Muslim Ummah is ever to assume its divinely ordained position as a witness to other nations.

NOTES

1. The reference here is to the verse in *Sūrat al-Baqarah*: "Thus We have made of you a median Ummah, that you might be witnesses over all people" (2:143).
2. Munīr Shafīq, *Al-Islām fī Maʿrakah al-Ḥaḍārah*, 12-13. See also Sayf ʿAbd al-Fattāḥ, *Al-Tajdīd al-Siyāsī wa al-Khibrah al-Islāmiyyah*. Ph.D. diss., Cairo University, College of Economics and Political Science, 1987.
3. Shafīq, *Al-Islām*, 36. See also ʿAbd al-ʿAzīz al-Khayt, *Manāhij al-Fuqahā'* (Cairo and Damascus: Dar al-Salam, 1406/1986), 7.
4. For a more detailed discussion, see *Islamization of Knowledge: General Principles and Work Plan* (Herndon, VA: International Institute of Islamic Thought, 1409/1989).
5. For the distinction between praiseworthy and blameworthy differences (*ikhtilāf*), see al-Shāfiʿī, *Al-Risālah*, ed. Aḥmad M. Shākir (Cairo: al-Ḥalabī and Sons, 1940), 560; al-Shāfiʿi, *Jimāʿ al-ʿIlm*, ed. Aḥmad M. Shākir, (Cairo: n.d.); and Tāhā J. al-ʿAlwānī, *Adab al-Ikhtilāf fī al-Islām* (Herndon, VA: International Institute of Islamic Thought, 1987).
6. ʿAbd al-Raḥmān al-Maḥallāwī, *Tashīl al-Wuṣūl ilā ʿIlm al-Uṣūl* (Cairo (Muṣṭafā al-Bābī, n.d.), 8-9.
7. See Al-Shaykh al-Murṣafī, *Bughyat al-Muḥtāj* (Cairo: Maktabah al-Azhar, n.d.), no. 1442, 4.
8. Among the stranger instances of ijtihad undertaken by such writers is their transferral of the day and the duty of the *jumʿah* prayer to Sunday in western countries, where Sunday is nearly universally a holiday. Likewise, some of these people have proclaimed that Muslims may now eat pork, for pigs are raised under carefully controlled conditions, whereas during the time of the Prophet they were allowed to run free. Another instance of such "ijtihad " is the opinion that polygamy is allowable only for the guardians of orphans, as they are the only ones mentioned specifically in the verse that legislated polygamy. A further instance is denying that jihad as one of the principles of Islam.
9. Some of the recent studies of ijtihad and *taqlīd* presented tentative discussions of these issues, inasmuch as they at least indicated that they were important. But such indications, though certainly important, did no more than present these issues in a scattered and fragmentary manner. Thus, they were not placed within the framework of an overall scheme for the study of *taqlīd* and ijtihad, or for understanding.
10. *Muwāfaqāt al-Shāṭibī wa Maqāṣid al-Sharīʿah* (by Shaykh Muḥammad al-Ṭāhir ibn al-ʿĀshūr) and *Maqāṣid al-Sharīʿah* (by ʿAllāl al-Fāsī) are two examples of such works. There are several recent dissertations and graduate-level studies on the subject as well, such as *Al-Ahdāf al-ʿĀmmah fī al-Sharīʿah al-Islāmiyyah* (by Dr. Yūsuf al-ʿĀlim), soon to be published by the International Institute of Islamic Thought, and *Naẓarīyāt al-Maqāṣid ʿinda al-Imām al-Shāṭibī* (by Dr.

Aḥmad al-Raᶜīsūnī), published in Morocco by the International Institute of Islamic Thought.

11. Among the studies that have dealt with this issue are the following: Muḥammad Muṣṭafā al-Marāghī, *Al-Ijtihād fī al-Islām* (Cairo: al-Maktab al-Fannī li al-Nashr, 1379 AH); Mu'tamar al-Fiqh al-Islāmī, *Al-Ijtihād fī al-Sharīᶜah al-Islāmiyyah* (Saudi Arabia: Jāmiᶜah al-Imām Ibn Saᶜūd al-Islāmiyyah, 1401/1981); Al-Mūsāwī, *Al-Naṣṣ wa al-Ijtihād*, ed. Abū Mujtabā (Beirut: Al-Dār al-Islāmiyyah, 1414 AH); Riḍā al-Ṣadr, *Al-Ijtihād wa al-Taqlīd* (Beirut: Dār al-Kitāb al-Lubnānī, 1976); Muḥammad Ibrāhīm Shaqrah, *Al-Raᶜī al-Sadīd fi al-Ijtihād wa al-Taqlīd* (1401/1981); and Aḥmad Ibrāhīm ᶜAbbās al-Darāwī, *Naẓarīyat al-Ijtihād fī al-Sharīᶜah al-Islāmiyyah* (Jeddah: Dār al-Shurūq, 1403/1979).

Taqlīd and Ijtihad

(Part Two)

THE LEXICAL AND TECHNICAL MEANINGS OF *TAQLĪD*

The lexical meaning and structure of the word *taqlīd* clearly indicate the negative connotations surrounding its technical meaning as well as its retention of much of the literal sense. The Arabic root *q-l-d* comes from *qald*, which means "to twist or to twine." As most necklaces were either twined or braided, the word came to refer to necklaces, and the active form of the verb (*taqlīd*) to putting on a necklace. An example from early Arabic poetry uses *taqlīd* in this sense:

> They placed on her (round her neck) amulets,
> To ward off evildoers and enviers.

The same word is also used to refer to the marking made around the neck of an animal destined for sacrifice during hajj. In addition, a camel is said to be "necklaced" (*muqallad*) when a rope is placed over its head and around its neck. In a less literal usage, this word has the sense of placing responsibility on an individual, as in "The sultan charged (*q-l-d*) someone with a duty," as charging a person in such a manner resembles putting a necklace around his/her neck. Here, the one who accepts the responsibility is as one who wears a necklace.[1]

The classical *fuqahā'* define *taqlīd* as one's "acceptance of another's *madhhab* without knowing the other person's justification." (In this definition, *madhhab* includes everything that falls within the purview of ijtihad.[2]) Although the *fuqahā'* give different definitions, all agree that it signifies the acceptance of and acting upon another's word without trying to substanti-

This "reflections" article first appeared in the *American Journal of Islamic Social Sciences* 9, no. 2 (summer 1992): 233-42. It has been slightly edited.

ate it. In other words, the determining factor is one's trust in or reverence for the scholar, or his/her own negligence or lack of interest in trying to establish the truth on his/her own.

Having defined *taqlīd*, we shall now explain what it means to follow someone. The lexical meaning of "following" stems from the word for walking behind or falling into step with somebody else as he/she passes by (i.e., the way Muslims follow an imam during prayer).[3] Following, which can be either physical or ideational, has been technically defined as "deliberating over the commands of Allah and His Prophet and considering the Prophet's deeds and statements for the purpose of obeying and emulating the same."

Abū ʿUmar ibn ʿAbd al-Barr (463 AH) discussed this issue in his *Jāmiʿ Bayān al-ʿIlm*, in which he quoted Abū ʿAbd Allāh ibn Khuwayz al-Mālikī as saying: "The legal meaning of *taqlīd* is to adopt someone's opinion despite his lack of any justification (for that opinion). This is clearly prohibited in the Shariʿah. Following, however, occurs when there is a justification for that opinion (*mā thabatat ʿalayhi al-ḥujjah*)." In the same book, Abū ʿUmar says: "Whenever you follow someone's opinion without any justification for doing so, that is *taqlīd*, a practice that is incorrect in Islam. Whenever you follow the opinion of someone based on its valid proof, that is following, which is permitted. But *taqlīd* is prohibited."[4] Abū Dāwūd quoted Aḥmad ibn Ḥanbal as having said: "Following involves adhering to narrations concerning the Prophet and his Companions. As regards narrations of the practices of the successor generation (the Tābiʿūn), one is free to decide for oneself."[5]

Thus, the difference between *taqlīd* and *following* is perfectly clear: *taqlīd* means to follow someone without any justification for doing so, while *following* involves following what can be justified through proof. This difference makes the former prohibited and the latter permissible.

THE LEGAL RULING ON *TAQLĪD*: THE COMPANIONS AND *TAQLĪD*

In an authentic narration of a conversation between ʿAlī ibn Abū Ṭālib and Kumayl ibn Ziyād al-Nakhaʿī, ʿAlī said:

> O Kumayl, hearts are like vessels: the best contain the most good. There are three kinds of people: knowers and people of the spirit, learners on the road to salvation, and the rabble who follow anyone who brays loud enough. This group is unenlightened by knowledge and has not sought support from anything substantial ...

This narration censures those who believe that they know the truth despite the fact that they have little or no insight (*baṣīrah*), a condition that causes them to be troubled by doubt when confronted by anything they cannot understand.

Undoubtedly, an ignorant *muqallid* (follower), unaware of the proof or justification cited by the one he/she imitates, is part of this rabble, for all he/she knows about Islam is that a certain respected imam said this or did that – he/she does not even know whether the imam's opinion was correct or not. As a result, the follower is neither lighting his/her path with the light of knowledge nor standing on solid ground, because he/she does not know what is right and what is wrong. In a prophetic hadith, the Prophet said:

> Allah will not strip away knowledge from your breasts all at once. Rather, He will strip it away by taking away (through death and by slow degrees) the scholars. People will then take as their leaders those who are ignorant (of the Shariʿah). When they are questioned, they will respond without really knowing the answers. In this way, they will go astray and lead others astray with them.[6]

It was related that Ibn ʿAbbās once said: "Woe to those who follow the mistakes of the learned!" When asked what he meant, he replied:

> When a scholar says something based only on his own opinion and then abandons it when he finds that someone more knowledgeable than he has given another opinion based on something related from the Prophet; while the person who asked for the opinion of the first scholar has gone away and knows nothing of the opinion based on the Prophet's hadith.

It was related that Ibn Masʿūd said: "Do not take the opinion of another in matters of religion so that if he believes you believe, and if he does not you do not. There can be no ideal in matters of evil."

Since both the Prophet and the Qur'an rejected *taqlīd*, the Companions and many others considered it an evil and also rejected it. Thus, scholars are those who give an opinion (fatwa) and then explain their proofs and evidences to the audience when questioned. In this way, those who ask become followers of evidence and not merely blind followers of certain respected personalities.

All of these citations indicate that *taqlīd* was forbidden. The successor generation (the Tābiʿūn) vigorously criticized it and warned people against it. ʿAbd Allāh ibn al-Muʿtamm said: "There is no difference between an animal that is led and a person who makes *taqlīd*." Thus, *taqlīd* is incorrect, unacceptable, and inadequate in terms of fulfilling one's religious responsibilities unless certain conditions are met. On the other hand, following is allowed, for it involves someone convincing another person, through valid evidence or proof, of the validity of his/her opinions. Ibn ʿAbd al-Barr said:

> There is no disagreement among scholars that *taqlīd* is corrupt ... that is why it was never widespread (among the early generations of Muslims). It was they who said: "If a *muqallid* respected and used his brain, he would never fall in behind another. Instead, he would use his own faculties to see for himself why it was that the great imams, even those within the same legal school, often differed."

THE IMAMS AND *TAQLĪD*

Imams Abū Hanīfah, Mālik, al-Shāfiʿī, and Ibn Ḥanbal warned people not to blindly follow what they said or did and denounced those who did so. Imām al-Shāfiʿī said:

> One who seeks knowledge without proof is like a gatherer of wood who goes into the forest at night to collect fallen branches and is bitten by a snake when, thinking it to be another branch, he picks it up.[7]

His student and the narrator of his knowledge, Ibrāhīm al-Muzanī, wrote in his *Al-Mukhtaṣar*:

> I have summarized all of this from the knowledge of Imām al-Shāfiʿī, and from the meaning of what he taught, in order to impart it to whoever wants it, along with notice of his prohibition of *taqlīd* (of his opinions) or of those of others, so that the reader will himself consider the evidence for the sake of his religion, and so as to be the more circumspect about it.[8]

The great *muḥaddith* Abū Dāwūd said:

> I once asked Aḥmad [Ibn Ḥanbal]: "Did Awzāʿī follow the Sunnah any closer than Mālik?" Ahmad replied: "In matters of religion, don't be a *muqallid* of any of those people. Take whatever is authentic from the Prophet, upon him be peace, and from the Companions. When it comes to the successor (Tābiʿūn) generation, you can choose."[9]

He also said: "Don't be a *muqallid* of mine, nor of Mālik, Thawrī, nor Awzāʿī. Rather, take from the same sources they took from."[10] Abū Yūsuf said: "No one may opine what we opine, unless they know the reasons why we hold that opinion."[11]

When Abū Ḥanīfah was asked what should be done if one of his legal opinions was found to contradict the Qur'an, he replied: "Abandon what I said in favor of what is in the Qur'an." When asked what should be done if his opinion contradicted something in the hadith, he replied: "Abandon what I say in favor of the hadith of the Prophet, upon him be peace." When asked what should be done if his opinion contradicted opined by the Companions, he replied: "Abandon what I say in favor of what was opined by the Companions."[12] On the same subject, Mālik said: "I am human. Maybe I am wrong and maybe I am right. So look into my opinions. If they are in accordance with the Qur'an and the Sunnah, accept them. But those that are not, reject them."[13] Ibn al-Jawzī wrote: "*Taqlīd* is a nullification of reason, for reason was created for consideration and contemplation. It is therefore unbecoming on the part of one given the lamp of reason to extinguish it and grope about in the dark."[14]

Taqlīd, in general, appeared only after the first generation and its successors had passed away. This is also true in the case of the Four Sunnī Imams, who only began to be objects of *taqlīd* after their deaths. In fact, they were no different from their predecessors in their censure and rejection of *taqlīd*.[15] The stories of how Mālik refused al-Manṣūr and of how Abū Yūsuf refused al-Rashīd, when those rulers wanted to command their subjects to follow a single *madhhab*, are well known.[16]

An example of the kind of argument given by the early scholars is recorded here from Ibrāhīm al-Muzanī:

> It may be said to one who passes judgment on the basis of *taqlīd*: "Do you have proof for your judgment?" If he says: "Yes," there was no *taqlīd*, for he arrived at his judgment on the basis of evidence. If he says: "No," he should be asked: "Why did you shed blood, legalize intercourse, and dissolve financial assets when Allah has prohibited all that, unless there be sound evidence as to why it should be done? Allah said: 'You have no proof of that' (10:68)." If he replies that he knew his judgment was correct, even if he did not know the evidence, because he is a *muqallid* of a great scholar who gave legal opinions only on the basis of sound evidence, it should be said to him: "Then you mean to say that your *taqlīd* of your teacher was legitimate, even though you did not know his reasons for adopting the opinion? Thus you consider it legitimate for your teacher to make *taqlīd* of his teacher, even if he did not know his teacher's reasons for a certain opinion? So are you a *muqallid* of your teacher or of your teacher's teacher?" If he answers that he is a *muqallid* of his teacher's teacher, he has abandoned the *taqlīd* of his teacher in favor of his teacher's teacher ... which means that he abandons the *taqlīd* of teacher after teacher until he finally goes back to the

> Prophet and his Companions (which is not *taqlīd*). If he denies this, he contradicts himself and may then be asked: "How do you legitimize your making *taqlīd* of someone whose knowledge and station are (relative to the Prophet's) so insignificant? That is clearly contradictory." If he replies: "Because my teacher, although of a lower station, combined his own knowledge with the knowledge he gained from his predecessors. Thus his opinions were more informed in terms of what he accepted and what he rejected," it may be said to him: "Then the same must be true of those who learned from your teacher, because they combined their knowledge with his and his predecessors' knowledge. You should, therefore, be the *muqallid* of your teacher's students. What this means is that you should be the *muqallid* of yourself, because you have combined your knowledge with that of your teacher and his predecessors."[17]

THE FORMS OF *TAQLĪD* AS DEFINED BY THE *FUQAHĀ'*

There are three forms of *taqlīd*: a) *taqlīd* in matters that either result in knowledge or likely assumption. Examples of this are accepting testimony or evidence (when the conditions for their authenticity have been satisfied), accepting a scholar's opinions on an issue of personal relevance (to the non-scholar), a blind person's facing the qiblah toward which he/she is directed by someone who can see, accepting another's word about the biographical data of narrators of hadith or about their reliability or lack of it. Personally, I have my doubts about whether this category actually falls under the heading of *taqlīd* [18]; b) *taqlīd* that results in neither knowledge nor in likely assumption, depending on how these are defined and what conditions are set for each[19]; and, c) *taqlīd* that is permissible and legitimate. Al-Rāzī and those *uṣūlī* scholars who followed him considered this as *taqlīd* of a scholar by a non-scholar, or *taqlīd* of a more knowledgeable scholar by a less knowledgeable scholar.[20]

* * *

It should now be clear from the opinions and statements of the learned Companions, Tābiʿūn, *fuqahā'*, and *uṣūlīyyūn* that *taqlīd*, generally speaking, is to be avoided and that its prohibition, if not a matter of ijmaʿ (consensus among the learned), is at least the opinion of the majority (*jumhūr*). The crux of the matter is that one should rely on sources from which legal judgments may be derived. Moreover, when an individual performs ijtihad for himself/herself without legal proof, his/her subsequent actions are permissible only as a matter of juristic license (*rukhṣah*) and may not, therefore, be blindly followed by another person, unless that person finds a legal basis (proof) for doing so.

If this is clear, then the first form of *taqlīd* mentioned above, if it can be considered *taqlīd* at all, is both acceptable and legally enjoined. Accepting testimony, for example, is enjoined in both the Qur'an and the Sunnah, while prohibiting the withholding of evidence is a matter of ijma[c]. The same is true for accepting the accounts of trustworthy narrators.

A non-scholar's questioning of a scholar is also enjoined, for Allah said: "Then ask the people of remembrance (scholars) if you yourself do not know" (16:43; 21:7). In the early days of Islam, the common people used to question the Prophet's Companions about rulings in cases that concerned them. When the Companions replied, the people would act in accordance with their replies. On another occasion, a person might ask a different Companion for his ruling, and then in complete confidence follow his advice.

Certain scholars considered the *taqlīd* of a scholar by an unlearned person not to be *taqlīd*, but rather following, for it is at least supposed that one who answers a question must have some kind of knowledge and that such a person would not give an answer unless there was evidence to support it. In a well-known hadith, the Prophet is reported to have said: "If they do not know the answer themselves, why do they not ask those who do? The only cure for ignorance is to ask questions."[21] Based on this, something resembling consensus arose on the unlearned's responsibility to question the learned when faced with confusing issues. After this, however, the question arose as to whether or not the questioner was required to learn the evidence in support of the scholar's answer. Must he/she know the reason for the answer? The majority of scholars opined that the questioner must ask for proof and that the scholar must mention it.[22]

What has been stated so far leads one to the certainty, or at least the likely assumption (*ẓann rājiḥ*), that the second type of *taqlīd* has no legitimacy and that we are responsible for making our own ijtihad and preparing ourselves to become capable of doing so. This form of *taqlīd* is prohibited, as any belief based upon it is no better than a guess, which is clearly unacceptable as the foundation for belief. Thus it also is unacceptable as the foundation for a legal ruling or legal advice (fatwa). Such *taqlīd*, whether of a living or a dead *mujtahid*, is expressly prohibited. The third form of *taqlīd* given above is no different from the first.

Scholars who hold that a certain form of *taqlīd* is permissible have differed among themselves as to whose opinions may be adopted. Some of their positions are:

- *Taqlīd* of classical and contemporary scholars more knowledgeable than the questioner is allowed, because Allah said: "Then ask the people of remembrance (scholars) if you yourself do not know" (16:43; 21:7).
- Some permit *taqlīd* of only the Companions and the Tābiᶜūn, because the Prophet said: "The best of the generations is my generation, then the ones who follow them."[23]
- Al-Shāfiᶜī (in an opinion that he later altered), Ibn Ḥanbal, Isḥāq ibn Rāhawayh, and Sufyān al-Thawrī said that only *taqlīd* of the Companions was permissible. In his early work, *Al-Risālah al-Baghdādiyyah*, al-Shāfiᶜī wrote: "The Companions were superior to us in every respect when it comes to knowledge, ijtihad, piety, and understanding. Accordingly, their opinions are better for us than our own." In the same work, al-Shāfiᶜī asked, after further extolling their many virtues: "So is it reasonable to expect that *taqlīd* of them should be the same as *taqlīd* of those who in no way measure up to them?"[24] Abū Dāwūd related that Ibn Ḥanbal said: "Following means that one follows what has come from the Prophet, upon him be peace, and from his Companions. After that, in relation to the Tābiᶜūn, one may make up one's own mind."[25]
- Some scholars held that *taqlīd* of the Companions was limited to the first four caliphs (*al-khulafā' al-rāshidūn*), for the Prophet stated: "Adhere to my Sunnah, and to the Sunnah of the rightly-guided caliphs who come after me."[26]
- Other scholars held that *taqlīd* may be made only of Abū Bakr and ᶜUmar, because the Prophet said: "Follow the two who come after me, Abū Bakr and ᶜUmar."[27]
- Muḥammad ibn al-Ḥasan (Abū Ḥanīfah's student and al-Shāfiᶜī's teacher) held that *taqlīd* by one less knowledgeable of one more knowledgeable is permitted.
- Another opinion is that one may make *taqlīd* only in regard to matters of immediate concern to oneself and not in matters that may be mentioned as fatwa to others.
- Ibn Surayj (of the Shāfiᶜī school) opined that a student may make *taqlīd* of his/her teacher on a matter of immediate personal concern, but only if there is not enough time for him/her to perform ijtihad before the opportunity to act accordingly is lost.[28]

The different opinions of the classical scholars on this matter are rather nicely summarized by Ibn Taymiyyah:

> As regards the particulars of law, the majority of theologians and jurists say that ijtihad is a responsibility placed upon every individual, even on the non-scholars. That, however, is not a tenable position, for if seeking knowledge of the evidence were the responsibility of every individual, it would only be so where there was the ability to do so, and such ability is clearly not possessed by the great majority of non-scholars. On the other hand, there are some who follow one legal school or another who say that *taqlīd* is the responsibility of everyone who comes after the [four Sunnī] imams, including the learned and the unlearned.
>
> The position adopted by most scholars is that, generally speaking, ijtihad and *taqlīd* are permitted. They do not require ijtihad of everyone while declaring *taqlīd* to be *ḥarām*, nor do they require *taqlīd* while declaring ijtihad to be *ḥarām*. Ijtihad is permitted to those who are capable of it, and *taqlīd* is permitted to those who are incapable of ijtihad. What, then, of the one who is capable of ijtihad? May such a one resort to *taqlīd*? There is a difference of opinion on this question. The correct answer, however, is that *taqlīd* is permissible for such a person when he/she is unable to perform ijtihad due to conflicting evidence, insufficient time, or a complete lack of evidence. This is because when one cannot undertake ijtihad, the necessity to do so no longer remains. Instead, the alternative is prescribed, which, in this case, is *taqlīd*. This is analogous to the person who cannot find water to perform his/her ablutions.[29]
>
> The same is true with regard to the non-scholar. If he/she can perform ijtihad for himself/herself on certain questions, it is permitted, because ijtihad is not an absolute – the pivotal point is ability or the lack thereof. Thus, a person might be able to perform ijtihad on certain questions and not on others. Nonetheless, this ability may be acquired only through the knowledge of those sciences that lead to an understanding of what is sought. It is hard to imagine, however, how one's knowledge of a single aspect of a discipline or a science would qualify one for ijtihad. Allah knows best.[30]

* * *

Islam, moreover, forbids us to follow any way other than that of knowledge. Allah says: "Do not pursue matters of which you have no knowledge. Surely every act of hearing, of seeing, and of the heart will be inquired into" (17:36). Thus, our responsibility in regard to every aspect of the divine law (*sharᶜ*), be it a command or a prohibition, is that we attain knowledge of its wisdom by whatever means possible. If sure knowledge is not possible, we have to reach an understanding based at least on the most likely possibility. This is why our scholars have not permitted *taqlīd*, except in the case of the most ignorant and incapable.[31]

NOTES

1. Entries in the dictionaries of classical Arabic may be consulted as follows: *Al-Miṣbāḥ*, 704; *Al-Muʿjam al-Wasīṭ*, 2:706; *Tāj al-ʿArūs*, 2:474-76; and *Mufradāt al-Rāghib*, 411.
2. For details of the classical *fuqahā's* various definitions, see al-Jurjānī, *Taʿrīfāt,* 57; al-Āmidī, *Iḥkām al-Aḥkām*, 4:221; al-Ghazālī, *Al-Musṭaṣfā*, 2:387; al-Māwardī, *Adab al-Qāḍī,* 269; and al-Shawkānī, *Irshād al-Fuḥūl*, 234.
3. *Al-Miṣbāḥ*, 1:99; and *Tāj al-ʿUrūs*, 5:385-88.
4. Ibn ʿAbd al-Barr, *Jāmiʿ Bayān al-ʿIlm*, 109-19.
5. Ibid., 2:117; Ibn al-Qayyim, *Iʿlām al-Muwaqqiʿīn*, 2:190-200.
6. Imām al-Bukhārī related it in the chapter of "Al-Iʿtiṣām bi al-Sunnah."
7. This was related by Abū Bakr al-Bayhaqī. See Ibn al-Qayyim, *Iʿlām al-Muwaqqiʿīn.*
8. Al-Muzanī, *Al-Mukhtaṣar*, 1 (printed on the margin of vol. 4 of al-Shāfiʿī's *Kitāb al-Umm*).
9. *Masā'il Abū Dāwūd li al-Imām Aḥmad*, 276.
10. Ibid.
11. Ibn al-Qayyim, *ʿIlm al-Muwaqqiʿīn*, 2:201.
12. Al-Shawkānī, *Al-Qawl al-Mufīd*, 54.
13. Ibid.
14. Ibn al-Jawzī, *Tablīs Iblīs*, 90.
15. Al-Shawkānī, *Al-Qawl al-Mufīd*, 5.
16. Ibn al-Qayyim, *ʿIlm al-Muwaqqiʿīn*, 2:187. The attempts by Manṣūr, Hārūn al-Rashīd, and others to codify and standardize the law represented, in the eyes of the imams who refused to sanction such undertakings, an attempt to limit their freedom to formulate their own legal opinions. In fact, they feared that any limitation would lead to the rulers' attempt to quell the freedom of thought in general, thus paving the way to political absolutism. Several scholars suggested that a ruler's confusion, resulting from the presence of so many varied and conflicting legal opinions, could be solved by endorsing a single *madhhab* while allowing all other legal opinions to be taught and used for formulating alternative solutions to current issues. Thus, while no one would be prevented from formulating his/her own opinions through ijtihad, the problem of standardization within the courts and legal system would be resolved.
17. Ibn ʿAbd al-Barr, *Jāmiʿ Bayān al-ʿIlm*, 2:204.

18. Ibn al-Qayyim, *Iʿlām al-Muwaqqiʿīn*, 2:254.
19. Knowledge might be defined as a certain perception that is in accordance with reality, whereas likely assumption (*ẓann*) may be understood as perception of the more likely of two possibilities.
20. Tāj al-Dīn al-Armawī, *Al-Ḥāṣil min al-Maḥṣūl*, unpublished manuscript, folio 3, 977.
21. This was related by Abū Dāwūd from Jābir. The same hadith was related by Aḥmad, al-Ḥākim, and Abū Dāwūd from Ibn ʿAbbās, though with the words: "Is not the cure for ignorance to ask questions?" See al-Suyūṭī, *Al-Fatḥ al-Kabīr*, 2:295.
22. Al-Āmidī, *Iḥkām al-Aḥkām*, 4:228; al-Shāṭibī, *Al-Muwāfaqāt*, 4:292. An opposing position was taken by Ibn Ḥazm. See al-Āmidī, *Iḥkām al-Aḥkām*, 1:151-53.
23. This hadith was related by al-Bukhārī, Muslim, al-Tirmidhī, and Aḥmad. See al-Suyūṭī, *Al-Fatḥ al-Kabīr*, 2:99. The scholars of hadith have spoken of this type of permission. See al-Māwardī, *Adab al-Qāḍī*, 1:27.
24. Ibn al-Qayyim, *Iʿlām al-Muwaqqiʿīn*, 2:261-62.
25. Abū Dāwūd, *Masā'il al-Imām Aḥmad*, 276.
26. Related by Aḥmad, Abū Dāwūd, al-Tirmidhī, Ibn Mājah, Ibn Ḥibbān, and al-Ḥākim on the authority of al-ʿIrbāḍ ibn Sāriyyah. See al-Māwardī, *Adab al-Qāḍī*, 1:271.
27. Related on the authority of Ḥudhayfah by Aḥmad, al-Tirmidhī, Ibn Mājah, and Abū Yaʿlā. See al-Suyūṭī, *Al-Fatḥ al-Kabīr*, 1:215.
28. This opinion was recorded by al-Māwardī in *Adab al-Qāḍī*, 1:262-63.
29. Under such circumstances, the legal alternative is to use dust under the conditions prescribed for *tayammum*.
30. Ibn Taymiyyah, *Majmūʿ al-Fatāwā*, 20:203-4.
31. Ibn al-Qayyim, *Iʿlām al-Muwaqqiʿīn*, 2:260.

The Crisis in Fiqh and the Methodology of Ijtihad

INTRODUCTION

The year 310/922, in which the last of the acknowledged *mujtahidūn*[1] died, may be marked as the beginning of the crisis of fiqh that continues even to this day. At that time, Islamic fiqh took a very serious turn and, near the end of the fourth Islamic century, its most negative effects began to be apparent: The thinking of scholars was seriously influenced by the apprehension that certain rulers, by means of citing permission obtained through the misuse of fiqh, were exploiting the things held dear by the Ummah.

Thus, the idea of closing the door of ijtihad was born out of fear. This essentially defensive notion was accomplished by stipulations to the effect that recourse might be had only to the ijtihad made by the scholars of the earliest generations, that no changes could be made to their ijtihad, and that any opinion that did not conform to their's should be rejected.[2]

So the sun set on true ijtihad, and in its place came mere *taqlīd*, which allowed legal and intellectual lassitude to become widespread. Moreover, the Ummah's ties to the two sources of legislation, the Qur'an and the Sunnah, and to the other sources weakened and then fell away entirely. Finally, *fiqhī* studies were confined to a few specific textbooks, commentaries on those textbooks, commentaries on the commentaries, and annotations on the commentaries on the commentaries.[3]

Let us see how al-Ghazālī (505/1111) described this situation, and how his explanation mentioned the most important developments in Shariʿah studies, in general, and in fiqh, in particular. He wrote:

This article first appeared in the *American Journal of Islamic Social Sciences* 8, no. 2 (September 1991): 317-37. It has been slightly edited.

You must know that the office of *khilāfah* after the Prophet of Allah, upon him be peace, was assumed by *al-khulafā' al-rāshidūn*, who were imams and Shariʿah scholars in their own right. Moreover, they were active in giving fatwas and making legal judgments. Therefore, only rarely if ever did they need to seek the opinions of the *fuqahā'*. The result of this was that the *fuqahā'* immersed themselves in knowledge of the next world and shunned all else. Thus, they were known for their refusals to give fatwas and legal advice on issues of worldly import, perferring instead to devote all of their deductive abilities to the worship of Allah Most High.

But when, soon after the deaths of *al-khulafā' al-rāshidūn,* the office of *khalīfah* passed into the hands of those unqualified to lead the Ummah and unlearned in matters of fiqh and fatwa, it became necessary to consult the *fuqahā'* and to seek their advice in nearly everything. At that time, there still remained of the successor generation (the Tābiʿūn) those who continued in the same way as before, practicing Islam in complete purity and following the example of the most learned and devout of their predecessors. Thus, if they were sought out (by those in power who would ask them questions), they would flee or otherwise evade them. The result of this attitude was that the rulers had to resort to pressuring scholars to accept positions as judges (*quḍāt*) and government officials. Thus, as the scholars repeatedly turned down the offers made by rulers and leaders, the people of those times witnessed the true nature of their scholarship. This, in turn, influenced many of them to go out and seek knowledge for themselves so that they too might earn the respect of the people and the notice of the rulers.

So people flocked to learn about the sciences of the fatwa. Thereafter, they did all they could to make themselves known to the rulers so that they could ask for positions and favors. Then, among them were those who failed and those who succeeded. But those who succeeded were unable to avoid the humiliation of sacrificing their dignity in order to ask. In this way, the *fuqahā'* went from being sought after to being seekers after, and from being respected for their spurning the offers of rulers to their being scorned for their opportunism. Of course, there were those true scholars of the religion (*dīn*) who were spared all disgrace by Allah Most High. But, in any case, the greatest interest in those times was in giving legal rulings (fatwas) and judgments (*qaḍā'*) because of the need for people to fill positions of authority in the courts and in government.

Thus, little by little, fiqh was transformed as a result of these mistaken practices. From acting as a means for the regulation of people's lives in accordance with guidelines from the Shariʿah, [it went] to functioning as a tool to be used for the purpose of legitimizing whatever was current or to satisfying purely intellectual desires to speculate on rulings that might be applied in conjectural situations.[4]

The state of fiqh in those days being what it was, it should come as no surprise that the Muslims felt uncomfortable and not a little confused. Oftentimes, something pronounced *ḥarām* by one *faqīh* would, at the same time, in the same place, and under the same circumstances, be pronounced *ḥalāl* by another *faqīh*. In order to have a sense of what really occurred in those times, it should suffice to note that a new and extensive chapter in jurisprudence was being written: *al-ḥiyal wa al-makhārij* (legal stratagems and dodges). Indeed, the mastery of this particular subject became a sign of the *faqīh's* erudition and academic preeminence!

So, as time passed and as Islam's influence decreased, people began taking more and more liberties with the Shariʿah. Some *fuqahā'* even went to the extreme of transgressing its bounds and its higher purposes (*maqāṣid*), explaining that they had done so either to simplify matters or to make them more difficult. Among them, one group was ever intent on finding new ways to make fiqh conform to whims and worldly desires, while another group was determined to pronounce only the most harsh and disagreeable rulings.

Moreover, until this period of stagnation, the fatwa had never been used to justify the government's policies or practices. But this is what happened during a period of weakness in Ottoman rule, and hereafter the affliction continued to spread.

THE DECLINE OF IJTIHAD

Under these looming shadows, ijtihad disappeared. Many of the pious, however, were concerned that unqualified and unscrupulous scholars would attempt to practice ijtihad anyway. Indeed, this duty had been undertaken by people who, in many cases, had been reared under the eyes of rulers and who had grown practiced in twisting the texts to suit their appetites. The other group comprised those who had been seized by blind loyalty to one school of legal thought (*madhhab*). Thus, they either abrogated or reinterpreted everything that appeared contrary to their *madhhab*, or argued and disputed with anyone who opposed their *madhhab*, or attempted to issue *fatāwā* based on another *madhhab*.

When the pious scholars turned their attention to remedying this situation, the only solution they came up with was *taqlīd*: strict adherence either to the opinions of a particular *faqīh* or to the teachings of a particular *madhhab*. Imagine what a crisis it must have been for the solution to be the fetters of *taqlīd*!

And so it was that the *fuqahā's* rivalry, incessant debating, and pedantic bickering and contradicting all led to the conclusion that the only way out of the resulting confusion was a return to the opinion of the earlier imams. Indeed, owing to the close ties between the judges and the rulers (who appointed and provided for them), and to the love of many judges for worldly things as well as their overlooking of many injustices, the people lost faith in them and their judgments. Ultimately, the only judgments respected among the people were those based on the opinions of one of the Four Sunnī Imams.[5]

And so the great Muslim masses followed these men, adhered to their opinions, and deduced what they had not said specifically from what they had said generally, believing this to be an adequate guarantee against the kind of judgments and opinions coming from Shariᶜah scholars who had no fear of Allah. This is why Imām al-Ḥaramayn (478/1086) claimed that there was ijmaᶜ (consensus) among the scholars of his day and that the *taqlīd* of one of the Companions was not acceptable. Rather, people were to adhere to the fiqh of one of these four imams, who had probed and examined the Shariᶜah, classified and given form to *fiqhī* questions, and had digested the teachings and opinions of the Companions and the Successors. This is what finally led to the dictum that the common man and woman, anyone other than a true *mujtahid*, is required to follow one of the four [Sunnī] *madhāhib*.[6]

Based on Imām al-Ḥaramayn's pronouncement and the claim of ijmaᶜ, Ibn al-Ṣalāḥ (643/1246) claimed that following one of these imams was obligatory (*wājib*), as only their teachings had been systematized, clarified, and preserved, while the opinions of the Companions and the Successors had never received such attention. Moreover, the four *madhāhib* had been passed on, in the form of common everyday practice, from generation to generation.

From this time onward, people began neglecting the Qur'an and its sciences, as well as the Sunnah and its associated disciplines. Instead, they satisfied themselves with quoting and arguing in favor of teachings from the different *madhāhib*, and, under what might be considered the best of conditions insofar as the exercise of legal acumen was concerned, using them as the basis for branching into details.

The decline continued, and the differences of opinion on legal issues increased and became more profound. Generations of scholars grew up under *taqlīd*, and thus all independent legal thought was stifled and the tree of ijtihad withered.

Consequently, people began to think of the *fuqahā'* as those who had memorized a portion of the earlier imams' teachings and opinions without ever developing the ability to distinguish between the sound and the unsound among them. Quite often, they had no knowledge of the evidence leading to the these teachings' formulation or of the methods used to deduce them from the sources.

Likewise, a *muḥaddith* became one who had memorized a number of hadiths and knew certain technical terms. A great scholar became one who had memorized the basic texts (*mutūn*) of a few of the major disciplines and had mastered the subtleties of one or another of the major *fiqhī* or *uṣūlī* texts to the point where he could speak or write at length on it. A great hadith scholar was one who could repeat what some of the early authorities had opined in regard to a hadith text's authenticity or its narrator's veracity.

In this atmosphere of pervasive intellectual gloom, however, a few shining lights were visible. Still, at the time the Ottoman Empire was established in 680/1342, this was the Ummah's condition. Thus, the Ottomans found themselves confronted with a people who retained very few elements of their true character; their beliefs (*ʿaqā'id*) were vague, their behavior was corrupt, righteousness was nearly nonexistent, thought was petrified, ijtihad was paralyzed, fiqh was defunct, infighting was commonplace, and divisions were widespread.

Accordingly, the Ottomans obliged the entire Ummah to accept the Ḥanafī *madhhab*. They chose Ḥanafī judges and other officials, designated Ḥanafī imams for their *masājid*, and appointed Ḥanafī hadith and fiqh teachers for their schools. In their opinion, this course of action was by far the most prudent, as a return to the texts of the Qur'an and the Sunnah would have required an undertaking that they considered impossible: a collective effort by the gifted and dedicated Sharīʿah scholars.

This important stage among the many stages of fiqh's development needs to be subdivided into several stages based on developments in politics, society, thought, and fiqh itself. This requires a very comprehensive study; however, this is not the place for it. What has been alluded to above will have to suffice, so that we may proceed to discuss another point.

FIQH AND INTELLECTUAL FREEDOM

Attempts to quell academic freedom, including freedom in fiqh, may be traced back to quite an early date. Some of those attempts took place under the Umayyads; others occurred under the Abbasids.

Perhaps the most well-known attempt was Abū Jaʿfar al-Manṣūr's (r. 754-75) decision to compel all Muslims to follow Mālik's teachings, as recorded in *Al-Muwaṭṭa'*, and prohibit them from undertaking ijtihad outside of or in contradiction to that work. A similar example may be seen in the agreement between Hārūn al-Rashīd (r. 786-809) and his chief legal advisor, the *qāḍi* Abū Yūsuf, to limit the appointments of judges and muftis to followers of Abū Ḥanīfah in order to compel the people to follow the Ḥanafī *madhhab*. Likewise, al-Ma'mūn told his subjects to adopt the Muʿtazilites' teachings in matters of theology.

Practically speaking, these attempts prepared the Ummah, mentally and intellectually, to tacitly accept that the door of ijtihad had been closed. Had the Ummah realized the danger of this matter or its negative consequences, or had the scholars been able to differentiate between the purely academic (in which various opinions are offered to answer questions) and the essentially administrative (in which *taqlīd* is less stifling), the Ummah might have been spared the ensuing chaos in its fiqh and the turmoil in its thought. If such had been the case, there would have been no need to suppress the free flow of ideas at every level.

The Ummah's intellectual decrepitude reached its lowest ebb under the Abbasid rulers in the fifth Islamic century, when closing the door of ijtihad became a matter of state policy and academic doctrine. Indeed, this was tantamount to proclaiming the Ummah's mental and intellectual inability to confront the factors of deterioration and decline. Finally, even though a few thinkers and *mujtahidūn* did appear after this period, the general torpor in academic and *fiqhī* circles had spread to such an extent that individual efforts could no longer preserve the Ummah from the elements of dissolution.

Thus, when the Ummah was caught unawares by the Crusaders, it was barely able to defend itself. As a result, the Crusaders captured many of the most important cities and territories and established their institutions there, after humiliating the Muslims and defeating their armies. After much reform, however, and many bitter experiences, the Ummah managed to reclaim something of its former vitality. It then repelled the Crusaders, and Ṣalāḥ al-Dīn (Saladin: d. 1193) retook the holy city of Jerusalem.[7]

In many parts of the Muslim world, however, the affairs of the Ummah had passed to the Mamalik (Mamluks: slave rulers), who represented the power bases and military leadership. The outcome of this situation was that academics and fiqh, as well as the means for their reform, were ignored. In particular, the Arabic language, the language of the Qur'an and hadith and the foremost means of exercising ijtihad, was neglected. *Taqlīd* continued to increase, ijtihad continued to be disregarded, and fiqh atrophied. Moreover, the common people held fast to their fathers' *madhāhib* and, what was worse, began to be fanatical in their partisanship for one *madhhab* or another. All of this, of course, only contributed to the Ummah's further dissolution and decline.

Then, in 656/1258, along came the Mongol armies, who found the way to Baghdad's destruction prepared for them by divisions resulting from differences in *madhāhib*, political schisms, and internal dissension.

FIQH IN THE OTTOMAN EMPIRE

After the Muslim Ummah had been made to suffer all manner of calamity and woes, the star of the Ottoman family began to shine above the horizon. Indeed, the establishment of the Ottoman Empire once again brought the Islamic world under a single banner. The Ottomans came to power in the seventh/thirteenth century, and soon much of the Islamic world was under their sway. In the following centuries, the Arab territories were added as the empire expanded and made major achievements in terms of leadership, military victories, power consolidation, and army organization.

The Ottomans won major victories in Europe and the Balkans, so that within a relatively short period their empire became the most powerful nation on Earth. Indeed, Europe was thoroughly preoccupied with the question of how to deal with the danger posed by the Ottoman Turks. Thus, the Muslims regained their lost honor and pride.

Owing to the Ottomans' martial character, however, they considered their military genius to be their greatest asset and the farthest limit of their ambition. Thus, they paid little attention to furthering their successes on the battlefield by reforming the Ummah's intellect or culture, or renewing the study of fiqh. Moreover, the Arabic language continued to be ignored, even though its script was adopted for writing Turkish.[8]

SIGNIFICANT FEATURES OF THE OTTOMAN PERIOD

In the field of fiqh, whatever freedom of thought had remained was finally dispensed with as the Ḥanafī *madhhab* was decreed to be the state *madhhab* and the only one referred to in court decisions. Scholars of the other three *madhāhib* were permitted to lead prayers according to the teachings of their *madhāhib* in certain mosques, but only if the worshippers were followers of that particular *madhhab*. Likewise, scholars could teach the fiqh of their *madhāhib* if there was sufficient interest in it. During this time, Abū Ḥanīfah was given the title of *al-Imām al-Aʿẓam* (the Greatest Imam), and his *madhhab* was called *Madhhab al-Imām al-Aʿẓam*. Thereafter, many *awqāf* properties were directed toward teaching and promoting the Ḥanafī *madhhab*. The other *madhāhib*, however (other than the four major ones), were ignored completely. This was especially true of the Shīʿī *madhāhib*, as relations between the Ottomans and the Shīʿī Safavids in Persia remained stormy for 350 years.[9]

However, the Ottomans were not the first ones to make the Ḥanafī *madhhab* the state *madhhab*: In 170 AH, Hārūn al-Rashīd had appointed Abū Ḥanīfah's pupil and close companion, Abū Yūsuf, chief *qāḍī* of his empire; therefore, the appointment of all judges and muftis had to be approved by Abū Yūsuf or done at his recommendation. Thus, all judges in Iraq, Khurasan, Syria, Egypt, or North Africa had been Ḥanafīs. Obviously, this policy played a great role in the Ḥanafī *madhhab's* spread.

Ibn Ḥazm is quoted as having said that two *madhhabs* became widespread due to official decree and authority: the Ḥanafī and the Mālikī. When the Ottomans adopted the Ḥanafī *madhhab*, however, there was a difference. The Tuks, the rulers, the governors, the leaders, and likewise the Albanians and other Balkan peoples, were Ḥanafīs to start with, and bigoted ones at that. So when this *madhhab* became the official court *madhhab*, the Muslims who followed the other imams really had no choice; either they became followers of Abū Ḥanīfah and made themselves eligible for positions in the military and civil service, or they contented themselves with limited opportunity, hardship, and obscurity.

THE CRISIS OF FIQH

The late Shaykh Maḥmūd Shaltūt, may Allah have mercy on his soul, described the beleaguered state of fiqh in those times as follows:

- The spirit of impartial academic inquiry was overcome by disputes over semantics and blind adherence to the words of authors and commentators.
- The opinions of earlier generations began to be treated as sacred, so that they were soon above criticism. As a result, new thinking was never taken seriously.
- Scholars became preoccupied with intellectual speculation about possible rulings on events and circumstances that had never actually taken

place, all the while ignoring the development of a practical fiqh that would address the needs of people in their daily dealings and legal affairs.

- Fiqh scholars became engrossed with inventing legal loopholes and stratagems that would allow people to avoid Shariʿah rulings. Indeed, stratagems were worked out for nearly every subject covered in fiqh. Unlike the early imams, who worked out legal stratagems solely for the purpose of sidestepping damage or loss, these scholars set out to invent ways to dodge legal responsibilities.
- Fanaticism in placing a certain *madhhab* over all others led to debates over such issues as whether or not salah was permitted behind an imam who followed a different *madhhab*. As a result, mosques were built with more than one *miḥrāb* so that the followers of different *madhāhib* could pray behind their own imams.
- Credence was given to the idea that all but the four major *madhāhib* should be banned. In this way, a vast body of legal scholarship, itself a mercy from Allah to the Ummah, was dismissed.

* * *

It appears that the Ottoman Empire, after contributing to fiqh's petrification and attenuation, became annoyed with it. Thus, the state often ignored both fiqh and the *fuqahā'*, choosing instead to solve its problems by means of institutions erected, or legislation promulgated, by the state. The first Ottoman ruler to thus "take matters into his own hands" was Muḥammad al-Fātiḥ (d. 1481), who ordered that civil and criminal codes be prepared to replace the Shariʿah's *ḥudūd*. Indeed, the movement in this direction was completed by the tenth Ottoman ruler, Sulṭān Sulaymān (d. 1566), who was called al-Qānūnī (the "Lawgiver"), owing to the great number of laws he enacted. Indeed, Sulṭān Sulaymān instituted major changes in administrative procedures as well as in the organization of the *ʿulamā'* and teachers of religious knowledge. He also made the mufti the highest religious official in the judiciary, rather than the *qāḍī*, which was the way things had been before Muḥammad al-Fātiḥ.

Thereafter, when legal contradictions began to appear, especially when Shariʿah judges would rule one way and government officials would rule another, both the people and the state were inconvenienced. So, it was finally decided that certain *fuqahā'* should be invited to reconcile all such contradictions by codifying the empire's laws. Thus, as a first step toward helping judges and officials to understand the Ḥanafī *madhhab*, a collection of legal rulings, known as *Al-Fatāwā al-Tatārkhāniyyah*, was compiled. This codification was concluded with the compilation of *Majallat al-Aḥkām al-ʿAdliyyah*.

Nonetheless, the petrification of fiqh, the general intellectual malaise, the misinterpretation of Islam, and the repeated mistakes made in attempting to apply Islamic teachings to changing situations were greater problems than any such fractional solutions could remedy. The proper remedy would have been a comprehensive intellectual and fiqh-based effort to return the Muslims to the original sources, the Book of Allah and the Sunnah of His Prophet, and, through them, to bring about change in every aspect of life. Indeed, it is inconceivable that a community that considers the exercise of ijtihad to be suspect behavior, or that supposes the appointment of a judge from another *madhhab* to be an invitation to trouble, could hold on to the reins of world leadership, progress, and civilization. On the contrary, such a community's fate can only be decline and the loss of its place a history to those who make better use of their genius, free their minds of all shackles, and confront their difficulties with learning and an understanding of the laws of the universe, life, nature, and humanity. This is how Muslims should be.

At that period of time, the Ummah had forgotten its sources, its heart had grown hard, and its people had become fatalistic. Philosophical notions and Sufi sentiments about one's needing only to trust in Allah had blurred the Ummah's vision. Then, having lost sight of its role in this life, the Ummah's chance to renew itself disappeared just as the winds of awakening and change were beginning to blow across Europe. How ironic that the reformist thought put forward by Europe's philosophers, writers, and thinkers came out, essentially, in reply to the challenge posed to Europe by Islam! In turn, then, the European Renaissance became the greatest of all threats to Islam!

One by one, the situations, questions, and issues brought to the fore by the Renaissance and then by the Industrial Revolution confronted the negligent Muslim Ummah. And, having no answer, the Ummah sank deeper into confusion, not knowing what to accept or what to reject. In such a state, its thought was useless and its fiqh was worthless. The spread of modern technology and inventions throughout the world left millions of Muslims stupefied. For many, this was surely the work of Satan or a sign of the Last Day's coming, and thus was to be resisted or confronted by increased recitation of such soporifics as *Dalāʾil al-Khayrāt.*[10] Others sought refuge in proclaiming everything new to be *ḥarām*. After the printing press was invented and the state announced that it would print the Qur'an, the *fuqahā'* disputed the matter until the majority ruled that such an undertaking would be *ḥarām*![11]

Nonetheless, the Ottoman-ruled lands contained people who advocated the reform of Muslim attitudes, thought, and fiqh. But the general trend was to reject all such calls to reform and amelioration. For example, the historian al-Jaburtī, while narrating the events that took place in Egypt during Ramadan 1711, wrote:

> A sermonizer of Turkish extraction sat in the al-Mu'ayyad Mosque in Cairo and exhorted the people to denounce such practices as turning to the graves of the pious, rubbing themselves with the dust they found there, and petitioning the saintly inhabitants for their intercession with Allah. Indeed, the sermonizer acquired a large following. But the scholars of al-Azhar opposed him. At last, the authorities stepped in and beat or banished the man's followers, so that finally the controversy was quelled.[12]

The attempts at reform during times of oppression have been many, and many attempts have been made to throw off the stifling yoke of *taqlīd* and free the Muslim mind from its influence. Nonetheless, that yoke continues to throttle the Ummah to the present day. Likewise, the yearning for true ijtihad continues to be just that: yearning, despite all of the attempts, many of which were truly inspired.

As I prepared this study, I returned to the writings of Muḥammad al-Khuḍarī, one of the best known authors on the history of Islamic law. In describing this period, from the fall of Baghdad (1258) to the present, he wrote: "It was not at all clear to me what I could possibly say about this period, because the stirrings of ijtihad had come to a standstill and there were no features of sufficient interest to write about."

Then he added:

> There was much to say about the first period, because that was the time when Allah revealed His commandments to the heart of the Prophet, upon him be peace, who then propagated the message and explained it to the people; and about the second and third periods, because those were when the Companions and the Successors clarified the methods of deducing legal rulings from the Book of Allah, the Sunnah of His Prophet, and by means of sound reasoning; and about the fourth period, because that was when the major imams and the greatest of the *fuqahā'* were active in recording and giving order to the detailed rulings of the Shariʿah; and about the fifth period, because that was when the Shariʿah rulings were sorted and pruned and selected and given preference, one over another. But what is there to say about this last period? Especially when there is nothing to distinguish it?

> Nonetheless, as this period includes our own, and as we are sorely in need of reforming ourselves as our pious predecessors had, I thought it would be useful here to list our shortcomings, for if these can be identified, our thinkers and scholars can devise solutions for them.

The most significant aspect of this period is the way that *taqlīd* has so dominated the Muslim mind that not a single scholar has aspired to achieve the level of *mujtahid.* He continues:

> From the outset of the tenth Islamic century to the present, the situation has changed, as have the landmarks, so that it has even been announced that no *faqīh* is to choose between the teachings within a *madhhab* (in cases where more than one opinion on a certain question has been recorded from the imam or from his companions) or to attempt to give preference to one over another, because the time for that has passed, and because a great deal of time has elapsed since the books of the early fiqh scholars were written, so that scholars today should rely only on works produced by the later generations.

The reasons for decline, as articulated by al-Khuḍarī, may be summarized as follows:

- The lack of ties between fiqh scholars from different Islamic lands.
- The lack of attention paid to, and outright ignorance of, the works of the earliest fiqh scholars.
- The debilitating trend toward abridgment, especially in textbooks (*al-mutūn*).
- Faulty and timeworn methods of teaching.

In my own estimation, and certainly Allah knows best, these are only a few symptoms of the true reasons for our decline. Essentially, the underlying cause is the backwardness of our thought, what I call "the crisis of thought," our loss of direct contact with the Book of Allah and the Sunnah of His Prophet, our loss of clear vision, and our complete ignorance of the testimony of reason.

It is interesting to note al-Khuḍarī's second reason, because it shows how unwilling our scholars have been to go back to the sources. What of their refusal to deal directly with the Qur'an and the Sunnah? They are loath to delve any further back than the fifth Islamic century! Moreover, when al-Khuḍarī mentioned the trend toward abridgment, he wrote:

> Near the end of this period, the trend toward abridgment took an unexpected turn. This was the attempt to cram as many questions of fiqh into as few words as possible. Then, as their facility with the Arabic language was limited (the authors of this genre of abridge *fiqhī* texts), their writing began to resemble puzzles, as if the authors had intended that their works should never be understood.

Indeed, I believe that they intended their works to be unraveled rather than understood, because the solving of puzzles was a sign of erudition among them! Al-Khuḍarī listed examples of this writing style from three of the most noted works still used as textbooks in many of our Shariʿah institutions. In them, the meanings are so briefly summarized that they have become enigmatic. In many of the sentences you will find the predicate mentioned on the page after the subject is mentioned, or you may have to search even further for it, or you may have to surmise what it is by means of implication! This is why the textbooks required commentaries, the commentaries required notes, and the notes required glosses. The situation is so bad in some of these texts that the teacher's attempt to explain the intended meaning of a single passage may take days on end!

At first, ijtihad was prohibited. Then, in the fifth and sixth Islamic centuries, scholars were restricted to *tarjīḥ* (preferring the opinion of one imam or another on questions of fiqh). But then *tarjīḥ* was prohibited, and scholars were restricted to choosing between the rulings within a single *madhhab* (in cases where more than one opinion on a certain question had been recorded from the imam or his companions). In this way, the door to independent legal thought was shut and then barred.

Having reviewed something of the historical background, we may now proceed to study ijtihad as a methodology that was affected by positive and negative factors in its historical development.

A METHODOLOGICAL PERSPECTIVE: IS THE DOOR OF IJTIHAD CLOSED?

Those opposed to an Islamic solution for contemporary society often charge that the door of ijtihad was closed long ago and that Islam teaches that no one can exercise ijtihad on issues not dealt with by the early imams. Of course, their intention is quite clearly to cause difficulties for the advocates of an Islamic solution by portraying them as incompetent people who cannot offer any reasonable answer to the numerous and complicated problems faced by the Ummah today. Furthermore, the opposition means to say that

Islam is essentially a historical phenomenon whose day has come and gone. Thus, they open the way for their own ideologies and pretensions.

In order to analyze this question properly, and in a way that clarifies its surrounding as well as resulting issues, it is necessary to study it from three separate viewpoints to discern the question with clarity.[13]

The First Viewpoint. All Muslims, specialists and non-specialists alike, agree that ijtihad is both a legal and vital necessity as well as a permanent religious responsibility. This understanding is substantiated by texts from the Qur'an and Sunnah, as well as by reason. All of this is documented in the *uṣūl al-fiqh* works dealing with ijtihad and its legal basis and importance.

Thus, the assertion that the door of ijtihad is closed is contrary to all of these sources of evidence. Indeed, at no time in the Ummah's history has there been a consensus among Muslims that this door had been closed. In fact, Muslims knew that the guarantee for the Shariᶜah's preservation and continuation lay in the vitality of ijtihad and the succession of qualified *mujtahidūn*, one after another, down through the ages.

As an institution, ijtihad suffered more from factors inhibiting the Muslim mind than it did from any imagined loss of the institution itself. There seemed to be no end to the kind of distorted thinking that produced the notions that the earlier generations had left nothing for the later ones, that ijtihad should be avoided because it included the possibility of error (and errors had to be accounted for), and that the door of ijtihad had to be closed to ensure that the unqualified not enter it, and so on. For various reasons and with different intentions, rulers and scholars alike were encouraged to adopt the position that the door needed to be closed. The rulers' intention was that the Ummah should not feel free to express opposing opinions, even in academic matters, lest the people make a habit of vocalizing all of their opinions, including the political ones.

Finally, the point was reached where certain rulers actually issued edicts banning even fully qualified scholars from undertaking ijtihad or issuing fatwas on particular questions unless the results agreed with what the ruler wanted.

The Second Viewpoint. Never in any stage of its unfolding did this claim rely on authentic Shariᶜah evidence or the argument that there was no need for ijtihad. In fact, the Shariᶜah scholars proved most emphatically, by means of both reason and revelation, that such a need would always exist. One of their major arguments was to point out that the texts of the sources of legislation are finite, while the occurrence of events requiring legal rulings is continuous. They also pointed out that every age must have a *mujtahid* capable of interpreting Allah's judgment[14] and that the Ummah is responsible for ensuring that such scholars continue to be produced; otherwise, the entire Ummah can be held responsible for having committed wrong. The Shariᶜah calls such group responsibility *farḍ kifāyah*, and it is possible that the claim of the door having been closed was aided, in part, by the common perception that ijtihad is a *farḍ kifāyah* and not an individual responsibility (*farḍ ᶜayn*). That being the case, as most people suppose, it is enough that a few specialized Shariᶜah scholars undertake this responsibility, and only those who are qualified may be held responsible.

This common perception, however, represents a faulty understanding of *farḍ kifāyah*. In fact, this type of *farḍ* is of great importance – of more importance, in reality, than the *farḍ ᶜayn* duties, because *farḍ kifāyah* is the concern of the entire Ummah, since its duties usually concern principles by which the Ummah proves to be the Ummah, contributes to civilization, and promotes humanity's mission as *khalīfah* (vicegerent of Allah). Indeed, the Eternal Lawgiver prescribed these duties for the Ummah in its capacity as the Ummah, and not as a group of individuals gathered together. In this way, the responsibilities of civilization and culture were divided equitably and with care.

The concept of ijtihad is similarly misunderstood. In the past, it was assumed to be limited to fiqh and jurisprudence. In the present, its meaning has been so diluted that it no longer retains its original Islamic content; rather, it is used to denote any sort of intellectual activity, regardless of its nature or the ideological base from which it originates or toward which it is directed. All of this has contributed to confusion regarding the term's original Islamic significance, especially among contemporary writers. To some of them, ijtihad means westernization, modernization, enlightenment, secularism, atheism, or change – even the nullification of all Shariᶜah laws and freedom from the teachings of the source texts! Thus, the question of whether or not the door of ijtihad is still open continues to divide people.

The Third Viewpoint. In order to clarify the two previously mentioned viewpoints, it is necessary to explain ijtihad's opposite: *taqlīd*. Moreover, it is interesting to note that almost none of the early scholars of *uṣūl* attempted, with any clarity, to trace *taqlīd* to a legitimizing source in the texts of the Qur'an and Hadith, or even to defend it or consider it an absolutely accepted

Shari^cah concept. Rather, the most that they had to say about *taqlīd* was that it was a legal concession based on necessity.[15]

Just as the progress of ijtihad was gradually impeded, until some of the later generations thought that it had been been discontinued and its door closed, *taqlīd* also came about gradually due to the materialization of several factors. Essentially, the reason for this was that *taqlīd* was alien to the Muslim mind and far removed from the nature of the *tawḥīd* that nurtured and enlightened that mind. Moreover, *taqlīd* was unknown in the first two centuries of Islam.[16] Nonetheless, circumstances were such that certain people supposed, albeit mistakenly, that *taqlīd* was a solution. Thus, the process of ijtihad was arrested.[17]

CONCLUSION

Taken jointly, the three viewpoints mentioned above form the essence of the methodological position on ijtihad. In short, ijtihad is a legal necessity and, therefore, no age may be without a *mujtahid*. Moreover, a *mujtahid* must meet certain qualifications such as possessing the legal expertise and erudition that transform ijtihad into an essentially exclusive process. Finally, the Ummah is jointly responsible for enabling ijtihad to continue in perpetuity; otherwise, every member will be held accountable as a doer of wrong.

Certainly *taqlīd*, as the opposite of ijtihad, has played a major role in obstructing ijtihad. Furthermore, if the Ummah's ijtihad-based mentality enabled it to undertake a civilizational renovation and respond to the demands of progress, then a *taqlīd*-based mentality incapacitated the Muslim mind so that it could no longer respond satisfactorily to events. Indeed, the manifestations of that mentality included state sponsorship of one particular *madhhab*, improper applications of *madhhab* rulings, stubborn adherence to the *madhāhib's* teachings, daring to issue fatwas without proper qualifications, and the muftis' wavering between severity and laxity without having recourse to any sort of Shari^cah guidelines to govern their responses.[18]

Those who called for closing the door of ijtihad needlessly backed themselves into a position for which there were alternatives. Likewise, they acted in haste when there was plenty of time to decide the matter. But, ultimately, they closed what should have remained open (ijtihad) and left open what should have been closed: (*kalām* [scholastic theology]).

Actually, they thought that ijtihad was a factor in dividing Muslims. But this was true only in regard to the kind of ijtihad exercised in the field of *^cilm al-kalām*. That is an area where all serious scholars agree that there is no scope for ijtihad and where there is no plurality of what can be correct. In matters of belief, truth is exclusive. And, the safest way to reach it is to take it directly (as it was revealed in the Qur'an) from the Eternal and All-Knowing. Delving into matters of belief caused schisms in the Ummah and destroyed its unity, so much so that its entire being was weakened and its very existence threatened. The end result of this was the appearance of sects and subsects: "Those who split up their religion, and became sects – each party rejoicing in that which is with itself" (Qur'an 30:32).

Certainly, the sects discussed in the books of sects, like al-Ashᶜarī's *Maqālāt Islāmiyyīn*, al-Shahrastānī's *Al-Milal wa al-Niḥal*, Ibn Ḥazm's *Al-Fiṣal*, al-Fakhr al-Dīn al-Rāzī's *Al-Iᶜtiqādāt*, al-Baghdādī's *Al-Firaq*, al-Isfarāīnī's *Al-Tabṣīr*, and al-Yamānī al-Zubaydī's *Al-Ḥūr al-ᶜĪn* – all of these sects grew out of opinions on obscure points of theology, rather than as any result of ijtihad exercised on issues of law or civilization.

Even the unfortunate events that took place in our history, events that may have seemed to be the result of differences over points of fiqh; in fact, had it not been for the questions of theology that were at the crux of these disputes, the differences in fiqh would never, on their own, have kindled the flames of open discord.

Obviously, our scholars must delineate the topics in which ijtihad may be practiced, describe the various fields, further explain the concept, and take care not to overstep the limits of excess or neglect. By doing this, ijtihad's true position will be clarified.

NOTES

1. Ibn Jarīr al-Ṭabarī.
2. If ijtihad had included an inherent capacity to reform itself and provide the necessary safeguards against abuse and against the Muslim *mujtahid's* being negatively influenced by outside pressures, then these scholars might have found another way out, one that did not involve closing the door of ijtihad and insisting on *taqlīd*.
3. Contrast this sorry state of affairs with how the earliest scholars approached fiqh. Muḥammad Zāhid al-Kawtharī wrote, in al-Bannūrī's introduction to *Naṣb al-Rāyah* by al-Zaylaᶜī: "The most obvious feature that distinguished the legal school of Abū Ḥanīfah was that it was a school of *shūrā* (mutual consultation)." Al-Kawtharī then cited several reports by the biographers of Abū Ḥanīfah. Those included a report that: "The associates of Abū Ḥanīfah, those who put fiqh down in writing with him, numbered forty; they were the greatest of the greatest (scholars). Among their number was Yaḥyā ibn Zakarīyā ibn

Abū Zā'idah who acted as their scribe for thirty years." Another report, related by at Muwaffaq al-Makkī, stated that: "Abū Ḥanīfah made his school of legal thought a school of *shūrā* such that he never monopolized the process of ijtihad to the exclusion of others. This was what his ijtihad on the matter had led him to believe; and this was the way that he emphasized his good will for Allah, for the Prophet, and for all the Muslims. Thus, he used to toss out questions, one after another, and listen to what the others had to say about them. Only then would he give his own opinion. Thereafter, they would debate back and forth, sometimes for as long as a month, before they would agree on something, and their decision would be recorded."
Most of the other great imams of fiqh in the early stages followed this method. See al-Zaylaʿī, *Naṣb al-Rāyah*, 2d ed. (Beirut: Dār Iḥyā' al-Turāth al-ʿArabī, 1973), 37-38.

4. In the early days of Islam, the only duties of a scholar or a *mujtahid* were *al-iftā'* (giving legal advice) and *al-qaḍā'* (giving legal filings, or formally passing judgment). The scholars also had to teach. Indeed, the great imams of fiqh considered teaching a form of purification, a way of remembering their Lord and Creator, and a method for gaining greater understanding of the *dīn*, in itself a form of worship. For these reasons, the early generations of scholars never sought payment from the authorities for their teaching, but only from the *awqāf* funds. Those who had to took as much as they needed and no more, and those who had no need taught solely for the pleasure of Allah. In fact, many teachers personally financed their students' education, and many contributed to the endowments of the schools in which they taught.
5. Namely, Abū Ḥanīfah, Mālik, al-Shāfiʿī, and Aḥmad ibn Ḥanbal.
6. See Imām al-Ḥaramayn, ʿAbd al-Mālik al-Juwaynī, *Al-Burhān* (Qatar: Maṭābiʿ Doḥah al-Ḥadīthah, 1399 AH), 11:1146.
7. Ṣalāḥ al-Dīn al-Ayyubī (Saladin) would never have achieved his political and military triumphs without the prior occurrence of several reforms in the spheres of fiqh, culture, administration, thought, and politics. Indeed, these reforms were first brought about by his predecessor, Nūr al-Dīn Zanjī. He brought them to fruition through his victory over the Crusaders, in which we Muslims take pride even today. This period and these reforms need to be studied seriously. For more information, see ʿImād al-Dīn Khālil, *Nūr al-Dīn Zanjī* and Mājid al-Kāylanī, *Kayfa Ẓahara Jīl Ṣalāḥ al-Dīn*.
8 Allah Most High chose the Arabic language as the vehicle of His message to humanity. Through the medium of Arabic, He revealed His Book. Moreover, He chose it to be the language of His Final Prophet and those entrusted with spreading the message of Islam worldwide. Thus, the revelational sources of Islam, the Qur'an and Hadith, are in Arabic. Furthermore, regardless of the translations' quality or the translators' expertise, it is still next to impossible to translate all Arabic's nuances, its denotations and connotations, subtle indications, figurative expressions, and metaphorical usages.

In addition, there is an inimitability to the Qur'anic text that makes it difficult to arrive at its true and intended meaning solely on the basis of a literal reading. Rather, a complete understanding of the text's stylistic qualities and syntactical elements is required. This being the case in regard to the native speaker of Arabic, what chance remains of faithfully conveying all such textual aspects in another language? Indeed, all translations of the Qur'an are works of interpretation (*tafsīr*) that depend, essentially, on the translator's ability to interpret what he/she understands. In no way can such a work be imagined to convey all shades of meaning, and in precisely the same way, as the original text. The *ʿulamā'*, both past and present, have much to say on translating the Qur'an's meanings. But regardless of their opinions as to whether or not the translation of its meanings is permitted, they all agree that it is impossible to convey the Qur'an's full meaning in another language. Thus, all scholars agree that anyone who attempts to study fiqh or master the disciplines necessary for ijtihad must be proficient in Arabic.

ʿUmar ibn al-Khaṭṭāb said: "Become learned in the Sunnah, and become learned in Arabic." It is also related that he said: "Learn Arabic, for it is a part of your religion." The early Muslims spread the Arabic language to every place they settled. In a few generations, it was spoken all through the lands previously held by the Persians and Byzantines. At the present time, there is great need for redoubling our efforts to make Arabic the language of all Muslims. Moreover, it is particularly important that those scholars and thinkers involved in Islamizing the social sciences gain as complete an understanding of Arabic as possible. This in itself will represent a very significant step in the Islamization of Knowledge.

9. The Safavid dynasty in Persia, founded in 1507, was essentially theocratic in nature, as the monarchs claimed to be representatives of the Shīʿī imams. Then, even though the majority of the people in that land had until that time been Sunnīs, Shīʿism was imposed as the state religion. Until their fall in 1732, their differences with the Ottomans, both political and religious, were a source of constant friction. In fact, much of the Ottomans' energy was expended in checking this Muslim neighbor, thus depriving themselves of the resources, military and otherwise, needed so badly on their western borders.
10. I do not mean to undermine the value of this book or its contents. Rather, I condemn the mentality of those who turn to its recitation, or to the recitation of *Ṣaḥīḥ al-Bukhārī* or of 10,000 *Subḥān Allāh*s, instead of dealing realistically with the problem at hand.
11. Al-Nabahānī, *Al-Dawlah al-Islāmiyyah*, 138.
12. Ṭāriq al-Bishrī, *Al-Mas'alah al-Qānūniyyah*, 669.
13. Sayf al-Dīn ʿAbd al-Fattāḥ, *Al-Tajdīd al-Siyāsī wa al-Khibrah al-Islāmiyyah*. Ph.D. diss., Cairo University, College of Economics and Political Science, 1987.

14. Jalāl al-Dīn al-Suyūṭī, *Kitāb al-Radd ʿalā man Akhlada ilā al-Arḍ wa Jahila anna al-Ijtihād fī Kulli ʿAṣr Farḍ*, ed. al-Shaykh Khalīl al-Mīs (Beirut: Dār al-Kutub al-ʿIlmiyyah, 1403/1983). See also ʿAlī al-Khafīf, *Al-Ijtihād fī al-Sharīʿah al-Islāmiyyah*, 210-11.
15. Al-Shawkānī, *Al-Qawl al-Mufīd fī Adillat al-Ijtihād wa al-Taqlīd* (Cairo: Muṣṭafā al-Bābī al-Ḥalabī, 1347 AH), 3; Ibrāhīm Ibrāhīm Jalāl, *Wilāyat Allāh wa al-Ṭarīq ilayhā*, a study and critical edition of al-Shawkānī's *Khaṭ al-Walī ʿalā Ḥadīth al-Walī* (Cairo: Dār al-Kutub al-Ḥadīthah, n.d.), 290; Rifāʿah Rāfiʿ al-Ṭahṭāwī, *Al-Qawl al-Sadīd fī Adillat al-Ijtihād wa al-Taqlīd* (Cairo: Wādī al-Nīl, 1387 AH), 11.
16. Shāh Walī Allāh al-Dahlawī, *Al-Inṣāf fī Bayān Asbāb al-Ikhtilāf* (Cairo: Maṭbaʿah Sharikat al-Maṭbūʿāt al-ʿIlmiyyah, 1329 AH), 18. The author quotes Abū Ṭālib al-Makkī as saying: "These books and compendiums are recent developments. Likewise, the same is true of quoting others as authorities, of issuing fatwas only on the basis of a single *madhhab*, of considering that *madhhab* to be the law, of relating only the opinions of that *madhhab* in regard to all that occurs, and of studying only that one school of fiqh." Certainly, that was not the way of the people in the first and second centuries.
17. Hishām al-Ayyūbī, *Al-Ijtihād wa Muqtaḍayāt al-ʿAṣr*, 147-53. Amīn al-Shinqīṭī points out that *taqlīd* of a *madhhab* is, in effect, tantamount to disregarding the Qur'an and the Sunnah. He writes: "This disregard for the Qur'an and the Sunnah, and the belief that they may be dispensed with through recourse to the recorded *madhāhib* followed by the great majority of Muslims, is among the greatest of calamities ever to befall the Ummah in the centuries of its history." See Amīn al-Shinqīṭī, *Al-Qawl al-Sadīd fī Kashf Ḥaqīqat al-Taqlīd* (Cairo: Dār al-Ṣaḥwah, 1985), 107.
18. For further reading on the subject of the door of ijtihad and the need to keep it open, see the following works: Yūsuf al-Qaraḍāwī, *Al-Fiqh al-Islāmī*, 39ff; Muṣṭafā al-Rāfiʿī, *Al-Islām: Inṭilāq Lā Jumūd* (Cairo: al-Majlis al-Aʿlā li al-Shu'ūn al-Islāmiyyah, 1386/1966), 174ff; Maḥfūẓ Ihrāhīm Faraj, *Al-Tashrīʿ al-Islāmī fī Madīnat al-Rasūl* (Cairo: Dār al-Iʿtiṣām, 1404/1983), 67ff; Muḥammad Suʿād Jalāl, *Al-Ijtihād fī al-Sharīʿah at Islāmiyyah* (Cairo: Dār Thābit, 1402/1982), 5ff; Muḥammad Sulaymān, *Bi Ayyi Sharʿ Taḥkum?* (Cairo: al-Maṭbaʿah al-Āmīriyyah, 1936), 12; Wahbah al-Zuḥaylī, *Tajdīd al-Ijtihād*, included in *Al-Ijtihād wa al-Tajdīd fī al-Tashrīʿ al-Islāmī*, Muṣṭafā Kamāl al-Tāzī et al. (Tunis: al-Sharikah al-Tūnisiyyah li al-Tawzīʿ, n.d.), 89-90, 95; Ẓuhūr Aḥmad, *Al-Ijtihād wa al-Shāʿir al-Islāmī Muḥammad Iqbāl*, published in the Proceedings of the Seventeenth Session of the Islamic Thought Forum in Algeria, Ministry of Religious Affairs, 1403/1983, 5; Ibrāhīm al-Qaṭṭān, "Al-Sharīʿah Ṣāliḥah li Kull Zamān wa Makān," *Majallat al-Dirāsāt al-Islāmiyyah* 6, vol. 17 (Nov-Dec. 1982): 48-49; Jamāl al-Dīn al-Afghānī, *Al-Aʿmāl al-Kāmilah*, 329; al-Sayyid Muḥammad Rashīd Riḍā, *Muḥāwarāt al-Muṣliḥ wa al-Muqallid wa al-Waḥdah al-Islāmiyyah* (Cairo:

Maṭbaʿah al-Manār, 1323 AH), 135-36; see also Muḥammad Zāhid al-Kawthārī, ed. Shams al-Dīn al-Dhahabī, *Ẓaghal al-ʿIlm* (Damascus: Matbaʿat al-Tawfiq, 1347 AH), 21, in which al-Kawthārī writes: "The door of ijtihad is wide open for all time, but shut in the face of any ingenuous incompetent incapable of verifying even a single chapter of fiqh," in commentary on the statement of al-Dhahabī: "...You don't need *uṣūl al-fiqh,* O *muqallid.* O you who suppose ijtihad to be over with, and that there will never be another *mujtahid.*"; see also Maḥmūd al-Sharqāwī, *Al-Taṭawwur Rūḥ al-Sharīʿah al-Islāmiyyah* (Beirut: al-Maktabah al-ʿAṣriyyah, 1969), 212-18.

The Role of Islamic Ijtihad in the Regulation and Correction of Capital Markets

I hesitate to speak on the role of ijtihad in an Islamic capital market, because this topic requires understanding two important but difficult areas whose primary sources are in different languages. The first area is ijtihad, which is connected with fiqh. Most of its sources are in Arabic. The second area is economics, which is connected with the analysis of capital markets. Most of its sources are in various European languages. Linking ethics and economics is necessary, because every economic choice has a spiritual dimension. But this is difficult, because secular economics severs the link by reducing values to tastes and arguing that different ethical values do not change the method of choice. Therefore, properly linking ijtihad and economics requires a determined effort to refute the secular separation of ethics and economics. I spent over 100 hours thinking, reading, and analyzing the essential points of both until I could establish a common ground between them.

Ijtihad, which is of central importance in *uṣūl al-fiqh,* is the method of implementing the spirit of the sacred texts in any environment. Since the third Islamic century, it has been the main theme of dialog between the different legal schools.To this day, scholars continue to debate the issue.

Economics is an important science that influences several other sciences. Since the capital market is a significant topic in economics, we must understand the strengths and weaknesses of the neo-classical analysis of capital markets in order to develop an Islamic capital market. In addition, we must understand the history of economic thought, how capital markets became an

This article first appeared in the *American Journal of Islamic Social Sciences* 14, no. 3 (Fall 1997): 39-66, and was translated by Waleed El-Ansary. It has been slightly edited.

important part of it, and why many neo-classical economists believe that their analysis is objective and spiritually neutral.

Since the ninteenth century, some of our *ʿulamāʾ* have tried to build a common ground between economics and ijtihad on matters of economic development by adopting many of the economists' views. Some *ʿulamāʾ* have called for imitating the West and its modernity to achieve prosperity and thus have adopted elements of western methodology. They believe that the Ummah resists change by clinging to such concepts of *ḥalāl* and *ḥarām* in economic activity, which hinder the community's development and prevent it from overcoming its economic problems. They have tried to justify this economic imitation on the community's *maṣlaḥah* (benefit), the relativity of fiqh, the absence of alternatives, or a combination of these.

However, this approach justifies *taqlīd* (blind imitation) of the West by erroneously combining ijtihad with western economics. A truly Islamic economics and ijtihad, on the other hand, must apply traditional principles to the contemporary world by combining the transmitted (*naqlī*) and intellectual (*ʿaqlī*) sciences. A precise understanding of Islamic principles must inform both disciplines to establish the true complementarity between them and then successfully apply the Islamic paradigm to economic problems. A bad economic analysis can misinform the best ijtihad, just as an erroneous ijtihad? can vitiate the best economic analysis. Those who call for *taqlīd* of the West often combine both errors.

Thus, failure to apply traditional Islamic principles to either ijtihad or economics creates a duality between the old and the new, between *naql* and *ʿaql*. And this duality creates a potential for opposition, which is a serious challenge to all Muslim thinkers, regardless of whether they are economists, political scientists, sociologists, or *fuqahāʾ*.

This challenge raises serious questions. Can Islam deal with this duality or not? Can the Shariʿah give us solutions for any problems – past, present, or future? The Ummah needs to see that the Shariʿah provides solutions by applying traditional Islamic principles to both *naqlī* and *ʿaqlī* sciences. Thus, the solution must come from the epistemological and methodological viewpoint that carefully defines and applies Islamic principles, not from *taqlīd* of the West. To build a solution based on traditional Islamic principles, we need to understand the *maqāṣid al-Sharīʿah* (the Shariʿah's higher values and causes). Without looking at all of these points, it is very difficult to answer questions of economic policy and the challenge of secular economic thought, especially on capital markets.

The Islamic paradigm is essential to building a common ground between ijtihad and economics, on which the Islamic solution is based. Our paradigm is based on three essential Islamic principles: *tawḥīd* (God is the Absolute and the necessary starting point of any Islamic analysis), *tazkiyah* (purifying humanity and society from evil), and *ʿumrān* (building a civilization in order to accomplish the good).

These principles form a complete and consistent set that can be applied to ijtihad and economics, for knowing that God is the Absolute requires eliminating the evil and accomplishing the good. Moreover, all three principles are necessary in a truly Islamic society. For example, it would be hypocritical to know the truth but not use it to purify oneself and society from evil and to neglect real needs in building a civilization designed to accomplish the good). Similarly, purification from evil is not possible without knowledge of the truth, and the existence of an Islamic civilization is crucial to enabling humanity to know and conform to that truth. Finally, building a civilization to accomplish the good is not possible unless it is based upon truth and reflects pure intentions rather than greed.

These essential Islamic principles or higher values are the pillars of our Islamic paradigm. They guarantee that our paradigm is characterized by *wasaṭiyyah* (avoids excess as evil and finds the good situated between two excesses), *tawāzun* (balanced), *ʿadl* (just), *istiqāmah* (direct, not winding), *rabbāniyyah* (from God), *ʿālamiyyah* (global), *al-ʿumūm* (universal), and *al-shumūl* (includes every part of life).

When these three principles are the common ground of ijtihad and economics, we can integrate both to develop an Islamic capital market. However, the references on ijtihad and economics are very different. Ijtihad is a central issue in *uṣūl al-fiqh* among all legal schools, and is the seventh chapter of any traditional *uṣūlī* book. All of these sources are in Arabic, which poses a major obstacle for many researchers. Ijtihad will be the first topic of our discussion.

Economics and the capital market will be the second topic of our discussion. Unfortunately, there are few books in Islamic languages on this subject, but many in European languages. In most of these books, neo-classical economists conflate values and preferences in order to separate ethics and economics, thereby excluding essential spiritual principles from their analysis. Neo-classical economists make the questionable claim that their analysis is objective and spiritually neutral. We will establish that ethics and economics cannot be separated, because values and preferences cannot be conflated. This is the basis for an Islamic theory of choice. Of course, a full treatment of this topic requires many researchers to deal with both Western and traditional Islamic sources from different viewpoints.

This introduction indicates how difficult it is to properly link ijtihad and economics and to deal with the capital market from an Islamic perspective. Nevertheless, we should try to deal with this challenge. At this point, I would like to emphasize that this paper will deal with the topics objectively and without an attempt to give legal rulings or recommend specific policies. We will try to discover the link between the two fields, dealing with those principles that will help others apply them to specific cases.

IJTIHAD

When we think about ijtihad in *uṣūl al-fiqh*, we cannot unequivocally say that its current format provides us with an effective methodology for deriving optimal solutions to all contemporary issues. We cannot make such a claim, whether or not there is anyone who can be a *mujtahid muṭlaq* (an expert qualified to make ijtihad in all areas of fiqh without conditions) and whether or not we can identify such a person. Therefore, we need to reconstruct the concept of ijtihad itself so that it can become a methodological tool capable of responding to the challenges and questions of our time and future generations. Ijtihad need not be a closed tool to be used only within a specialized methodology.

To reconstruct ijtihad, we need to take note of the following. First, in its *fiqhī* dimension, ijtihad is limited to the genius of a scholar who can formulate the appropriate question, given the event(s), and go to the text of the Qur'an and Sunnah for a ruling. If he/she cannot find a direct answer, then he/she must look for an answer in the rulings derived from ijmaᶜ (consensus), *qiyās* (analogy), or articulate his/her own considered legal principle.[1]

But in our time, the unprecedented and ongoing explosion of knowledge and communication has made this impossible. With the advent of the social sciences in world affairs and their continued spread into different spheres, there is even more information to incorporate into ijtihad. Similarly, the collapse of the idea of the "limitedness of the text and the unlimitedness of the events" in the face of the holistic thought and purposes of the Qur'an and Sunnah (which exemplifies Qur'anic principles) makes it necessary to apply Islamic principles within ijtihad. In turn, this application requires information from other sciences, meaning that ijtihad can no longer be limited to the *fiqhī* sphere or to one person. Thus, we have to establish a strong connection between the social sciences (as a tool for understanding the event[s] in order to formulate the relevant ethical question) and fiqh (as the science according to which these formulated incidents have moral value and meaning).

Second, due to the difficulty of individual ijtihad, we must adopt the principle of collective or institutional ijtihad based on diverse disciplines and specialists outside the framework of current fatwa committees or fiqh councils, despite their continuing importance. Ijtihad should be undertaken within the framework of establishing qualified research institutions featuring dedicated scholars from all *fiqhī* and *uṣūlī* schools, law, Hadith, and *tafsīr*, as well as social scientists, linguists, and community leaders. Guidelines may be established to determine the team's constitution depending on the issue. This does not negate the individual's role in ijtihad; rather, it emphasizes it and gives it direction.

Whenever such an institution for collective ijtihad develops, the nature of ijtihad itself will change. First, it will no longer be a process based on an individual *mujtahid's* theoretical dialog between the text and dictionaries in order to deduce a ruling established on an inference based on the semantics to which the scholars of *uṣūl* and logicians are accustomed.

Second, this institution will need to utilize all of the available social science methodological means, and possibly some of the available natural science methodologies, to understand, analyze, and better define the event. Such an approach includes, in addition to the linguistic method, the statistical, quantitative, and qualitative methods as well as other tools. Even the linguistic method will have to be modified to make better use of new developments that have taken place in the study, analysis, and deconstruction of the text in order to gain a deeper insight into its purpose.

Third, the Shariʿah's characteristics and the nature of its universal textual proofs (*al-adillah al-kulliyyah*) will have to be brought to the forefront. Thus, it will become imperative to understand the particular textual evidence within the framework of the universal textual proofs. It is no longer sufficient to collect only those particular proofs relevant to the issue; rather, such proofs or evidence need to be understood within the context the Shariʿah's universal textual proofs, goals, and purposes, as well as the nature of its originating source (the Qur'an) and its particular, clarifying, and binding source (the Sunnah).

Fourth, understanding the precise relationship between the Qur'an and the Sunnah will become apparent. This relationship shall consider the Qur'an as the only originating source of law and the Sunnah as the only clarifying and binding source. Such a relationship does not allow one source to be separated from the other. In addition, it calls for understanding the nature of *bayyinah* (evidence), its characteristics, and how it details the general, interprets the vague, specifies the generic, and generalizes the particular. All of this is done to reveal the methodology used to apply the text to reality in the Prophet's time, and to show how such a methodology could be generalized for all ages so that humanity may be guided by the values and regulations of the Qur'an and the Sunnah until the end of time.

Fifth, after these centers and research academies are established, its members will have to reexamine "controversial legal indicators" (*al-adillah al-mukhtalaf fihā*) and leave behind those that are no longer relevant. Other indicators may be renewed, developed, and further regulated by the originating and clarifying sources.

Sixth, the Shariʿah's higher values, *tawḥīd* (the unity of God and acknowledgment that God is the Absolute), *tazkiyah* (purification from evil), and *ʿumrān* (building of civilization to accomplish the good) shall be the guiding lights, regulating standards, and just scales against which the outcome of institutional ijtihad shall be evaluated.

Seventh, after such institutional ijtihad has become widespread, people will realize that no matter how many safeguards and means have been put into place, ijtihad cannot be presented as producing binding rules for future generations or that these rules respond to their needs. This ijtihad should not lead to new schools of thought and sects that may erode the Ummah's unity, impede its future development, and hinder future generations from practicing ijtihad. The most we can expect from any generation's fiqh is to offer solutions to crises and challenges that face a specific society in a certain time, place, and circumstance. The outcome of such ijtihad cannot be absolute and should only be binding on that generation and whoever chooses to adopt it. If a consensus exists among the people of a region or a certain time about a previous ijtihad ruling, it shall become binding upon them but not necessarily upon the people of other regions or other times. Only the Qur'an and the Sunnah have binding authority. Thus, we recover ijtihad's effectiveness, vitality, and continuity and make it an integral part – not an exception – of the Ummah's psychological and mental state.

Eighth, ijtihad conducted by academic and research centers will reveal Islam's universal characteristics, which are not merely virtues but rather items to be applied as methodological guidelines when formulating collective ijtihad. Islam's universality, which is at the forefront of these characteristics, is indicated by the fact that the Shariʿah is a law of ease and mercy, based on the Qur'an's authority, connected with prophethood's finality, and provides a necessary methodology. This universality indicates that Islam's message is for all of humanity, regardless of time or place, until the Day of Judgment. Its rapid spread took place according to a perfect methodology that began by preparing the final Prophet, tasking him to warn his relatives (the people of Makkah and the surrounding area), and then building an Ummah that provided a model for the rest of humanity to emulate.

Islam's mission is global, although it addresses humanity through a specific social entity in its own language (Arabic) and deals with the community's needs and problems. These are not necessarily problems common to all of humanity in all times and places; rather, other societies can use them as a model for meeting their own different needs and problems by drawing on the Qur'an's methodology, values, and purposes. The Qur'an is so resourceful that it provides answers to specific questions regardless of time or place. At one level, it gives an answer for the Prophet's time, while at another level it applies the link to the Prophet's community to project the answer into the future. The text's multiple meanings and applications are fascinating, and this is how the Qur'an communicates absolute values in a relative environment, links the transient to the eternal and the specific to the general. This correlation between the relative and the absolute has been achieved in the Qur'anic text, for if it had ignored the problems of the Prophet's community, it could not have projected these absolute values forward. In other words, there would have been no example of how to apply the message.

In a short period of time, Islam incorporated many other civilizations due to its universal vision, thereby proving its beneficial power in every time and place. This final message, characterized by the Absolute Book and the Last Prophet, contains categories that integrate the continuous and the temporary, the general and the specific, and the global and the local to satisfy its goals and objectives.

Unfortunately, our current religious teachings and studies do not prepare us to understand these essential principles. As a result, some people approach the Qur'an as if it were meant only for themselves, like a closed letter that our ancestors carried without opening. This leads some people to misinterpret the Qur'an based on their current viewpoint, such as equating jinn with bacteria, or money with capitalism or socialism. Some people take the opposite position, holding that the Qur'anic message was meant for our ancestors and simply provides us with general directions but no specific instructions. Both positions represent extremes that do not reflect a true understanding of the Qur'an, for they place limits on the methodology used to understand it. A deep understanding requires a knowledge of the dichotomies in Islamic discourse, namely, the absolute and the relative, the general and the specific, the continuous and the temporary, and the local and the global in the Qur'anic teachings. In the absence of this discourse, we cannot understand the sacred text.

Our ancestors understood these categories and incorporated them into *uṣūl al-fiqh* as "chapters of terminology" and "chapters of what is common in the Qur'an and Sunnah." These chapters include discussions of the general and the specific, the absolute and the limited, Qur'anic veses (*āyāt*) with locked and flexible meanings, abrogation and the abrogated, and other topics. In addition, they established some constraints and criteria to distinguish between the discourse's different levels, the legislative and the non-legislative, as well as the obligatory (*farḍ* or *wājib*), and the forbidden (*ḥarām*) or the reprehensible (*makrūh*). Our ancestors understood these distinctions so clearly that they formulated five categories for action: forbidden, reprehensible, indifferent, recommended, and obligatory. They even distinguished between two types of reprehensible categories: *makrūh tanzīh*, which implies unsuitability, and *makrūh taḥrīm*, which leads to the border of *ḥarām*. They also classified necessities into three categories: essential needs, means to these needs, and embellishments or accessories to support these means.

In order to serve and carry Islam's message, as well as prove its applicability and usefulness for every time and place, we need to build upon this great legacy. We must use our knowledge to go back and rethink what should be included in the different categories discussed above. This is an essential, dangerous, and difficult journey, particularly for a mentality that has been used to *taqlīd*, instead of ijtihad, for several centuries. To help us with this undertaking, we should also establish centers for collective ijtihad.

Let's consider one example of how a specific incident develops into a general legal principle so that we can understand how principles guide ijtihad. Take the case of adoption. The Qur'an deals with this through the example of Zayd (the Prophet's adopted son), declaring that the Prophet had no sons. Even though this message applied to a specific Arab community, the principle that adoption does not entail changing the child's name and literally creating new parents (although the Qur'an emphasizes the great rewards and spiritual virtues of caring for orphans) still applies today. There are many other examples of establishing a principle through specific events in fiqh, such as emancipating slaves and dividing war booty.

Since our ancestors understood that the Qur'an communicates principles through specific incidents, they did not need the Qur'an to tell them:

"This is relative, this is absolute. This is general, this is specific. If the circumstances change, do this or that." But Allah revealed the Qur'an as He wills, and He revealed it to the Ummah in this way, thereby placing the heavy responsibility of textual interpretation on the people of dhikr (remembrance) and the scholars:

> [Here is] a Book that We have sent down to you, full of blessings, that they may meditate on its signs, and that men of understanding may receive admonition. (38:29)

> Nor should the believers all go forth together; if a contingent from every expedition remained behind, they could devote themselves to studies in religion and admonish the people when they return to them – that thus they [may learn] to guard themselves [against evil]. (9:122)

Our ancestors produced many great achievements with this understanding. If our generation could function at the same level of ability without stopping ijtihad, we could understand correctly the Qur'anic categories mentioned in our *uṣūl al-fiqh*. If we pursue deep thought and illuminate our minds, we can build on our ancestors' great achievements.

Their *mujtahidūn* deduced many principles for making legal judgments and deriving appropriate solutions, such as alleviating legal hardship, blocking licit means to illicit ends, choosing the most prudent course, limiting the matter to make options more plentiful, and realizing that difficulties attract facility, that the illicit can be rendered licit by necessity or overwhelming circumstances, that the public's needs may be considered the same as the individual's needs, and that there may be acceptance in continuation for matters unacceptable in initiation. These rules represent deep jurisprudential and legal thought, and past generations may have considered them more than enough to deal with their problems. Through these partial rules that are based on the Shariʿah's total objectives, they could properly understand those rules related to specific situations. They did not necessarily articulate the framework they used to derive these partial rules or how to apply the holistic viewpoint involving different levels of Qur'anic discourse and instruction.

In this regard, how the Qur'an dealt with alcohol and slavery, both of which were widepread at the time of its revelation, is important. The Qur'an gradually prohibited alcohol, and the Muslims were expected to end slavery shortly afterward. However, the failure to eliminate slavery during the Prophet's time does not mean that it was left to continue. The ruling to eliminate slavery was in the Qur'an, but its full application took some time. Since all of the Qur'anic rulings related to emancipation, not slavery, we know that slavery must ultimately end. Indeed, slaves were to be considered as the master's brothers and sisters, to eat what they eat, wear what they wear, and work as they work (not to be given overbearing tasks). All of this let people know that slavery was only a temporary situation. Moreover, people were forbidden to call others "slaves" and had to address them more affectionately. People have talked a lot about how Islam released slaves, but nobody talks about why slavery lasted until the recent universal emancipation. Why did we not reach global prohibition? We should have reached this conclusion ourselves, since we did not have any rules for enslaving people.

The truth is that slavery was a sensitive issue. The *fuqahā'* went around it – we did not find somebody to "break the egg." The Abbassids and Ottomans were more powerful than other civilizations of their time, but they did not abolish slavery because they did not understand the nature of the sacred text. For example, the texts require that a slave be freed to atone for an accidental killing. According to Nasafī's *Tafsīr*, freeing a slave is like giving life to what is dead. Indeed, slavery is associated with *kufr* in the Days of Ignorance, and *kufr* is related to spiritual death; a person who accepts Islam is like a person who was dead and to whom God gave life.

Moreover, the analogy between charity and freeing a slave is erroneous, because the essence of money is an object for use, whereas the essence of a person is to be free. Our ancestors supported emancipation, saying that slavery was like death and *kufr*. They came so close to, but did not embrace, the prohibition of slavery. But if it is our job to resist *kufr* and end every trace of it in our society, why did we not eliminate slavery in our society and the rest of the world? We had the power. Even if other civilizations continued with slavery, we could have at least eliminated it in ours. The whole question goes back to our inability to deal with what is continuous and limited, and with what is global and specific in the Qur'an. This is why we left it to the West to abolish slavery. We now turn to economics.

ECONOMICS AND THE CAPITAL MARKET

The Islamic tradition of economics contains a rich history of economics as applied ethics. Muslim intellectuals were well aware of the distinction between tastes and values, and that values determine the methodology one uses to make a choice, whereas tastes do not. Since values cannot be reduced to preferences or tastes, differences in the content of desires, due to values, imply different methodologies of choice. Thus, Muslim scholars recognize that ethics and economics are inseparable, for, since God is the Absolute, every choice has a spiritual dimension.

Secular neo-classical economic thought, on the other hand, denies that a "distinction between tastes, preferences, values and ethics can coherently be made."[2] The theory conflates values and tastes, argues that different values do not change the methodology of choice any more than tastes do, and thereby separates ethics and economics.[3] This is why Milton Friedman could declare at his Nobel prize acceptance address: "The great saints of history have served their 'private interest' just as the most money grubbing miser has served his interest."[4]

But if neo-classical theory does not logically distinguish between tastes and values, how can it contribute to Islamic economic policy, which does? We will pursue this question by suggesting that secular neo-classical theory cannot accommodate Islamic values and that an Islamic theory of choice, which recognizes the distinction between tastes and values, can better inform collective ijtihad on capital markets. In addition, we will draw out the policy implications of the essential Islamic principles of *tawḥīd*, *tazkiyah*, and *ʿumrān* for the capital market and respond to potential objections from neo-classical economists.

Let's begin with the neo-classical theory of choice, as espoused by Milton Friedman, Gary Becker, and the Chicago School of Economics, because they have won the most Nobel prizes in economics for the past decade and provide a good starting point for the neo-classical approach. While their approach attempts to answer essential economic questions, it lacks spiritual neutrality, for it is based on the doctrine that the only thing anyone can desire or pursue as an end in itself is one's own self-interest or utility, in which pleasure, satisfaction, and happiness are used as synonyms.[5] The theory admits that people sometimes desire the happiness of others, but insists that this desire is only a means to their own happiness. Purely altruistic and benevolent actions and desires, therefore, do not exist. In other words, according to neo-classical theory the noble actions of the Prophet or the *muqarrabūn* (those who are close to Allah) are disguised forms of self-serving behavior rather than models of conforming to the truth. It is one thing to suggest that people often "put their own interests first," which Islamic economics takes into consideration, but quite another thing to assert that they are capable of nothing else and thereby deny a person's ability to be motivated by the truth or God, rather than utility. As the Qur'an states, God is the Truth (*al-Ḥaqq*) because He is the Real.

While the Chicago School's neo-classical approach denies a person's spiritual nature (read their literature on the economics of crime, marriage, fertility, and so on), Islamic economics recognizes that the believers' ultimate motivating cause is not utility or happiness, but the truth, for although happiness accompanies conformity to the truth, it is an effect rather than a motivating cause. "Our willing is not inspired by our desires alone. Fundamentally, it is inspired by the truth, and this is independent of our immediate interests."[6] If a person meets his/her spiritual needs fully by conforming to the truth with his/her whole being, the result is spiritual virtue, or "beauty of soul."[7] With spiritual virtue comes true happiness, for beauty and the love of beauty give the soul happiness. Indeed, "sensible beauties are situated outside the soul, and their meeting with it is more or less accidental; if the soul wishes to be happy in an unconditional and permanent fashion, it must carry the beautiful within itself."[8] Happiness, therefore, is an effect that accompanies spiritual virtue. This explains why a pious person with few means is far happier than an impious person of great wealth. As the Prophet said: "The Muslim is happy [*bi khayr*] in every situation."

The Chicago School erroneously inverts cause and effect by subordinating truth to utility and declaring utility to be the sole motivating cause. It is a theory of choice appropriate for the *nafs al-ammārah* (the soul that commands to evil), for only the *nafs* would reduce values to tastes, subordinate the truth to utility, and ignore the reasons behind preferences. This reduction applies to both spiritual complements (e.g., physical needs) and opposites (e.g., anti-spiritual desires). For example, the Chicago School's neo-classical approach suggests that a spiritually inclined person should allocate his/her time between complementary needs (e.g., praying, eating, and working) such that the utility of the last moment spent in each of these activities is equal. This would maximize utility, since any discrepancy would mean that the individual could increase utility by reallocating his/her time. This principle also applies to allocating time to different questions on an exam.

But this approach to a hierarchy of spiritual and other needs is only appropriate for the *nafs*, because these needs are qualitatively different (points on an exam are not). Lumping "spiritual utility," "eating utility," and "working utility" into one utility is not possible, because doing so requires that spiritual and other needs to serve as substitutes for each other. Such a relationship would create tension between them. This view is further mistaken because a different type of "spiritual utility" accompanies both eating and working. As the Prophet said, a person working to feed his/her family is performing an act of worship, just as if he/she were praying. A person's life can be integrated around a sacred center only if qualitatively different types of utility exist simultaneously. Such integration explains how the sacred is always present and not in conflict with a person's other needs. Islam holds every aspect of life to be sacred, because nothing is outside of the Absolute. Moreover, no aspect of life is profane, because everything is attached to God. Given this, believers have no need to allocate resources between the sacred and profane, or between spiritual and other needs, because everything has a spiritual context. They find the ultimate purpose of any action in God, because no end is beyond Him and no end has sufficient reason if it stops short of Him.

Thus, the neo-classical approach to spiritual and other needs collapses into one type of utility, creating trade-offs that do not exist in reality, but only as an illusion of the *nafs*. Indeed, such trade-offs could exist only if one does not recognize the spiritual nature of all activities on the one hand, and one vitiates spiritual activity with an inferior intention on the other. Through such false trade-offs, the Chicago School's neo-classical approach sets the stage for the sacrifice of spiritual needs.

The same principle applies when this approach is applied to the opposition between spiritual needs and anti-spiritual desires. For example, the Chicago School's literature on the economics of crime suggests that its spiritual costs can be traded off against its material benefits in a single measure of utility. Obviously, this is a theory of choice for the *nafs*, for such costs and benefits are incommensurable. Believers recognize that spiritual benefits cannot be traded off against criminal gain, for this would require the existence of an end beyond God, Who aggregates both. Such a proposition contradicts the truth that God is the Absolute. And so they do not engage in this particular type of calculation.

Unlike the *nafs*, the *rūḥ* (spirit) recognizes that good and evil are qualitatively different, given that they are related to different intentions, because there are qualitatively different criteria upon which to make a choice. The *rūḥ* judges the alternatives not with respect to utility, but with respect to the truth, by examining the reasons behind the various good and evil desires. Indeed, the *rūḥ* would not adjust its estimate of a "mono-utility" if the material benefits of crime increased. Moreover, not only is the neo-classical approach irrelevant for the *rūḥ*, it is also unstable for the *nafs*, since ignorance of the truth is not necessarily permanent. God saves whom He wills, and the *rūḥ* can overcome the *nafs al-ammārah* with the truth, transforming it into the *nafs al-muṭma'innah* (soul at peace). Thus, this neo-classical approach to both spiritual complements and opposites corresponds to a theory of choice for the *nafs*, not the *rūḥ*.

Economists attempt to make all choices commensurable, reducing them to a single intention, by employing the concept of "indifference." For example, if a person rates options A and B as being equally good, the person is "indifferent" to them. This indifference is only possible, however, when there is one intention – multiple intentions would lead a person to prefer option A to B, or vice-versa, depending on which intention has the higher priority. In other words, indifference is impossible and preference is necessary when there are two or more intentions. When many options are compared, a set of points that a person ranks equally form what economists call an "indifference curve." These curves are central to neo-classical economic analysis, because advanced mathematics can be applied to them (i.e., maximize utility according to the shapes of indifference curves). Given this, the saint and the money-grubbing miser simply have differently shaped indifference curves.

While this may be true for tastes that reflect a single intention, it cannot be true for values that reflect multiple intentions. Only by reducing values to tastes can the Chicago School claim to have a theory of choice that is independent of ethics. But this theory of choice itself incorporates bad ethics into economics and is only appropriate for the *nafs*. In fact, it even denies that there is an inner battle between the *rūḥ* and the *nafs*, for it maintains that everything is reducible to a single intention under indifference curves. In other words, the Chicago School denies the Prophet's teaching that we must continuously engage in the inner jihad, because no such battle exists for them.

Some economists recognize that this is obviously false and that there are major problems with the Chicago School's neo-classical approach. They attempt to limit the application of indifference curves to situations in which the alternatives are qualitatively similar and morally neutral, such as optimally allocating one's time to questions on an exam in order to maximize one's score. Since a variety of further intentions are consistent with this goal, such situations accommodate multiple intentions. While this approach to limiting the use of indifference curves is spiritually neutral, it suffers from a particular defect: These situations are too few to cover essential economic choices, since spiritual considerations appear everywhere. For example, how much wealth one strives for and the nature of economic institutions are spiritual choices in traditional Islamic civilization, for nothing is profane. Without explaining the "budget constraint" and the institutional environment, economic theory is fatally incomplete, abstracting from the essence of the problem it seeks to solve.

Moreover, applying indifference curves only to such goods as food and clothes does not eliminate the problem of spiritual neutrality. For instance, when one is overeating or buying way too many clothes simply to gratify his/her pleasure, indifference curves can exist between such tastes. But when one is directing needs for food and clothes to support spiritual work, they are not substitutes and thus indifference curves do not exist – one cannot wear food or eat clothes. They can only be viewed as substitutes toward a single intention, such as pleasure, if the *nafs*, instead of the *rūḥ*, is in control. In this sense, the incommensurability of real needs is based on values, whereas the commensurability of arbitrary desires is based on tastes. By reducing those needs that are not substitutes for desires, which are determined through indifference curves, neo-classical theory once again reduces values to tastes and violates spiritual neutrality. The range of spiritually neutral economic choices to which indifference curves apply is far narrower than any neo-classical economic approach accepts. Indeed, economists who recognize that indifference curves do not exist for spiritual needs must justify why they should exist between other qualitatively different needs.

Hence, these very indifference curves, which are central to neo-classical theory, force economists to choose between spiritual neutrality and logical completeness. Economists can either apply their theory of choice in a spiritually neutral way, leaving essential economic questions unanswered and the theory incomplete, or they can provide answers to essential questions by using a theory of choice that is not spiritually neutral.

Islamic economics does not have this problem, because it denies the existence of indifference curves between a hierarchy of qualitatively different spiritual and other needs on the one hand, and between spiritual needs and anti-spiritual desires on the other. Islamic economics recognizes the existence of indifference curves within each qualitatively comparable "level" and applies an ethical analysis to determine the differences between levels. Since only the *nafs* conflates values and tastes, by ignoring the reasons for these "preferences," neo-classical economics is only a theory of choice for the *nafs*. While indifference curves reflecting a single intention can exist for different tastes, they do not exist for different values. Whereas "there is no arguing about tastes," since they do not depend on the truth or require justification, there is an ethical argument about values that depend on truth and require justification. Islamic economics recognizes these crucial distinctions, and thereby combines ethics and economics in a theory of choice for the *rūḥ*, which is spiritually neutral (it recognizes God rather than utility as the Absolute) and logically complete.

Any effort at collective ijtihad on the capital market should, therefore, beware of neo-classical errors. Developing an Islamic capital market requires both a correct understanding of ijtihad and a correct vision of economics with which to inform ijtihad. One cannot base economic analysis on secular economic fallacies any more than one can base ijtihad on anti-Islamic principles. Indeed, modernists usually substitute *taqlīd* of the great imams like Abū Ḥanīfah and his school of law with *taqlīd* of some economists like Milton Friedman and the Chicago School. It is useful to remember that not too long ago many people were arguing for *taqlīd* based on Karl Marx rather than Abū Ḥanīfah, despite the fact that many religious leaders recognized and predicted that communism must fail because it inverts spiritual principles.[9]

The point is not that the Islamic world should blindly follow the imams of the past, but that one should not simply replace them with secular economists today. Indeed, blindly following Milton Friedman instead of Karl Marx may simply replace one error with another. Adopting the neo-classical fallacy, which inverts spiritual principles, necessarily leads to self-destruction, for the Qur'an and Hadith continuously warn humanity of spiritual indifference, regardless of whether it is applied to communism or any other economic system. In short, it is more dangerous to base *taqlīd* on secular economic thought than on past Islamic thought, and understanding the latter can play a key role in refuting the former to correctly inform ijtihad.

In brief, the danger of blindly following neo-classical economics in developing an Islamic capital market is illustrated by the secular analysis of *ribā*. (Regardless of how one defines *ribā* – "preferences" may generate either extremely high or low interest rates – the point is not to examine Islamic arguments on interest, but to examine whether the neo-classical justification of it is spiritually neutral.) Secular economists usually attempt to justify the morality of *ribā* by arguing that consumption today gives more utility than consumption tomorrow, so that a lender must restrain himself/herself in order to lend money. This theory was popularized by Irving Fisher, a major economist on capital markets, and is taught in economics courses on savings and investment. (While we recognize that this is not the only neo-classical justification for *ribā*, it is a popular one. Our purpose is simply to illustrate that it is not spiritually neutral.)

According to this argument, the lender's "effort" at self-restraint deserves a reward, just as the effort of labor in production deserves a reward. This secular economic argument equates not consuming too much, which a Muslim is supposed to do even without compensation, with the jihad of a person working to support his/her family. These two types of "effort" are not, however, comparable from the Islamic point of view. Abstaining from such an evil as over-consumption is not something that morally requires a payment, whereas accomplishing a good (e.g., working to support one's family) deserves compensation. As the Prophet said: "Pay the laborer his/her wages before the drying up of his/her sweat." He did not say to pay the person who has more money than he/she needs today extra money tomorrow so that he/she will not commit the sin of consuming too much today.

The real effort is to abstain from *ribā*, not simply restraining oneself from consuming too much today. Secular economists often respond that abstaining from *ribā* will ruin the economy. The Qur'an counters this by stating that Satan threatens the Muslim with poverty when he/she abstains from *ribā*, whereas God promises him/her blessings. God's promise is empirically verifiable by the simple fact that stock investments are far more profitable than bonds in the long-run. For example, statistics from Ibbottson Associates show that $1 invested in long-term government bonds in 1926 would be worth $33.73 today, whereas $1 invested in stocks on the New York Stock Exchange would be worth $1,370.95 and $1 invested in the smallest 10 percent of stocks on the exchange would be worth $4,495.99.[10] If someone objects that the stock market cannot accommodate small or short-term investments in order to offer superior returns to capital, the response is that in these cases, abstaining from *ribā* does not lead to the dire poverty envisioned by the economists.

On the contrary, guaranteed interest actually burdens future Muslim generations. As any natural resource economist will testify, maximizing the value of such non-renewable resources as oil requires selling practically everything within 50 to 100 years. Discounting the consumption of future generations places the value of their consumption of these nonrenewable resources at practically zero. The "optimal" sales plan is to exhaust nearly all of the resource within a few generations, after which the resource will have little economic value, because a positive interest rate makes $20 for a barrel of oil today worth far more than $20 for the same barrel 50 years from now. Therefore, future generations are not properly represented in the economic equation, a case of "missing markets" in the language of economists.

Moreover, labor has a spiritual purpose ultimately directed toward God in conformity with the truth, whereas *ribā* does not, for the Prophet said that a person working to feed his/her family is performing an act of worship just as if he/she were praying. Indeed, the Shariᶜah makes the effort to earn one's daily bread a religious act that is just as obligatory as specifically religious duties, and gives religious meaning to all acts that are necessary for a Muslim's life, but not to those that are exploitative luxuries, such as *ribā*. This is why the Qur'an implies that working for a living and being charitable to one's family, the opposite of hoarding wealth with *ribā*, is tantamount to defending the faith.[11]

The Prophet stressed this fact when a young man with a strong physique was running to his shop through the area where the Prophet was marshalling his troops to repel an enemy assault. Someone remarked that he wished the young man would use his body and health to run in the way of God by enlisting to defend the faith. The Prophet responded:

> If this young man runs with the intention of not depending on others and refraining from begging, he is following God. If he strives for the livelihood of his weak parents or weak children, he is following God. If he tries to show his health out of pride, he is following Satan.[12]

By defining *maṣlaḥah* as the effect of conforming to the truth, Islamic economics opposes the erroneous neo-classical definition of it as personal desire. Only a vision of economics that correctly recognizes the spiritual possibility of the truth as a motivating cause, and *maṣlaḥah* as an effect can inform the ijtihad necessary to develop Islamic capital markets.

This brief example suggests how *taqlīd* of such western economists as Milton Friedman can lead to ruin in formulating Islamic capital markets.[13] Indeed, *taqlīd* based on an older but truly Islamic ijtihad is preferable to the modern *taqlīd* of western economics based on a secular ijtihad. Even if this *taqlīd* is accidental, Muslims must never forget that blindly following secular economic thought, whether neo-classical or Marxist, eventually leads to ruin. Moreover, this accidental *taqlīd* is the real danger in the current environment. While some modernists argue that Muslims do not need a fatwa to justify the *taqlīd* of western financial institutions, other Muslims often unknowingly confuse a fatwa that supports such *taqlīd* with real ijtihad. The two are obviously completely different, just as an occupied territory is different from an independent state.

However, *taqlīd* of past legal rulings on economic matters is also dangerous. While the Islamic view of humanity as God's servant (*ʿabd)* and vicegerent (*khalīfat Allāh fī al-arḍ*) has not changed, the circumstances according to which people fulfill these roles and make their choices have. In today's complex environment of industrial production and institutional trade, *taqlīd* is no longer possible. Early fatwas dealt with relatively simple economic situations in which exchange was more individual than institutional, and production was more agricultural than industrial. Since questions about just and unjust transactions were simpler, the *faqīh* (expert in Islamic jurisprudence) did not need the expertise of others and could make legal deliberations alone.

This is extremely difficult, for the knowledge required to deal with today's complex environment is enormous and requires specialized investigation in several areas. Moreover, early fatwas dealt with transactions within *dār al-Islām* at a time when Islamic civilization was politically and economically dominant, and did not address the international trade of today, when many Muslim countries are dominated economically if not politically. For all of these reasons, past fiqh on economic matters does not necessarily apply to the current environment. As a result, we must look to the Qur'an and the Sunnah for guidance.

The correct methodology is to apply Islamic principles to economic policy in order to integrate ethics and economics around the three essential principles of *tawḥīd*, *tazkiyah*, and *ʿumrān*. Each principle has important implications for the Islamic view of wealth and, by extension, the role of capital markets in an Islamic society. Applied to wealth, the truth that God is the Absolute requires that people recognize that wealth is a means that serves their spiritual interests, and that it is not an end in and of itself. If the Absolute is that which requires no further justification, then the first principle excludes the possibility of money or anything else being viewed as a self-sufficient end. Moreover, the first principle obviously requires that believers have God, rather than any other good, as their ultimate end, for God can never be a means to a further end. To suggest otherwise is to deny that He is the Sovereign Good "requiring no justification in terms of a higher good."[14]

The second principle, *tazkiyah*, requires that people's will and sentiment be pure and willing, and that they love all things for God's sake. Purity requires that the will of *homo Islamicus* should keep the Sovereign Good in view and consider all things in their connection with this Good. Their sentiments should be objective in loving all things in their divine context. It would be illogical and against the truth for *homo Islamicus* to will or love things outside of their Divine Cause, for that would constitute the sin of idolatry, defined as "to hate indirectly the Cause from which all perfection and all love derive."[15] The second principle, therefore, requires that people must not be passionately attached to wealth; must be grateful to God for their *rizq* (provisions) and view nature as an *āyah* (sign) of Allah; and must be generous when dealings with others. The fact that zakah is based on the same root as *tazkiyah* shows just how intimately generosity is connected with purity.

The third principle, *ʿumrān*, requires that people accomplish the good in building civilization. In other words, they should not waste their God-given talents and resources either through underutilizing them and neglecting to fulfill their real needs or through exploiting them in the service of greed rather than God. In accomplishing the good, the third principle requires humanity to be vigilant and not slothful, build wealth and civilization to fulfill real spiritual and other needs, and not to abuse them for the sake of passion.

These three principles show that Islam recognizes the importance of wealth in a hierarchy of humanity's spiritual and other needs (*maṣāliḥ*). The Islamic economic hierarchy recognizes that such external goods as wealth are means to attain goods related to the body, such as health and beauty, which, in turn, is the physical support for the spiritual work that manifests itself in intrinsic virtue, the "goods of the soul." The Islamic principles of *tawḥīd*, *tazkiyah*, and *ʿumrān* regulate this hierarchy and integrate humanity's spiritual and other needs into a meaningful whole, thereby realizing and implementing the *shahādatayn* (the fundamental testimonies of faith). In this sense, Islamic economics recognizes the possibility that people can be motivated by the truth or God, rather than by utility or happiness, to eliminate the evil and accomplish the good.

Given all of the above points, we can say that Islam clearly recognizes the role of capital markets in raising funds for companies and projects designed to help the community fulfill its physical and other needs while also providing the necessary liquidity. But the capital market cannot betray the purpose of its existence, which is determined by these three essential Islamic principles. Islamic values must be in the marketplace as well as the mosque, for God is the witness to all contracts. Therefore, companies and investors must use resources ethically in a way that is consistent with these principles. This raises many questions, such as how the capital market can be used as a means to wealth or development that supports society's spiritual ends. Such questions cannot be answered by simply assuming that the capital market or wealth is an end in and of itself. Indeed, the principles imply that freedom is not an unconditional right, but rather the result of fulfilling one's responsibilities. It is self-contradictory to argue that human dignity gives unlimited rights to the basest of people, for this would allow such people to destroy what makes up a person's real dignity: his/her attachment to God.

Several questions that suggest the kinds of responsibilities these principles imply for companies and investors are given below. They are intended to be suggestive (not exhaustive) and relate directly to the equity (not the debt) market. Although several questions apply to both, they are placed in the context of the stock (rather than bond) market, for the latter ultimately contradicts essential Islamic principles. More investigation is needed to determine distinctions between bond types and which types are Islamically acceptable (e.g., bonds for such public works projects as airports).

Turning first to companies, these principles raise questions about corporate responsibility to customers, employees, and shareholders. For example:

- Is it Islamically acceptable for companies to use money raised in the capital market to create entry barriers that inhibit competition so that they can charge their customers higher prices? Islamic principles say it is not. But this has occurred in several American industries.[16]
- Can companies treat some shareholders differently, even when they make similar investments? Justice requires that investors be treated equitably and that arbitrary treatment be considered unacceptable.
- What type of technology will the companies buy with their raised capital? Case studies by the Appropriate Technology Institute reveal that the West often sells technology to developing countries that cannot be transplanted and is often inappropriate. E. F. Schumacher, an economist famous for popularizing appropriate technology, has demonstrated that large-scale western technology is often not in the people's best interests.[17] Some economists may object that the market always produces the most efficient types of technology, but the Appropriate Technology Institute's research shows this is not always the case and that inappropriate technology can conflict with spiritual principles. After billions of dollars have been loaned to developing countries to buy inappropriate technology with such dismal results, it is time to consider more appropriate technologies.
- What is a company's responsibility to the environment and future generations with respect to pollution and resources? For example, can companies use capital from the stock market to deplete non-renewable resources within 50 or 100 years in order to maximize financial gain? Once again, this violates Islamic principles. However, this is the regular practice of the oil industry, which represents some of the world's largest publicly traded companies. In short, capital must be used according to

Islamic principles if the idea of an Islamic capital market is to have any meaning.

Although these questions highlight some of the differences between Islamic and secular stock markets, there are several areas of common concern. Of particular concern is givng investors complete information on corporations so that unscrupulous brokers and companies cannot mislead them into purchasing practically worthless shares, as was common in the early days of the American stock market and, to some extent, today.

Only in the last decade did the U.S. Securities and Exchange Commission close such notorious brokerage firms as Blinder and Robinson, known to experienced investors and industry experts as "Blind'em and Rob'em." This brokerage firm routinely created companies in which it was the only "market-maker," or transactor of sales, and created an enormous spread between the "bid" price and the "ask" price, thereby making an enormous profit on the difference. To trick potential investors into buying shares, the brokerage firm would tell them that the company manufactured something morally commendable, like Bibles. It would then manipulate the stock price by sending it higher and higher, moving investors into and out of the stock (known as "churning the accounts"). On each transaction, it made a huge profit. The firm would continue to manipulate the stock price higher before bringing it crashing down and wiping out the remaining investors. The process would then begin again with a new round of investors. Certain types of stocks are still notorious for scandals, such as "penny stocks" in gold or oil companies, which attract investors with false promises of vast discoveries of gold or oil deposits. Thus, a large drop in a stock's price should be investigated to ensure that there has been no manipulation.

Similarly, unscrupulous brokers must be prevented from selling their own shares to customers at unnecessarily high prices by buying shares for themselves before their customers. However, eliminating these swindles is not sufficient to make the market "Islamic," because the Islamic market is concerned with other ethical questions as well. Moreover, the function of all participants (e.g., market-makers and dealers) must be examined and justified in light of Islamic principles.

Turning to investors, Islamic principles raise questions about the investments available to them. Of course, any investments in liquor and casino stocks, for example, are forbidden. But what about futures and options trading on companies selling *ḥalāl* products? Futures contracts on stocks require more study and should be stopped until they are properly analyzed. Of course, futures contracts on commodities require the seller to actually have the commodity specified in the contract. Similarly, options are questionable because they allow one investor to buy shares from or sell shares to another investor before a given time and at a pre-determined price in exchange for a fixed, irretrievable payment. Many scholars argue that such a transaction encourages speculation and allows exploitation, both of which are against Islamic principles.

Similarly, one must determine how much leverage is Islamically permissible when investing in stocks? Can investors put down 10 percent in the hope of greater profits and pay interest on the 90 percent balance? This was the New York Stock Exchange's policy before the stock market crash of 1929. Afterwards, the minimum investment was increased to 50 percent, because such a high leverage contributed to the prices' collapse and so created instability by encouraging speculation. Such destabilizing speculation is clearly against Islamic principles and is the major reason why some modernists argue that bonds are necessary, since stocks are unstable.

But many economists have pointed out that debt financing and speculation are major causes of stock market instability.[18] This is especially important in the current market environment, when price-earnings ratios are at extremely high levels. In the past year, Alan Greenspan, chairman of the U.S. Federal Reserve, repeatedly warned investors to invest cautiously, clearly discouraging leveraged investments that increase market volatility. This is good advice, because price-earnings ratios and market volatility have now reached levels similar to those before the market crash of 1987. Some economists argue that the stock market's volatility is not rational, and that information systems on company performance and stock prices must be better utilitzed. Therefore, trading rules that limit leverage are critical to stabilizing the stock market and maximizing investor safety. Short-selling also increases instability and is clearly against Islamic principles. Under trading rules that allow leverage and short-selling, both of which decrease stability, fewer investors will prosper from the growth of publicly traded companies and fewer funds will be available for the capital market in the long term.

In general, neo-classical economists often argue that regulations that reduce choices for investors and companies are harmful. They argue that one must contradict the essential Islamic principles of the Qur'an or Sunnah because of the community's *maṣlaḥah*, fiqh's relativity, the absence of alternatives, or a combination of all three. However, those engaged in collective ijtihad must defend the Islamic economic approach which uses applied ethics from these erroneous charges. We will make a few suggestions in this regard.

Let's begin with the last argument: the lack of alternatives. Actually, this is a variation of the *maṣlaḥah* argument, since it derives its force from the harm that would befall the community if it abstained from the economic activity in question. As the earlier discussion on the principles of an Islamic capital market showed, alternatives do exist, but our lack of creativity and desire to realize this goal prevent their implementation. Therefore, this section focuses on the neo-classical economists' first two arguments: the community's *maṣlaḥah* and fiqh's relativity.

As pointed out earlier, what is relative must conform to the absolute, not vice-versa. Scholars in *uṣūl al-fiqh* have maintained that arguments based on what is relative (such as *maṣlaḥah* and time) are not valid against arguments based on what is absolute, namely, the Qur'an and Sunnah, as well as the principles that they necessarily imply. Erroneous arguments that contradict the absolute based on the relative make the relative absolute, and thereby contradict the first principle of *tawḥīd*. Without absolute and eternal standards based on *tawḥīd*, there is no basis upon which to evaluate either *maṣlaḥah* or changes in time. Consequently, there is no basis on which to purify individuals and society from evil or to accomplish the good, thereby contradicting the second and third principles of *tazkiyah* and *ᶜumrān*, respectively.

The argument that humanity can determine what is in its best interests by thinking about *maṣlaḥah* without referring to revelation is absurd. The Qur'an commands us to think about our interests with an intelligence that is pure (*salīm*). But this is only possible if we follow the Shariᶜah. When passionate desires control us and we break the Shariᶜah, our intelligence alone is not sufficient to determine what is in our best interests.

Similarly, the fact that some parts of fiqh are relative cannot be used to argue that all parts are relative. This erroneous argument implies that everything is relative, which itself is self-contradictory. One scholar answers this absurd proposition in the following manner:

> Relativism sets out to reduce every element of absoluteness to relativity, while making a quite illogical exception in favor of this reduction itself. In effect, relativism consists in declaring it to be true that there is no such thing as truth, or in declaring it to be absolutely true that nothing but the relatively true exists; one might just as well say that language does not exist, or write that there is no such thing as writing. In short, every idea is reduced to a relativity of some sort, whether psychological, historical, or social: but the assertion nullifies itself by the fact that it too presents itself as a psychological, historical, or social relativity. The assertion nullifies itself

> if it is true, and by nullifying itself logically proves thereby that it is false; its initial absurdity lies in the implicit claim to be unique in escaping, as if by enchantment, from a relativity that is declared alone to be possible.[19]

Thus, arguments that contradict the absolute because of *maṣlaḥah* or time are fallacious. Unfortunately, secular economics combines both errors in a way that is even more extreme than that of Najm al-Dīn al-Ṭūfī, who argued that *maṣlaḥah* has priority even over the Qur'an and Sunnah. Secular economists and some Muslims have used this type of argument against developing a truly Islamic capital market. Of course, specialists in *uṣūl al-fiqh* recognize the danger of al-Ṭūfī's argument and have developed an extensive literature on the appropriate use of *maṣlaḥah* in legal arguments. The scholars have strongly rejected radical interpretations of *maṣlaḥah*, as the following quote from Zāhid al-Kawtharī's criticism of al-Ṭūfī illustrates:

> One of their spurious methods in attempting to change the *Sharᶜ* in accordance with their desires is to state that "the basic principle of legislation in such matters as relating to transactions among men is the principle of *maṣlaḥah*; if the text opposes this *maṣlaḥah*, the text should be abandoned and *maṣlaḥah* should be followed." What an evil to utter such statements, and to make it a basis for the construction of the new *Sharᶜ*!
>
> This is nothing but an attempt to violate the divine law (*al-Sharᶜ al-Ilāhī*) in order to permit in the name of *maṣlaḥah* what the *Sharᶜ* has forbidden. Ask this libertine (*al-fājir*) what is this *maṣlaḥah* on which you want to construct your law? ... The first person to open this gate of evil ... was Najm al-Ṭūfī al-Ḥanbalī ... No Muslim has ever uttered such a statement ... This is naked heresy. Whoever listens to such talk, he partakes of nothing of knowledge or religion.[20]

Although al-Ṭūfī was clearly unsuccessful in his attempt to abuse the concept of *maṣlaḥah* and create heretical legislation, unfortunately, in the West, his British counterpart Jeremy Bentham, who was reacting to the injustices of the church, was far more successful. Bentham played a key role in developing the secular economics that now oppose the development of a truly Islamic capital market. Bentham defined *maṣlaḥah* in terms of individual desires, regardless of whether they are from the *nafs al-ammārah* or not. Modern economics uses the same approach by defining *maṣlaḥah* as any voluntary choice. According to this theory, more choice is always better because any voluntary exchange supposedly increases the society's *maṣlaḥah* (assuming that it does not create a negative "externality" or negatively affect others). According to this theory, Islamic rules on ethics in the capital market are wrong, because they reduce the people's choices. Modern economics claims to be for the *maṣlaḥah* of society by maximizing these choices in accordance with the Pareto principle that "nobody can be made better off without anybody being made worse off."

From the Islamic point of view, this definition of *maṣlaḥah* is absurd and simply replaces serving God with serving one's passions in terms of utility. The theory makes the relative absolute by subordinating truth to desire, not distinguishing between "the mental states involved in believing something that really is true and a successful deception."[21] This neo-classical definition ignores whether an action or an intention conforms with the truth of the Absolute, thereby allowing an egoistic illusion to be preferable to the bitter truth, and a complete delusion that one has realized the meaning of existence to be the same as actually doing so. Thus it is irrelevant to economics if the perceived *maṣlaḥah* is false in relation to its object or level. In the latter case, "the object can be good, but happiness can be wrong if it cuts it[self] off from its Divine context..."[22]

Such false happiness or *maṣlaḥah* is unacceptable from any spiritual point of view. If the *nafs al-ammārah* is making the choices instead of the *rūḥ*, then fewer choices are better for both the individual and society. As al-Ghazālī said, some people have to be driven to heaven with a whip. Conforming capital markets to Islamic principles by eliminating evil choices and creating good choices is the true definition of *maṣlaḥah*. Unfortunately, many Muslim scholars believe that western economics can guide the Ummah to develop its capital markets. Therefore, it is vital to show how these economic arguments make *maṣlaḥah* absolute instead of God, and how they invert essential Islamic principles.

Indeed, the economic definition of *maṣlaḥah* destroys the Islamic integration of the Ummah's spiritual and other needs by inverting the three key principles. The definition clearly inverts the first Islamic principle (*tawḥīd*) by making *maṣlaḥah* absolute, instead of God. It denies that God is the Sovereign Good "requiring no justification in terms of a higher good," and replaces God with *maṣlaḥah*.[23] According to economics, wealth can be an end in and of itself because *maṣlaḥah* is not subordinate to the truth.

In replacing truth with error, economics similarly inverts the second Islamic principle (*tazkiyah*). By making *maṣlaḥah* absolute, economics denies the need for purity in willing and loving all things for God's sake, and makes its inversion unavoidable. Rather than eliminating evil, acting according to the economic definition accomplishes it. Without truth to regulate *maṣlaḥah* and our desires, we are bound to be passionately attached to wealth, ungrateful, and greedy (*tazkiyah* requires detachment, satisfaction, and generosity), as the Qur'an and Hadith testify.

Similarly, this definition perverts the third principle (*ʿumrān*), substituting accomplishing the good with an exaggerated concept of development that resembles an irrational swelling more than an intelligible civilization. Unlimited greed leads to the exploitation of nature and, inevitably, to an environmental crisis. Moreover, society decays from the pursuit of immoral pleasures associated with this economic definition. This is obviously inconsistent with the third principle of building civilization to accomplish the good, because it implies a wealth motivated by greed rather than spiritual principles.

In fact, this is the very starting point of western economics, beginning with Adam Smith, who examined the wealth of nations, in his book of the same title, from the point of view of material pursuits.[24] As a Deist, he believed that God was detached from the world. Similarly, John Locke believed that God was unknowable and that civilization had to be based on human reason rather than revelation. For him, the purpose of government was to facilitate the unlimited accumulation of money and exploitation of nature for material prosperity. "The negation of nature," he argued, "is the way toward happiness."[25] Such doctrines are a parody of the Islamic concept of *ʿumrān*.

Such contemporary scholars as Muḥammad Saʿīd Ramaḍān al-Būṭī correctly argue that utilitarian philosophy, of which economics is the central application, represents nothing short of an attempt to destroy Islam.[26] To better understand this dangerous character of secular economics, it is helpful to understand more about Jeremy Bentham, the "founding father" of modern utilitarianism.[27] Bentham hated God and religion, and attacked both vehemently. John Colls, a former disciple of Bentham who later turned against him, described Bentham's volumes on religion as "volumes of blasphemy and slander ... against the Author of Christianity and His people."[28] Bentham attacked the Church's teachings, arguing that bans against practices that do not "harm others," such as sexual indulgence and homosexuality, actually decreased utility. For him, questions about the truth of religion were irrelevant and relegated to second-order considerations if divorced from justifications in terms of utility.

His book, *An Introduction to the Principles of Morals and Legislation*, established the utilitarian principles on which the state should replace religious laws so that it could govern society with secular laws based on the science of legislative utilitarianism. After trying to influence others with the book before its publication, Bentham dreamed that he was "a founder of a sect, of course a personage of great sanctity and importance."[29] Bentham dreamed of himself as the savior of England and possibly the world. When asked by "a great man" what he should do "to save the nation," Bentham replied: "Take up my book, and follow me." Bentham implied that his book should replace scripture as the best plan to save the world, for it is a book with "the true flavour of the fruit of the tree of knowledge." The angel who delivered it to him said that Bentham "had no occasion to eat it ... as St. John did his: all I had to do was cram it as well as I could down the throats of other people."[30]

Given this account of Bentham's source of inspiration, one should have no questions about applying secular economics to the development of Islamic capital markets. Unfortunately, many Muslim scholars call for help from secular economists, not understanding the dangerous assumptions behind their economic policy recommendations. Secular economics has no category for motivation by the truth, because utility is absolute. Muslim economists can refute this approach by drawing on the valuable literature in *uṣūl al-fiqh*, which had a parallel refutation of al-Ṭūfī. Scholars in *uṣūl al-fiqh* must also be aware of the dangerous assumptions underlying neo-classical economics. Both groups of scholars can generate truly Islamic alternatives and refute the modernists' arguments that an Islamic economy does not serve society's *maṣlaḥah*.

CONCLUSION

Hence, *taqlīd* of secular economics and institutions is even more dangerous than *taqlīd* of scholars in Islamic law. Contemporary Muslim scholars must acquire an accurate understanding of both ijtihad and Islamic economics on which to base their capital markets policy. Bad economic analysis can misinform the best ijtihad, just as erroneous ijtihad can vitiate the best economic analysis. A correct understanding of both disciplines must be achieved by applying the three essential Islamic principles: *tawḥīd*, the truth that God is the Absolute; *tazkiyah*, the purification of humanity and society from evil; and *ʿumrān*, the building of civilization to accomplish the good.

By recognizing that truth is the believers' motivating cause in purifying themselves from evil and accomplishing the good, authentic ijtihad and Islamic economics can be combined in order to develop a truly Islamic capital market. The same analysis must also refute the erroneous legal and economic arguments of those who favor *taqlīd* of the West with a fatwa. If current ijtihad fails to apply such essential Islamic principles, the Ummah will face a more perilous situation in the future, for nothing useful can be accomplished without the truth.

The most important cause of our current economic problems is the lack of wisdom. Consequently, we do not know how to properly use our God-given resources. The secular economist's argument that scarcity is necessary because everyone must have insatiable desires is a myth propagated by the West. God's justice must be the source of our guidance, for wealth is God's wealth, and humanity is God's creation. We are His vicegerents and must fulfill our duty to Him. God says the truth, and may He guide us.

NOTES

1. For example, that avoiding evil is prior to doing good.
2. Geoffrey Brennan, "The Economist's Approach to Ethics: A Late Twentieth Century View," in Peter Groenewegen, *Economics and Ethics?* (New York: Routlege, 1996), 124.
3. Ibid.
4. Quoted from Tibor Machan, "Reason in Economics versus Ethics," *International Journal of Social Economics* (1996): 21.
5. C. Dyke, *Philosophy of Economics* (Englewood Cliffs, NJ: Prentice-Hall, 1981), 10-11.
6. Frithjof Schuon, *Spiritual Perspectives and Human Facts* (Middlesex: Perennial Books, 1987), 93.
7. For example, humility comes from one's total dependence on God. This awareness prevents people from overestimating themselves and underestimating others.
8. As Seyyed Hossein Nasr notes, Marxism is Christian charity without Christ. See his *The Need for a Sacred Science* (Albany: State University of New York Press, 1993), 152.
9. Frithjof Schuon, *Esoterism as Principle and Way* (Middlesex: Perennial Books, 1981), 94.
10. Ibbotson and Associates, *Stocks, Bonds, Bills, and Inflation: 1997 Yearbook* (Chicago: Ibbotson and Associates, 1997).
11. Muhammad Abdul-Rauf, *A Muslim's Reflections on Democratic Capitalism* (Washington, DC: American Enterprise Institute), 5.
12. Al-Ghazālī, *Iḥyā' ʿUlūm al-Dīn* (New Delhi: Kitab Bhavan, n.d.), 2:54.
13. As the paper's first section clarifies, it is important to point out that an interest-free capital market does not by itself guarantee that the capital market is Islamic, for it is possible to have an un-Islamic capital market that is interest-free.

14. E. F. Schumacher, *Guide for the Perplexed* (New York: Battam, 1997), 58.
15. Frithjof Schuon, *Stations of Wisdom* (Bloomington: World Wisdom Books, 1995), 94.
16. The breakfast cereal industry, represented by such companies as Kellogg's and Post, is a recent example. Only after the American government applied heavy legal pressure did the industry's companies respond by reducing their prices. See F. M. Scherer's *Industrial Organization* for these and other examples.
17. E. F. Schumacher, *Small Is Beautiful: Economics as if People Mattered* (New York: Penguin, 1973).
18. M. Umer Chapra, *Towards a Just Monetary System* (Leicester: The Islamic Foundation, 1985), 95-100.
19. Frithjof Schuon, *Logic and Transcendence* (Middlesex: Perennial Books, 1984), 1.
20. Muhammad K. Masud, *Shatibi's Philosophy of Islamic Law* (India: Kitab Bhavan, 1997), 163.
21. James Griffin, *Well-Being: Its Meaning, Measurement, and Moral Importance* (Oxford: Clarendon Press, 1986), 13.
22. Schuon, *Esoterism*, 102.
23. Schumacher, *Guide for the Perplexed*, 58.
24. Harry Landreth and David Collander, *History of Economic Thought* (Boston: Houghton Mifflin Co., 1994), 67.
25. Jeremy Rifkin with Ted Howard, *The Emerging Order: God in the Age of Scarcity* (New York: G. P. Putnam's Sons, 1979), 30.
26. Masud, *Shatibi's Philosophy*, 132.
27. The following account of Bentham draws from an article by Waleed El-Ansary on "The Spiritual Significance of Jihad in Economics," *American Journal of Islamic Social Sciences* (June 1997): 251.
28. Quoted from James Crimmins, *Secular Utilitarianism: Social Science and the Critique of Religion in the Thought of Jeremy Bentham* (Oxford: Clarendon Press, 1990), 148.
29. Ibid., 287.
30. Ibid., 315.

Part III:

Human Rights

The Testimony of Women in Islamic Law

The only Qur'anic verse to equate two women's testimony to that of one man is Qur'an 2:282, the so-called "verse of debt" (*āyat al-dayn*). This verse contains a significant amount of material that later jurists categorized as recommended or merely instructional (*irshād*) and without legal import. However, a very few jurists opined that recording debts, witnessing, and all other matters dealt with in the verse may be categorized as obligatory (*wājib*).

Whether we agree or disagree with a particular school, there is near unanimity among all jurists that the Qur'an's mention of testimony in relation to transactions was revealed to advise Muslims about how they might reduce the possibility of misunderstandings arising among themselves. Therefore, the entire matter of testimony was revealed to humanity by way of instruction. Obviously, instruction is one thing, while binding legal precepts are another matter entirely.

The verse of debt, moreover, may be seen as connecting testimony, the taking of witnesses, the agreement of both parties to the contract at the time of its ratification, and the judge's (*qāḍī*) acceptance of testimony given by the witnesses, as follows:

> ... and call upon two of your men to act as witnesses; and if two men are not available, then a man and two women from among such as are acceptable to you as witnesses ... (2:282)

The verse goes on to explain the reason for seeking testimony from two women in place of the testimony of one man, by saying "... so that if one of them should make a mistake, the other could remind her" (2:282).

This article first appeared in the *American Journal of Islamic Social Sciences* 13, no. 2 (Summer 1996): 173-96 and was translated by Yusuf DeLorenzo. It has been slightly edited.

Thus, the verse clearly indicates that there are differences in the ability of women to serve, under the prevailing social conditions, as competent witnesses and givers of testimony in cases involving financial transactions. The relevant wording implies that, in general, transactions were not often matters of concern to women at that time. It also indicates that the actual witness would be one woman, even though her testimony might require the support of another woman who would "remind" her if necessary. Thus, one woman acts as a guarantor for the accuracy of the other woman's testimony.

Obviously, then, the two are not on the same level, for one witness is supposed to be knowledgeable and aware of that to which she is testifying. As such, her testimony is legally acceptable. The other witness is considered merely a guarantor, for the basis of all legal testimony is that it should aid the judge in reviewing the case as if he/she had been an actual witness thereof. Moreover, testimony is considered a legal responsibility so as to instill within the witness a heightened sense of his/her awareness of God and the importance of the undertaking, so that he/she will not be careless with the testimony or swayed by emotions or personal feelings. If the verse were understood in this way, probably many of the past and present disputes surrounding it could have been avoided, for the main cause of such disputes has been the belief that the verse has binding and legal significance.

Furthermore, classical scholars appended another matter to the verse's guidelines concerning testimony, one that had absolutely nothing to do with the distribution of responsibilities addressed in the verse: their assumption that the verse pointed to women's natural inferiority, especially in terms of their mental and physical abilities, despite its clear reference to women living at the time of revelation – a time when there were few or no opportunities for women to receive an education, occupy positions of responsibility in society, or undertake work that would increase their experience in ways that would make "being reminded" unnecessary. However, once society passes beyond that stage and women are allowed to participate more fully in its affairs, and in transactions in particular, there should no longer be a need for such arrangements.

The question for consideration is whether or not, on the basis of the verse's circumstantial context (*ʿillah*), the testimony of one woman may be accepted even when the verse states that two women should testify. Before dealing with this question, however, and before examining whether or not it is legitimate or whether it may be answered in the affirmative or the negative, we must reflect on several other issues.

The First Issue. The Qur'an, as discourse, was directed toward a people who, before its revelation, had little or no regard for women and did not allow their inclusion in matters considered the domain of men. In fact, pre-Islamic Arab society sanctioned female infanticide:

And they ascribe daughters unto God, who is limitless in His glory, whereas for themselves [they would choose, if they could, only] what they desire; for, whenever any of them is given the glad tidings of [the birth of] a girl, his face darkens and he is filled with suppressed anger, avoiding all people because of the [alleged] evil of the glad tiding that he has received, [and debating with himself:] shall he keep this [child] despite the contempt [which he feels for it] – or shall he bury it in the dust? Oh, evil indeed is whatever they decide! (16:57-59)

According to the Qur'anic commentator Fakhr al-Dīn al-Rāzī:

During *jāhiliyyah,* men would hide when they knew that their wives were about to give birth. If they were told they had fathered a son, they rejoiced. But if they learned that the newborn was a girl, they were saddened and would stay in seclusion, trying to make up their minds about what they should do with the child: *Shall he keep this [child] despite the contempt [which he feels for it] – or bury it in the dust?* Should he keep the child alive, as an object of perpetual disdain, or simply do away with it?[1]

Nor was this phenomenon very far removed from the period of revelation. In fact, some early Muslims had killed their infant daughters. Qays ibn ᶜĀṣim once said to the Prophet:

"O Prophet of God! In the days of ignorance I buried alive seven daughters." The Prophet replied: "For each one of them, set free one slave." The man said: "But I have only camels." So the Prophet told him: "Then for each one, sacrifice a camel (at the hajj)."[2]

Another man told the Prophet:

"I have never been able to taste the sweetness of faith, even though I have accepted Islam. In the days of ignorance I had a daughter. One day, I told my wife to dress her up. When my wife sent her out to me, I took her to a distant valley in the desert where nothing grew. At that place, I threw my daughter down from my camel, and rode away. When I left her, I heard her calling to me: 'Father! You have killed me!' Now, whenever I think of her and what she said, I find that nothing helps me." The Prophet replied: "Whatever wrongs took place in the days of ignorance are abolished by Islam. And whatever wrongs take place in Islam may be abolished by repentance (*istighfār*)."[3]

The Qur'an transported the people of those times to the realm of faith in absolute gender equality. This single article of faith, perhaps more than any other, represented a revolution no less significant than Islam's condemnation of idolatry and its censure of blind faith passed, without examination, from one generation to another. Theoretically, such equality may seem a relatively simple matter to accept. But when it comes to the practical implementation of any new social model, problems are certain to arise. In the case of early Muslim society, given the long-established customs, attitudes, and mores of pre-Islamic Arabia, it was necessary to implement such changes in stages and to make allowances for society's capacity to adjust itself accordingly. For example, if God had prohibited wine by degrees, as related by ʿĀ'ishah,[4] it follows that He would do the same in the case of an issue of far greater importance and sensitivity in that society, namely, the equality of men and women.

It would appear that the Qur'an sought gradual change via prudent and judicious means, rather than all at once, in which case the possibility of rejection and negative reactions might have been greater. Thus, its initial intent was to instruct Muslims in the ways of a truly civilized society, one in which economic, social, or other changes would be integral to its development. Such change, moreover, is designed to occur in accord with the Qur'anic teachings for introducing reform on the basis of the two readings: that of revelation and that of the natural universe. And this is what the verse of debt brings to us.

In its own subtle manner and with characteristic sagacity, the Qur'an places the reclassification of women as fully participating members of society on its agenda for reform. By establishing a role for woman in the witnessing of transactions, even though at the time of revelation they had little to do with such matters, the Qur'an seeks to give concrete form to the idea of woman as participant: "… and if two men are not available, then a man and two women from among such as are acceptable to you as witnesses" (2:282).

The objective is to end the traditional perception of women by including them, "among such as are acceptable to you as witnesses," and to bring about their acceptance as full partners in society by means of this practical recognition. In this way, the Qur'an seeks to overcome the psychological impediments that prevent men from accepting women as their equals in society. At the time of revelation, the question of numbers was irrelevant, as it was the equality of women that the Qur'an sought to emphasize. Even the matter of witnessing served merely as a means to an end or as a practical way of establishing the concept of gender equality, for what was critically significant was the Qur'an's application of the principle of equality not only on a religious or otherworldly level, but on the levels of human society, interpersonal relations and, most pointedly, commerce. Under the prevailing circumstances, all of this was extremely important.

Thus, it was as if the Qur'an, in its subtle attempt to bring about major change in a society whose customs constituted a major obstacle in the way of that change, sought to address that society in an "acceptable" manner by implying that women were somehow less important as witnesses in such matters. As a result, the testimony of two women would equal that of one man. It was as if the Qur'an had recognized society's view that women, in general, are quicker to forget matters related to affairs with which they had little or nothing to do, especially when these were usually conducted and concluded orally.

Furthermore, the society's oral culture was dominated by two cultures: that of pagan Arabia and its female infanticide and that of the People of the Book (Christian and Jewish inhabitants of Arabian towns) who considered woman the chief reason for humanity's fall from Paradise. Under those circumstances and by means of this approach, the change sought by the Qur'an was not change that would completely overturn the society's customs, but rather a modification or a judicious laying of foundations for accepting its teachings about equality in general. Otherwise, it is more than obvious that the "forgetfulness" taken as a circumstantial context for the legal ruling regarding the acceptance of two women's testimony in place of one man's is a trait shared equally throughout the world. From the beginning of history, each man and woman has been subject to it. In fact, Adam is characterized as having forgotten the covenant of his Lord, a matter of far greater importance.

Both the pagan Arabs and the Arabian People of the Book believed that women were somehow a lesser breed than men. Indeed, the dominant culture on the Arabian peninsula at the time was that of the Christians and the Jews, both of which refused to grant equality to women.[5]

The Second Issue. Christian, Jewish, and Muslim scholars have neglected the wisdom of their respective revelations concerning the equality of the sexes. Qur'anic commentators and jurists in particular seem to have ignored the broader intellectual aspects of a woman's testimony. In addition, some seem to have allowed themselves to completely overlook the basic Qur'anic principle of gender equality, even though this teaching is mentioned in literally hundreds of Qur'anic verses. Instead, they have engrossed themselves in studies emphasizing biological and psychological differences, thereby attempting to derive evidence from divine revelation to support the attitudes and customs of their pre-Islamic heritage.

Such a decidedly un-Islamic bias has prevented Muslim scholars from considering the issue of a woman's testimony in light of the broader Qur'anic teachings of equality. Instead of looking at the issue as a mere division of labor, they considered it as one based on natural incompetence. Taking their cue from Jewish, Christian, and pagan Arab traditions and attitudes, they dwelt on a "woman's natural tendency to be forgetful and fall into error" and her physical "disabilities." Did God not say, they argued, that "if one of them should make a mistake, the other could remind her" (2:282), thereby reading no more than the letter of revelation and without taking into consideration the verse's context or attempting a balanced reading of woman or of nature?

In essence, Muslim jurists and Qur'anic commentators allowed their cultural prejudices to color their discussions on women. In their ignorance, they used those verses declaring the competence and equality of women to "prove" the contrary. Using the same perverted logic, they dealt with the subject of the shares due to women through the laws of inheritance.

The Third Issue. Let us turn now to a discussion of the meaning of "mistake" (*ḍalāl*) in the verse in question. According to the *Arabic Lexicon*,[6] the underlying meaning is "absence." Later, the word was used to indicate any turning from the right way, whether intentionally or otherwise.[7] The word came to be used in the sense of "to forget," for one who forgets is one for whom the right way is absent. The wisdom in the Qur'an's choice of this word, rather than the one usually chosen to mean "to forget" (*nisyān*) or "to err" (*khaṭa'*) is perhaps that the meaning of *ḍalāl* is broader and more comprehensive than the other two, as a mistake in testimony may be either intentional or unintentional.[8]

The Fourth Issue. Since most commentators have explained that the meaning of *ḍalāl* in this verse is probably "to forget," it would be best here if we paused to consider the meaning of the infinitive, "to forget," which is oversight and dereliction. This also may come about either intentionally or unintentionally.

The Fifth Issue. Commentators differ in their interpretations of "reminding" in the verse "if one of them should make a mistake, the other could remind her" (2:282). For example, Ṣufyān ibn ʿUyaynah opined that a woman who gives testimony and who is helped through another woman's reminding becomes legally equal to a man. Other commentators, including al-Ṭabarī, rejected this view on the grounds that the other's "reminding" has the effect of causing the first woman to remember something she had forgotten:[9]

> Clearly, the mistake that might be made by one of the women in the testimony she gives would be her forgetting, like the mistake made by a person in a matter of religion, when they are unsure of something and stray from the truth. So, if one woman should become this way, how is it possible that another's reminding her will make her as if she remembered the testimony she had forgotten and mistaken?

Qur'anic commentators who came after al-Ṭabarī did not go beyond these two positions, namely, that the woman remembered after being reminded (and could then be legally equal to one man, but only with the help of a "reminder") or that the combination of the reminding woman and the forgetful woman is, in legal terms, equal to one man who remembers.

In his *Aḥkām al-Qur'ān*, Ibn al-ʿArabī, first mentioned the opinions summarized above, then asked rhetorically: "What if there is one woman with one man, so that the man can remind her if she forgets?[10] What is the wisdom in that?" Immediately, however, he goes on to nullify the question by stating: "The answer is that Allah legislates what He wills, and He knows better what wisdom lies behind His legislation. It is certainly not essential that His creation should know and understand the wisdom in what He legislates for their betterment and welfare."

In their interpretations of "mistake" and "remind," Qur'anic commentators have approached the issue from a perspective based on the assumption that the division of testimony for women into halves is somehow connected with women's inherent inequality to men. This idea has been shared by classical and modern commentators alike, so that generation after generation of Muslims, guided only by *taqlīd* (imitation), have continued to perpetuate this faulty understanding. Certainly, the attitudes engendered by such a misunderstanding have spread far beyond the legal sphere.

Based on the above, I would like to say that the purpose of this particular article of legislation was to emphasize the Qur'anic principle of gender equality by means of a practical formula. The subject of this principle is, furthermore, by no means limited to witnessing and legal testimony, regardless of whether we consider this a right, a responsibility, or a partnership in the affairs of society. The important thing is that the presence of two women as witnesses to such affairs is held to be essential, even if one is there only to remind the other in the event that she forgets.

Thus, Ibn al-ʿArabī's question is valid: "What if a man is there to remind the female witness?" If the point is to remember the event after it has been forgotten, it should suffice that a man remind a woman if she forgets. The emphasis, however, on the necessity of having two women is so that they may support one another in the testimony and in breaking down the psychological barriers erected by society, regardless of their numbers. All of this is a part of the miraculous nature of the Qur'an, which has paved the way for major social changes in economics, law, relationships, and social structure in a single verse.

The Sixth Issue. But how was this "miracle" perverted into the indictment (or the insinuation) that it became, and one that generations of Muslims have had little success in refuting? There are several reasons for this, among them the following:

- The dominant culture at the time of revelation was, as mentioned earlier, a mix of pagan Arab, Christian, and rabbinical Jewish, all of which had little regard for women, minimized their role, stressed their natural inferiority to men, and refused to grant them equality.
- The prevailing social customs were dictated by an oral legal tradition passed down from generation to generation by the male elders of the tribes. This tradition was perpetuated via the proverbial Arab veneration of their elders and their ancestors.
- The prevailing social structure was predicated on military and commercial success, and both, owing to their physical nature, were the domain of men – military success depended on the force of arms and commercial success depended on caravans traveling across vast expanses of desert.
- Family honor was a key element in that society, and women were perceived as weak links in the chain that preserved that honor. Thus, men felt it was their duty to control women.

These and other factors led Islamic-Arabic thought to dwell upon the physical and mental differences between men and women whenever it encountered texts from the Qur'an or the Sunnah that dealt differently with men and women, especially in matters of witnessing, inheritance, and indemnity for bodily injury. For example, consider al-Rāzī's extraordinarily biased commentary, written in the seventh Islamic century, on Qur'an 2:282[11]:

> The nature of women is dominated by forgetfulness, owing to a predominance of cold and wetness in their physical constitution. The joining of two women in forgetting is less likely than the occurrence of forgetting in just one woman. This is why two women are to take the place of only one man.

He also maintains that the verse in question can be read in different ways, namely, "so that when one makes a mistake," as if making a mistake is a foregone conclusion, and, "willing that when one makes a mistake," as if to say that it is God's will that one of them make a mistake. He justifies this bizarre assertion by saying:

> Here, there are two purposes. The first is to bring about testimony, and that will not take place unless one of the two women reminds the other. The second is to explain that men are better than women, so that it becomes clear why it is just to equate two women to one man. This explanation will be served only if one of the two women actually forgets. Moreover, if both purposes are to be served, and there is no way that will happen unless one of the women forgets and the other reminds her, then, without doubt, that is what is sought.

The reader will note how this greatly respected scholar attempted to put words in the mouth of the Qur'an for the sole purpose of supporting prevalent social ideas, despite the fact that this would destroy a principle that the Qur'an seeks to establish as one of its most important principles – gender equality! But consider how a scholar of al-Rāzī's stature could state with authority that God stipulated that there be two female witnesses just so He could cause one of them to forget and thereby establish the principle of male superiority!

Before discussing the evidence presented in the Sunnah, I should explain that witnessing (*shahādah*) and legal authority (*wilāyah*) are two totally separate matters. However, many jurists ignore this point when discussing why a woman's testimony is equal to only half of a man's. Rather, witnessing should be understood as an attempt to present the judge with an objective acount of an event so that he/she can make a fair judgment. All of the ten or more conditions stipulated by the jurists for witnesses were formulated in such a way that the ruling could not be dictated to the judge. Since Islam considers the ruler as God's deputy (*khalīfah*) and as being responsible for carrying out His will by implementing the Shariʿah (i.e., the ruler has no sovereignty in his/her own right), then how can one say that a witness has legal authority over, or dictates the judgment to, the judge?

To summarize, then, there is no difference between men and women in terms of their abilities and propensity to forget, the possibility of colluding to present false witness, or their ability to speak either the truth or fabrication. Moreover, the Qur'an's objectives do not include anything that would indicate otherwise. Therefore, no evidence suggests that there is anything other than equality between the sexes.

THE EVIDENCE OF THE SUNNAH

I shall examine the evidence of the Sunnah as it pertains to this issue. But before doing so, I would like to emphasize that preeminence in this matter, and in all others, belongs to the Qur'an alone, for only the Qur'an is without blemish, as its text is protected by God.[12] Furthermore, Prophet Muhammad was ordered to recite it to the people, impart its wisdom, and purify them by means of it. After this, the people were commanded to learn it, ponder its meanings, and disseminate its knowledge openly. The Qur'an was revealed "to clarify everything" (16:89), and therefore no other source can share in its qualities and attributes. Thus, it is to be consulted whenever differences occur: "... and on whatever you may differ, the verdict thereon rests with God" (42:10). The Sunnah, on the other hand, clarifies the Qur'an and helps us understand and interpret its meaning. It does not overrule the Qur'an, overstep its bounds, abrogate its texts, contradict it, or violate its principles.[13]

Therefore, the Sunnah does not transgress the bounds set by the Qur'an in regard to the principles of the equality of all human beings and of men and women. Rather, this is a firmly established principle, one of the highest of all Islamic values and a fixed methodological and epistemological truth. Furthermore, many hadiths emphasize this point. For example, Abū Dawūd related a hadith in which the Prophet is reported to have said: "Verily, women are the partners of men."[14] Likewise, al-Bukhārī related a hadith in which ʿUmar ibn al-Khaṭṭāb said: "In the Days of Ignorance, we considered women to be worthless. But when Islam came and God mentioned them, we realized that they had rights over us."[15] Another version of the same hadith states: "By God! In the Days of Ignorance we never used to consider women to be important. But then God revealed what He revealed concerning them, and granted them what He granted them."[16]

If the Qur'an equated, in absolute terms, the humanity of both sexes and said that men and women are equal, no one has the right to say otherwise. In addition, they certainly have no right to say that the Sunnah states otherwise, for the Sunnah is there to clarify the Qur'an, not to contradict or reject its basic principles. Such "rights" cannot be tolerated, especially when the Prophet dealt with the issue in his final message, which was delivered to the Muslims on the occasion of the farewell pilgrimage:

> Verily the Almighty has distanced you from the time of ignorance and its aggrandizement of your male forebears. All people come from Adam, and Adam came from dust.

In his commentary on the Qur'anic verse concerning the creation of each soul from a male and a female, al-Zamakhsharī writes:

> ... that is, from Ādam and Ḥawwā' (Eve). And the Almighty said that He created every one of you from a father and a mother, so that there are none among you who may claim other than that he or she was created like every one else was, in exactly the same way.[17]

There is no basis, then, for claiming that one is somehow less than the other. Such a view only manifests its holder's ignorance of the Sunnah and its true relationship to the Qur'an, for, in effect, it states that the Sunnah contains something that refutes, ignores, or contradicts the Qur'anic principle of absolute gender equality.

Hadith scholars expended a great deal of effort on the Sunnah during the classical period. In fact, had the *'ulamā'* continued to refine these scholars' methodologies, the Muslim world might not have fallen into the intellectual difficulties and pitfalls that robbed it of its vitality and impeded its progress to such an extent that, even today, it continues to suffer from the effects of intellectual stagnation.

The inability to use these methodologies has persisted since the advent of the herd mentality encouraged by *taqlīd* (imitation). Moreover, this same mentality has led the Muslims to neglect the differences between the concepts of service to God and slavery to despots, so that the one was equated to the other with disastrous consequences for Muslim society. While *taqlīd* legitimized the abandonment of performing ijtihad (effort to determine the actual meaning) and renew their faith, both of which resulted in the Muslim world following a handful of imams in matters of fiqh, it also prompted them to accept the opinions of a few selected scholars concerning the degree of authenticity, or lack thereof, of hadiths and what could and could not be accepted from the Sunnah.

The methodologies for dealing with the Sunnah remained the same as those used by their initial developers, and underwent little or no change. Thus, it is as if they were used in the first age of ijtihad and then abandoned. Such an oversight has resulted in the Muslim world's continued acceptance of an understanding of the Sunnah based on the individual efforts of a few classical-era scholars or from the first three Islamic centuries. In terms of women's testimony, any discussion on this subject was abandoned early on in our history and at a time when prevailing social attitudes were antithetical to women. For the last several centuries, whenever the subject came up, reference was made to the thinking of earlier generations and the matter was closed.

Let us consider the differences, in the classical period, between ijtihad on questions of fiqh and ijtihad on questions of certain hadiths' authenticity. Entire schools grew up around the imams of fiqh. For example, Abū Ḥanīfah never ruled on an important question until he had presented it to his dozens of students and discussed it with them at length, often for an entire month.[18] On the other hand, hadith scholars worked as individuals to collect, remember, and transmit narrations. As the majority of hadiths were transmitted by certain individuals to other individuals, the criteria and methods used were highly individualized. For example, in regard to a certain hadiths' authenticity, we read that "this was authenticated in accordance with the conditions (established by) al-Bukhārī" or by some other hadith scholar. These conditions, of course, represent the scholar's own preferences and criteria based on personal experience and taste. All of this points to major differences between the *fuqahā'* and the *muḥaddithūn*.

Within fiqh, an entire body of knowledge (viz., *uṣūl al-fiqh*) gradually to studying the methodological principles and guidelines regulating the actual processes involved in deriving juridical rulings and classifications from the Shariᶜah. Owing to its theoretical nature and importance in the eyes of scholars, *uṣūl al-fiqh* passed through several stages of development and refinement as a discipline in its own right. The "conditions" of the hadith scholars, by comparison, largely remained the result of individual efforts and thus never attained the sophistication of *uṣūl al-fiqh*. Any attempt to discern a comprehensive methodological framework would take a great deal of effort to collect and piece together an assortment of methods and criteria from the works of various hadith scholars. No single set of "conditions" would ever yield anything approaching a comprehensive methodology.

There is a world of difference between the existence of such "conditions" throughout the corpus of classical Hadith literature and their being ordered in such a way as to facilitate a formal process of ranking hadiths in accordance with established methodological criteria.

Over the centuries, many controversies have arisen over the Sunnah and its validity as a source of Shariʿah classifications and rulings, for while its validity is obvious, the methodology for dealing with it has remained difficult.[19] Furthermore, while the integrity of the Qur'anic text is guaranteed by God, the Prophet insisted that the Companions memorize and preserve it. So great was his insistence that he once prohibited them from collecting his sayings (hadiths) and treating them as they treated the Qur'an. Nonetheless, several Companions memorized and transmitted what the Prophet had said and done. In many cases, however, they used their own words to convey what he had said, as they were concerned with the meaning rather than the exact wording. Such changes opened the way to possible further distortion, for other narrators felt free to express the hadith's meaning rather than its exact text. This, in turn, increased the possibility of intentional distortion. Moreover, as the meaning grew further from the one originally intended by the Prophet, whether intentionally or otherwise, the sense of context was also lost and, in many cases, the hadith's true import became impossible to discern.

With the rise of theological disputes and sectarianism, a great deal of spurious Hadith literature was circulated. This caused the great hadith scholars to look for a way to preserve the Sunnah, which involved stipulating methods and procedures for sifting sound narrations from those that were unsound. While their efforts continue to enrich all Muslims, the methods they used were determined by the age in which they lived and the available methodological tools.

In fact, the methods they employed were quite varied, and some even became widespread. Chief among these were the methods developed for classifying and authenticating the chain of transmission (*isnād*). Highly specialized and technical studies were conducted on every person who related even a single hadith, so that his/her strengths and weaknesses as a narrator could be known and used in assigning a rank to the hadith related. Volume upon volume of biography, in the forms of history (*tārīkh*), ranking (*ṭabaqāt*), and biographies (*siyar* and *rijāl*) were written to cover the intellectual life histories of hundreds of thousands of narrators. Even so, as the "conditions" or criteria differed from biographer to biographer, there was a great deal of disagreement over which narrators could be (or could not be) considered trustworthy or accurate, especially in regard to those who came after the first generation.

In addition, these scholars developed methods for criticizing the text and exposing what they considered "fatal" textual faults that would disqualify the hadith in question from serious consideration, even if no fault could be found in its method of narration or chain of narrators. The hadith scholars emphasized that a hadith could not be cited as a proof (legal indicator) until it had satisfied all of the methodological criteria used to authenticate both its chain of transmission and its text. Had this been the case in regard to what the Sunnah had to teach regarding women, their status in the Muslim world today would very likely be quite different.

Muṣṭafā Sibāʿī, who sought to summarize the methodological considerations devised by the hadith scholars for criticizing the texts of hadiths, counted around seventeen.[20] Not every hadith scholar accepted all of these criteria, however, and there were significant differences in how they applied the criteria that they did accept. Some of these criteria may appear to overlap, while some seem more concerned with the chain of transmission than with the actual text. Nevertheless, the important thing is that the hadith scholars recognized the need for such criteria, in addition to the criteria they developed for classifying the chain of transmission.

In recent years, Muṣfir Gharām Allāh has done some important work regarding the criteria used in hadith textual criticism. He has summarized the criteria collected by Sibāʿī into seven,[21] as follows:

1. It should not contradict the Qur'an.
2. Its different versions should be in agreement.
3. The practice (Sunnah) recorded in the hadith should agree with what is known about that particular practice.
4. It should concur with known historical facts and events.
5. It should be free of grammatical and stylistic weaknesses.
6. It should not contradict established Shariʿah principles or Islam's universal truths.
7. It should not contain material that is impossible to imagine as having originated with the Prophet.

Even so, the Muslim mind is still confronted with material from the Hadith literature that clearly contravenes the natural laws formulated for the universe. For example, several Hadith collections include the narration by Asmā' bint ʿUmays, who reported that the Prophet would receive revelation while his head was in ʿAlī's lap. Once, the revelation took so long that ʿAlī was unable to perform the *ʿaṣr* prayer until the sun had set. Then the Prophet said: "O God! He was busy obeying You and Your Prophet! So, please, return the sun." Asmā' said: "I saw the sun go down and then I saw it come back above the horizon after it had set."

It appears that the intention of those who fabricated this hadith was to compete with the Jews. If the Jews could boast of a miracle when the sun remained on the horizon long enough for Joshua and his army to defeat their enemies and bring victory to Banū Isrā'īl, then why should Prophet Muhammad's nephew not have a similar miracle attributed to him? Many hadith scholars, including Aḥmad ibn Ḥanbal, Ibn Kathīr, Ibn Taymiyyah, al-Dhahabī, Ibn al-Jawzī, and Ibn Qayyim, say it is a fabrication. Even so, many others have upheld its authenticity, including such learned and respected imams as al-Bayhaqī, al-Ṭaḥāwī, Ibn Ḥajr, Qāḍī ʿAyāḍ, al-Haythamī, al-Qusṭalānī, al-Suyūṭī, ʿAli al-Qārī, and others.[22]

But how could this have happened? How could the Muslim mind have accepted a single-narrator narration[23] of such an incredible event? How did such a hadith escape their scrutiny or pass their criteria for textual criticism? Why did they not compare it with another hadith that has been authenticated by both al-Bukhārī and Muslim, in addition to many others? This particular hadith related that during the Battle of Aḥzāb, when the fighting was so intense that the Muslims were unable to perform the *ʿaṣr* prayer, the Prophet said: "May God fill their (the idolaters') homes and their graves with fire, for they have prevented us from performing the *ʿaṣr* prayer!" God did not stop the sun's progress or return it to the horizon after it had set so the Prophet and his Companions could pray the *ʿaṣr* prayer, even though they had been engaged in jihad.

Among contemporary hadith scholars, Muḥammad ʿUmrānī Hafashī has completed an excellent study in which he applies the *muḥaddithūn's* methodology to both the hadith's chain of transmission and text as related by al-Bukhārī and Muslim and held by both to be authentic. Hafashī, however, establishes that this hadith is unquestionably a fabrication. The hadith in question, related by Abū Dharr al-Ghifārī:

> One day the Prophet said to his Companions: "Do you know where the sun goes (at night)?" They replied: "God and His Prophet know best." So the Prophet replied: "It continues on its path until it comes to its resting

place beneath the Throne, where it falls into *sajdah* (prostrates itself). It remains in this position until it is told to rise and return from whence it came. It gets up and goes back, so that it rises from its place on the horizon. It then continues on its way until it again reaches the Throne and falls into *sajdah*. Again it stays in that position until it is told to rise and return to its place of rising on the eastern horizon. Again and again it will do this, and no one will notice anything wrong until, one day, when it is in the *sajdah* position, it will be told to rise from the western horizon. Do you know when that will be?" the Prophet asked his Companions. "That will be on a day when faith will avail no one who has not previously had it or earned by means of it some good."

Hafashī writes:

No one today who knows even a little about geography or astronomy will doubt that this hadith is unsound, especially if they consider the two principles for rejecting hadiths: first, that the hadith should not contradict what can be sensed and witnessed, and second, that it should not contradict the laws of nature or the natural order of the universe. The hadith, moreover, is not open to explanation as it clearly speaks of the sun below the Throne, waiting for permission to rise. Thus, the hadith cannot possibly be the words spoken by the Prophet, as he never spoke out of caprice. Rather, since most of the hadith scholars knew nothing of the natural sciences, I shall employ their own methodology for authenticating both the text and the chain of transmission of hadiths to establish that the hadith is spurious.

He then reexamines its chain of transmission as related by al-Bukhārī, Muslim, and other major hadith scholars, as well as the works of those Qur'anic commentators who related it. During his analysis, he found fourteen versions and demonstrated that its chain of transmission, as recorded by al-Bukhārī and Muslim, revealed serious weaknesses when subjected to the methodology and criteria developed by the hadith scholars themselves. He went on to show that the same was true of each version. Applying this criteria to the criticism of the text itself, he pronounced the hadith a fabrication. Hopefully, the International Institute of Islamic Thought will be able to publish this study in its series of methodological studies on the Sunnah.

All of this emphasizes the need for a close examination of the hadiths related in the "authentic" collections before all others. This exercise must be carried out by qualified experts in accordance with the methodology and criteria developed by the *muḥaddithūn* so that the Sunnah may be cleansed of everything that contradicts or opposes the Qur'an's authority, the laws of nature, reason and logic, or historical fact. In addition, linguistic, sociological, and psychological studies of the Hadith literature are needed in order to consider the impact of sectarianism and/or theological and ideological orientations. Only if this is done will the subject of gender equality receive its due from the Hadith literature.

The neglect of criteria for textual criticism of the Hadith, as well as the lack of sufficient interest in this subject, have led to many of the Sunnah-related problems facing Muslims. A prime example is that of gender equality, or the place of men and women in terms of their common humanity, their intellectual and psychological constitution, and controversies as to their roles in society. Nearly all of the legislation that arose in regard to inheritance, witnessing, marriage, divorce, and indemnity (for bodily injury) is based on differences perceived in men's and women's religious and social roles and functions. Obviously, there will be significant differences in the opinions and positions of those who adhere to a worldview based on an intellectual paradigm formulated by the Qur'an (with its concepts of divinity, worship, covenance, trial, vicegerency, creation, unicity, the oneness of humanity, the oneness of the universe that was created as the abode of humanity and as a mist, and the oneness of the ultimate destination) and the positions taken by those whose worldview may best be represented by the following verse: And yet they say: "There is nothing beyond our life in this world. We die as we come to life, and nothing but time destroys us" (45:24).

One of the greatest calamities to befall Muslim society, and one that led to a truly dangerous rift, was when the religious legacy of the Jews and Christians, with all of its twisted notions concerning women, was taken as a source for interpreting the Qur'an and the Sunnah. An even greater catastrophe occurred when certain hadith narrators began adding words and expressions carrying Jewish and Christian concepts to their narrations and then presenting these as having come from the Prophet. In fact, many hadiths were misunderstood or given interpretations based on that time's dominant cultural influences, even if they were untenable or incompatible with the originally intended spirit and meaning. All of these factors, in turn, influenced the legislation or judicial opinions governing the institution of the family, which is the cornerstone of all existence, creation, and humanity, and of the totality of each person's role as a *khalīfah*.

The first home of the Prophet's message, the cultural environment of Makkah with its pagan practices and attitudes, represented a major obstacle to social change and a real challenge to establishing a sound family system. In addition to female infanticide, other practices were even more insidious in terms of the family structure, such as sons inheriting the wives of their fathers and other customs that debased and degraded women. As a result, the pagan Arab concept of family was confused and ambiguous at best.[24]

All of these factors constitute a backdrop against which certain hadiths need to be read in order to acquire an accurate understanding. The Prophet was a wise and practical man when it came to education and upbringing. Thus, when Islam began to restructure the family by teaching the principle of gender equality, the Prophet was forced into the role of a mediator between the forces of the newly liberated and those of traditional reaction. In this capacity, he was regularly called upon to educate, advise, and caution his followers about many of the details occasioned by the ensuing social revolution. In some instances, he needed to correct people. Such corrections, taken out of context, have led to the misinterpretation of certain hadith texts that became "key" to the classical understanding of issues concerning women.

One such hadith was related by both al-Bukhārī and Muslim on the authority of ʿAbd Allāh ibn ʿUmar, who reported that the Prophet, after performing a special prayer (*ṣalāt al-khusūf*) during a solar eclipse, said:

> "The sun and the moon are among God's many signs and do not go into eclipse for the death or the life of any person. When you see an eclipse, remember God." On that occasion, the Companions said: "O Prophet of God. As you were standing there, it appeared to us that you were taking something, and then we saw you flinch." He replied: "Verily, I had a vision of Paradise, and I reached for a bunch of grapes ... Had I been able to grasp them, you would have eaten from them for as long as the world remains. Then I had a vision of the Fire. To this day, I have never seen a more horrible sight. And I noticed that most of its residents were women." The Companions asked: "Why, O Prophet?" He replied: "For their ingratitude." They asked: "For their ingratitude to God?" The Prophet replied: "No, for their ingratitude to their husbands. If you do something good for one of them, and then you displease her with the slightest thing, she'll be the first to tell you that you've never done anything good for her."

On this occasion, it seems clear that the Prophet took the opportunity to direct a few words of advice to the female Muslims. His words were certainly not intended to drive them to despair or lead them to think less of themselves. On the contrary, the intent was to caution and advise. In fact, the Hadith literature is filled with thousands of examples of such admonitory narrations, sometimes directed toward individuals and sometimes stated generally. In regard to this particular hadith, Ḥāfiẓ ibn Hajr wrote that another version indicated that the women seen in the Fire were those who exhibited serious character flaws, for the other version included: "I noticed that most of its residents were women who, if entrusted with something would betray that trust, or if asked for charity would refuse to give it, or if given something would not appreciate it."

Clearly, this particular hadith is an example of admonition and instruction that exhorts all Muslims to strive for Paradise and avoid Hell. It then went on to explain to the women how one aspect of their behavior might need their attention. On other occasions, the Prophet addressed various shortcomings among men, merchants, soldiers, husbands, and fathers.

Abū Sa^cīd related another hadith, included in the collections of al-Bukhārī and Muslim, in which he reported that the Prophet went out on the Day of ^cĪd to the place of prayer and passed by a group of women. He said:

> "O you assembly of women. Never have I seen so intellectually or religiously deficient a person, or one more capable of driving away the good judgment of a man, than one of you." The women asked: "And how are we intellectually and religiously deficient?" The Prophet replied: "Is the testimony of one woman not equal to the testimony of half a man?" They replied: "Quite right, it is." The Prophet said: "Then, there is your deficiency of intellect. And is it true that you do not pray or fast when you have your period?" The women answered: "Quite right, it is true." So the Prophet replied: "There is your deficiency of religion."

Such hadiths have contributed to basic misunderstandings in regard to gender equality. Moreover, these misunderstandings have resulted in serious legal and intellectual consequences, even to the extent of confining and overshadowing the Qur'anic principle of equality. In addition, the ensuing misconceptions have served as the basis on which the practical Islamic position on women's issues was formulated. Thus, the Qur'anic teachings about equality and the general principles derived from those teachings were ignored, and very nearly buried, save for the conclusions derived from the verse "then a man and two women." The matter was further complicated when the classical jurists considered the relevant Hadith literature as having significant legal import, for it is clear that a legal ruling has real consequences not only for the law, but for history, society, and culture as well.

The positions of the classical legal schools were summarized by Ibn Rushd, as follows:

> The entire legal community agrees that the testimony of women will not be accepted in *ḥudūd* cases. The Ẓāhirī jurists, however, opined that the testimony of more than one woman can be accepted if it is corroborated

by (testimony from) one man, because this is what the verse literally says. Abū Ḥanīfah said that their testimony may be accepted in financial matters and in non-*ḥudūd* matters having to do with the person, such as divorce, marriage, manumission, and the like. Imām Mālik, however, held that their testimony may not be accepted in matters related to the person. The testimony of women on their own, in which only women (and not men) give testimony, is accepted by the entire legal community in matters related to the person on the condition that the matter is of the nature that only women would have knowledge of it. Such matters include childbirth, monthly courses, hidden physical defects, and the like. There is no disagreement on this matter, save in regard to suckling and establishing foster relationships.[25]

Ibn Ḥazm wrote:

It is not lawful to accept, in cases of adultery, the testimony of fewer than four men who are both Muslim and deemed trustworthy (*ʿudūl*) by the court. Two trustworthy Muslim women may, however, take the place of each man. In all cases involving rights, like *ḥudūd*, blood, *qiṣāṣ*, marriage, divorce, return to marriage (*rajʿah*), and financial affairs, only the testimony of two men, or one man and two women, or four women may be accepted. In all such cases, except for those of *ḥudūd*, if the one seeking rights gives an oath, then the testimony of only one trustworthy male witness will suffice, or one male and two female witnesses, or four female witnesses. Likewise, in all such cases, except for those of *ḥudūd*, the testimony of one man or two women will be accepted if it is accompanied by an oath taken by the plaintiff. In matters of suckling only, the testimony of one trustworthy woman or man will be accepted.

Ibn Taymiyyah wrote:

The verse – "and if two men are not available, then a man and two women from among such as are acceptable to you as witnesses, so that if one of them should make a mistake, the other could remind her" – indicates that the reason for equating the testimony of two women with that of one man is so that one woman may remind the other if she makes a mistake. Generally speaking, the sort of mistake that will take place is forgetfulness and the inability to remember. This is what the Prophet alluded to when he said: "... as to the deficiency in their intellect, it is (attested to by the fact that) the testimony of two women is equal to that of one man." Thus, he clarified that the reason for halving their testimony is attributable to a deficiency in their intellect and not in their religion. From here, we learn that the trustworthiness of women as witnesses is the same as the trustworthiness of men, but that their intellect is inferior. Thus, in regard to testimony on matters in which it is not feared that they will make mistakes, their testimony is not equal to half the testimony of men. As for matters on which the sole testimony of women is accepted, these are matters that women have an opportunity to witness by themselves, or hear, or otherwise sense, so that their intellects play no part in the testimony. These are matters like childbirth, monthly courses, hidden physical defects, suckling, and the like. Usually, such matters are neither easily forgotten nor require great intellect to comprehend, as opposed to words spoken in acknowledgment of a debt and the like, all of which are complex and generally require a great deal of experience before they can be understood. Having established this point, we may say that the testimony of a man and two women is accepted in every case in which the testimony of a man and the oath of the plaintiff are accepted. Both ᶜAṭā' and Ḥammād ibn Sulaymān held the opinion that the testimony of one man and two women will be accepted in cases of *ḥudūd* and *qiṣāṣ*. And, according to one narration, they accepted such testimony in cases of marriage and manumission as well. The same was related about Jābir ibn Zayd, Iyās ibn Muᶜāwiyyah, al-Shaᶜbī, al-Thawrī, and others from the rationalist schools of jurisprudence. The same holds true, according to another narration, in regard to cases involving damages and reparations.

The passages quoted above should suffice as examples of how the classical scholars of Islam understood the Qur'anic verses we are considering and the Hadith literature on the subject. Clearly, the legal rulings derived from these texts came not only from statements made in the imperative or prohibitive mode, but from every aspect of the reported texts.

It also appears that the word for "make a mistake" in the verse was interpreted as a deficiency when considered in conjunction with the relevant Hadith literature. The reader will recall that the meaning of the word was interpreted variously by Qur'anic commentators and lexicographers as either "to forget" or "to overlook." Also, the hadiths related by ᶜAbd Allāh ibn ᶜUmar was interpreted in various ways. For example, Imām Muslim related it in a chapter entitled "An Explanation of Deficiency in Faith by Means of Deficiency in Devotion, and an Explanation of How the Word 'Kufr' Does Not Always Mean Disbelief in God But Is Sometimes Used To Denote Ingratitude."

Sharaf al-Dīn al-Nawawī, when explaining Abū Saᶜīd's hadith concerning a woman's "intellectual deficiency," stated that the meaning of the Prophet's statement, "there is your deficiency of intellect," should be understood as meaning "there is a sign of your deficiency."[26]

In any case, when we examine the classical commentaries on these hadiths, we find that none of them applied the criteria that they or their predecessors established for textual criticism. The *muḥaddithūn* themselves stated that the authenticity of a hadith's chain of transmission alone does not guarantee the text's authenticity. So, in what follows, I will apply some of these criteria to authenticate the hadiths' texts. For the purposes of this paper, I shall deal only with the texts and the classical criteria for their criticism.[27]

The difficulty in the hadith alleging women's "intellectual and religious inferiority" is that it ascribes to the Prophet a statement that indicates the religious inferiority of people who do no more than what God has commanded them to do, both in the Book of Nature and in the Qur'an. Therefore, the assertion that women are deficient in their religion because they cannot pray or fast during their menstrual periods is clearly suspect. Several hadith commentators have attempted to explain this in one way or another, but the fact remains that God ordered women not to fast or pray during such times. Thus, when they follow these instructions they are rewarded for obeying His commands, and He "does not lose sight of the labor of any who labors, be it man or woman" (3:195).

In comparison, the Shariʿah considers the shortening of prayer while on a journey to be the original state of affairs. In one hadith, ʿĀ'ishah related: "When prayer was first prescribed as a duty for Muslims, the number of *rakʿahs* was two. Later on this was increased to four for those not traveling, while the number for those on journeys remained the same."[28] So the shortening of prayer for a traveler has nothing to do with deficiencies on the part of anyone.

In addition, it is extremely difficult to reconcile the matter of "intellectual deficiency" with the Qur'anic principle of equality between the sexes. Had it been a matter of deficiency in testimony, there might not have been a problem. But when the hadith mentions "intellectual deficiency" in clear contradiction to the evidence of both nature and the Qur'an's unequivocal texts in regard to equality, a problem arises. Furthermore, the difficulty does not become any less important just because it has come to light only in modern times. The message of Islam is, after all, universal and applicable to every time and place. These truths are beyond dispute.

Western intellectual trends, including the scientific method, are now widespread and have led to the development of important critical and analytical skills and tools. Modern thinkers are very reluctant to consider anything that cannot be subjected to their various critical methodologies. This has led to reservations and doubts about nearly everything related to religion and religious experience. In order to counter these doubts, we must develop methodologies based on Qur'anic paradigms and strive to develop our methodologies for critiquing hadiths, rather than leave our intellectual legacy to the depredations of others. What the Muslim world expects of its hadith scholars, hadith colleges, and university departments of hadith studies is not a mere rehash of what was produced in the past, but a renewal, in the sense of further development based on the foundations laid in the past, so that these can be strengthened by modern methods of criticism. If we want to serve the Sunnah, this is the direction we must take.

We know that the early imams of hadith rejected some hadiths with sound chains of transmission because their texts were unsound, and that they rejected hadiths with sound texts because their chains of transmission were unsound. In addition, they allowed their rulings on those hadiths' authenticity to be swayed by the fact that they had been included in al-Bukhārī's and Muslim's collections. Al-Bukhārī, for example, selected the 2,602 hadiths in his collection from over 600,000 hadiths. Nor does it detract from his efforts to include only the most authentic hadiths if later scholars discover that some were not actually authentic or that some did not meet the criteria he had established for their authenticity.

If the ijtihad performed by the four major imams of fiqh was disputed by others, why should it be difficult to imagine that there might be criticism of the ijtihad performed by al-Bukhārī and Muslim in ascertaining which hadiths were authentic and which were not? In fact, their work was corrected by many great hadith scholars, among them Abū Masᶜūd al-Dimashqī, Abū ᶜAlī al-Jiyānī al-Ghassānī, and Abū al-Ḥasan al-Darquṭunī, who found 200 hadiths in al-Bukhārī's and Muslim's collections that did not measure up to the criteria for authenticity set by these two collectors. Likewise, the two great *rijāl* biographers Abū Zurᶜah al-Rāzī and Abū Ḥātim listed the mistakes made by al-Bukhārī in his biographical works. Abū Ḥātim even wrote a book on the subject: *Bayān Khaṭā' Muḥammad ibn Ismāᶜīl al-Bukhārī fī Tārīkhihi*. Al-Khātib al-Baghdādi did the same in his *Muwaḍḍiḥ Awhām al-Jamᶜ wa al-Tafrīq.*[29]

Thus, the real problem is one of methodology. There is a very real need today for developing a methodology for dealing with the Sunnah and then applying it carefully so that balance may be maintained in regard to the Hadith literature. Only in this way can we protect the Sunnah from baseless attacks and incorrect applications (through assumptions or deductions drawn from less-than-authentic hadiths). In order to address this problem in a suitable and effective manner, the gulf between the classical scholars' criteria and today's methodologies must be bridged by building upon the classical era's foundations and developing these in light of the Qur'anic epistemology. Once these issues have been clarified, it will be possible to review much of Islam's legal legacy in regard to women and issues of gender equality.

It is not my intention to cast doubt upon the works of al-Bukhārī and Muslim. Rather, I am concerned with serious scholarship and devoted academic attention to using modern methods to criticize and analyze hadiths. Finally, our current problems with the Hadith literature are not the result of anything done by the classical *muḥaddithūn*, but rather with the failure of our scholars to follow up their predecessors' work and develop it further. If today's scholars would apply as much energy to studying and critiquing hadith texts as the classical scholars applied to studying and critiquing hadith chains of transmission, we would be able to join our reading of the Qur'an with our reading of the Sunnah, and our reading of the Qur'an with our reading of the "book" of the real-existential.

These are some of my reflections on the subject of women's testimony. I hope that they may inspire others to ponder that subject and those related to it in greater detail and from the perspectives of their respective disciplines. Clearly, owing to shortcomings in our intellectual history, our attitudes toward women and their roles in society have been less than the Qur'anic ideal. If we are to make progress in this particular matter, or in any other of the imbalances that exist in our societies, we have to reconsider the teachings of the Qur'an and the Sunnah and how we deal with them.

NOTES

1. Fakhr al-Dīn al-Rāzī, *Al-Tafsīr al-Kabīr* (Cairo: Maṭbaᶜah al-Bahiyyah, n.d.), 12:54-56. Italics added for emphasis.
2. Ibn Kathīr, *Tafsīr al-Qur'ān al-ᶜAẓīm* (Cairo: at Maktabah al-Ṣalafiyyah, n.d.), 4:478; al-Rāzī, *Al-Tafsīr al-Kabīr.*
3. Al-Rāzī, *Al-Tafsīr al-Kabīr.*
4. Al-Bukhārī, "Kitāb Faḍā'il al-Qur'ān" (Virtues of the Qur'an), in *Al-Jāmiᶜ al-Ṣaḥīḥ*, hadith no. 4707.
5. Numerous passages can be cited from the Bible, such as the following: "I will put enmity between you and the woman, between her seed and your seed" (Genesis 3:15) and "Let the woman learn in silence with all subjection" (Timothy 2:11-12). The Qur'an exposes something of these attitudes in its story of how Mary's mother vowed that the fruit of her womb would serve God and how she was startled to learn that she had given birth to a girl. See Qur'an 3:35-37. [Trans.]
6. Aḥmad ibn Muḥammad al-Fayyūmī, *Al-Miṣbāḥ al-Munīr*, 3d ed. (Egypt: al-Maṭbaᶜah al-Āmiriyyah, 1912), 496.

7. Al-Ḥusayn ibn Muḥammad al-Rāghib al-Aṣfahānī, *Mufradāt fī Gharīb al-Qur'ān*, 297.
8. For a detailed discussion of the uses of the word, compare Abū Zakarīyā al-Farrā', *Maᶜānī al-Qur'ān* (Cairo: Dār al-Kutub al-Miṣriyyah, 1955), 1:184 and 2:181. See also Muḥammad ibn Jarīr al-Ṭabarī, *Jamiᶜ al-Bayān fī Tafsīr al-Qur'ān*, 2:62-67 and 16:132-33; and Abū Bakr al-Jaṣṣāṣ al-Rāzī, *Aḥkām al-Qur'ān*, 1:507-14; and Ibn al-ᶜArabī, *Aḥkām al-Qur'ān*, 1:252-56.
9. In other words, these jurists refused to equate a woman's testimony with that of a man because neither she nor her partner could deliver reliable testimony; not her's, because she might forget, and not the other's, because her role is merely to remind and not to give testimony. [Trans.]
10. In other words, under those circumstances, is the woman's testimony to be considered equal on its own as a result of the man's reminding her or equal in combination with the man's reminding? See Abū Bakr ibn al-ᶜArabī, *Aḥkām al-Qur'ān* (Cairo: Dār Iḥyā' al-Maktabah al-ᶜArabiyyah, 1958), 1:252-56.
11. Al-Rāzī, *Al-Tafsīr al-Kabīr*, 2:366-67.
12. Qur'an 42:41.
13. Muḥammad ibn Idrīs al-Shāfiᶜī, *Kitāb al-Umm* (Cairo: Maktabat al-Kulliyyah al-Azhariyyah, 1961), 7:264-65.
14. Nāsir at Dīn al-Albānī, *Ṣaḥīḥ al-Jāmiᶜ al-Saghīr* (Beirut: al-Maktab al-Islāmī, 1969), hadith no. 2329.
15. Muḥammad ibn Ismāᶜīl at Bukhārī, *Al-Jāmiᶜ al-Ṣaḥīḥ*, "Kitāb al-Libās."
16. This version was related by both al-Bukhārī and Muslim.
17. Abū al-Qāsim Jār Allāh al-Zamakhsharī, *Al-Kashshāf ᶜan Ḥaqā'iq al-Tanzīl* (Būlāq, Egypt: al-Maṭbaᶜah al-Āmiriyyah, 1318 AH), 3:569.
18. See the introduction written by Zāhid al-Kawtharī on Zaylaᶜī, *Nasb al-Rayah* (India: al-Majlis al-ᶜIlmī, 1936), 1:37-38.
19. The number of Qur'anic verses attesting to the Sunnah's validity is such that there is hardly a chapter in which this fact is not mentioned. Significant among these, however, are the following: Qur'an 4:105, 59:7, 4:59, 4:80, 16:64.
20. Muṣṭafā Sibāᶜī, *Al-Sunnah wa Makānatuhā fī al-Tashrīᶜ al-Islāmī* (Damascus: al-Maktab al-Islāmī, 1979), 271.
21. Muṣfir Gharām Allāh al-Damīnī, *Fī Maqāyis Naqd Mutūn al-Sunnah* (Riyadh: Imām Muḥammad ibn Saᶜūd University Press, n.d.), 127-29.
22. Ibn Qayyim, *Al-Manār al-Munīf fī al-Ḥadīth al-Ḍaᶜīf* (Aleppo: Maktabat al-Maṭbūᶜat al-Islāmiyyah, 1970), 58.
23. The term *single-narrator narration* (*khabr al-wāḥid*) refers to a hadith transmitted, at some point, by only one narrator. The authenticity of such transmissions was disputed among the hadith scholars and the *fuqahā'*, many of whom held that such narrations were acceptable only as corroborative evidence. [Trans.]
24. Al-Bukhārī relates a lengthy hadith from ᶜĀ'ishah, in which she narrates the variety of forms taken by pagan marriages. See hadith no. 4835.
25. Ibn Rushd, *Bidāyāt al-Mujtahid* (Cairo: n.d.), 2:174.

26. Sharaf al-Dīn al-Nawawī, *Sharḥ Ṣaḥīḥ Muslim* (Beirut: Dār al-Fikr, 1990), 5:226.
27. ʿAbd al-Ḥalīm Abū Shuqqah, *Taḥrīr al-Mar'ah fī ʿAṣr al-Risālah* (Kuwait: Dār al-Qalam, 1990), 1:271-91.
28. lbn Abū Shaybah, *Al-Muṣannaf* (Beirut: Dār al-Fikr, n.d.) 14:132.
29. See the introduction by Ibn Ḥajr al-ʿAsqalānī to his commentary, *Fatḥ al-Bārī* (Beirut: Dār al-Fikr, n.d.), 346, 375-76, 465.

Naturalization and the Rights of Citizens

Naturalization, an integral part of the concept of identity and its related problems, has been an issue in the Muslim world since its first contacts with western thought, culture, military, and politics. Even though the matter was decided, in practical terms, by the emergence of ethnic and geographic nation-states out of the wreckage of the Ottoman Empire, it remains an open topic at the cultural and academic levels. Whether it is addressed as a challenge, an excuse, or as a means to an end, it remains a major and very sensitive question. As new ethnic and regional Muslim nation-states begin to show signs of instability, the subject grows more complex: It takes on new aspects of identity and affiliation and seeks to discover the best way of ordering relations between the peoples of each region or between them and the (factional, military, or otherwise) elitist governments controlling them.

With the stirrings of a new Islamic movement and its members' belief that Islam represents a viable political alternative, the question of naturalization has become a major challenge. In fact, it is often thrown in their faces by their secularist opponents. Thus, the question has become instrumental in the current political struggle taking place in the Muslim world. Many Muslim governments cite indigenous non-Muslim minorities as an excuse to deprive their Muslim majorities, who often represent 98 percent of the total population, of the right to be ruled by the Shari^cah. These are the same governments that discredit Islamic movements by viewing their very presence, principles, demands, and objectives as threats to national unity. To counteract such "threats," they promulgate "emergency measures" and suspend constitutional legal codes.

This "reflections" article first appeared in the *American Journal of Islamic Social Sciences* 11, no. 1 (Spring 1994): 71-78, and was translated by Yusuf Talal DeLorenzo. It has been slightly edited.

Naturalization is the basis of nationalism, which gives identity to the modern state and may be defined as an affiliation with a geographically defined region. All people who trace their lineage to that region are subject to all accompanying rights and responsibilities. Thus, the bond between them is secular and worldly. The same is true of bonds between states, for they are entirely secular and measured in terms of profit and loss. It is considered essential that all citizens, regardless of their religious, ethnic, or sectarian background, melt into this regional and profitable affiliation by casting off those parts of their background that might lead them into conflict with the state. In this sense, then, naturalization must occur in an atmosphere in which secular concepts, order, and methodology reign supreme. This is why secularists in the Muslim world saw the presence of non-Muslim minorities as a powerful argument that could be used to quell the demands of the Islamic political agenda. As a result, they opposed the Islamists and called for a "civil society," or what they suppose to be the opposite of a "religious society."

Several Islamist leaders have emphasized that the Islamic agenda can create the desired civil society, but within an Islamic framework. They have also asserted their readiness to accommodate many of the foundations of western society, as it is considered the best example of civil society. Even so, many secularists remain unconvinced. For their part, Islamist leaders have given a great deal of thought to the secularists' objections to the Islamic agenda. Many Islamists have written on democracy, proclaimed their acceptance of it, and found precedents for it in authentic Islamic sources. They have even announced their acceptance of political pluralism, as one of the foundations upon which democracy is built, and of civil liberties, though some have done so with certain reservations. In his *The Rights of Citizens*, Rāshid al-Ghannūshī states clearly that Islam can accept naturalization, as it is popularly understood, and then cites and explains the reasons for his claim and gives precedents for it. However, some secularist groups continue to reject and fear the Islamic political agenda. It seems that they prefer to live in the shadow of dictatorship and repression rather than accept the Islamic political agenda, regardless of how it may be altered.

We now come to a point of fundamental importance: understanding that the logic of Islamic thought (i.e., the basis of the Islamic agenda for civilization) is based on the constants, and not the variables, of Islam. In other words, the Islamic agenda for civilization looks at these variables within the framework of those constants. In addition, borrowing concepts from a civilization with pagan roots and a significantly different system of principles is not the same as borrowing a few simple words or translating mechanical, agricultural, industrial, and other terminologies. Certainly, underlying ideas must not be overlooked in terms of their effect on thought and culture. Still, there is less danger in borrowing terms from such fields than there is in borrowing such terms based on underlying ideas and values that may have an effect on practical life, such as "nationalism" and "democracy."

In what follows, I will give some examples of the dangers inherent in borrowing key concepts from entirely different civilizations. There is clearly a need to establish suitable regulations and standards for this type of borrowing so that the division between a society's variables and constants remains intact.

First, the word *citizen* did not appear until after the French Revolution of 1789. Before that time, people were grouped in terms of religion, language, ethnicity, or tribal background. Nowhere did people affiliate themselves with the land on which they lived. Second, secularism sought to minimize or overcome all differences between people, as differences cause problems for secularism and detract from its ability to establish comprehensive organizations based on expediency, pleasure, and worldly benefits, all of which it venerates in place of religious and moral values.

Third, the relevant texts of the Qur'an and the Sunnah, as well as the actual implementation of these concepts (i.e., the Covenant of Madinah and the resulting decisions of the first four caliphs and the Companions), indicate that Islam is especially concerned with helping those who have not yet converted to preserve their religious, cultural, and ethnic characteristics.

All Muslims are guaranteed five basic necessities. Upon entering into a *dhimmah* (covenant of protection) contract, all non-Muslims are guaranteed the same rights as Muslims, as well as official recognition, defense, and protection of their communal or racial traits. If these are threatened, Muslim soldiers are duty-bound to defend them. Thus, non-Muslims enjoy the freedom of thought and comparison so that they may decide for themselves whether to adhere to their old ways or to convert. In fact, Islam views non-Muslims from the perspective of a universal message that rejects compulsion: "Let there be no compulsion in religion" (Qur'an 2:256).

Islamic law protects non-Muslims in two ways: It offers them the same protection and rights given to Muslims, and it protects their cultural and ethnic characteristics by guaranteeing the armed protection enjoyed by Muslims. It would seem, then, that non-Muslims enjoy a privilege not enjoyed by Muslims. How is it that a privilege may be viewed as a sign of contempt on the part of those who granted it? Islam grants respect and privilege to *dhimmī* (i.e., protected non-Muslim people) subjects because it is a universal religion that views each individual in exactly the same way: a descendant of Adam, who came from dust, with some special characteristics that distinguish him/her from all others. This is why Islam attaches such importance to all relationships, particularly those binding followers of the Abrahamic religions – Judaism, Christianity, and Islam – to each other and to the rest of humanity. Ultimately, this diversity is to be used as a means of mutual recognition and acquaintance among the children of Adam.

Fourth, the scholars of Islam, particularly Muslim social scientists, should engage in ijtihad and thereby participate in building an ideal Islamic society. In matters of legal significance and creativity, the Islamic movement needs ijtihad in order to address issues of social significance and to lay the foundations for an Islamic civilization. Its practitioners must be careful not to embrace unfounded ideas or draw analogies between Islam and other religions, for ijtihad is a human undertaking and therefore subject to error. It is also essential to understand that earlier rulings cannot be nullified – new rulings are no more than additions to existing *fiqhī* knowledge.

Fifth, among the most consistently misunderstood and misinterpreted rulings are those related to *dhimmīs*[1] and the division of the world into two warring camps: *dār al-ḥarb* and *dār al-Islām*. Many classical legal scholars misinterpreted the verses related to the *dhimmīs*, especially the following one: "Fight against such of them as have been given the scripture until they pay the tribute [*jizyah*] readily, having been brought low" (9:29). They overlooked the simplest meaning: Once vanquished, the new subjects would abide by Islamic rule and pay the *jizyah*. Instead, classical jurists interpreted the phrase "having been brought low" to mean that the vanquished should be humiliated as they pay the *jizyah*. Undoubtedly, this outlook created many doubts and questions as to how a Muslim majority today would treat a non-Muslim minority.

These rulings have generated a great deal of criticism from modern secularists. If their original sources were considered anew and in light of the progress made in the social sciences, however, they might well provide solutions to long-standing problems and offer the basis for a harmonious blend of divergent elements, and then be transformed into sources of strength instead of tension (i.e., racial tension in the United States). Indeed, owing to gaps in American social thought, ethnic, religious, and racial conflict can never be entirely dismissed.[2]

The peace and outward sense of tranquility found in the United States, for example, and the relative ease in relations between the different ethnic, religious, and racial groups, are only apparent. Such harmony seems to be based on the principle that an individual's freedom ends where the group's freedom begins and on the open acceptance of each person's individuality and special characteristics as part of their human rights. This concept of freedom, however, is erroneous. Likewise, this ideal of human rights leaves much to be desired. The balance found in American society and in those that have followed its example may best be described as a balance of tigers,[3] for western thought and philosophy, based on the rejection and attempted destruction of the "other," are inherently dualistic, argumentative, and contentious. Balance, if ever it occurs, is only a temporary stalemate among opposing forces or interests of equal power. For example, Europeans overcame the weaker Native Americans and then decimated them and took their lands. Thereafter, Europeans discriminated against people of color, women, and all other minorities. So whenever they speak of balance, they do so in terms of temporary solutions imposed upon them by the force of transient interests. The corollary to this is that such solutions are always subject to deterioration and breakdown.

Given this, if the breakup of the Soviet Union is explained by the inability of Marxism, which is based on class struggle, to overcome the individual's natural inclination for self-expression, the other western model carries many of the same seeds. The idea of freedom alone may be transformed into a paradigm for a temporary balance that may well collapse under pressure, making of freedom a negative means that can be used to destroy any true balance between various groups.

What brings Americans together is the shared perception that they are a diverse group of people from different countries who have come together under a social contract to which they have access as taxpayers. Thus, a citizen's proper characteristic is the regular and timely paying of taxes, while at the same time benefiting from the facilities that those taxes provide. Marxism was essentially an attempt to treat maladies in western thought and civilization. But it failed. This does not mean, however, that the patient has been cured and restored to health. On the contrary, it is far more likely that the illness has become more serious, and that the need for treatment has become more acute.

But Islam, with its community-based organization and codified placement of each individual within the framework of the group, addresses the psychological and spiritual needs of those living within its borders. Thus, no majority has the right to suppress a minority or erase a minority's special or distinguishing characteristics. By the same token, no minority has the right to establish its uniqueness by detracting from the majority's rights or destroying its distinguishing features. Thus, the Islamic concept of social balance is based upon a mutual recognition of all of a given society's traits and characteristics and upon their codification in a way that allows both the majority and the minority to develop and prosper. This allows a society's differing traits and characteristics to be transformed into a positive social diversity.

If understood in a conceptual context, Islam's treatment of non-Muslims contains much that may be of value in treating the hidden crises of modern societies, especially of those societies based on the American pattern. Historically, minorities in the Muslim world maintained their cultures and ways of life because the Islamic system legislated and codified their special characteristics and thus accorded them state protection. In this way, non-Muslim minorities coexisted with Muslims for centuries and even played important roles in Muslim societies. In the Muslim world, there is hardly a city without its Christian or Jewish quarter. In the West, however, despite repeated waves of immigrants, all of their religious and other distinctions seem to have been lost in the melting pot of worldly secularism, which strips everything of its sacred nature.

Colonialism brought about attacks on all indigenous thought, both Muslim and non-Muslim. Gradually, the colonialists gave their own interpretations to many concepts, thereby confusing and misleading people on matters of religion. As a result, Islamic legislation for minorities came to be understood as degrading and segregationist, and certain minorities sought to destroy the system in the belief that only the majority would be adversely affected. However, both groups were harmed, for all religious and cultural distinctions fell victim to the foreign secularist agenda. Members of majority and minority groups would do well to remember the past before trying to block Islamic legislation.

Presently, Muslims are suffering from serious rifts in their cultural and intellectual lives as a theoretical war rages around them. One side features the factions of the secularists, modernists, and atheists, and the other side features those of the fundamentalists and traditionalists. The Ummah does not need any of these factions or their compromises to reach some imagined political equilibrium. What it needs is to discover its own unique self and define the frame of reference from which all of its factions may derive their principles, legitimacy, and standards. While the various factions may agree on the need for freedom, democracy, renaissance, and nationalism, they cannot agree on a single interpretation or method of implementation. Look at how democracy was rejected in Tunisia and Algeria when national polls showed that the

Islamists had won. The reason in both cases was differences in standards. In the wake of those rejections came a strong secularist current that preferred military dictatorship to Islamic rule. Clearly, the Ummah's need to agree on a single standard and frame of reference, as well as the rectification of its thought and its intellectual, cultural, political, and social foundations, is far greater than its need for accommodation and compromise, for these fade away as quickly as the circumstances that caused them.[4]

We do not want to be forced by political pressures to accept a median solution involving concessions by the secularists or nationalists in exchange for a proportional concession from the Islamists. We are fully aware that this takes place within the framework of the secular-materialist western culture that has imposed itself on every other civilization. The new center of this culture, the United States, views the acceptance of its culture and worldview as an essential condition for the success of what it calls the "New World Order."

Had Muslim intellectuals sought to understand such concepts as naturalization and democracy within a universal Islamic milieu, a central Islamic culture, or at least within a self-sufficient Islamic culture, they might have avoided many of these [negative] observations or found satisfactory answers. Under the present circumstances, however, caution is required. For the most part, secularist and atheist intellectuals in the Muslim world, particularly in the Arab world, contribute nothing more than translations of western criticism of Islam. They have cleverly altered these works in order to direct them against the Qur'an, the Sunnah, and Islamic law in general. Thus they have nothing new to say. It also follows that Muslim thinkers and intellectuals would be wasting their time if they tried to refute these borrowed criticisms.

When secularists see Islamists engaging in innovative and independent thought, they quickly adopt traditional orthodox positions and hide behind the same texts as the orthodox. For example, one of them has said: "We know, naturally, that the absolute equality spoken of by the revolutionary Islamic groups is incorrect from the standpoint of Islamic law. The texts of the Qur'an and the Sunnah speak unambiguously about differences in rank."

When Shaykh Nadīm al-Jisr published an article in the Lebanese daily newspaper *Al-Nahār*, one that sought to find a theoretical connection between the modern theory of light and supernatural beings (i.e., angels and jinn), Ṣādiq Jalāl al-ʿAẓm refuted him by writing a book entitled *Naqd al-Fikr al-Dīnī* (A Critique of Religious Thought). In it, he asserted that the Qur'anic texts could be interpreted only according to the rulings of the first generations of Muslim scholars. Moreover, he argued that the knowledge spoken of in the Qur'an and enjoined upon Muslims is knowledge of the Shariʿah and nothing more. In support of his argument, he cited the definition of knowledge given by al-Ghazālī (d. 1111) in his *Iḥyā' ʿUlūm al-Dīn*.

To follow up on this sort of scholarship done by the secularists would require a separate study. What is clear, however, is that it is very unlikely that the secularists will pay serious attention to the Islamists' arguments. But that in itself does not detract from the value or need of Islamist thought, especially when it is placed in context and used to deliver the Muslim mind from the crisis with which it is presently beset. Ijtihad, in the sense of independent and innovative thinking, is what Islamists need.

And now for my final point: From the beginning of our contact with the West until only a few decades ago, the Muslim mind was often occupied with the idea of rapprochement – an attempted bridging of the gulf between Islamic thought and western ideas and civilization. This idea's time has now passed, for its negative ideas clearly far outweigh the positive. It has proven to be a failure. This is also true of comparative thought and of considering issues in Islamic thought from the perspective of western thought. If the idea of rapprochement helped to weaken the Muslim character and rob Muslims of their intellectual and cultural heritage, then the idea of considering issues from a western perspective has coerced Muslims into modernization or forced them to seek refuge in the past – to "progress backwards." Obviously, the consequences in either case have been to further widen the gulf between Muslims and the modern age, as well as between Muslims and their counterparts in the modern world.

NOTES

1. In *Towards an Islamic Theory of International Relations* (Herndon, VA: IIIT, 1993), ʿAbdulḤamīd AbūSulaymān writes: "In classical jurisprudence, this term (*al-dhimmah*) is defined as a sort of permanent agreement between Muslim political authorities and non-Muslim subjects which provides protection for Muslims and peaceful internal relations with non-Muslim subjects. In return, the latter accepted Islamic rule and paid the *jizyah* as a substitution for being drafted into the army. Jurists were fully aware that, in turn, the Muslim state was obliged not only to tolerate with sincerity the non-Muslims' faith, religious practices, and laws, but also to provide them with protection for their lives and properties: 'Their blood is as our blood, and their possessions are as ours'" (p. 28).

2. Refer to Abdelwahab Elmessiri's *Al-Firdaws al-Arḍī* and his series of articles on the recent racial violence in Los Angeles in "*Hākadhā Taḍīᶜ al-Aḥlām,*" in *al-Muṣawwar* (Cairo: 1993). Compare these with what Fahmī Ḥuwaydī has written on these events.
3. This phrase was first used by Ismāᶜīl al-Fārūqī in his lecture "The West and Us."
4. See the excellent analysis by Ṭāriq al-Bishrī, "*Mustaqbal al-Ḥiwār al-Islāmī al-ᶜIlmānī,*" in *Mushkilatān: Wa Qirā'atān Fīhimā* (Herndon, VA: IIIT, 1992).

The Rights of the Accused in Islam

(Part One)

INTRODUCTION

As a faith and a way of life, Islam includes among its most important objectives the realization of justice and the eradication of injustice. Justice is an Islamic ideal under all circumstances and at all times, one that is not to be affected by one's preferences or dislikes or the existence (or absence) of ties of blood. Rather, as the Qur'an states, it is a goal to be achieved and an ideal to be sought: "Surely, Allah commands justice and the doing of good" (16:90); "And I was commanded to deal justly between you" (42:15); and "Do not allow your rancor for a people to cause you to deal unjustly. Be just, for that is closer to heeding" (5:8). Many hadiths also command justice and prohibit wrong. Moreover, achieving justice is one of the objectives toward which human nature inclines, while its opposite – injustice – is something that people naturally abhor.

Allah has ordained measures by which justice may be known and distinguished from its opposite. He has clarified the means by which all people might achieve this objective, facilitated the ways by which it may be accomplished, and made those ways (the most important of which is the institution of judgment [*qāḍā*]) clear to them.

Allah prescribed the institution of legal judgment so "that people may stand forth in justice" (57:25). This institution ensures that everything will be measured by the same criteria, which would make it impossible for one

---

This article first appeared in the *American Journal of Islamic Social Sciences* 11:3 (Fall 1994): 348-64, and was translated by Yusuf DeLorenzo. It has been slightly edited.

Translator's Note: In view of the recent interest shown by scholars of human rights and how they are neglected in many lands, the journal presents the following study. Among all of the rights accorded to individual human beings, perhaps those of the accused are the ones most often transgressed. Owing to the study's length, it will be published in two installments.

to be unjust to another's person or wealth. As a result, all people will live in the shade of peace and justice, where their rights are protected and contentment envelops their hearts, souls, persons, honor, and wealth.

HISTORICAL DEVELOPMENT OF THE JUDICIARY

The judiciary has been a firm religious responsibility and a form of worship from the time the Prophet initiated it by establishing the first Islamic state in Madinah. This is clear from the treaty between the Muhājirūn and the Anṣār and their Jewish and polytheistic neighbors. This treaty states: "Whatever occurrence or outbreak is feared to result in corruption shall be referred for judgment to Allah and to Muhammad, His Prophet."[1]

During the Prophet's reign, Madinah was small and the community's legal problems were few and uncomplicated. And so only one judge (*qāḍī*) – the Prophet – was needed. But as the territory ruled by Muslims began to expand, the Prophet began to entrust some of his governors with judiciary responsibilities and permitted some of his Companions to judge cases. He sent them to different lands and advised them to seek justice for the people and oppose inequity. ʿAlī was sent as a judge to Yemen, and others, among them Abū Mūsā and Muʿādh, became judges.[2] The Prophet's judgments were always based on what Allah had revealed to him.

In most cases, the two disputing parties would agree to present their case to the Prophet. After listening to both sides, he would tell them that he was deciding their case solely on the basis of the externals (i.e., evidence and testimony).[3] He was careful to explain that his decisions should not be cited in order to permit what was prohibited or prohibit what was permitted. He explained the proof and evidence as well as the means of defense and denial:[4] "Proof is the responsibility of the claimant; whereas, for the claimed against, an oath is sufficient."[5] In other words, confession, with all of its conditions, is proof against the confessor, and no judgment is to be passed until both parties have been heard. The Prophet had no apparatus to collect and verify evidence to the advantage or detriment of either party.

When Abū Bakr became the political ruler (*khalīfah*) upon the Prophet's death, he entrusted the judiciary to ʿUmar ibn al-Khaṭṭāb. Owing perhaps to ʿUmar's reputation for severity, two years passed without his having to judge a single case. When he became the ruler, however, the situation changed. During his reign, Islam's major conquests were underway and the territory under Islamic rule was becoming truly vast. Thus, legal issues began to come to light for the first time. In response, ʿUmar laid the foundations for an institutionalized juridical order in which judges, chosen by the ruler on the basis of certain criteria and functioning as his deputies, would hear cases, arbitrate disputes, and pass legal judgments. He appointed Abū al-Dardā' judge of Madinah, Shurayḥ ibn al-Ḥārith al-Kindī judge of Kufa, Abū Mūsā al-Ashʿarī judge of Basrah, and ʿUthmān ibn Qays judge of Egypt. For the territories of Sham (Greater Syria), a separate institution was established.

ʿUmar set a remarkable example for his judges to follow and warned then not to deviate from it. In his letter to Muʿādh, he wrote:

> As to what follows: Verily, legal judgment is an established religious responsibility and a practice (*sunnah*) to be emulated. So if it is assigned to you, remember that speaking the truth when there is nothing to back it up is useless. Make peace between people in your sessions, in your countenance, and in your judgments, so that no decent person will ever have anything to say about your unfairness and so that no oppressed person will ever despair of finding justice with you.
>
> The burden of proof is on the claimant, and for the defendant there is the oath. Arbitration is lawful between Muslims, except in cases where the lawful (*ḥalāl*) is made unlawful (*ḥarām*) and vice versa. If someone claims a right to something that is not present and has no proof of it, then set him something like it. If he describes it, give him his due. But if he cannot do so, then you have solved the case for him in a most eloquent and enlightening manner.
>
> Do not be impeded by your prior decision to change your mind about the truth if you reconsider and are guided by your understanding to take another decision. Indeed, the truth itself is eternal and nothing can change it. It is better for you to change your mind about it than to insist upon what is false.
>
> With the exceptions of those Muslims who are guilty of perjury, who have been lashed in accordance with *ḥadd* punishments, or who are suspect because of their relationship to the accused, all Muslims are reliable witnesses. Only Allah knows the secrets of His servants, and He has screened their misdeeds, except for those that are attested to by evidence and witnesses.
>
> You must use understanding when a question that has not been mentioned specifically in either the Qur'an or the Sunnah is raised. Make use of analogy and know the examples that you will use. And then undertake the opinion that seems more pleasing to Allah and closest to the Truth.

> Avoid being angry, annoyed, irritated, or upset by people. Do not be hostile when hearing a case (or "towards one of the parties to a case," [the narrator, Abū ʿUbayd was unsure]), for surely a right decision is rewarded by Allah and is something that will be spoken well of. Thus, one whose sincere intention is to serve the truth, even if it were to go against him, will be sufficed by Allah in what transpires between him and others.
>
> One who adorns oneself with what one does not possess will be shown to be unsightly by Allah. For, indeed, Allah accepts from His servants only that which is done for His sake. So keep in mind Allah's rewards both in this life and in the Hereafter. May Allah grant you His peace, blessings, and mercy.[6]

The institution of legal judgment during the times of the four rightly guided caliphs remained simple and uncomplicated. Judges had no court scribe or written record of their decisions, for these were carried out immediately and under the individual judge's direct supervision. No detailed procedures were worked out for the judicial process, registering claims, delineating jurisdictions, or for any other matters that would arise later, for the people's lives were not yet complicated enough to require such refinements. Even the Shariʿah specified no details, but left them to be determined by ijtihad. In other words, the juridical system was allowed to develop in a way that would be the best suited for the peoples' circumstances and customs.[7]

Under the four rightly guided caliphs, the judiciary was limited to resolving civil disputes. Other types of disputes, such as *qiṣāṣ* (where capital punishment may be prescribed), *ḥudūd* (where punishment, including capital punishment, is prescribed by the Qur' an), or *taʿzīr* (where punishment, including capital punishment, is left to the discretion of the judge or the ruler) were decided by the ruler or his appointed governor.

Not a great deal of change in this institution took place under the Umayyads, particularly under the early rulers, and so the procedures remained uncomplicated. Major developments were confined mostly to recording decisions in order to avert evasion and forgetfulness. In fact, such an incident occurred during the reign of Muʿāwiyah ibn Sufyān, when Salīm ibn Muʿizz, the judge of Egypt, decided a case of inheritance. When the heirs reopened the dispute and returned to him, he recorded his decision in writing.[8] This period also saw agreement upon a judge's qualifications, where the judicial procedure would be carried out, and the development of a system to address injustices in public administration.[9]

With the coming of the Abbasids, the judiciary made significant progress. Its sophistication grew both in form and procedure, and its vistas increased with the variety of cases heard. The court register was introduced, the judge's jurisdiction was increased, and the state established the position of chief judge (*qāḍī al-quḍāh*), which today is comparable to the office of the chief justice. One negative development, however, was the increasingly infirm nature of ijtihad, which limited the judges to following the previous rulings of the four established Sunnī schools of legal thought: *taqlīd.* Thus in Iraq and the eastern territories, judges ruled according to the rulings of Abū Ḥanīfah; in Syria and Spain according to Mālik; and in Egypt according to al-Shāfiʿī.[10]

After the Mongol destruction of Baghdad and the subsequent end of the Abbasid Empire in 606/1258, several smaller states emerged and developed their own legal institutions. While these legal institutions differed hardly at all in their foundations and the principles upon which they were established, they did differ significantly in matters of organization, procedures, criteria for the appointment and removal of judges, and in the schools of legal thought that they followed.

Ibn al-Ḥasan al-Nabahī portrayed the judiciary of Muslim Spain during the eighth Islamic century as follows: "The authorities who deal with legal rulings are first the judges, then the central police, the local police, the appellate authority, the local administrator, and then the market controller."[11] Ibn al-Qayyim described the contemporaneous institutions of the eastern Islamic states, after mentioning questions of rulings on claims, by saying that,

> ... the maintenance of authority in matters not connected to claims is called *ḥisbah*, and the one responsible for it is called the *ḥisbah* commissioner. Indeed, it has become customary to assign a commissioner especially for this type of authority. Likewise, a special commissioner, called the appellate commissioner, is assigned to the appellate authority. The collection and spending of state funds comes under the authority of a special commissioner called the *wazīr*. The one entrusted with calculating the wealth of the state and seeing how it is spent and how it should be controlled is called the performance commissioner. The one entrusted with collecting wealth for the state from those who possess it is called the commissioner of collections. The one assigned to deciding disputes and upholding rights, making decisions on matters of marriage, divorce, maintenance, and the validity of transactions is called the *ḥākim* or judge.[12]

JUDICIAL ORGANIZATION AND ITS SOURCES

It should be clear from the historical survey presented above that the Shariʿah did not specify a particular juridical framework. Rather, it established the principles, general foundations, objectives, and sources of legislation. Organizational details (i.e., the extent of a judge's jurisdiction,[13] limitations of his authority in terms of time and place, the assignment [or lack thereof] of another judge to work alongside him) were to be determined by the people's customs, needs, and circumstances. As there is nothing in the Shariʿah that entrusts the juridical process to an individual or an institution, it was left up to the Muslim leadership to decide. The responsibility could be spread among several officials or confined to one, as long as the sole requirement was met: The ruler must ensure that those entrusted with this responsibility meet the Shariʿah's conditions.[14]

It is also clear that the responsibility for judging criminal cases was divided among such different authorities as the ruler (*khalīfah*), the appellate authority (*wālī al-maʿālim*), the military authority (*amīr*), the police commissioner (*sāḥib al-shurṭah*), the market authority (*ḥisbah*), and the judge (*qāḍī*), in the limited sense represented by Ibn al-Qayyim above.[15] The responsibilities of each were not always exclusive or well-defined, for they differed in scope and overlapped. In fact, certain responsibilities associated with one sometimes would be entrusted to another in accordance with the ruler's desires or as a result of his policies.[16]

Usually, the governor or the police commissioner was responsible for investigating such serious crimes as *ḥudūd* or *qiṣāṣ*. Likewise, the market authority was usually responsible for assigning a punishment designed to deter an action (*taʿzīr*) for crimes against the general public interest or misdemeanors. This authority was often called the "market controller," as most of the cases were related to crimes committed in the market place. The judge, sometimes called the *ḥākim*, was responsible for settling civil disputes that involved upholding rights and making sure that these were enjoyed by those entitled to them.[17]

Scholars of the procedural systems used in criminal cases divide these systems into three categories:

- *The System of Accusation.* Criminal cases are heard to resolve a dispute between two equal parties. Such cases are brought directly to the judge, who has conducted no prior investigation, so that he can weigh the evidence of both sides, decide which argument seems stronger, and rule in accordance with his findings.

- *The System of Investigation.* The accusation is investigated before the actual trial starts. It resembles the present system, under which the state apparatus (i.e., the police in cooperation with the district attorney) undertakes these responsibilities. The authorities have enough power and authority to discharge their responsibilities. The accused's defense consists of gathering evidence to refute the charges.
- *The System Combining Both of the Above.* This system involves an investigation in its first (pretrial) stage and an accusation at the final, courtroom stage.

Modern systems of legal procedure combine, to a greater or lesser extent, aspects of these systems. At certain stages, features of one will appear dominant, while at other stages, features of another will appear dominant.[18]

We mentioned earlier that the Shariʿah does not provide a specific procedural system, but leaves such details to the ijtihad and understanding of those responsible for ensuring that justice is done. History shows that rulers used one system or a combination of these systems, depending upon their preference. And even though the Shariʿah did not specify details of a legal system, it did put forth general principles, the most obvious being that its laws must be enforced and that justice must be done in accordance with it.[19]

THE ACCUSED

The Rights of the Accused at the Investigative Stage. The word *muttaham* (accused) comes from the root *t-h-m*, meaning "to taint or decay" in the case of spoiled milk or meat. The Arabs also used it to say that "the heat is rotten," meaning that the air was still and the temperature was very high. The area known as Tihamah, in present-day Saudi Arabia, most probably got its name from the second meaning.

The word *tuhmah*, or *tuhāmah*, means "doubt" and "uncertainty." The initial "t" is no doubt a substitute for the letter *wāw*, because the root of the word is *w-h-m*, which connotes suspicion or misgiving. The Arabs used to say that "the man gave rise to suspicion" when someone gave other people reason to suspect himself/herself or his/her actions.[20]

In legal terminology, the word can be traced to several hadiths. For example, Ibn Abū Shaybah related in his collection *Al-Muṣannaf*, on the authority of Abū Hurayrah, who said:

> The Prophet of Allah, may Allah bless him and grant him peace, sent someone to call out in the market place that the testimony of a party to a dispute, like that of one who is suspect, is not admissible. When the Prophet was asked what he meant by one who was suspect, he replied: "One concerning whose religion you have misgivings."[21]

Ibrāhīm used to say: "The testimony of one concerning whom you have misgivings is not acceptable."[22]

The jurists (*fuqahā'*) used the term *the claimed against* instead of *the accused.* In other words, they used the root for *claim*, which is one's seeking to establish that one has more of a right to something than somebody else.[23] The word for claim, *daʿwah*, has the meaning of the infinitive. Thus, if Zayd claims a right over ʿAmr in the case of money, Zayd becomes the claimant, ʿAmr the claimed against, and the money the claim or claimed. Lexically speaking, however, a claim and an accusation are different things, for a claim is essentially notification.

The jurists understand this in the following ways: The Ḥanafis, a claim is one's notification of one's right to something over another person present in the court[24]; the Mālikīs say that it is a statement that, if accepted as true, will entitle the one making it to a right[25]; the Shāfiʿis say that it is notification of one's right to something over someone else before a judge[26]; and the Ḥanbalīs define it as a person's ascribing to himself/herself an entitlement to something in the hand or in the safekeeping of another.[27]

The jurists also disagree in their interpretations of the words *claimant* and *claimed against.* Some have defined *the claimant* as one who is left alone if he/she leaves his/her claim alone, while *the claimed against* is one who is not left alone even if he/she leaves the claim alone. Others, however, have defined *the claimant* as one who claims that something is not as it is and effaces something that is evident, while *the claimed against* is one who establishes that something evident is as it is. Still others define *the claimant* as one who is not required to enter into a legal dispute, and *the claimed against* as one who is required to do so.[28]

The words derived from *claim* are used by jurists in cases pertaining to financial rights and personal law, such as loans, usurpation, sales, rentals, collateral, arbitration, bequests, criminal malpractice related to wealth, marriage, divorce, allowing a wife to leave her husband (*khulʿ*), manumission, lineage, and agency. These were the kinds of cases that were usually referred to a judge for a decision.

There is nothing, however, to prevent the use of the word *accused* in criminal cases. On the contrary, its use there is more suitable, particularly in view of what we have discussed above regarding its lexical derivation and legal significance.

Categories of the Accused in Criminal Cases. Jurists divide those accused in criminal cases into three categories: someone well-known for his/her piety and integrity and thus unlikely to have committed the crime; someone notorious for his/her wrongdoing and profligacy and who is thus likely to have committed the crime; and someone whose circumstances are unknown, so that nothing may be surmised concerning the likelihood of his/her committing the crime.

In reference to the first category, the accusation will not be accepted unless it is accompanied by legally valid evidence. No legal action may be taken against such people on the basis of an accusation alone. In this manner, decent people may be protected from the deprecations of those seeking to dishonor them. There are two differing opinions regarding the punishment for those who make false claims or accusations against such people: that of the majority of the jurists, which says that the person should be punished, and that of Imām Mālik and Ashab, who held that punishment should not be meted out unless it can be proved that the accuser intended to harm or otherwise discredit the accused. The legal principle upon which the majority's ruling is based is that consideration must be given to the circumstantial state of innocence.

As regards the second category, the principle of considering the circumstantial evidence and following the principle of abiding by what is most prudent, the accused may be deprived of personal freedom. Thereafter, an investigation must be made of the alleged crime to determine whether the accusation should be upheld or rejected. The accused's denial of the charges is not sufficient as evidence, nor is his/her sworn oath. Rather, it is essential to prove or disprove the truth of the accusation. In such cases, the court authority (i.e., the ruler or the judge) has the right to detain the accused for the duration of the investigation.

In regard to the third category, one whose circumstances are unknown, the ruler or the judge may detain the accused until his/her circumstances are better known. This ruling, which was accepted by the majority of scholars, including Mālik, Aḥmad, Abū Ḥanīfah, and their companions and students, was derived from a hadith in which it is related that the Prophet detained someone accused of a crime for a day and a night.[29] The meaning of detention, as understood by classical jurists, is to hinder and limit freedom, regardless of whether this is accomplished by confinement in a prison, surveillance, or being required to stay within a defined area. The permissible period of detention is also disputed. Basically there are two opinions: some have determined it to be one month, while others have opined that the matter should be left to the legal discretion of the official.[30]

PRINCIPLES THAT MUST BE CONSIDERED

The Shari^c^ah is concerned with the circumstantial state of a person's innocence, and jurists have based several legal rulings on it. Moreover, this principle may only be overruled if there is irrefutable evidence. Thus, it is connected closely with the principle that certainty may not be erased by doubt. Indeed, the relationship of one principle to the other resembles the relationship of a branch to a trunk, for the two are found together throughout jurisprudential literature. In addition, they must be reconciled to the principle of protecting society, by implementing preventative measures, from perceived dangers with a high likelihood of occurrence. The same is true with protecting what is considered essential to society.

May the principle of circumstantial innocence be superseded by something that is likely to harm society if the principle is abandoned? Part of that answer can be found in the above threefold division of the accused. Perhaps the rest of the answer may be found in the principles of opting for what is most prudent, for limiting opportunities for wrong, and for doing away with what is detrimental.

Islam, which seeks to protect the rights of the individual, also seeks to protect the rights of society as a whole. Therefore, no individual may presume to overstep the rights of society while hiding behind the veil of personal rights and freedom, and society may not trample on the rights of the individual or deprive him/her of his/her rights on the pretense of some alleged peril. Islam honors and exalts humanity and has given human beings many rights, above all the right to life, physical well-being, honor and respect, personal freedom, freedom of movement, and many others. Thus, an individual's home and personal life are sacred. No one has the right to enter another person's home without permission or to look inside his/her home, eavesdrop on private conversations, open one's mail, or do anything else that infringes upon those rights.

Society, in its capacity as society, enjoys similar rights. It is essential that peace and security be maintained for society, that its interests be upheld, and that crime be eradicated. If it becomes necessary to maintain these rights by temporarily curtailing or suspending the rights of an individual, then such an act will be done based on the nature of what is dictated by necessity, which is determined by the extent of the necessity. What is dictated by necessity represents the limit of power, set by the authorities, given to the investigator over the accused. Thus, the investigator's power is essentially a departure from a legally established principle for the purpose of realizing another legally established principle that cannot otherwise be realized.

If the Sharᶜiah allows the investigator or the judge to place certain restrictions on the rights of the accused to maintain the principle of the rights of society, it has also placed restrictions on the power of the investigator, which represents guarantees to the accused.

The Authority of the Investigator. The authority enjoyed by the investigator in relation to the accused is limited and, if it encroaches on some of the accused's rights, it certainly does not extend to any of his/her other basic rights. This is why the Prophet called such a person a "prisoner."[31] This also establishes that the accused will be maintained at the state's expense.

Ibn al-Qayyim defined detention as "preventing the individual from dealing with others in any way that would lead to their being harmed."[32] Other jurists considered detention as being in the same class of punishments as the *ḥudūd.* Accordingly, they opined, it should not be prescribed on the basis of suspicion alone. In fact, the overriding principle here is that the individual is guaranteed personal freedom and the right of free movement: "He it was Who made the earth tractable for you; then go forth in its highlands" (67:15). Thus, a person cannot be detained or deprived of freedom of movement without a legally valid reason.[33]

Islam has shown a great deal of consideration for the prisoner and his/her affairs. For example, the Prophet once left a prisoner in the care of a certain individual. He ordered the latter to care for and show respect to the former and, thereafter, often visited the man and inquired after the prisoner's welfare. ᶜAlī ibn Abū Ṭālib used to make surprise visits to the prison in order to inspect its condition and listen to the inmates' complaints.[34]

It is the state's responsibility to provide ample food, clothing, and medical treatment for all prisoners and to ensure that their rights are protected. Moreover, Shariᶜah scholars have ruled that a judge's first responsibility, upon assuming his position, is to go in person to the jails and free all who have been detained unjustly. He should go to each prisoner and ascertain the reasons for his/her imprisonment. In certain cases, he may meet with the accusers to determine whether the reasons for imprisonment are still valid and if justice was done.

When someone is imprisoned, the sentencing judge must record the prisoner's name and ancestry, the reason for imprisonment, and the beginning and ending dates of the period of imprisonment Likewise, when a judge is retired and another takes his place, the new judge must write to the old judge and ask him about the people he sent to prison and why he did so.

The Authority for Sentencing Someone to Prison. Jurists have differed over who has the right to sentence someone to prison. Al-Māwardī wrote that an investigator's authority differs in accordance with his position. For example, if the investigator is an official or a judge, and someone accused of theft or adultery is brought before him, he cannot imprison the accused until he learns more about the individual, for mere accusation is not sufficient grounds for imprisonment. If the investigator is a ruler or a judge in a criminal court, however, and if he deems the evidence to be sufficiently convincing or incriminating, he may arrest and detain the accused. Later on, however, if the accusation should prove to be unfounded or untenable, he must release the accused. In these details, most legal scholars accepted al-Māwardī's opinion.

The Period of Imprisonment. Scholars also differed over how long a person can be confined. Some said that it should not exceed one month, while others felt that it should be left to the discretion of the imam or the relevant court official. Indeed, the latter view is the more reasonable.[35]

By now, it should be apparent that precautionary detention is allowed only when the need for it is great and when certain conditions are satisfied, such as matters related to the objective for which the accused was detained, the position of the one doing the sentencing, the sentencing itself, and the length of the sentence.[36] All of these are matters in which there is a great deal of scope for the concerned court official to organize things in accordance with the dictates of the legal policies of a particular time or place. In other words, these are not fixed matters that are closed to change or development.

Investigating the Accused's Person, Residence, and Conversations. Allah has protected and honored humanity and prohibited the touching of an individual's person, skin, or honor.[37] Likewise, He has declared that a person's home is sacred and must not be violated:

> O you who have faith! Do not enter the homes of others without first seeking permission, and then wishing peace upon its inhabitants. That is better for you, so that you may remember. If you do not find anyone at home, do not enter until permission is given to you. If it is said to you, 'Go back,' then go back, for that will be purer for you (24:27-28),

and "O you who have faith! Avoid being overly suspicious; for suspicion in some cases is wrong; and do not spy on one another" (49:12).

The Prophet said: "Everything about a Muslim is sacred to another Muslim; from his blood, to his wealth, to his honor"; "Those who listen to what people say about another, even when [they know] those people are unfriendly toward that person, will have molten lead poured into their ears on the Day of Judgment"; and "If the amir seeks to uncover the doubtful things about people, he will ruin them."

There are also other instances. Once, Ibn Masʿūd, when he was governor of Iraq, was told that "Walīd ibn ʿUqbah's beard is dripping with wine." He replied: "We have been prohibited from spying. But if something should become obvious to us, we will take him to task for it." It is related that one time ʿUmar ibn al-Khaṭṭāb was informed that Abū Miḥjan al-Thaqafī was drinking wine in his home with some friends. ʿUmar went straight to Abū Mihjan's house, walked inside, and saw that there was only one other person with Abū Miḥjan. This man said to ʿUmar: "This is not permitted to you. Allah has prohibited you from spying." ʿUmar turned and walked out.

ʿAbd al-Raḥmān ibn ʿAwf related:

> I spent a night with ʿUmar on patrol in the city (Madinah). A light appeared to us in the window of a house with its door ajar, from which we heard loud voices and slurred speech. ʿUmar said to me: "This is the house of Rabīʿah ibn Umayyah ibn Khalf, and right now they're in there drinking. What do you think?" I replied: "I think we are doing what Allah has prohibited us from doing. Allah said not to spy, and we are spying." So ʿUmar turned away and left them alone.

Clearly, the privacy of the individual and all other types of privacy must be respected and preserved. This is true unless something occurs that requires otherwise.

The meaning of "suspicion" in the above verse is "accusation." The famed authority on legal interpretations of the Qur'an, al-Qurṭubī, said that what the verse was prohibiting is an accusation that has no basis in fact, such as accusing someone of adultery or drinking wine in the absence of any supporting evidence. He wrote:

> And the proof that the word *suspicion* in this verse means *accusation* is that Allah then said: 'And do not spy on one another.' This is because one might be tempted to make an accusation and then seek confirmation of one's suspicion via spying, inquiry, surveillance, eavesdropping, and so on. Thus the Prophet prohibited spying. If you wish, you may say that what distin-

guishes the kind of suspicion that must be avoided from all other kinds of suspicion is that the kind of suspicion for which no proper proof or apparent reason is known must be avoided as *ḥarām*. So if the suspect is well-known for goodness and respected for apparent honesty, then to suspect him/her of corruption or fraud for no good reason is *ḥarām*. The case is different, however, in relation to one who has achieved notoriety for dubious dealings and unabashed iniquity. Thus there are two kinds of suspicion: that which is brought on and then strengthened by proof that can form the basis for a ruling and, secondly, that which occurs for no apparent reason and which, when weighed against its opposite, will be equal. This second type of suspicion is the same as doubt, and no ruling based on it may be given. This is the kind of suspicion that the verse prohibits.

This indicates that an individual may not be subjected to a search of his/her person or home, surveillance, the recording of conversations over the phone or elsewhere, the invasion of privacy in any manner, or the disclosing of any confidences merely on the basis of a dubious suspicion that he/she may have committed a punishable crime. This is because unfounded suspicion is the worst possible kind of suspicion, and the one who holds such a suspicion is a wrongdoer. It adds nothing to the truth, and nothing may be built upon it unless there is information to indicate it, grounds to confirm it, and evidence to prove it.

It should be noted here that Qur'anic commentators and authorities on the legal interpretation of the Qur'an have all followed the legal scholars in allowing arrest and precautionary detention. In fact, they distinguished between those whose apparent lifestyles indicated their honesty or dishonesty. Thus, they considered the prohibition to apply only to spying on honest and decent people. In relation to others, however, these scholars felt that spying on them was lawful.

The Qur'an and the Sunnah prohibit spying in general – not specific – terms. One's previous record of having transgressed or being accused is not sufficient to violate the sacredness of his/her person or privacy in the absence of hard supporting evidence. This view was upheld by ᶜUmar when he refrained from spying on Abū Miḥjan al-Thaqafī and Rabīᶜah ibn Umayyah, for both were well-known for their love of strong drink. The same was true when Ibn Masᶜūd did not spy on al-Walīd ibn ᶜUqbah, although he was notorious for his drinking habits.

Based on these principles, the Shari ᶜah does not allow the searching of a person or of one's home, surveillance of personal conversations, censorship of personal mail, and violation of one's private life unless there is legally valid evidence to show his/her involvement in a crime. Such evidence must be considered by the authority responsible for carrying out the Shariᶜah's rulings. This authority, obviously, must also be able to interpret correctly the Shariᶜah's teachings and higher purposes, realize that these rights are guaranteed by the Qur'an and the Sunnah, and that any attempt to alter or particularize them is a violation of what those two sources have established. Therefore, the above actions are permitted only if they can help determine the circumstances a crime, protect society by ensuring that criminals are not punished, and ensure that the innocent are not punished.

In short, the investigating authority may not go beyond what is absolutely necessary. Moreover, those in authority should always maintain proper Islamic behavior. For instance, if the person in authority is male, he should not conduct a body search of a woman or enter a house in which women are present. In addition, personal property that has no relation to the alleged crime should not be destroyed or confiscated.

Questioning the Accused. The investigator may question the accused on any topic that will help to reveal the truth, and may confront the accused with the accusation. The accused, however, does not have to answer those questions, as will be seen in the following article.

NOTES

1. Ḥasan Ibrāhīm, *Tārīkh al-Islām al-Siyāsī,* 1:102.
2. Ibid., 1:458.
3. The Prophet said: "I rule on the basis of externals." The same meaning may be derived from several other hadiths, many of which are authentic. For details, see the author's footnotes in his edition of al-Rāzī's *Al-Maḥṣūl* (Beirut: Mu'assasat al-Risālah, 1992), 80-83.
4. The hadith was related by al-Tirmidhī, Abū Dāwūd, al-Nasā'ī, al-Bayhaqī, and al-Ḥākim. See al-Shawkānī, *Nayl al-Awṭār* (Beirut: Dār al-Jīl, n.d.), 9:220.
5. The general juristic principle says that "evidence is for him who affirms, the oath is for him who denies," and thus lays the burden of proof on the affirmer or claimant. [Trans.]
6. Ibn al-Qayyim, *Iᶜlām al-Muwaqqiᶜīn,* 1:85; al-Māwardī, *Al-Aḥkām al-Sulṭāniyyah,* 71-72; al-Bayhaqī, *Al-Sunan al-Kubrā,* 10:115.
7. Ibn al-Qayyim, *Al-Ṭuruq al-Ḥukmiyyah,* 218.
8. *Kitāb al-Qaḍā',* 309; Maḥmūd Arnūs, *Al-Qaḍā' fī al-Islām,* 49; Ibrābīm Najīb Muḥammad Awad, *Al-Niẓām al-Qaḍā'ī,* 48.
9. Ibn Khaldun, *Al-Muqaddimah,* 741.
10. Ibid., 1150. See also Ibrāhīm, *Tārīkh al-Islām al-Siyāsī,* 2:55, 3:306.
11. Ibrāhīm, *Tārīkh al-Islām al-Siyāsī,* 4:377-86; Awad Muḥammad Awad, *Al-Majallah al-ᶜArabiyyah li al-Difāᶜ al-Ijtimāᶜī,* no. 10 (October 1979): 98.

12. Ibn al-Qayyim, *Al-Ṭuruq*, 215-16.
13. Al-Māwardī, *Al-Aḥkām al-Sulṭāniyyah*, 69-73; Ibrābīm, *Tārīkh al-Islām al-Siyāsī*, 4:377-86.
14. These are faith in Islam, maturity, the ability to reason intelligently, freedom and trustworthiness, having all of one's faculties, and knowledge of the Shariʿah's sources.
15. Ibn al-Qayyim, *Al-Ṭuruq*, 215.
16. Ibn Khaldūn, *Al-Muqaddimah*, 740.
17 Ibid., Ibn al-Qayyim, *Al-Ṭuruq*, 218-19.
18. Ibn Khaldūn, *Al-Muqaddimah*, 740-43; Awad, *Al-Majallah al-ʿArabiyyah*, 101-3.
19. Ibn Khaldūn, *Al-Muqaddimah*.
20. *Al-Miṣbāḥ*, 107, 129; See "T-H-M" in al-Zabīdī, *Tāj al-ʿArūs*.
21. Ibn Abū Shaybah, *Al-Muṣannaf*, 8:320; al-Bayhaqī, *Al-Sunan al-Kubrā*, 10:201; al-Tirmidhī, *Al-Sunan*, hadith no. 2299; al-Khaṣṣāf, *Adab al-Qāḍī*, 2:112, 1:229.
22. Ibn Abū Shaybah, *Al-Muṣannaf*, 8:321.
23. Aḥmad ʿAbd al-Razzāq al-Kubaysī, *Al-Ḥudūd wa al-Aḥkām*, 228; Abū al-Walīd ibn Shahnah al-Ḥanafi, *Lisān al-Ḥukkām*, 226; ʿAlā al-Din al-Tarabulsi, *Muʿīn al-Ḥukkām*, 54.
24. Al-Kubaysī, *Al-Ḥudūd*, 288.
25. Al-Jurjānī, *Kitāb al-Taʿrīfāt*, 93; al-Muṭṭarizī, *Al-Muʿarrab min al-Mugharrib*, 164.
26. Al-Kubaysī, *Al-Ḥudūd*, 287.
27. *Sharḥ Ḥudūd Ibn ʿArafah*, 468.
28. *Ḥāshiyat Qaylūbī wa ʿUmayrah*, 4:334.
29. Ibn al-Qayyim, *Al-Ṭuruq*, 101, 103.
30. Al-Māwardī, *Al-Aḥkām al-Sulṭāniyyah*.
31. Ibn al-Qayyim, *Al-Ṭuruq*.
32. Ibid.
33. Ibn Ḥazm, *Al-Muḥallā*, 11:141.
34. Abū Yūsuf, *Kitāb al-Kharāj* and its commentary *Fiqh al-Mulūk*, 2:238.
35. Ibn al-Qayyim, *Al-Ṭuruq*, 103.
36. Awad, *Al-Majallat al-ʿArabiyyah*.
37. This is part of an authentic hadith. See al-Suyūṭī, *Al-Fatḥ al-Kabīr*, 3:256.

The Rights of the Accused in Islam

(Part Two)

Under the law of Islam, the accused enjoys many rights. These will be summarized below.

THE RIGHT TO A DEFENSE

The accused has the right to defend himself/herself against any accusation by proving that the evidence cited is invalid or presenting contradictory evidence. In any case, the accused must be allowed to exercise this right so that the accusation does not turn into a conviction. An accusation means that there is the possibility of doubt, and just how much doubt there is will determine the amount and parameters of the defense. By comparing the evidence presented by the defense with that of the accuser, the truth will become clear – which is, after all, the investigation's objective.

Therefore, self-defense is not only the right of the accused to use or disregard as he/she pleases, but it is also the right and the duty of society as a whole. If it is in the best interests of an individual not to be convicted when he/she is in fact innocent, the interests of society are no less important. Society must ensure that the innocent are not convicted and that the guilty do not escape punishment. This is why the Shariʿah guarantees the right to a defense and prohibits its denial under any circumstances and for any reason.

In a well-known hadith, the Prophet is reported to have told ʿAlī, who he had just appointed as governor of Yemen: "O ʿAli! People will come to you asking for judgments. When the two parties to a dispute come to you,

This article first appeared in the *American Journal of Islamic Social Sciences* 11:4 (Winter 1994): 504-18, and was translated by Yusuf DeLorenzo. It has been slightly edited.

do not decide in favor of either party until you have heard all that both parties have to say. Only in this manner will you come to a proper decision, and only in this way will you come to know the truth." It is related that ʿUmar ibn ʿAbd al-ʿAzīz said to one of his judges: "When a disputant comes to you with an eye put out, do not be quick to rule in his favor. Who knows, maybe the other party to the dispute will come to you with both eyes put out!"

The basic rule in regard to defense is that it should be undertaken by the accused, as it is his/her right, if he/she is capable of doing so. If not, he/she may not be convicted. This is why some jurists have opined that a deaf mute cannot be punished for *ḥadd* crimes, even when all of the conditions regarding evidence have been satisfied. The reasoning here is that if the deaf mute were capable of speaking, he/she might be able to raise the sort of doubts that negate the *ḥadd* punishment (for a lesser, *taʿzīr* punishment or amercement), and by means of sign language only, he/she may not be able to express all that he/she may want to. So, under such circumstances, if the *ḥadd* punishment is administered, justice will not have been served, because the *ḥadd* will have been administered in the presence of doubt.

THE ACCUSED'S SEEKING LEGAL DEFENSE FROM A LAWYER

I know of no opinions from the early jurists that permit the accused to seek the help of a lawyer. Books dealing with Islamic procedural law (*aḥkām al-qaḍā'*) and the behavior of judges (*adab al-qāḍī*) do not mention this issue. This apparent omission might be due to the fact that, historically, court sessions were public. As these sessions were widely attended by legal scholars and experts, whose presence represented a true and responsible legal advisory board that actively assisted the judge in dispensing justice, there was never any need for professional counsel.

Nonetheless, Abū Ḥanīfah ruled that one who appoints another to represent him/her before the court is responsible for whatever ruling is passed, even though the one represented may not be present when the ruling is made. Other jurists have given similar opinions. An authentic hadith relates that the Messenger said:

> I am only human, and some of you are more eloquent than others. So sometimes a disputant will come to me, and I will consider him truthful and judge in his favor. But if ever I have (mistakenly) ruled that a Muslim's right be given to another, then know that it is as flames from the Hellfire. Hold on to it or (if you know it belongs to another) abandon it.

Many Shariʿah texts stress the need to settle disputes by whatever means necessary. When we consider the great disparities in talent and ability (particularly the ability to argue and debate effectively) between the disputants, even those brought before the Prophet, we realize that any method that will lead to a just settlement may be considered legally valid. Therefore, the accused's decision to ask for help in defending himself/herself may also be considered valid, provided that the help comes from an impartial and independent counsel. With the help of such counsel, the accused may acquire a proper understanding of the charges against him/her, what the law says, the weight of the evidence presented, and what may be used (and how it may be used) to rebut that evidence. When taking all of this into consideration, we may assume safely that the accused has the rights to defend himself/herself and to seek the help of someone else.

Some people might object to this on the grounds that while such a counsel might be a more capable defender than the accused, it is also true that he/she might be more capable than the other party. As a result, a just settlement might never be reached. But, one could counter this view by saying that what is being sought is a settlement that is as just as possible, and that it is better to allow one the choice of counsel than to deprive the accused of help in articulating his/her case and refuting the other party's arguments. It is also better than leaving any doubt in the judge's mind about what kind of punishment should be given. As mentioned above, there should be no room left for doubt about the final verdict's validity.

In his *History of the Qadis of Qurtuba*, al-Khashinī reports that two men brought their dispute before Aḥmad ibn Bāqī. Believing that one of the disputants seemed to know what he was talking about while the other (who appeared to be honest and truthful) did not, he advised the latter to find someone to speak on his behalf. When the man replied that he spoke only the truth regardless of the consequences, the judge replied: "It couldn't be worse than [your opponent's] murdering the truth." According to al-Marīdī, however, if the judge tells the disputant to seek the help of someone else, the individual chosen to serve as counsel may only assist in establishing (not refuting) a claim. The judge may not appoint an individual to represent someone else.

So, here we have two judges: one who advises a disputant to seek defense counsel and another who considers such advice improper. Obviously, then, this is a question of ijtihad. In such a case, it is quite possible that the best opinion and the one closer to the spirit of the Shariʿah is the one that allows a disputant to seek legal counsel. It is even more likely that the right to legal counsel is indicated in cases of penal law, whether in *ḥudūd* cases (where only the rights of Allah are involved) or in cases where the alleged crime involves the rights of both Allah and His subjects.

Under the procedures in contemporary courts of law, the accused is certain to encounter an opponent, usually an attorney or a public prosecutor, who is far more eloquent and capable of making legal points than himself/herself. Under such circumstances, the accused will obviously need the services of someone who can present his/her case and rebut the arguments put forth by the accuser. The question that arises here, however, is whether the accused is entitled to counsel while the case is under investigation or only when it actually comes to court? If the question is subjected to ijtihad and it is determined that the accused is allowed to seek legal counsel, then it may be best for the accused to have legal counsel at both stages. This also would help to establish the facts of the case. In addition, if one is to prepare an effective defense, it is necessary to acquire a complete understanding of the alleged crime and the evidence so that the charges can be refuted. In addition, information proving the accused's innocence must also be gathered and then presented effectively. This would indicate that the accused should be allowed to seek legal counsel from the time that charges are filed.

THE ACCUSED'S RIGHT TO REMAIN SILENT AND TO BE HEARD

The accused has the right of free expression without the fear of reprisal or the use of truth serum, drugs, or hypnotism to obtain information that he/she would otherwise not give.[1] The accused may choose not to respond to questions. If he/she does respond and it is later determined that the answers were false, he/she may not be charged with, or punished for, bearing false witness. If the accused acknowledges liability or confesses to a *ḥadd* crime, he/she may retract his/her statement and thereby nullify the earlier confession.

STATEMENTS MADE UNDER DURESS

The accused may not be pressured to confess. Ibn Ḥazm writes:

> Therefore, it is unlawful to subject someone to tribulation, either by blows, imprisonment, or threats. There is nothing to legitimize such treatment in the Qur'an, or the established Sunnah, or ijmaʿ, and nothing may be said to be of the religion unless it comes from one of these three sources. On the contrary, Allah Most High has prohibited this and caused His

> Messenger to say: "Verily, your blood, your wealth, your reputations, and your skins are sacred to you." So when Allah made both the body and the reputation sacred, He prohibited the physical and verbal abuse of Muslims, except when required by law as prescribed in the Qur'an and the Sunnah.[2]

Among the most important conditions to be satisfied before a confession may be accepted is freedom of choice. A confession submitted of one's own volition will be considered valid, as its truth is more probable than its falsehood. This assumption is based on the fact that it is inconceivable that a rational person would admit to something harmful unless there was a good reason to do so. If the confession or admission of guilt or liability is obtained through coercion, the probability of its being false will be considered greater than its truth owing to the factor of duress. As it was given in the hopes of avoiding a greater (or more certain or immediate) evil, it cannot be considered as having been given freely. Therefore, the majority of *fuqahā'* have ruled that any admission of guilt or liability obtained under duress is invalid and legally inadmissible.

In the Qur'an, we read "... save he who is compelled, though his heart be content with faith (16:156)." Here, Allah has said that compulsion is grounds for canceling the sin of unbelief and the prescribed punishment for apostasy. Therefore, it may be considered grounds for canceling other matters. A hadith says that the Prophet said: "The responsibility for mistakes, forgetfulness, and duress has been lifted from my Ummah."[3] Abū Dāwūd related that:

> Goods were stolen from the Kalāʿī tribe, who accused certain weavers [of the crime]. When they brought the matter to Nuʿmān ibn Bashīr, the Prophet's Companion, he imprisoned the weavers for a few days and then let them go. The tribesmen went to Nuʿmān and said: "How could you let them go without beating them or otherwise subjecting them to tribulation?" Nuʿmān replied: "What did you want? Did you want me to harm them? If your goods appeared [after they had been forced to confess their whereabouts], that would have been that [and you would have your goods back]. Otherwise, I would have had to take [as much skin] off of your backs [in lashing them to get a confession] as much as I had taken from theirs." The tribesmen said: "So that is your ruling?" Nuʿmān said: "That is the ruling of Allah and His Messenger."[4]

ʿUmar said: "A man is not responsible for himself if he is starved, fettered, or beaten."[5] Shurayḥ said: "Confinement is duress, a threat is duress, prison is duress, and beating is duress."[6] Shaʿbī said: "[Subjecting people to] tribulation is a [blameworthy] innovation."

It should be clear from the foregoing that the scholars never considered the authorities' use of force against the accused to be justified by the Shariᶜah. On the contrary, such behavior was clearly prohibited by Allah, who had His Messenger say: "Verily, every part of a Muslim is sacred to a Muslim; his blood, his wealth, and his reputation."

It is related on the authority of ᶜUrāk ibn Mālik that he [ᶜUrāk] said:

> Two men from the Ghaffār tribe approached an oasis, fed by the waters of Madinah, at which members of the Ghaṭfān tribe were grazing their camels. When the Ghaṭfān tribesmen awoke the next morning, they discovered that two of their camels were missing and accused the two Ghaffārīs. When they took the two to the Prophet and told him what had happened, he detained one of them and said to the other: "Go and look." The man in custody was treated as a prisoner until his companion returned with the two camels. The Prophet said to one of them, or to the one he had kept with him: "Ask Allah to forgive me." So the Ghaffārī tribesman said: "May Allah forgive you, O Messenger of Allah." And then the Prophet said: "And you. And may He grant you martyrdom in His way." Later, at the Battle of Uḥud, the man died a martyr.[7]

It is related on the authority of ᶜAbd Allāh ibn Abū ᶜĀmir that he [ᶜAbd Allāh] said:

> I set out with some riders. When we arrived at Dhū al-Marwah, one of my garment bags was stolen. There was one man among us whom we thought suspicious. So my companions said to him: "Hey, you, give him back his bag." But the man answered: "I didn't take it." When I returned, I went to ᶜUmar ibn al-Khaṭṭāb and told him what had happened. He asked me how many we had been, so I told him [who had been there]. I also said to him: "O Amīr al-Mu'minīn, I wanted to bring the man back in chains." ᶜUmar replied: "You would bring him here in chains, and yet there was no witness? I will not recompense you for your loss, nor will I make inquiries about it." ᶜUmar became very upset. He never recompensed me nor did he make any inquiries.[8]

In the first example, the Prophet sought forgiveness from one he had detained on the basis of no more than an accusation. ᶜUmar considered the rights of one whose property had been stolen to be invalid, for the man told him that he wanted the accused arrested even though there was no evidence to indicate his guilt. As for the invalidity of something said under pressure, the majority of scholars have opined that a confession obtained under duress is similarly invalid and that nothing may legally result from it.[9]

Even so, certain scholars did consider a confession obtained under duress as valid if the accused was known for corruption and evil doing, such as theft and the like. They cited the hadith of Ibn ʿUmar, in which he reported that the Prophet fought the inhabitants of Khaybar until they were forced to take refuge in their fortress. Seeing that their land, crops, and orchards had fallen into Muslim hands, they signed a treaty that their lives would be spared and that they could take with them all that they could carry. All of their gold and silver, however, would be left to the Prophet. All of this was dependent on the condition that they hide nothing. If they ignored this understanding, they would have no treaty and no protection. Nonetheless, they hid some musk with the money and jewelry belonging to Ḥuyayy ibn Akhṭab, which he had brought with him when he was banished with the Naḍīr tribe. The Prophet asked Ḥuyayy's uncle: "What happened to the musk that your nephew brought with him from the Naḍīr?" He replied: "The wars and other expenses took it." The Prophet replied: "But he arrived very recently, and there was more money than that..." So the Prophet turned the man over to Zubayr, who subjected him to some punishment.[10] Ḥuyayy, in the meantime, was spotted hiding in the midst of some ruins. So they went there and searched, and found the musk hidden in the ruins.[11]

This hadith, however, concerns Jews in a state of war who had broken one agreement (by fighting) only to seek refuge in another one, which they also broke. How does this compare with inflicting pain on an innocent Muslim whose guilt has not been established?

Some later Ḥanafī scholars upheld the validity of a confession obtained under duress. Sarkhasī wrote, in his *Al-Mabsūṭ*: "Some of the later scholars from among our shaykhs gave fatwas upholding the validity of confessions obtained under duress in cases of theft, for the reason that thieves, in our times, do not willingly admit their crimes."

It is related that ʿIsām ibn Yūsuf, an associate of Abū Ḥanīfah's two companions,[12] was asked about a thief who denied (having committed a theft). ʿIsām replied: "Let him take an oath to that effect."[13] But the amir objected: "A thief and an oath? Get the whip!" Before ten lashes had been administered the man confessed, and the stolen goods were recovered. ʿIsām said: "Praise Allah! Never have I seen injustice appear so similar to justice than in this case."

In Bazāziyyah's collection of fatawas, the validity of confessions obtained under duress is also upheld. When Ḥasan ibn al-Ziyād was asked if it was permitted to beat a (suspected) thief until he/she confesses, he replied: "Unless the flesh is opened, the bone will never show through."[14]

Ibn ᶜĀbidīn wrote: "Beating one accused of theft is a matter of politics. So opined al-Zaylaᶜī. A *qāḍī* may do what is politic, as politics are not the exclusive domain of the imam."[15] Yet there is nothing to support the opinions offered by these scholars. It should suffice (by way of refutation) that a Ḥanafī, ᶜIsām ibn Yūsuf, described it as an injustice.

Moreover, none of these reasons refutes or even weakens the evidence gathered by the majority of jurists that it is illegal to obtain a confession through the use (or threat) of force. Their opinions would be valid only if there were contributing circumstances that clearly indicated the accused's guilt, that he/she had hidden the stolen item(s), and if the evidence stipulated (for prosecution as a *ḥadd* case) was not available. In such a case, a judge could use force to recover what had been stolen.

But even then, there is no evidence to support their opinion. In fact, Ḥanafī scholars agreed with the majority that a confession made under duress was always invalid, except in the case of theft. Even in cases of theft, they held that duress might be resorted to only in order to recover stolen goods. Otherwise, the *ḥadd* penalty of severing one's hand may not be carried out even when there is suspicion that force had been used.[16]

Ibn al-Qayyim, following the opinion of his shaykh, Ibn Taymiyyah, upheld the beating of those who were accused of theft if they already had a notorious record of evil deeds. But this was only done in order to recover the stolen goods. In his opinion, this admission under duress was not the reason for carrying out the *ḥadd* penalty, as the thief's possession of the stolen goods was sufficient reason to punish him. He wrote:

> If the accused is beaten in order to obtain his confession and he does confess, and then the stolen goods are found where he said they would be, his hand may be severed. The sentence will not be carried out as a *ḥadd* penalty on the basis of the confession obtained under duress, but because the stolen goods were found where he, in his confession, had indicated they would be.[17]

Ibn Ḥazm wrote:

> In a case, if there is no more [evidence] than a confession obtained under duress, then this will amount to nothing, for such a confession is condoned by nothing in the Qur'an, the Sunnah, or ijmaᶜ. Moreover, the sacredness of a person's flesh and blood is an established certainty. Thus, nothing of that may be made lawful save by virtue of a text or ijmaᶜ. If, however, in addition to the confession there is evidence that proves what the accused had confessed to, and that he had undoubtedly been the per-

petrator, it then becomes obligatory to carry out the *ḥadd* penalty against him.[18]

I do not suppose that Ibn al-Qayyim intended anything other than what Ibn Ḥazm intended when he mentioned conclusive evidence obtained by other means, so that the case may be decided by that rather than on the basis of the confession alone. As mentioned previously, the majority of jurists held that a confession obtained under duress was invalid. Moreover, they maintained this to be so even when circumstantial evidence indicated the contrary, as in the presence of the stolen goods in the accused's home, owing to the possibility that the goods may have been placed there by someone hoping to implicate the accused.[19]

Undoubtedly, the majority's opinion must be considered preponderant in terms of prohibiting duress and nullifying the legal effect of whatever is obtained under duress. This opinion is consistent with the teachings of the Qur'an and the Sunnah in relation to the need to uphold truth and justice. A confession obtained under duress cannot be considered truth, and punishment carried out because of it cannot be considered justice. Moreover, the only true deterrent to the dangers that threaten society is the guarantee that truth and justice will prevail. Therefore, duress must be considered a source of innumerable evils.

CONFESSIONS OBTAINED BY DECEIT

The use of deceit to obtain an admission of guilt from the accused was preferred by Ibn Ḥazm, who cited a hadith[20] in which the Prophet was reported to have used deceit to ensnare a Jew who had crushed the head of a girl with a stone. In that instance, the Prophet interrogated the man (after determining from the girl before she died that the man had attacked her) and continued to question him until he ultimately relented and admitted his guilt.[21]

Ibn Ḥazm likewise mentioned that the Companions used deceit to obtain admissions of guilt. As there is no coercion or torture involved, Ibn Ḥazm considered it a good method. Earlier, Mālik had opined that deceit was reprehensible, but Ibn Ḥazm disagreed and refuted his arguments. However, it is more likely that Mālik's position is closer to the principles of Islamic law, for deceit, after all, invalidates one's choice and the voluntary nature of the confession, even if it does not involve harm or the threat of harm to the accused. In fact, prohibiting duress owes less to the factor of harm than it does to the matter of free will, a matter upon which Islam is adamant.

THE ACCUSED'S FREE CONFESSION AND RIGHT TO RETRACT

In terms of the validity of the accused's retracting his/her confession, one's rights are of two varieties:

First: There are rights for which the retraction of a confession is valid. These are the *ḥudūd*, which are the rights of Allah and may be waived whenever doubts arise in relation to them. Thus if a person accused of a *ḥadd* crime retracts, there is the chance that the original confession was false and that the retraction is true. As *ḥadd* penalties must be waived whenever doubts arise, one who has confessed to adultery, for example, can have this punishment waived if he/she retracts his/her confession. All of the classical jurists agreed with this, with the exceptions of Ibn Abū Laylā, ʿUthmān al-Battī, Ibn Abū Thawr, and the Ahl al-Ẓāhir (the literalists).[22] Imām Mālik, however, is reported to have said that a retraction is acceptable only if it leads to doubt. Actually, there are two versions of Mālik's opinion on when a retraction does not lead to doubt. The best known version is that it will be accepted, while the lesser known is that it will not.[23]

This difference of legal opinion occurred in regard to the *ḥadd* penalties for theft and intoxication. The jurists generally agreed that a retraction may not be accepted in the case of false accusation (*qadhf*). They also differed on highway (armed) robbery. One opinion held that any retraction in such a crime may not be accepted, because the rights involved were those of people in need of protection, as in the case of false accusation (where the rights of the innocent are to be protected). The second opinion is that retraction should be accepted, just as a retraction in the case of adultery may be accepted.[24]

The evidence for accepting a retracted confession comes from the hadith in which Mūʿiz is prompted by the Prophet to retract his confession to adultery: "Maybe you simply kissed, or felt, or looked ..." Had retraction not been an option, the Prophet would not have prompted him in the manner reported. Retracting such a confession may be made by declaration, as in stating: "I retract my confession," or by indication, as when one flees from the place where the penalty is to be applied. Likewise, a retraction may be made before or after the judge rules.

Second: There are rights, financial or otherwise, for which retracting a confession is not valid. These are the rights of people. Clearly, the one confessing has no rights of disposal over another's property. However, since the confession has the effect of establishing such a right for someone else, it follows that its retraction invalidates someone else's right. For this reason, such a retraction, either by declaration or indication, may not be accepted.

THE ACCUSED'S RIGHT TO COMPENSATION FOR MISTAKES IN ADJUDICATION

Certain scholars hold the opinion that the Shariʿah allows compensation to the accused who is detained as a precaution, but whose innocence is later established. As proof, they cite ʿAlī's ruling for compensation (*ghurrah*) to be paid to the mother when miscarriage resulted from an official's mishandling of her case.

It was reported to ʿUmar ibn al-Khaṭṭāb that a woman whose husband was away had been entertaining male visitors. Finding this reprehensible, ʿUmar sent someone to question her. When she was told that ʿUmar had summoned her to explain her behavior, she exclaimed: "Woe unto me! What chance do I have with someone like ʿUmar!" On her way, she was overcome with fear and began to have pains. Unable to continue, she stopped at a house and immediately gave birth to a baby who, after delivery, screamed twice and died. ʿUmar sought the counsel of several Companions. They told him that he was not responsible for what had happened. Then he turned to ʿAlī, who had remained silent, and asked his opinion. ʿAlī replied: "If they have spoken on the basis of their opinions, then their opinions are mistaken. If they have spoken to please you, their advice will not benefit you. My opinion is that you are responsible and must pay blood money (*diyyah*). After all, you were the one who frightened her. If you had not frightened her so, she would not have given birth prematurely." So ʿUmar gave instructions to pay the money.[25]

The Ḥanbalī school says that the ruler must pay the blood money. If the mother dies for the same reason, the ruler also has to pay her blood money.[26] On this point, the Shāfiʿī jurists agreed with the Ḥanbalī, arguing that the child died through no sin of its own and pointing out that the ruler is responsible for blood money in case a pregnant woman miscarries as a result of a *ḥadd* punishment.[27]

Imposing a *ḥadd* punishment is the ruler's duty. If he is remiss in carrying out this duty, he will have sinned against Allah and His Prophet. As visits by strange men to the home of a woman whose husband is away is a questionable matter, the authorities should look into it so that it will not lead to any social evils. In the case described, it is possible that ʿAlī took the position he did because he felt the matter should have been dealt with in a different manner. For example, the woman could have been counseled in her home and in a non-threatening manner. So, perhaps what ʿAlī meant to say was that if a ruler needs to talk to someone, he should summon the individual in a polite and dignified manner, not harshly. Otherwise, a ruler's summoning the accused in an appropriate manner should never subject the ruler to such a responsibility, unless he oversteps his right and transgresses the rights of the accused.[28]

It should also be noted that the woman gave birth before she had been accused of anything and before knowing why ʿUmar had summoned her. Therefore, it is difficult to use her case as a precedent for saying that a ruler is responsible for paying blood money when an individual dies while in custody. Still, the Shariʿah's principles are certainly not averse to the government's doing a good turn for those who suffer as a result of its mistakes while it seeks to protect the rights of society and its subjects. This could take the form of an apology or material or juristic recompense. In fact, it is likely that these principles encourage such acts. The Prophet apologized to the Ghaffārī tribesman he had detained and then asked the tribesman to pray and ask Allah's forgiveness for him. When he did so, the Prophet immediately prayed for the man and asked Allah to grant him martyrdom. That was certainly more than a simple apology by the Prophet, and it indicates the correctness of the opinion that the accused should be recompensed for whatever suffering he/she undergoes due to an unproven accusation.

As regards the tyrannical and despotic procedures used by certain rulers who transgress rights and privileges granted to humanity by Allah, the entire Ummah agrees that they and their officials are responsible for both the harm they intend and that which they do not, and that they must be held accountable for it, just as anybody else would be. After all, the Prophet took himself to task.

Finally, the jurists were divided on whether payment for the ruler's mistakes or transgressions should be made from his personal funds, those of his family and neighbors (*ʿaqīlah*), or from public funds (*bayt al-māl*). Each option had its supporters.[29]

CONCLUSION

It was not my intention to enumerate each right of the accused in Islam, but rather to point to some of the more important ones. Otherwise, it would have been necessary to review all of the legal procedures, conditions, and etiquette designed to protect the accused's person and dignity. It shames us today to see that certain Muslim-majority states are not at all concerned with human dignity and rights, and that they willfully ignore the guarantees designed to protect those rights. Many of those associated with Islam in certain Muslim countries have become a curse on Islam and Muslims. Their tyranny serves only to distort the truth of Islam and the ways in which it upholds justice, as well as to turn the lives of their subjects into a living hell. If the rest of the world views Muslims as generally cruel and despotic, it is because of these rulers' barbarism and disregard for human decency. For these reasons, the world community is always ready to join with the enemies of Islam for whatever cause, simply because they believe that the Muslims must be the aggressors. After all, how can those who transgress the rights of their own citizens and violate their sanctity not be expected to be the aggressors against their enemies and opponents?

NOTES

1. Samīr al-Janzūrī, *Al-Majallah al-ᶜArabiyyah*, no. 7 (March 1978): 119.
2. Ibn Ḥazm, *Al-Muḥallā*, 11:141.
3. There are several versions of this hadith, some of which are authentic. For details, see my edition of al-Rāzī's *Al-Maḥṣūl* (Beirut: al-Risālah, 1992), 1:233.
4. Abū Dāwūd, *Sunan*, hadith no. 4382. The same was related by al-Nasā'ī, hadith no. 4878.
5. ᶜAbd al-Razzāq, *Al-Muṣannaf*, 10:193.
6. Ibid.
7. Ibid., 216.
8. Ibid.
9. See Ibn Qudāmah, *Al-Mughnī*, 15:12; Al-Bāhūtī, *Kashshāf al-Qinā*ᶜ, 6:454; Al-Baṭlayūsī, *Al-Insāf*, 12:133; Al-Shaharābādī, *Mughnī al-Muḥtāj*, 2:240; Al-Fayruzabādī, *Al-Muhadhdhab*, 2:362; Al-Kaysānī, *Badā'i*ᶜ *al-Ṣanā'i*ᶜ, 7:189; Al-Mīrghanānī, *Al-Hidāyah*, 3:275; Al-Sarkhasī, *Al-Mabsūṭ*, 9:184-85; Al-Dasūqī, *Hashiyat al-Dasūqī* ᶜ*alā al-Sharḥ al-Kabīr*, 3:348; Al-Kharāshī, *Al-Kharāshī*, 6:87; Ibn Ḥazm, *Al-Muḥallā*, 2:288; and Ibn al-Matūrīdī, *Al-Baḥr al-Zakhkhār*, 5:3.
10. For example, in order to force information or a confession. This part of the hadith, however, is mentioned in only one of the several versions related. See the following footnote.
11. This version was related by a sound chain of narrators in Bayhaqī's *Sunan al-Aḥkām*, 9:137. Abū Dāwūd related it (3006), but without mention of the uncle being turned over to Zubayr. This is how it was related by Ibn Ḥajr in his *Fatḥ al-Bārī*, 7:366-67. See also Ibn ᶜĀbidīn's *Ḥāshiyyah*, 3:270; and Ibn al-Qayyim's, *Al-Ṭuruq al-Ḥukmiyyah*, 7-8.

12. These were Abū Yūsuf and Muḥammad ibn al-Ḥasan al-Shaybānī, the two of his companions most responsible for ensuring the preservation and dissemination of his legal thought and opinions. Otherwise, it is well known that Abū Ḥanīfah was surrounded by companions who jointly participated in the process of ijtihad. See Zāhid al-Kawtharī. *Fiqh Ahl al-ʿIrāq wa Ḥadīthuhum.* [Trans.]
13. The general rule in cases involving a claim is that the case may be decided, if the claimant cannot produce evidence, by an oath taken by the party denying the claim. This accords with the juristic principle that "evidence is for those who affirm, and the oath for those who deny." This was not used often in cases involving a *ḥadd* punishment, such as theft, and explains why the *amīr* objected to the ruling. [Trans.]
14. See al-Rifāʿī, *Tanwīr al-Abṣār* and Ibn ʿĀbidīn's commentary on it, 3:270.
15. See Ibn ʿĀbidīn's *Ḥāshiyyah*, 3:259.
16. Ibid., 4:651. The general rule in regard to *ḥadd* penalties is that they may not be administered if there is the least doubt about the case. [Trans.]
17. See Ibn al-Qayyim, *Al-Ṭuruq al-Ḥukmiyyah*, 104.
18. Ibn Ḥazm, *Al-Muḥallā*, 11:142.
19. See al-Zarqānī, *Sharḥ al-Muwaṭṭā'*.
20. This hadith, related by Anas ibn Mālik, was included in the collections of Bukhārī, Muslim, Abū Dāwūd, Ibn Mājah, Imām Aḥmad, and others. [Trans.]
21. Ibn Ḥazm, *Al-Muḥallā*, 11:142.
22 See *Al-Ifṣāh*, 2:406; *Kashf al-Qināʿ*, 6:99; *Al-Qawānīn al-Fiqhiyyah*, 344, *Bidāyat al-Mujtahid*, 2:477; *Mughnī al-Muḥtāj*, 4:150; *Badā'iʿ al-Ṣanā'iʿ*, 7:61; and *Al-Mabsūt*, 9:94.
23. See Ibn Rushd, *Bidāyāt al-Mujtahid*, 2:477.
24. See al-Nawawī, *Al-Muhadhdhab*, 2:364.
25. This incident was narrated in the following works: ʿAbd al-Razzāq, *Al-Musannaf*, 9:454, 10:18; 11:18; Ibn Qudāmah, *Al-Mughnī*, 9:579; Ibn Ḥazm, *Al-Muḥallā*, 11:24; al-Nawawī, *Al-Muhadhdhab*, 2:192.
26. Ibn Qudāmah, *Al-Mughnī*, 9:579.
27. Of course, a pregnant woman is not to be given a *ḥadd* punishment until after she has given birth and weaned her child. However, if a mistake is made and she is punished, then the imam is responsible for whatever results. [Trans.]
28. The opinion of the Ẓāhirī jurists was that the ruler or his representative cannot be held responsible in such cases. See Ibn Ḥazm, *Al-Muḥallā*, 11:24-25. Both al-Māwardī and Abū Yaʿlā differed between *ḥadd* and *taʿzīr* punishments, holding the ruler responsible only when the latter led to the prisoner's death. See al-Māwardī, *Al-Aḥkām al-Sulṭāniyyah,* 238 and Abū Yaʿlā, *Al-Aḥkām,* 282.
29. See the sources listed at the end of the previous footnote.

Part IV:

Political Thought

Political Science in the Legacy of Classical Islamic Literature

In my own limited knowledge, I know of no specialized studies in our classical legacy that could be described today as political thought, or as treatises on political systems, international relations, systems of government, the history of diplomacy, political development, methods of political analysis, political theory, political planning, or any of the other categories currently studied as a part of contemporary knowledge.

Nonetheless, many of the issues raised in these subjects were treated in the classical legacy through the medium of fiqh (laws of Islam), which, in its long history, touched upon many of the subjects studied today in the social sciences. Likewise, many of the questions dealt with in political science were addressed by the early scholars of Islam within the framework of the classical fiqh *al-aḥkām al-sunniyyah* (the precepts of power). Perhaps Ibn Taymiyyah's *Al-Siyāsah al-Sharʿiyyah*, was one of the most distinctive efforts in this direction, as well as al-Khatīb al-Iskāfī's *Luṭf al-Tadbīr*, which also dealt with certain issues that remain relevant today. Similar to such works are *Sulūk al-Mālik fī Tadbīr al-Mamālik*, *Badāʾiʿ al-Silk*, and others.

These works show that the meaning of politics to the Muslim mind, and, as envisioned by Islam, involves making arrangements for humanity in accordance with the values prescribed by Allah, to realize His purposes in creation and to fulfill the trust of vicegerency, the duties of civilization, and the responsibility of the Ummah to act as a witness to humanity in its capacity as the "middlemost nation."

This article first appeared in the *American Journal of Islamic Social Sciences* 7, no. 1 (March 1990): 9–14, and was translated by Yusuf DeLorenzo. It has been slightly edited.

"Making arrangements" includes reading the past and learning its lessons, as well as interpreting, understanding, and analyzing the present in the light of those lessons. Other elements include planning for the future and benefiting from all scientific knowledge that clarifies the particularities of the present. In such an endeavor, a certain kind of penetrating, striving intellect is necessary. This particular kind of genius and ability is what the *fuqahā'* called *fiqh al-nafs* (inherent religious/legal acumen), an attribute of someone for whom understanding and analytical capacity have become second nature.

CHALLENGES FACING MUSLIM SCHOLARS

Significant challenges confront Muslim scholars of political science. Two fundamental issues often prevent the development of a comprehensive and objective view of matters. First, these scholars have an inherent difficulty in separating the political aspect from other scholarly aspects (e.g., the sources of Islam [the Qur'an and Sunnah], the source-methodology employed to interpret these texts, or the comprehensiveness of fiqh legislation). It is difficult, perhaps impossible, to place well-defined divisions among these aspects as is done today with the social sciences.

This point was made all the more obvious by the recent experiences of certain Islamic universities that have newly established departments of *al-siyāsah al-sharʿiyyah* (the science of Shariʿah-based principles and conduct of government). They have had a very difficult time presenting material on political science in the Islamic tradition in a methodical manner befitting the educational and academic purposes for which they were established. Indeed, such factors as the models of application from Islamic history, the variety of experience in terms of how closely (or otherwise) these models approximated the stated Islamic ideal, the traditional scholars' different positions vis-à-vis such models all give credence to the statement that Islamic culture and learning are bereft of a science of Islamic political thought.

Second, this intellectual void forced the imposition, by default, of the West's political perspective and experience as authoritative sources in the field of Islamic political science. Yet this political perspective is based on values that, when applied by Muslim scholars, actually impede their understanding of the Islamic political system. In addition, those values are unsuitable agents for change or development in an Islamic context. Among the most prominent values espoused by western thought, and those that obstruct an understanding of the proper Islamic perspective, are the following:

- Islam is a religion like any other, and therefore it should not differ in any significant way from the Christianity of the Middle Ages in Europe, in the sense that the church was duty-bound to stand in the way of progress. From this perspective, human development and progress only became possible after the split between church and state. After a long and bitter struggle, the West emerged triumphant over the church and all that it represented. Thus, it is inconceivable that a Westerner could imagine a link between knowledge and religion, to say nothing of accepting the concept of basing the humanities and social sciences on religion or giving them a religious perspective.
- Islam is a religion, and religion, which relies solely on revelation, relegates reason and empirical knowledge to marginal roles. Proponents of such a view consider it absurd to suggest that a social science could be based on religion, particularly a discipline like political science, which gives weight to human experience and empirical knowledge.
- The sources of religion, which are based on revelation, are thus subject to interpretation primarily by means of the language in which the religion was revealed. Therefore, determining its truths is said to depend entirely on that language.
- The sources of religion are historical, in the sense that they are linked with the events of a particular time. According to this view, the historicity of those sources stands between any serious academic work produced within the framework of that religion and, furthermore, negates any attempt at generalization.

These misconceptions demand that contemporary Muslim political scientists, today more than ever, mobilize all available resources to pursue the introduction of a revolution of thought in the Ummah and establish sound academic foundations for an Islamic science of Shariʿah-based principles and conduct of government. In this way, Muslims may regain their identity and be encouraged to work for the Ummah's regeneration as an influential international power capable of wresting the reins of leadership from the forces of evil and from self-assumed superiority on Earth.

STEPS ALONG THE WAY

Perhaps the proper beginning for those Muslim political scientists who are aware of the truths expressed above would be a comparative study of some of the topics listed below:

- *Tawḥīd*, the absolute Oneness of Allah (SWT) as Divine Entity and Lord (*Rabb*).
- The absolute sovereignty of Allah and exclusiveness of revelation (*waḥy*) as the source of legislation.
- Revelation and the universe as sources of knowledge.
- Reason, the senses, and experiment as means of attaining knowledge.
- Unity in the Ummah and the uniqueness in its character and meaning.
- The concept of vicegerency (*khilāfah*), the dignity of humanity and that which distinguishes humanity from the rest of creation.
- Affliction and its repulsion.
- The permanence of the source of values.
- The oneness of ultimate truth and reality.
- *Taskhīr*, in the sense of utilization rather than exploitation.

When we consider these principles, it is hard to perceive any real resemblance between them and those upon which other civilizations are based.

As a second step, these Muslim scholars should work on presenting a complete conception or design, based on the principles indicated above, of how Muslims may practice politics in the contemporary world; how politics are linked to Shariʿah obligations; and how present-day political practices and institutions may be considered Islamic, or at least capable of substantiating Islamic objectives; and in such areas as individual political expression, *shūrā*, and enjoining the good and prohibiting the evil. They must also answer the question of how to implement truly Islamic alternatives in current political configurations.

Islamic civilization produced various examples of polity that approximated, in some cases, the ideas of justice and good government and, in others, the worst forms of oppression, injustice, and tyranny. Certain scholars of fiqh were lenient in their acceptance of the latter circumstances, while others adopted positions of suitably steadfast opposition, struggled against the rulers' tyranny, and maintained the integrity of Islamic values and the lucidity of Islam's purpose. However, this history has not left us with an integral understanding of those questions considered to be of contemporary importance. Among these are the following:

> What is the true nature of *shūrā*? How is the principle to be expressed, and how may it be participated in? What sort of institutions need to be

> established in order to realize *shūrā*? How is the Ummah to be prepared to make use of *shūrā*? How are the circumstances of the Ummah's history to be analyzed in order that lessons may be drawn from it? What is to be the effect of fiqh on Islamic political thought, practice, and institutions? How is the Ummah to be involved practically in the political process? What are the means of bringing the Ummah to a state of political competence? What kind of institutions are needed for such an undertaking? What guarantees can contemporary scholars of political science glean from the teachings of Islam, which could be presented at a legislative and institutional level, about preventing a ruler from abusing his/her office and toying with the Ummah's rights? What guarantees and fundamental concepts can be presented to the non-Muslim minorities living in Islamic states? How can they participate in the politics and government of a clearly Muslim-majority state?

During the nineteenth century, several serious attempts were made to establish Islamic states within the traditional Muslim homeland. Yet, many of these failed because, among other reasons, Islamic political thought could not meet the contemporary Islamic state's fundamental conceptual needs. In addition, the Muslim thinkers of that time could not present a contemporary Islamic fiqh of government and politics that could serve as a base for establishing a sound and distinct Islamic policy.

Still, through the medium of various Islamic movements, Muslims, as a people, have exhibited their ability to spur the Ummah on to achieve its goals and to engender within it the spirit of jihad so that it is willing to make the greatest of sacrifices. There are many examples of this, but perhaps the most obvious are the jihad in Afghanistan and the intifada in Palestine. But in spite of this ability, the Muslim mind still cannot capitalize on these advances and put them to good use. The revolutions in the Islamic world are the best example of this phenomenon. Political scientists and scholars of fiqh, despite the differences in their disciplines, are clearly in the best position to suggest solutions to these problems.

The fiqh of politics and government, which is needed by the Ummah at present, must turn to the goals and purposes of Islam, its general principles, and its precepts. In this way, a complete system of political thought may be developed, one that can interact with contemporary realities in order to realize Islam's greater purposes. In this endeavor, all theories must be derived from the basis of accepted Shariʿah source-evidence, while drawing upon humanity's historical and contemporary experience.

The necessary source-evidence for contemporary Muslim scholars involved in this endeavor will, of course, begin with the Qur'an and the

Sunnah, ijma^c (consensus of the scholarly community), and *qiyās* (analogical reasoning). Beyond these four sources, there are other less known, but certainly valuable, sources of Islamic law: *maṣlaḥah mursalah* (the greater good), *istiṣḥāb* (assessment of circumstances), *barā'ah* (legal license), *ʿādah* (custom), *aʿrāf* (legal convention), *istiqrā'* (induction), *istidlāl* (deduction), *istiḥsān* (legal preference), *sad ad-dharā'iʿ* (obstruction of pretexts), and *akhdh bi al-akhaff* (acceptance of the least imposing).

Muslim scholars who study these additional methods will soon realize that there is a great scope and suitable benefit for exercising the intellect in establishing the fiqh of government and politics.

Missing Dimensions in Contemporary Islamic Movements

INTRODUCTION

This paper examines several dimensions that I believe are totally or partially absent from the thought or practice of many contemporary Islamic movements. However, I acknowledge that the majority of these movements are only extensions of those reform and independence movements that played a pioneering role in safeguarding the Ummah's identity and resisting colonial penetration and hegemony at the turn of the twentieth century. This paper seeks to remind them of some missing dimensions on the grounds that "remembrance does the believer a world of good" and that "wisdom is the quest of believers; wherever they find it, they should cherish it."

I fully realize the sharp distinction between the discourse characterizing the stage of liberation and safeguarding the Ummah's identity, and that of the post-colonial stage that, by necessity, must be distinguished by mature reconstruction. This implies that examining the missing or underemphasized dimensions in contemporary Muslim discourse requires considerable effort and meticulous attention and objectivity.

In this study, I will uncover these missing dimensions in the hope of contributing to the development and maturity of Islamic discourse. If I succeed, then praise be to Allah, the Bestower of merit in this life and the Hereafter. If I fail, my excuse is that humanity is prone to oversight and forgetfulness. I ask for His pardon if I forget or err, and ask Him to make us benefit from what He has taught us and to teach us what is beneficial. He is the All-Knowing, All- Responding.

Since Allah created Adam, taught him all concepts, and made him vicegerent on Earth, human history has been progressing toward the goal

---

This article originally appeared as number 9 in the IIIT's "Occasional Papers." It was translated by the IIIT Department of Translation in 1996.

ordained by the Creator. Meanwhile, people have fallen into two groups: those who perform their roles according to the divine teachings, and those whose roles emanate from their own (or their ancestors') conceptions and desires. The first group sees history as the product of a sanctified dialectic between Allah, humanity, and the universe, whereas the second group views it as the outcome of conflict between humanity and nature. As a result, they ignore, deny, or bypass the central place of Allah in His divine plan, or worship false deities to which they ascribe Allah-like roles. Islam endeavors to correct such people's basic assumptions, revamp their vision, help them find peace of mind, and provide them with the ultimate answers to their quintessential questions.

THE CONTEMPORARY ISLAMIC DISCOURSE: MISSING DIMENSIONS

Viewing Islam as the foundation for both thought and practice in all aspects of life is the Muslims' prime aim and driving force. Islam takes an abiding interest in human issues and humanity's destiny. Therefore, Allah has revealed a perfect text that answers the questions of existence, both as issues and courses of events and also at the level of humanity as vicegerent or the universe as home and instrument. In the final analysis, the Qur'an is the Word of Allah, the all-encompassing miraculous Book that He has described as a mercy to humanity:

> On the day We shall raise from all peoples a witness against them from among themselves. And We shall bring you [Muhammad] as a witness against these [your people]: and We have sent down to you a Book explaining all things, a guide, a mercy and glad tidings to Muslims. (16:89)

TESTIMONY AND RESPONSIBLE WITNESSING

After the Messenger fulfilled his mission, the task of responsible witnessing and testimony, as the Qur'an predicted, was passed on to the Ummah at large: "Thus have We made of you an Ummah justly balanced, that you might be witnesses over the nations ..." (2:143).

Through the Messenger's testimony and that of the justly balanced Ummah, whose collective effort is geared to doing good deeds and achieving universal harmony, Allah will make His purpose prevail: "He has sent His Messenger with guidance and the religion of truth that he may proclaim it over all religion, even though the pagans may detest [it]" (61:9).

Bearing witness is a responsible act, one that is both conceptual and actual. Thus, its need to be transmuted into the living world is paramount. Each application has its own economic, social, and intellectual components that, in turn, are based on a specific cultural order as well as on a specific order in terms of scientific and research methodology. The Qur'an contains and rectifies all methodologies, because it is by nature a perfect, divine text. It is equally equipped to engender and guide all cultural orders due to its message's universality. In addition, being Allah's final revelation to humanity, Islam can cope with humanity's cultural crises as well as the methodological problems inherent in branches of human knowledge. Thus, it can reconstruct their methods of reasoning and, eventually, solve these problems in the light of divine guidance and the religion of truth. Our responsibility in witnessing, then, is much greater than what we have envisioned or put into practice so far.

MISSING DIMENSIONS: A DISCOVERY PROCEDURE

Several important dimensions are absent from our perspectives and practices. These may be uncovered through a critical evaluation of our current practices and applications. For this, we need to weigh them against the objectives inherent in our active witnessing as a justly balanced Ummah. These objectives are laid down in the Qur'an:

> *Alif lām rā'*. A Book that We have revealed to you so that you might lead humanity out of the depths of darkness into light – by the leave of their Lord – to the Way of [Him] the Exalted in Power, worthy of all Praise. (14:1)

The purpose of such guidance is to lead us to the straight path of *tawḥīd*, which should enable us to rebuild ourselves and reconstitute our Ummah so that it might overcome the deficiencies of current methodologies, their human-made limitations, and atomistic introversions.

The new darkness of contemporary civilization is manifold, for it engulfs all processes, cultures, and sciences. Negative experiences accumulate, for the West as well as for others, and require people to acquire a general awareness of how to confront them. Otherwise, Muslims will be starting from where the West started and eventually end up in a similar confusion and stagnation:

> Like the depths of darkness in a vast deep ocean overwhelmed with billow topped by billow, topped by [dark] clouds: depths of darkness, one

> above another. If a man stretches out his hand, he can hardly see it. For any to whom Allah gives no light, there is no light. (24:40)

Against this compound darkness is the light to which Allah guides those who seek it:

> Allah is the Light of the heavens and Earth. The parable of His light is as if there were a niche and within it a lamp; the lamp enclosed in glass; the glass, as it were, a brilliant star lit from a blessed tree, an olive, neither of the East nor of the West, whose oil is well-nigh luminous, though fire scarce touched it, light upon light. Allah guides whom He wills to His light, sets forth parables for people, and knows all things. (24:35)

TOWARD A COMPREHENSIVE AWARENESS

The issue of reform and change is both complex and universal, a fact that calls for a comprehensive awareness to match the challenge. Due to its complexity, this comprehensive awareness must be methodological, one geared to examine all the "depths" of darkness, whether cultural or scientific, at both the level of theory and of application. Its goal must be to understand the characteristics of the flux and the agents that affect change and induce (or obviate) crisis. This exercise seeks to deal with those agents by using a comprehensive method, one unconstrained by reductionism or compartmentalization.

UNIVERSAL CRISIS, UNIVERSAL SOLUTION

The factors affecting the variables of the current state of affairs are not confined to the geographic locale of Muslim societies. In fact, the crisis' universal aspect emanates from the all-out interaction among nations and peoples in the wake of the contemporary information explosion. A proper understanding of these factors, which infiltrate our minds through our interaction with other cultural orders and methodologies of science, is an essential precondition for comprehending developments in our present state of affairs. These scientific methodologies and cultural orders have not only been transferred to us in the form of government systems and socioeconomic institutions, but have also contributed to shaping our worldview in the image of their paradigm.

Given this, every epistemological paradigm has the potential for taking over another one via an intellectual or institutional invasion, particularly when we are vulnerably located on the margin of an influential and central civilization that is universally dominant in terms of its civilizational and epistemological orders. If this situation continues unabated, the end-product will be total absorption into this dominant cultural and epistemological order.

THE TENDENCY TO COMPROMISE OR REJECT: ITS ORIGINS

As a result of the above, the tendency to align oneself with the victor (*al-ghālib*) – as the jurist, sociologist, and historian Ibn Khaldūn (d. 1406) states in *Al-Risālah*[1] – or to reject the victor out of hand has emerged. Aligning oneself with the victor starts with making concessions and compromises. One example of this is approximating western democracy to Islamic *shūrā* (mutual consultation), thus neglecting the major differences between these two cultural and epistemological paradigms. Democracy emanates from liberal individualism and rests on containing conflict; *shūrā* is based on communal unity and rejection of conflict altogether. Another example is approximating social justice to socialism, for this tends to ignore the fact that socialism is rooted in class conflict, while the Islamic doctrines of social justice are based on the principles of wealth distribution between the individual and the community in terms of zakah,[2] inheritance regulations, and the prohibition of hoarding wealth for its own sake. All in all, the present situation is an outcome of falling under the influence of a cultural and epistemological order that pervades our consciousness and practices in the name of universalism.

Those who opt for outright rejection of the other's dominance defend their rejectionism by contrasting the Islamic heritage with that of the victor. They go to great lengths to glorify that heritage and portray it as the be-all and end-all. This defensive self-glorification has blinded Muslims to the need to examine their history in a critical and analytical manner in order to explore its weak points. In fact, our current grasp of the Islamic legacy and, by extension, of the modern world cannot solve our contemporary crisis. This is attested to by the fact that Islamic culture has been severely marginalized and demeaned on the world scene today. I have discussed that phenomenon elsewhere.[3]

To recapitulate, the problem is rather complex and multifaceted, for it encompasses numerous epistemological issues and goes beyond the regional to the universal. Thus, the IIIT was established to research these complex and composite dimensions within an objective and universally valid framework of an interactive Islamic universalism. The institute does not preach Islam's basic principles to the world, important as that task is, but seeks to generate an Islamic methodology that can reconstruct the Muslim mind so that it may overcome its crises.

THE NEED FOR METHODOLOGY

The need for such a methodology is paramount. Its conspicuous absence from the Muslim and global scenes leaves both the humanities and the sciences vulnerable and accident-prone. Belief in Islam's basic tenets are deeply embedded in Muslim hearts, and principles of worship, transaction, and Shari[c]ah policies are likewise lucidly prescribed and articulated in various sources and references. If we just confine ourselves to the formalities of belief and practices, then there is no need for such institutions as the IIIT. Nevertheless, a concerted effort is needed to establish a new dimension (that of methodology) by means of which other missing dimensions can be uncovered.

THE ACQUISITION OF POWER: IS IT A SOLUTION?

Acquiring political power, on its own, neither solves the Ummah's problems nor provides a methodology for its reform. The quest for power in order to apply our legal heritage is futile, for it belies oversimplification and is a gross error of judgment. Had our problems started immediately in the wake of the West's encroachment and the caliphate's demise, then there would have been some justification (however tenuous) for viewing access to political power as a solution. But our crisis started well before then and under various Muslim regimes. The simultaneous Mongol invasion from the East and the Crusades from the West some seven centuries earlier, which were succeeded five centuries later by the Muslim expulsion from Spain, and – more recently – the pathetic outcome of such contemporary causes as the Palestinian and Afghan independence struggles, were nothing but tokens of an inner failing, one disguised by such august names as *khilāfah* and *salṭānah*.

Thus, acquring political power alone cannot be a prelude to reform. Rather, reform starts by addressing ourselves to the problems that caused our degeneration. In this sense, focusing on the treatment should prepare the ground for reform. However, we must remember that the roots of the crisis lie in our thought and practice, which have deviated from the true teachings of the Qur'an and the Sunnah – themselves often misconstrued by Muslims and non-Muslims alike.

Much ink has been used to explain why Muslims should rise, but little has been written on the causes of their deterioration and collapse. Most writers rarely go beyond saying that Muslims declined because they parted company with the law of Allah, and that, as stated by the Prophet: "The well-being of this Ummah in its latter days will be based on what brought its well-being in the beginning." This is true; but we need to know what caused the Ummah's well-being in the beginning and then apply it to the present. In other words, we need to know how to change that understanding into a viable methodology that can be applied to the present.

CONSTITUENTS OF WELL-BEING IN THE PAST

Several factors gave the Ummah its healthy integration and vitality in the past: a supreme sacred text, a final prophet, a tolerant Shariʿah, a universalist discourse, and an appeal to reason and one's *fiṭrah*.[4] Clearly, this did not materialize out of a vacuum, but was brought about by the Divine Will enacted in time and space. Allah, may He be praised, brought together in harmony hearts and souls that otherwise could not have been united:

> And [moreover] He has put affection between their hearts. If you had spent all that is in the Earth, you could not have produced that affection. But Allah has done it, for He is Exalted in Might, Wise. (8:63)

Allah made the message ultimate and final, for there would be no more prophets or human infallibility after Prophet Muhammad:

> Muhammad is not the father of any of your men, but [he is] the Messenger of Allah, and the seal of the prophets. Allah has full knowledge of all things. (33:40)

Moreover, Allah made the Qur'an the supreme authority and reference, which is so conclusive that no other is needed to supplement it:

> And unto you [O Prophet] have We vouchsafed this divine writ, setting forth the truth, confirming the truth of whatever there still remains of earlier revelations and determining what is true therein ... (5:48)[5]

In addition, Allah made the Shariʿah a law of tolerance and mercy in the context of which Muslims are enjoined to do what is just and refrain from what is evil:

> ... those who shall follow the [last] Apostle, the unlettered Prophet whom they shall find described in their Torah, and [later on] in the Gospel, [the Prophet] who will enjoin upon them what is right and forbid them what is wrong, make lawful to them the good things of life and forbid them the bad things, and lift from them their burdens and the shackles that were upon them [aforetime]. Those, therefore, who shall believe in him, honor him, succor him, and follow the light that has been bestowed from on high through him – they shall attain to a happy state. (7:157)[6]

Fallible human beings were to carry the message and endeavor to form bonds of mutual affection and dependence, rather than rely on His direct intervention to incline the hearts to one another. But Allah's grace was to continue, and the message would win over billions of hearts and minds across time and space:

> He has sent among the unlettered a messenger from among themselves, to rehearse to them His Signs, purify them, and instruct them in the Book and Wisdom, although they had been before in manifest error, along with others of them, who have not already joined them. He is Exalted in Might, Wise. (62:2-3)

WRONG ANALOGY

Those Islamic movements that measure themselves by past models and ignore time and distinctive features, and yet expect identical results, need to reassess and correct their perspective. In this way, a fair and proportionate amount of interaction with the past can be made, instead of vainly trying to resurrect it, body and soul.

THE UMMAH'S DECLINE: UNDERLYING CAUSES

The question, then, is how did the Ummah's great vigor and creativity end and how did a chasm appear between it and its divinely inspired role? This came about and sowed the seeds of later or further decline despite the presence of the *khilāfah* and the relative absence of outside pressure.

SECULARISM VS. REFORM

Secularists in the Muslim world maintain that the idea of transcendence should be excluded from human affairs. This is perhaps based on several false assumptions: the Qur'an has served its purpose and there is nothing further to be gained from it, the Sunnah has been totally consumed and can in no way benefit the development of modern jurisprudence, and the human effort on which Qur'anic and Sunnah studies rest can no longer expand or renew itself. This view has engendered a trinity directly opposed to the instruments of the divine plan, thus resulting in further weakness and decline.

The secularist trinity can be contrasted with the several constituents of the Ummah's early well-being. First, in contradistinction to the concept of "united hearts and souls," pre-Islamic fragmentation has reasserted itself in such forms as tribalism, regionalism, territorialism, racism, sectarianism, and denominationalism. As a result, Muslims have multiplied into mutually opposing sects and movements, even to the point of trading charges of treason and claiming that their party is the sole custodian of truth and salvation. Such Muslims have not heeded the Qur'anic warning:

> And do not be like a weaver who breaks into untwisted strands the yarn that she has spun after it has become strong, using your oaths to deceive one another, lest one party should be more numerous than another. For Allah will test you by this, and on the Day of Judgment He will certainly make clear to You [the truth of] that wherein you disagree. (16:92)

In other words, Muslims have retreated from Islam's universality and the need for unity, and have fallen to the level of warring tribes.

Second, despite the Qur'an's authority and the irrefutable authority of the Sunnah within the revelation's comprehensive context, Muslims have approached the Qur'anic verses and hadiths in a highly selective manner. They have emphasized what they wanted to emphasize and have ignored what they imagined should be ignored for the benefit of some narrow, ephemeral interests on which they conferred legitimacy. In other words, they approached the Qur'an in the same way as some long-ago Israelites approached the Torah: "... and which you treat as [mere] leaves of paper, making a show of them the while you conceal [so] much" (6:91).[7]

In consequence, Muslims have lost sight of the Qur'an's comprehensive totality and its methodology, thereby losing the opportunity to relate to reality and control the inevitable changes in time and circumstances as the Qur'an expects us to do. Rather, Muslims have made circumstance dictate to the Qur'an and the Sunnah, and, by selection, have justified their deviation. Instead of improving the condition or situation by referring to the divine message's totality, they have accommodated it to the situation in question and have justified that circumstance by recourse to the divine text. This undertaking, however, contravenes the natural postulate that a divine text projected onto reality is not meant to justify it, but rather to change, improve, and eventually reform it. The current practice of making circumstance the master of the sacred text is obviously wrong.

The interaction of these negative factors caused the Muslims to virtually dismantle the order of their belief and civilization. They have so misused the divine text that they have lost sight of the purpose of witnessing to humanity, a task with which Allah has entrusted them. In fact, they have lost touch with the Almighty Himself, may He be praised and exalted above all else. Would He bring them together, hearts and souls, as He did in the beginning, even though they have cut themselves off and severed their links with the requirements of religious and cultural witnessing?

Muslims must fully realize their responsibilities toward Islam and humanity. With this must come a commitment to witness based on the supremacy of the divine text in its entirety, its relation to reality, and its totality. But what does that mean and how can it be actualized? What is needed is "human action": to make "conscious" contact with the "divine action" that initiated the divine plan and brought humanity from darkness to light through the Revelation and the practice of the Prophet and the early Muslims. But is it enough to retrieve the fruits of ijtihad (endeavor in legislation and other matters) as practiced in early years of Islam and apply them now? Or, is there a qualitatively different situation that requires further ijtihad? How can we create the appropriate milieu for this latter ijtihad? To what extent does the new (and changing) state of affairs breed new difficulties in actual practice? What problems, if any, cannot be resolved merely by *qiyās* (analogical reasoning)? Such problems would inevitably require a fresh recourse to the totality of the Divine revelation in the Qur'an and the Sunnah.

A further question arises: To what extent can we respond, through revelation, to new problems never posed before? This matter requires contemplating the idea of the relative and the variable in the Qur'anic sense, with the Qur'an being the perennial light applicable to every time and place and presiding over social and historical change.

All of the above questions could be irrelevant if the changes taking place in the modern world were quantitative rather than qualitative, namely, changes in degree rather than substance, for the latter would require a quantitative change in research methods as well as in the criteria governing induction and deduction and the study of human and natural phenomena.

Those who claim that the changes in the real world are quantitative in essence adopt a static view, one that is oblivious to and unperturbed by changes in time or place. Their intellectual activity never ventures beyond analogical reasoning, for they continue to apply the traditional problem-solving methods to modern problems and resort to ancient rules governing induction and deduction. Their scope of research does not reach beyond the specific phenomenon being examined, which is cut off from a more complex reality, and which is commented upon by a principle lopped off from the great expanses of the Qur'an and the Sunnah.

This approach is at odds with the method of examining the real world in its objective totality, as well as with the Qur'an in its comprehensiveness and the Sunnah in terms of its methodological guidelines.

TOWARD A COMPREHENSIVE VIEW OF THE REVELATION AND THE WORLD

On what grounds does this comprehensive and dynamic view stand? Ibn Khaldūn explained civilization's foundations in terms of environmental factors and within the framework of a society based on agriculture and handicrafts (i.e., the society of natural economy). His method relied on inductive reasoning, and his metaphors were of growth and decline (viz., birth, maturity, and old age).

Contemporary western studies have brought home to us an understanding of the foundations of industrial civilization, one in which humanity has gone beyond the stage of "natural civilization," controlling natural phenomena by discovering their properties and laws of interaction to such an extent that physical labor has been replaced by, successively, steam, oil, nuclear, and solar power, and has gone on to exercise technological control over soundwave frequencies and image dissemination. As a result, our position in the production process has shifted from handicraft to cerebral and technological expertise.

This quantitative and qualitative change in the nature of human civilization has resulted in new concepts in human thought and social relationships. These have come about in a way radically different from what existed earlier. As a result, humanity's view of itself, as well as people's relationship with the natural universe, human society, and the system of values and ethics that existed during earlier phases of human development, have undergone major changes.

NEW LOGIC

A new logic shaped by technology is taking over the world, not because the world has moved on to a very high technological level, but because certain dominant and highly visible centers of culture, armed with advanced scientific research methodologies, have overwhelmed the world's cultural and epistemological orders and gained control of minds and perceptions *en masse*.

The most significant change to date is that cognitive processes are no longer confined to mental hypotheses, sense-based observation, intuition, or surface experience. In fact, all of these have been subjected to systematic doubt and scientific reasoning, which found their way into the natural sciences and then into the human and social sciences. Science has even surpassed empirical thought, transforming it into "illogical empiricism" in place of "mental empiricism," and thus subjecting us to rarefied laws of logic as a substitute for rational thinking.

Some confusion has arisen with regard to distinguishing between the development of human societies in the material sense and their qualitative changes in the historical sense. Our concern here is with the latter. This view was embedded in the writings of both Ibn Baṭṭūṭah (d. 777) and Ibn Khaldūn. The former started by linking natural phenomena to social phenomena, while the latter merged both in the context of birth, maturity, and old age in his early attempts to establish a philosophy of history and civilization.

The foregoing underscores the need for a dynamic, rather than a static, understanding of human societies. The word *statis* connotes stagnation and unchangeable constants, while *dynamism* suggests perpetual movement. Ibn Khaldūn ranked these two concepts (the constant and the variable) as equal in his perception of civilization's three historical stages.

The variable, whether human or natural, cannot be conceived without understanding its actualization's specific laws, which reformulated the natural and human sciences and then synthesized them into an overall methodological bond that threads all sciences together. This is exactly where science as a whole converges and runs in tandem with the structure of the universe as a whole. These two wholes, in turn, run in concert with the wholeness of the revelation, as embodied in the Qur'an, the Absolute Book that oversees the universe's existence and movement through all time.

METHODOLOGICAL UNDERSTANDING AND THE COMBINED READING OF THE QUR'AN AND THE UNIVERSE

Using the Qur'an to reflect on reality and improve it requires a comprehensive understanding of the Qur'an and the real world. IIIT was established to undertake such a methodological inquiry. This holistic and disciplined inquiry is most alarmingly absent from the thought and practice of contemporary Muslim movements, which seem resigned to a static view of the universe and a fragmentary treatment of the Qur'anic text.

A holistic reading of the Qur'an corresponds to a holistic reading of the universe. Dispersed throughout the universe are wondrous signs, the comprehensive system and organic unity of which can be discovered by the human mind. By the same token, there are miraculous signs and *āyāt* (verses) in the Qur'an, whose comprehensive system, methodology, and organic unity are there to be discovered. This perhaps explains why the Prophet was inspired to arrange the chapters and verses not in terms of chronology, but in accordance with a subtle methodology decreed by the Almighty:

> When We substitute one verse for another – and Allah knows best what He reveals [in stages] – they say you are but a forger. But most of them are lacking in knowledge. Say the Holy Spirit has brought the Revelation from your Lord in truth in order to strengthen those who believe, and as a guide and glad tidings to Muslims. (16:101-2)

The "strengthening" is only a circumstantial event geared to resolving a tense situation. This is further explained by the fact that the circumstances for a particular revelation, sign, or verse (*āyah*) are not prerequisites for that particular verse. In the Qur'anic context, "glad tidings" can only be futuristic. Therefore, the Qur'an has been arranged in a specific sequence so that it can assume its comprehensive methodological unity and thus facilitate bearing witness to the human mind's development. Discerning that methodology in a comprehensive manner requires an examination of the "signs" within the overall pattern of their movement, whether in the form of the Qur'an's miraculous signs or revelations or of nature's miraculous signs:

> And [of Our sway over all that exists] they have a sign in the night: We withdraw from it the [light of] day, and they are in darkness. And [they have a sign in] the Sun: it runs in an orbit of its own – [and] that is laid down by the will of the Almighty, the All-Knowing; and [in] the Moon, for which We have determined phases [that it must traverse] until it becomes like an old date-stalk, dried-up and curved. The Sun cannot overtake the Moon, nor can the night usurp the day, since all of them float through space [in accordance with Our laws]. (36:37-40)[8]

The Overseer controls all phenomena, from the infinitesimally small atoms and subatomic particles to the infinitely large galaxies and the universe. This is where we begin to reestablish our methodological engagement with the Qur'an, which is absolute in its methodological unity. This can be achieved by examining how the Revelation handles, through its numerically limited verses, the universe's unlimited reaches and innumerable aspects, and how it handles the relative through the absolute:

> That which We have revealed to you of the Book is the truth, confirming what was [revealed] before it, for Allah is assuredly, with respect to His servants, well acquainted and fully observant. Then We gave the Book for inheritance to such of our servants as We have chosen. But some among them wrong their own souls, some follow a middle course, and some, by Allah's leave, are foremost in good deeds. That is the highest Grace. (35:31-32)

Are we not people – all of us – who either wrong our own souls, follow a middle course, or, by supplication to Allah endeavor, as fallible human beings, to exert our utmost in the way of good?

To start our reading of the Qur'an and the Sunnah on the basis of that holistic vision, in 1982 we chose the Islamization of Knowledge as a means toward that goal. We assumed the need for Islamizing the methodologies of the natural and human sciences through the Qur'an in order to make them the key to understanding the sacred text. In effect, this was a twofold and reciprocal process: The Qur'an was to rectify the prevailing methodologies of knowledge, and the rectified methodologies of knowledge were to provide a means of delving deeper into and engendering a better understanding of the universe of the Qur'an. In fact, this logic underlay our call to combine the two readings, the divine text and the matured universe (both of which require human intellect), as the first revealed verses urge:

> Proclaim [read] in the name of your Lord and Cherisher, Who created – created humanity out of a leach-like clot. Proclaim. And your Lord is Most Bountiful, He Who taught [the use of] the pen, taught humanity that which it knew not. (96:1-5)

Through this combined reading, which brings together the miraculous signs of the Revelation and nature, we discover the dimensions of interaction that must reject any static thought that ignores the laws of the universe and the logic of change:

> You [Allah] cause the night to gain on the day, and the day to gain on the night. You bring the living out of the dead, and the dead out of the living. And You give sustenance to whom You please, without measure. (3:27)

By combining both readings and emphasizing interaction and formation, as well as the historical logic of change, we may become better equipped to deal with the Qur'an according to a clear methodology, one that should enable us to overcome such impasses as those found in Ibn Rushd's (d. 1198) *Faṣl al-Maqāl fī mā bayn al-Ḥikmah wa al-Sharīʿah min al-Ittiṣāl* or al-Ghazālī's (d. 1111) *Tahāfut al-Falāsifah*, which induced Ibn Rushd to retort with *Tahāfut al-Tahāfut*. Such tensions also drove ʿUthmān ibn ʿAbd al-Raḥmān Abū ʿAmr ibn al-Ṣalāḥ (d. 1246) to prescribe logic as an "unlawful" activity, and Ibn Taymiyyah (d. 1328) to try to reconcile a measure of logic to another from the Qur'an in order to avert the contradiction between tradition and reason. Instead, the Qur'an's totality should be addressed without recourse to any discipline or approach that relies on selectivity in its treatment of the sacred text.

What is required is not "striving by reaction," but striving by a positive intellectual endeavor that is guided by the Qur'an's epistemological methodology. All contemporary crises of the methodologies of the sciences (whether of scientific dialectics or positivistic logic) based on relativity and probability, when added to the crises of international cultural orders and their inherent conflicts, boil down to one fundamental crisis: the deconstructivist approach of the methodologies of sciences and cultural orders that can no longer undertake the kind of reconstruction informed by the cosmic laws elucidated so wonderfully by the Revelation.

As a result of this double failure (reduction with no reconstruction) on both the scientific and cultural planes, hedonistic individualism has been reinforced. In reality, this is no more than a reversion to the primitive times, when people, heedless of the divine laws of mercy, fairness, and responsible trusteeship, killed and pillaged at will.

Within the context of the Islamization of Knowledge, we do not propose to initiate any new sciences or cultural orders; rather, we propose to reformulate the sciences and reorient cultural orders within a specific methodology. In other words, we seek to inspire the natural sciences, which are presently atomistic and deconstructive, to take a universal and reconstructive direction, one that relates natural and human phenomena to their global ambit and ultimately divine origin. Thus, findings derived from the methodologies, tools, and instruments of limited, situational research may be augmented by spiritual considerations, whose impact on both the psyche and the body cannot be ignored. Nature itself interacts and manifests its Allah-given wonders between two poles, infinitely great and infinitesimally small:

> Those who dispute about the Signs of Allah without any authority bestowed on them, there is nothing in their hearts but arrogance, which

> they shall never attain to. Seek refuge in Allah, Who hears and sees all things. Surely the creation of the heavens and Earth is greater than the creation of humanity. Yet most people do not know. (40:56-57)

At the scientific level of application, the Islamization of Knowledge removes researchers from the atomistic examination of the natural or human phenomena and enables them to examine the universe wherein these phenomena were formed. Current scientific theories are reluctant to examine phenomena within a larger purposeful context, for they do not realize the dialectic of the infinite regenerative cycle of creation, its interactions and fulfillment: bringing the living out of the dead and the dead out of the living, and manifesting the miracle of infinite variety from the simplest elements.

The Islamization of Knowledge is the solution for the modern sciences' current impasses, for it will enable science to generate a new, cosmic understanding of the philosophy of the natural sciences, an understanding that is closely connected with *tawḥīd*, where the meaning of the following *āyah* is made clear: "Those who are truly aware of Allah's Presence and Might are those who have knowledge" (35:28).

In this sense, the Islamization of Knowledge is not only confined to natural phenomena that derive their signs from the Qur'an, but extend the scope of research to cover those human phenomena that interact with their natural correlates. Since contemporary science avoids research in this universal and cosmic framework or these complex phenomena, scholars of the Islamization of Knowledge must do so not from a spirit of defiance or a desire to avert the contradiction between the traditionalists and rationalists, but to seek the truth, in all of its complexity and infinitude, guided by the Qur'an's holistic methodology in an age of inadequate methodologies. This is particularly pertinent and urgent in view of the epoch in which we live and whose means of communication and exchange of information – however disproportionate – are instantaneous and global.

IMPASSES OF CONTEMPORARY MUSLIM ACTION

Having identified what is required, we now consider our problems in a rapidly changing world and how to solve them.

These problems crystallized immediately after the early centuries of the hijrah,[9] around the beginning of the tenth century CE. However, this general estimate does not exclude the occurrence of problems shortly after the

Prophet's death, problems centered around such issues as succession, the nature of the political system, documentation, and why the various schools of fiqh (Islamic jurisprudence) and sects emerged.

If we draw a detailed diagram of the types of problems Muslim reformers confronted, it becomes clear that they were all issues that struck at the roots of our thought, whether jurisprudential, historical, political, social, philosophical, economic, or even linguistic. Our cultural atrophy, to quote Ibn Khaldūn, did not ensue from one single source; rather, it was the result of a multi-dimensional failure that entailed multi-dimensional problems.

COLLECTIVE IJTIHAD AND COLLECTIVE ACTION

Over the centuries, some reformers have tackled problems related to Qur'anic interpretation (*tafsīr*). They have weeded out Biblical fabrications, legends, and myths. Some focused of political tyranny, while others dealt with the nature of government and political order.

However, scholars whose research and intellectual endeavors should contribute to reforming the structure of Islamic thought have not yet sought to reform its methodology. Among these scholars are linguists, sociologists, historians, and researchers into the epistemological impasses of the methodology of contemporary science. Thus, a linguist who penetrates to a certain text's semantic heart and reviews its interpretation and use within one or more historical contexts, a researcher who examines the cultures of agrarian societies, a historian or archaeologist who studies the experiences of past civilizations, may all, in unison, enrich collective ijtihad. In this light, we remember the important contributions of Ibn Baṭṭūṭah and Ibn Khaldūn to ijtihad.

This supports our call for collective ijtihad. Of course, this does not imply that each researcher's individuality and unique skills have to be sacrificed, for each will achieve that which he/she strives. Rather, this concept envisages the integration of all branches of knowledge within a comprehensive framework so that the new "endeavor" can deal more equitably with human and natural phenomena.

By the very nature of its comprehensive logic, this methodology presupposes variety and a successful integration of its research inputs so that it can diagnose objective reality as it exists, and further understand the text's import as well as reanimate the relevant tradition in a critical and scientific manner – one that could articulate the sacred text from within. In this way, IIIT hopes to harness various scientific initiatives so that they may yield a collective harvest responding to all problems of life and further the Islamization of Knowledge in such fields as psychology, economics, sociology, and the natural sciences. We noted earlier that the possibility of mutual interaction between the Islamization of the sciences (on the basis of the Qur'an and the Sunnah) and the rechannelling of these sciences, once Islamized, into an interpretive reading of the Qur'an and the Sunnah already exists. In this manner, the sciences should derive solutions to their problems from the Revelation, and those scholars dealing with the Islamic text can perceive it better in terms of the epistemological dimensions (of the sciences) and scientific observations.

Reforming methods of thought, as a prelude to rectifying practices, is not necessarily confined to researching the grounds on which earlier scholars approached the Qur'an and Sunnah or of studying the then-prevalent rules of ijtihad, for these rules have changed immensely due to the development of epistemological methodologies and research instruments, including research relevant to human cognition. Indeed, some researchers perceive things in their multiplicity, polarity, or unity. In the same vein, some scholars deal with such things by using descriptive interpretation, while others employ epistemological analysis.

Collective ijtihad, which can embrace all constituents of actual life and methods of epistemology, should spare us the delusion of possible reform through exclusively or predominantly political or economic efforts within a highly complex actuality.

To be candid, our experiences at IIIT, over a period of approximately ten years of collaborative work on the intellectual plane, have revealed the depth and breadth of the Ummah's crisis and have convinced us of the dire need for collective ijtihad. With such experience on the purely intellectual level, one can only wonder about the magnitude and intensity of the effort needed to change the status quo on a political, intellectual, and socioeconomic scale and within a complex and ever-changing regional and international context.

GOING IT ALONE: THE PITFALL OF EXCLUSIVENESS

The concept of an exclusive or one-dimensional organization, be it political or intellectual, has wreaked untold damage on the Ummah. It has erroneously led such organizations to believe that they embody the Ummah's will and consciousness, a mistaken concept that does not realize the depth and ramifications of its implications. Such organizations cannot function as substitutes for the Ummah's collective endeavor. Rather, they will become mere factions on a long list of past and present adversarial groups.

Allah warns us of the dangers of narrow-minded pretension to exclusiveness both at the individual and social levels. Accordingly, He commands us to form the Ummah that enjoins what is right and forbids what is wrong. This command harmonizes with two other exhortations to Ummah-wide unity and collective thought and action. There are, however, certain conditioning factors mentioned in the Qur'an:

> Let there arise out of you an Ummah inviting to all that is good, enjoining what is right and forbidding what is wrong. They are the ones to attain felicity. (3:104)

The first guideline stipulates:

> Hold fast, all together, to the bond of Allah, and do not draw apart from one another. Remember the blessings that Allah has bestowed upon you: how, when you were enemies, He brought your hearts together so that through His blessing you became brethren; and [how, when] you were on the brink of a fiery abyss, He saved you from it. In this way, Allah makes clear His messages unto you so that you might find guidance. (3:103)[10]

The second guideline follows:

> Do not be like those who are divided among themselves and fall into disputations after receiving clear signs. For them is a dreadful chastisement. (3:105)

The claim to sole representation of the entire Ummah is not sanctioned by the Qur'an and the Sunnah. In fact, both sources caution against such tendencies on account of their divisive nature. "Good intentions" must not be invoked as an excuse for such tendencies. Rather, let all good intentions operate within the framework of constructive interaction with the Ummah. Enriching and complementing this collective effort, while giving due respect to other groups, should be a common policy and objective. This agrees with the divine exhortations to unity and mutual love. Significantly, the group addressed in these verses is not a faction, but one described as an Ummah, a whole nation, or one that bears in its conscience the universal Ummah's aspirations and concerns and is working to fulfill them. The term *Ummah* itself alludes to *umm* (mother), from which it is derived, and thus hints at the ideal mother-child relationship as well as the relationship between the children themselves. The members of such an Ummah should seek to reform it through collective and concerted action.

The Qur'an treats factionalism and division as serious moral and social evils, the consequences of which pollute the human psyche and the body politic. Partisanship, fanaticism, hypocrisy, and unfairness are among the many ensuing ills. Hence, the path leading to such pitfalls is clearly marked off and condemned as incompatible with the Islamic message. But those who persist, even with a "good intention," in endorsing or legitimizing factionalism are accomplices – however unwittingly at times – to a colossal act of mischief:

> There is the type of man whose speech about this world's life may dazzle you, and he calls Allah to witness about what is in his heart. Yet is he the most contentious of enemies. When he turns his back, his aim everywhere is to spread mischief throughout the land and destroy crops and progeny. But Allah does not love mischief. When it is said to him: "Fear Allah," he is led by arrogance to more crime ... O you who believe, enter Islam [the creed of peace] wholeheartedly and do not follow Satan's footsteps, for he is your avowed enemy. (2:204-8)

Discovering and then implementing the formula for collective action should be the quest of Muslims, for it will enable them to enter Islam wholeheartedly, as Allah commands. A coherent and viable Ummah, one that addresses itself energetically and intelligently to internal and external challenges, should be the outcome of such a collective effort.

The complex crises facing Muslims require complex and collective solutions. Human sciences have become so finely specialized that their methodologies and research instruments penetrate all social and human phenomena. This is in marked contrast to the time when an encyclopedic scholar could possess all the knowledge of medicine, astronomy, mathematics, and philosophy of his/her time.

At that time, such scholars were often accepted as the supreme authority on the knowledge they had acquired. Nowadays, however, the sources of knowledge have ramified and become complementary to each other, resulting in the unquestionable need for collective effort. Moreover, cultural orders have become closely connected with scientific disciplines, thus giving a global dimension to issues and alternatives that effectively places them outside the grasp of any single entity. Given these facts, we emphasize collective action without, of course, neglecting distinctive features and abilities. However, the tendency to go it alone in organization and action, albeit with "good intentions," remains a very serious threat to our collective aspirations.

THE GENESIS OF EXCLUSIVE THOUGHT

Exclusive thought sets out in the mistaken belief that it alone has been called upon to reform the current state of affairs. This simplistic notion carries deep within it the delusion of possessing the whole truth. In most cases, this is due to ignorance of the complexities of reality as well as of the nature of truth itself. This mistaken belief results in oversimplifying the proposed reform program for the benefit of potential recruits, in the hope that a more mature engagement with the more substantive issues can be deferred to a nebulous point in the distant future.

This results in "organization" preceding thought itself, and in rigorous intellectual and educational endeavor being replaced by superficial and simplistic "dictation" or rote learning. The major issues are subsumed by formal "programs" that focus on mere slogans. By necessity, this entails accessing readily available ideas from existing and commonplace sources, as well as developing a spirit of abject compliance and imitation, all of which contravene Allah's command:

> Do not pursue that of which you have no knowledge, for every act of hearing, seeing, or (feeling in) the heart will be inquired into (on the Day of Judgment). (17:36)

It follows that both the propensity for methodological criticism and the potential for creativity disappear, while blind imitation becomes institutionalized; that the movement's elements dissolve into a quantitative whole; and that thought and reflection are replaced by a preposterous concept: Leadership, which now occupies the pinnacle of the hierarchy, is infallible. This not only leaves the door wide open to fanaticism, but also perverts the person, both as a leader and a follower.

Such an organization, asserting that it alone possesses knowledge and legitimacy, alienates all members of the Ummah and accuses them of apostasy and ignorance. It starts with the wrong premise of introducing Islam to the world anew, ignoring all history and precedence. The lapse of fourteen centuries and the practices of many generations of Muslims cannot be encapsulated in one group, party, or organization. To claim otherwise is an act of intellectual violence that precipitates and justifies actual violence.

The majority of Muslims, no matter how pronounced their deviations or weakness, live and practice Islam, even if they only meet the minimum requirements. No faction or individual can claim sole representation of the Ummah or a monopoly of truth. Nor is there any justification for resorting to violence, whether by opposition groups or governments. When all is said and done, Allah never assigned power over the Ummah to one person or faction. It is, therefore, most salubrious that some wise and responsible Islamic movements reject violence. However, other movements claiming to possess the truth instill in their young and impressionable followers the legitimacy of violence when dealing with other members of the Ummah. Even established members of such movements are prone to banishment if they disagree with the leadership's dictates. This leads to the absence of diversification or a free exchange of views – an intellectual straitjacket.

In short, Islam is based on the unimpeachable authority of a perfect Islamic text, a universal discourse, and a tolerant and merciful Shariʿah. The true realization of such a composite reality requires a collective awareness and will. Contemporary Muslims, all of whom are in the grip of an awesome and complex crisis, need to focus their efforts, which by nature must also be composite, on the task at hand. There is no room for narrow partisanship or exclusive formulations.

SUMMARY

To sum up, our scholars need to consider some of the Ummah's basic characteristics when surveying those dimensions that are missing from the perspectives of current Islamic movements. These characteristics can be encapsulated as follows: the Qur'an, which is divine in origin and supreme in authority; belief in Muhammad as the seal of all prophets; a universal discourse; a versatile and tolerant Shariʿah; and a combined reading of both the Revelation and the universe. These five characteristics make it incumbent on the Ummah to develop a collective will that is aware of the requirements related to each characteristic and of the means to project all of them onto the Islamic movement, as well as, more generally, onto human effort and reality.

The distinctive features, both present and missing, of existing Islamic movements, can be summarized as follows:

- Islamic movements have become tainted with a partisan mentality and are now at odds with the Ummah's higher interests. Since they cannot carry out any form of collective work, they have become easy targets for those seeking to isolate or destroy them.

- Some of these movements have confused the sacred texts with human interpretations and jurisprudence derived from ijtihad based on these texts.
- This confusion of the divine and the human has resulted in some of these movements claiming that only they have the truth, thus conferring on their own human thought and ijtihad the sanctity of fundamental texts. In addition, they have expropriated the Ummah's historical achievements and taken credit for them by claiming that they are the only extension or embodiment of that historical reality.
- Some movements mistakenly believe that they can do without intellectual effort or ijtihad as long as they have the Qur'an and the Sunnah. Thus, they fail to link the Islamic text with the real world and lose the ability to actualize the faith. Some of them launch themselves as fully fledged "organizations" well before determining or reforming the world of their thoughts. As a result, they begin to haphazardly select notions from the real world and Muslim tradition in order to respond to the requirements of their organizations and everyday activities, instead of proceeding by sound and rational judgment.
- They have claimed to embody, through organization and membership – and to the exclusion of all other groups – the whole Ummah. This is no more than intellectual immaturity and a juvenile fondness for exclusiveness and theatrics.
- Despite their untiring verbal commitment to the Qur'an and the Sunnah, these movements have not drawn up any appropriate programs for themselves and thus display their members' poor grasp of the methodological foundations of Islamic doctrines and the Shariʿah. As we know, methodology constitutes the cornerstone leading to the development of a comprehensive Islamic discourse that can implement Islam's ultimate objectives.
- Since the beginning of modern contacts with the West, the Islamic discourse has been stranded between high and low tides, between progression and retrogression. At times when an all-out mobilization of effort and resources was needed to ward off an outside danger, it rose to the occasion. However, during times of construction and development, the Islamic discourse seemed almost everywhere to be pathetically lacking in

vigor and wholeness. Be that as it may, an analysis of the present Islamic discourse's salient characteristics ought to instill in us more awareness toward rectifying its form and content in order to make it more viable in an age fraught with intellectual and other challenges.

TOWARD A RESOLUTION OF THE CRISIS

The Islamic discourse's general features were discussed during our survey of the dimensions missing from contemporary Muslim discourse. In this section, we shall elaborate on these absent dimensions and explore ways of retrieving and incorporating them into the Islamic discourse so that it can regain its effectiveness and overcome its crisis. In this connection, Islam's most salient characteristics need to be borne in mind: the Shariʿah's comprehensiveness and tolerance; the very general approach to humanity, time, and place; the purposefulness of creation; the Islamic discourse's universality; the Qur'an's supreme authority; the conclusive nature of Muhammad's prophethood; and the belief in humanity's capacity to renew its Allah-given ability to discover the divine pattern (and mechanics) of perpetual renovation – a knowledge that would enable people to offer a sound and balanced reading of both revelation and the cosmos.

COMPREHENSIVENESS

Comprehensiveness implies a balanced depiction of quintessential facts. In the Islamic context, these are the fundamentals of the faith, the methodology of thought, the way of life resulting from such faith and thought, the methodology of research, and the approach to humanity and the universe at large. It also implies that all principal issues (e.g., the reality of the divine, the sanctity of life, and the vicegerency of humanity) have been explained by the Divine Revelation, and that all aspects of human activities (e.g., worship and transaction) are described and provided for from within the framework of this vicegerency. This worldview contains no such thing as aimless, nihilistic action; rather, a person's actions, which emanate from or conform with that comprehensive system, are a form of *ʿibādah* (worship). The very "bread" that a person earns for his/her dependents, the love (both physical and spiritual) that exists between husband and wife, is a form of worship. Such sanctity secures humanity's dignity and prevents people from falling to the level of that which was originally created to serve them, be it animals, plants, or objects. In this way, humanity rejoices in a sense of peace and security with its Lord, thus escaping such feelings as nihilism and alienation. In short, it is a divine, comprehensive methodology for life as a whole.

THE GENERAL APPROACH TO HUMANITY, TIME, AND PLACE

This implies that Islam is not confined to a specific community, time, or place. Its message was never meant to be addressed to a particular community located in a particular place at a particular time. Rather, it is a call to humanity, which, within the Islamic methodology, is seen as an indivisible whole. This approach views human unity as a fact of life and an attribute of the living, irrespective of race or any other consideration. One of its features is the Muslims' inherent belief in the unity of all revelation and all prophets. Another is the belief in humanity's common origin and its destiny to seek after the truth and form (re-form) the requisite bonds of love and cooperation.

PURPOSEFULNESS

The notion of a purposeful creation becomes clear upon a close or clear-sighted observation of the universe. Each creature, whether large or small, has been created to play a particular role in this life, whether humanity is aware of it or not. The Qur'an makes this abundantly clear: "Did you think that We had created you in jest, and that you would not be brought back to Us [for account]?" (23:115) and "Does humanity think that it is to be left to itself, to go about at will?" (75:36).[11]

Nothing in this universe can be described as accidental, without purpose, reason, or role. Belief in blind chance is a feature of backward and primitive thought dating back to the time of humanity's emergence. In contrast, Islam has brought humanity out of that time's darkness and transferred people to a mode of thought based on rational and methodological thinking, which should enable them discover the relationship between various phenomena and between cause and effect. Islam engenders a state of mind that should help them to discover the presence of the beneficent Creator in the universe and in humanity, as well as the marks of His purpose and design in every aspect of creation. In turn, this intellectual (cognitive) activity should generate the sciences and branches of knowledge that organize the human mind, equip it to bypass the merely partial significance of objects and phenomena, and link them all together in order to discover their interrelationship and purpose:

> We did not create the heavens, Earth, and all between them, merely in [idle] sport. We created them only for just ends, but most [people] do not know. (44:38-39)

UNIVERSALITY

Understanding this crucial aspect of Islam and realizing its significance at this stage in human history is of extreme importance and benefit. The Qur'an was revealed in Arabic to a messenger, a man who lived among his own people in Makkah. The Revelation was completed in Madinah, and with it, Islam was perfected. The Arabs then carried the Qur'an to the basin of ancient civilizations in the Middle East and elsewhere not of their own accord or any natural inclination; in reality, they were galvanized into action by a divine impetus that overruled tribal and racial allegiances. Their relationship with the Qur'an and the message was based on the fact that they were molded by Islam, rather than the other way around. They set out to achieve two objectives: call for belief in Allah and become "the best nation (Ummah), evolved for humanity, enjoining what is good and forbidding what is evil" (3:110).

This call to achieve common human objectives can be summed up as moving people away from worshipping demagogues to worshipping Allah alone, from the oppression practiced by other religions to the justice of Islam, and from the confinement of narrow worldly affairs to the expansiveness and infinite possibilities of the world and the Hereafter. All of these matters benefited everyone who heard this discourse, which is inherently free of any national or individual interest. Rather, with its altruistic and tolerant outlook, it embraced peoples of all cultures and allowed them to freely and creatively express their various cultural experiences, which greatly enriched Islamic civilization. Such peoples enjoyed equal status in upholding the message and shouldering the responsibility of communicating it to others. In the course of a few decades, Islam shed its light from southern Europe to southern China. It incorporated erstwhile pagan nations, such as the Mongols, Persians, Turks, and Berbers, in a massive all-sweeping movement that took place within the framework of, and in accordance with, the system and nature of relationships existing among the nations of that time.

The People of the Book entered, if they so wished and of their own free will, into covenants with the Muslims. Thus, they were allowed to keep their national identities, religions, and cultural characteristics intact and were, in turn, enfolded within the Islamic state in their own right. Byzantine power in Greater Syria collapsed, as did the Persian Empire, and the light of

Islam soon took the region's ancient civilizations under its purview and began to construct the first universal state. Muslims managed to transcend the duality of East and West and to enfold all religious and cultural pluralities within the universality of the Islamic discourse.

Despite contemporary civilization's ability to accommodate plurality, the Islamic discourse's universality has always been characterized by accepting plurality, but only after injecting its ideals into that same plurality and pushing it toward universality so that it could function and develop within a positive universal framework that welcomes variety and shuns sectarian division. In this way, Islam has always functioned as a force of attraction rather than of rejection and discrimination, as is the case with contemporary western centralism.

The Qur'anic promise of victory and ascendancy for the voice of truth is contingent upon pursuing divine guidance and truth. Indeed, the word *Islam* is never used when the promise is stated in the Qur'an, so that people will not be confused or misled into assuming that the promise applies to the triumph of early Islam in Arabia and the ancient world, or to any nominally Islamic movement at any given time. This is because it is not a prophecy to be fulfilled, regardless of reasons or conditions, or an event to be activated by factors duplicating those of the ancient past. Rather, historical change is governed by laws that Allah has set down and that humanity needs to discover and observe.

Humanity has reached an advanced level of scientific knowledge and methodology. The march of science has been long and arduous. Of late, however, people have started to doubt some contributions of the scientific mind and are coming to the realization that although the scientific mind has enabled humanity to deconstruct reality through analysis, it has been unable to help humanity to synthesize or reconstruct it. In addition, humanity has begun to realize the danger of this stage of development, feeling that continuing on this course will lead to nihilism and, eventually, the end of history. And so tension and anxiety, which are common among the educated in the West and elsewhere, have now reached new heights. No doubt, Islam is the solution. In other words, Muslims can introduce the Qur'an as a civilizing substitute on a global level. But how can this be done?

OBSTACLES ON THE WAY TO ISLAMIC UNIVERSALITY

The historical model has entrenched in the Muslim mind certain patterns used in the early phases of Islamic expansion. The notions that the Muslim

Ummah should establish a state like the one founded by the Prophet in Madinah and that Muslims need constant mobilization to make that dream a reality are widely held. Contemporary Islamic discourse has remained captive both to this wish and to the imagined scenarios that are dependent upon it, instead of paying proper attention to the contemporary world and forward thinking. The desire to attain political power and "establish the state" to the exclusion of everything else has become the norm. This has paradoxically (but predictably) made that goal even more remote.

The collapse (or dismemberment) of the Ottoman Empire resulted in every Muslim community mobilizing all of its potential, including religious beliefs, to resist colonization and hegemony. This led to a sharp enhancement of tradition's status and role, while consolidating the mood of rejecting everything associated with the adversary. Such paradigms became ingrained in the modern Muslim mind. Although there have been many contributions in the intellectual or polemical field, they have been largely influenced by those paradigms. Several generations of Muslims have regarded these contributions as essential to the Ummah's integrity and survival, and thus have maintained that they should be defended and adhered to *en masse*, whether justified or not, and without any kind of revision or scrutiny.

Furthermore, the loser usually becomes interested in emulating the victor. At the same time, the loser's behavior assumes the form of mere reaction, particularly if the loser is living in a state of chronic intellectual crisis and mental stagnation, as is the case with the Ummah today. This has made the process of presenting the Qur'anic model of civilization as an alternative a most formidable task.

ISLAMIC UNIVERSALITY VS. WESTERN UNIVERSALISM

The intellectual characteristics of current western universalism or centralism may be summed up as follows: It is a positivistic universalism enhanced and shielded by scientific methodology that has successfully (though not fully) galvanized humanity's potential for critical and analytical thought. In addition, it has inculcated in humanity a tendency to reject whatever influences its freedom of choice and selection. This universalism has spread all over the world, imposing itself, as well as its values and products, on everyone by using the whole world as its zone of influence. It has also encouraged suspicion of all things religious and ecclesiastical by offering the model of the medieval Catholic church as a dire warning. Given this scenario, how can Islam and its sacred book be introduced as a source for a cultural alternative?

If Islam is presented in the way Muslims and Islamic religious movements are now presenting it, the global response can only be one of rejection, even repression. Furthermore, if Islam is introduced as a comprehensive heading for the geographical area in which Muslims now live, not to mention its self-professed adherents, representatives, and heirs to its historical and cultural legacy (itself conveyed in an antiquated expression), then Islam will be viewed as a distorted image of Judaism or Christianity, albeit free from several of their negative elements and geared to offer a functional religion that could satisfy people's spiritual and other needs.

Be that as it may, Islam is invariably presented in a form that does not match its greatness and potential. It is routinely introduced through a thick tangle of transmitted fiqh more suited to a simple agrarian society and a basic exchange of benefits than to the complex realities of our time. Even if we are assured that this legacy can respond to the complex needs of modern societies and their economies, we are, in effect, burdening it with something that it cannot withstand. This will reflect badly and negatively on Islam and its universality so much so that it might negate its globalism and create the impression that Islam is applicable only to unsophisticated agricultural societies.

This will be most regrettable, for it contradicts the very spirit and teachings of Islam. It is also unfair to actual history, which saw Islam branch out to connect the Atlantic to the Pacific and to occupy a central position that joined Asia, Africa, and Europe and merged diverse civilizations, cultures, and races in one human framework. This Islamic universality has always represented a force for global interaction, doggedly removing barriers all the time, while the secular concept of universalism is invoked only when nationalistic or regional crises erupt and when regional orders begin to atrophy and wither away. In the case of Islamic universality, however, its order for good and unity is sustained by divine order and promise, both of which need to be enacted through human agency.

CONTEMPORARY WESTERN CIVILIZATION: BACKGROUND AND DISTINGUISHING FEATURES

Ancient Asian and African civilizations never managed to constitute a universal dimension comparable with Islam's universality. Western Europe, however, produced versions of universalism through the Hellenic and Roman models – the first taking shape in the wake of Alexander's conquest of large Asian territories, and the second by virtue of its inheritance of the Greek Empire. The contemporary West considers itself heir to both.

The Hellenic and Roman civilizations were pagan, deriving their power from the deities on Mt. Olympus in the case of Athens and from the deified Caesars in Rome, before that city converted to a pagan-tainted Christianity. Both civilizations had grown within a cultural order that had its own view of humanity. Both worldviews allowed slavery (if the person was not a "citizen") to exploit the person's labor, which was forced and unpaid, and made the slaves implacably subordinate to the interests of Athens or Rome. The most valued slave was the gladiator. The modern inheritors of these two civilizations have not developed a significantly different alternative, as evidenced by their enslavement of people in the mines and other industries in ways that resemble their ancient paragons, who enslaved people to build their temples and row their ships.

This cultural order, both in its original and modern forms, is based on a view of humanity that is conducive to conflict, aggression, and mutual animosity. Contrasted with this is Islam's universality, which transcends such positivistic approaches, be they Greek, Roman, or contemporary western. The Islamic approach is manifested in the following:

First, as opposed to the coercive Greek and Roman models, Islam came as a liberator. History does not record an instance of Muslim armies fighting the peoples of the countries they liberated. All wars were waged against the armies of emperors and tyrants. The liberated peoples supported the Muslim conquerors against their oppressors. These Muslims were the first in history to be welcomed by the peoples of the conquered countries as liberators. As such, they were committed to a divine scripture that disciplined them ethically and morally to such an extent that they would not permit themselves to become arrogant or "do mischief in the land." In this way, Islam established the first universal fraternity, as opposed to the high-handed and selective "universalism" that prevailed at that time.

Second, the major centers of Islamic civilization (e.g., Madinah, Damascus, Baghdad, Cairo, and Istanbul) were characterized by a vigorous adherence to *tawḥīd*. Allah was not the deity of a race or a faction, but was the Lord of humanity. In fact, Islamic civilization was very much shaped by its uncompromising stance against polytheism as well as by building bridges to other monotheistic traditions, their deviations notwithstanding. Thus, Judaism and Christianity remained and were accepted by Islam. Adherents of other creeds in Persia and India were tolerated and offered protection within the overall structure. In other words, Islam was the first system to accommodate the faiths emanating from the Abrahamic heritage, in addition to others, and never forced people to change their religion, for: "There is no compulsion in religion" (2:256).

Third, the Islamic model of civilization was characterized by the non-enslavement of the conquered peoples. Unlike Athens and Rome, Madinah, Damascus, Baghdad, and Cairo were not built by unpaid slaves brought over from colonies. Zakah was distributed in the areas where it was collected, and thus benefited those non-Muslims who were allies of the Muslims or who depended on Muslim aid. The Islamic model (in its pure form) was certainly at odds with the Hellenic and Roman models, for it was based on retrieving the heritage of all prophets, emancipating it from all additions, and fusing it into a truly universal and open-ended structure. It sought to emancipate and ennoble humanity by placing believers in direct relation with their Creator, instead of enslaving or demeaning them.

The centralized European civilization, whether it branched out from eastern or western Europe, came about after Muslim power declined after the Mongol sacking of Baghdad and the European reconquest of Spain. The onslaught against the Muslim heartland by wave after wave of "crusading" armies confirmed the West's ascendancy. In passing, we should note that Muslims called these events the "Frankish wars," as can be seen in all contemporary Muslim accounts. Islam does not endorse wars between the "crescent" and the "cross" or between the East and the West, for its nature opposes that kind of antagonistic perspective. Be that as it may, that particular period was a prelude to a later penetration, which culminated in the rise of western colonialism and then imperialism.

In consequence, the concept of universalism that has been imposed on Muslim (and other) regions is shaped after the western fashion in order to produce a world in its own image by creating a new "world order," under which the three constituents of Greco-Roman universalism are reborn: a central universalism rooted in the West but enveloping the world at large; a positivistic centralism in which religious values have no place, despite the lip-service accorded to the Judeo-Christian heritage; and an order based on conflict and appropriation.

Nevertheless, Muslims, along with others in the West and elsewhere, need to help transform the current conflict-ridden situation into a more congenial and agreeable world, one in which humanity may settle down to enjoy peace and security by moving along the path of divine guidance and truth.

THE LOGIC OF ENTERING INTO THE PEACE OF ISLAM

Islam's condemnation of aggression and racial prejudice is unambiguous. As a faith, Islam addresses humanity and recognizes no superiority or distinction, except in good deeds, which only Allah can evaluate correctly. To inveigh against the West or the East is both un-Islamic and counterproductive, for all it does is blind Muslims to the complexities of reality while sharpening and deepening the present duality. Both fairness and commonsense will take a back seat, and complacency and self-satisfaction will prevail, to the detriment of global peace and unity.

Allah Almighty is the Lord of all Muslims as well as of all Europeans, Americans, and all other people. He has provided for a new Islamic universality, one which is far more comprehensive and equitable than the presently dominant norm. It is a universality of mercy and fairness at a truly global level. In order to explain this further, the following observations are germane.

First, Islamic universality is blessed by the Creator of the cosmos. Its *raison d'être* is the world's desperate need for solutions to its ecological, intellectual, economic, and political crises, all of which will worsen as the world's social and moral order continues to decline. Thus, the Islamic outlook will provide solutions and bring relief not only to Muslims, who in their present state of stagnation and blind imitation are in dire need of succor and reform, but also to humanity in its moral and social decline.

Second, Muslims need to address their discourse to the whole world. Addressing it to the West in particular is also crucial and may take priority, since western culture dominates much of the world's moral, cultural, social, and human behavior due to its universal centrality and advanced technology. In our view, Islamic universality can respond to western anxiety and confusion. On the other hand, the Ummah can only find its way to salvation by adopting this universal message and carrying it forward. The Muslim mind has to recall this dimension in order to address the appropriate Islamic discourse to humanity and to understand and be aware of its own role in life.

Third, the triumph of Islamic universality, once articulated and enacted by responsible human agency, is inevitable. When Muslims start working toward that goal, they will do so in response to their duty to be Allah's vicegerents on Earth and to witness to humanity. This is a responsibility, not an indulgence. Carrying it out will determine the measure of their freedom as well as of their success in overcoming their own crisis. What they do for others will reflect on them, since the Almighty has ordained that they shall carry His Message and witness to humanity. If they continue to fail in this task, they will not improve or progress beyond the present impasse. This is the special relationship of understanding and honor between them and Allah. Nevertheless, they should not give others the impression that they are above them or are doing them a favor when they carry His message to them. He is the One who bestows favors on His servants entrusted to elevate His word. In their turn, Muslims need to be utterly humble and self-effacing, for they must work to make His word the most supreme and Earth a better and safer place for everyone.

Western culture, its awesome global dominance notwithstanding, realizes, as its own thinkers and philosophers testify, that it cannot extricate itself from its present impasse. This is due to the following reasons:

- While western civilization seeks further technological advancement, following its two industrial revolutions, it suffers from the social, cultural, and moral deterioration for which it has found no adequate solutions. The conundrum persists. Cultural advancement, which is truly consistent in all domains, should move simultaneously and at all levels to enhance humanity in terms of values and ethics. However, we do not see this in western civilization. In fact, sciences progress while people decline, their values vanish, and their suffering, coercion, and calamities increase.
- All modern secular attempts to control human destiny have foundered, despite all the optimism before and after the two world wars. Hopes had been high, and yet those conflagrations erupted and saw the most appalling acts of barbarity. What can avert the recurrence of such horrors in the absence of a guided mechanism to control that destiny, except divine guidance? In fact, what is happening at present is merely a change in the tactics and instruments of conflict, for the conflict itself and the coercion of humanity continue relentlessly.
- All modern attempts to build civilizations, whether on a socialist or a capitalist ideology, have been punctuated by dissent and rebellion. Under materialistic dominance, people continue to search for their identity, retrogressing first into nationalism and eventually delving into questions concerning destiny, which leads them back to religion. This has recently, and most dramatically, happened in the former Soviet Union. Still, humanity cannot find solutions, within the context of western liberalism and positivism, for liberalism imparts only fragmented, selective thought. Within this context, humanity looks for its inner self and does not find

it; people focus on truncated details and become prey to depression and alienation, even from their own family roots. Western people's obsession with freedom is without content, for humanity exists without commitment to anything or anyone. It is a kind of freedom that verges on nihilism and self-destruction. Its major icons, Darwin, Marx, Freud, and Einstein, emphasized doctrines and areas of interest that were pursued but led to no real fulfillment.

- This order, which is based on conflict and survival of the fittest, is proving to be even more hostile to the real interests of average people not only in the West, but in the rest of the world as well, than previously thought. Such people find themselves coerced, under a barrage of advertisements and other devices of persuasion, to buy products and make decisions that they would not otherwise have bought or made. Large companies so dominate the consumer's psyche that they choose the educational model, food, and clothing to be used. Accordingly, people exist and behave under these pressures. But for how long?

DETERMINANTS OF THE CRISIS IN THE WESTERN MIND

Much has been written on this subject, thus offering ample evidence (and confirmation) of the problem. If we were to organize this evidence, we would discover the following determinants:

First, Christian theology, having been expropriated by the Greco-Roman heritage, can no longer give the western mind a universal view that transcends the concept of an embodied God. In this way, Christian theology has ended the purity of *tawḥīd,* replaced it with polytheistic incarnation, and expunged the metaphysical concept that transcends nature and philosophy. Subsequently, human mental endeavor has been restricted to a narrow area, because the concept of the Godhead (the first basis of universality) has been reduced to the level of the natural object. Thus, Christian theology, which should have helped expand the western mind's horizons, has hindered it. Despite the sorry situation in which they find themselves, Muslims should still encourage people to enter, as they themselves should, more comprehensively into Islam.

The return to God, according to Christian theology, does not go beyond the narrow self. The concept of God's supremacy, which is philosophically absent in Christian theology, represents the purity and supreme sovereignty of the concepts of the divine and *tawḥīd* and, *inter alia*, provides a solution for the crises stemming from cultural prejudice and arrogance. That inference, contained within the proclamation of *tawḥīd,* is of crucial importance. However, many people do not recognize this fact.

In the Christian worldview, God became embodied by taking the form of His creation, or by appearing to be similar to it or personified in it. This leads to the idea that God needs humanity to recognize Him, even if only to receive love and fealty. It also follows that humanity can embody itself in the divine form in order to gain God-like power. As such, humanity can do without the power of the embodied God, and thus become independent of Him and go beyond His teachings and codes to become self-sufficient unto himself, a tyrant. Thus, western civilization dismissed God the Omnipotent. When it rediscovered Him and attempted to find a new place for Him within its new fundamentalism, it wanted Him to come back on its own terms.

Given these facts, Christian theology lies at the root of this cultural and intellectual conundrum, which cannot be solved without introducing the concept of *Allāh Wāḥid – Allāhu Akbar* (God is One – God is most supreme) into western civilization. God, being greater than any natural event occurring in time or space, cannot be taken over by either of these elements, not even by the force of action at exceptional events (e.g., Jesus' miracles). In this way, we can distinguish between the methodology of divine creation and that of making things and determining their functions.

Since Christian theology does not recognize monotheism or believe in God as the most supreme, its concept of creation and the methodology of creation is confused. Thus, western thought has produced philosophies of natural sciences in an equally fragmented and arcane way, making them both limited and obscure. By negating or ignoring the element of the divine, they have lost much potential for expansion.

Second, there is the problem of the natural mind vis-à-vis the scientific mind. The natural mind emancipated itself from Christian theology and, supported by the scientific mind's principles and postulates, attempted to justify this action. The end result was a parting of the ways between science and theology, with culture either adopting this separation or remaining neutral. The Materialists exploited the situation to confirm or consolidate the neutralization of God, while the Positivists made the very concept of God archaic and irrelevant.

Third, there is the issue of deconstruction and the inability to reconstruct. After developing both the natural and scientific mentalities in confrontation with a narrow Christian theology, the scientific mentality, supported by the powers of criticism and analysis, set out to thoroughly and deeply research and examine the "metaphysics" of everything. Thus, it referred all postulates to their basic components in keeping with the logic of industrial civilization. A considerable measure of success was achieved. However, the overriding problem now is reconstruction.

Reconstruction in the field of matter and power has been successful, though at a high ecological and human cost. Such repercussions impinge on reconstruction attempts, most significantly and crucially in the cultural order and the structure of historical and social development. The western cultural order, based on the Greco-Roman experience, has established itself on the linchpins of conflict and superiority. This order is exclusive and founded on the dominance of power and the logic of might in almost every field. Given this, the West finds it difficult to apply moral practices, except where they cannot produce effective and comprehensive reform. For example, you may pray to God however you wish, but you cannot act socially or economically or in a way that contravenes the interests of those in power or goes against their social philosophy or economic thought. It is because of this that world orders, old and new, have sought to eliminate (or subvert) all distinctive features of other nations and peoples.

Here the issue seems to be one of cultural order, rather than religion or morality as such. One may witness about Jesus in many forms, but working to implement his teachings in a comprehensive way may well be condemned as a political act that is both fundamentalist and extreme.

COURSE OF ACTION

What should Muslims do to bring about a beneficial interaction between Islam's universality and the West? The task is not easy, but it is possible.

It is not easy because the West is prone to resist vigorously any reformation, particularly if it emanates from religious (especially Islamic) thought, since the West has a long history of resisting religious dogma coupled with a collective memory of conflict with Islam. In fact, both Christian theology and Islamic doctrines are hardly distinguishable from a secularist perspective. In addition, the West's cultural order rejects calls for any value system that is not commensurate with its own, particularly after the Soviet collapse. This event is seen to have given the western liberal system a clean bill of health and confirmed the righteousness of its stance.

Three approaches can be attempted. First, given the West's chronic crisis in the aftermath of analytical deconstruction and the failure to reconstruct, Muslims must arm themselves with the Qur'an's epistemological methodology and then form close relations with the West's analytical schools, regardless of their trends or directions. These schools, along with their philosophical, intellectual, and cultural bases, continue to expand and provide a salubrious entry into epistemological contact with the West for the benefit of humanity.

Second, Muslims should give all possible support to the Islamization of Knowledge, when it comes to guiding the natural sciences and reconstructing the human and social sciences. Developing these sciences in their universal unity will constitute an impetus for most westerners to open their minds to our methodology so that they may explore and use it.

Third, a dialogue can then take place within a scientific methodological framework to which Muslims can bring their awareness of the Qur'an coupled with the awareness of universal laws. Circumstances permitting, the new Islamic universality will be epistemological and methodological; it will operate more fairly and persuasively on a global scale. Throughout, Muslims should avoid raising (or being entrapped by) sensitive issues or those that activate the West's historical memory. Rather, they should resort to research and scientific studies that address contemporary issues, crises, and problems on the basis of the Qur'an's epistemological methodology and the Prophet's Sunnah.

But to what extent can contemporary Islamic movements understand (or undertake) this significant task?

DETERMINANTS OF THE CRISIS IN THE MUSLIM MIND

Islamic movements based on historical and cultural pretensions have bound their minds and visions to the Muslim past and thereby eschew present realities – especially in times of crisis and insecurity. Whenever they project the Islamic legacy onto their contemporary situation, they do so with a static mentality that pays little attention to the Qur'anic text's characteristics and its general and timeless pronouncements. Thus, they confine the Qur'an and the Sunnah to the limited framework prescribed by earlier generations of scholars who worked within defined methodological and epistemological constraints and even, at times, with poorly documented material. This approach does not try to analyze those constraints and imperfections in order to discern or calculate the enormous changes that may affect those limitations through human interaction, or the variables of time and place together with the laws of historical change. Such an analysis would provide an insight into the value and volume of local and international interaction in a coherent, free-flowing context.

The West's crisis is the result of a deconstructive mode that cannot reconstruct, because it has excluded the concepts of God, transcendence, and revelation. The crisis in the Muslim world is manifested in the flawed methodology of dealing with a justifiably comprehensive heritage, one that is nevertheless always meets up with a static mentality when it comes to interpreting that heritage. This reality prevents it from coming to terms with the concepts and methodologies of a contemporary and vibrant world. Since Islamic movements fail to effect change through an Islamic epistemological methodology, they resort to the moral violence of branding others as "apostates"; cling to the more triumphant features of early Islamic history; and refer matters to the world of the Unseen and the Unknown, while neglecting Islam's methodology of interaction between that world, humanity, and the cosmos. Alternatively, they may gain political power in order to introduce change by setting up a cleric as a ruler under divine jurisdiction and to appease the Almighty by applying the Islamic penal code. Within the context of this oversimplification – indeed trivialization – of Islam, political programs are established to support the claim that they represent, express, and speak for Islam.

The world sees such Islamic movements as trying to change all forms of government and all regimes, even those within which they work, irrespective of whether or not their political legitimacy is derived from Islamic law. Even so, Islamic movements continue to squabble among themselves with each one claiming that it is the most legitimate. In the process, they try to embarrass and upstage all other movements and systems in terms of their conception and practice of Islam. Avowing their uncompromising opposition to liberal plurality, they strip other systems and regimes of their legitimacy, for only they possess or confer such a concept upon others. Accordingly, they become mesmerized by the dream of gaining power, and so ignore the concept of universality as well as the methodologies or tools to achieve them. Thus, they overlook a basic aspect of Islamic discourse. Their obsession with narrow political goals makes them identify any success in terms of political power achieved. Some hold this to be a springboard for universalism; but the logic of this argument, if raised at all, is quite fatuous and ignores the eternal laws of cause and effect.

Many Islamic movements have attained several Islamic objectives, but they have failed to build a paradigm that links these objectives with the laws and ways of social change. In consequence, they have resigned themselves to recruiting new members and expanding horizontally, for their concept of change is linked to forming a numerically large *jamāʿah.* Addressing the laws of social and historical progress, the laws and norms of change, as well as the reality of cultural and intellectual development and their universal directions – all of this simply falls outside their sphere of interest, because many of these movements treat thought and science as beneath their dignity and classify them as contrary to belief.

Nevertheless, there have been numerous attempts to overcome this impasse and free the Muslim mind from these vicious circles. But these attempts still cannot provide the right impetus for overcoming the crisis. Various bids to reform *uṣūl al-fiqh* (sources of jurisprudence) or fiqh itself, or to revive and modernize such disciplines as *ʿilm al-kalām* (scholastic philosophy), cannot connect the definite statement in the sacred text and the actual world, which is subject to the laws of historical change and the peculiarities of time and place. Neither laxity nor the rigidity of custom-made fatwas can help in this context; it can only result in more confusion and fabrication.

When things reach this stage, the idea of assuming political power becomes an attractive solution for, or a way out of, a crisis that intellectual methodologies have failed to address. The idea becomes a goal toward which all efforts are focused and which, once achieved, all efforts are exerted to maintain. The underlying assumption is: Since thought has failed, why don't we use the stick?

The divine discourse addressed to humanity, even before the Muhammadan mission, is coherent, challenging, and cannot fall behind the historical development of human societies. If humanity is progressing rapidly toward universalism, then how can the discourse of the ultimate universal message retreat to a state of regionalism, nationalism, or narrow interest? This cannot happen; nor can the coveted goal of universal unity come about without an awareness of divine laws and patterns.

Muḥammad ibn ʿUmar Fakhr al-Dīn al-Rāzī (d. 1210) reported in his *Tafsīr*, on the authority of ʿAbd Allāh ibn Aḥmad Abū Bakr al-Qaffāl al-Marrūzī (d. 1027), that the jurisprudents' division of the world into *Dār al-Islām* (Land of Islam), *Dār al-Ḥarb* (Land of War), and *Dār al-ʿAhd* (Land of Treaty) is no longer acceptable. According to him, it is preferable to divide the world into *Dār al-Islām* and *Dār al-Daʿwah* (Land of the Call for Islam). We may substitute the division of the world into a Muslim Ummah and non-Muslim nations by classifying humanity into *Ummat al-Ijābah* (a nation that upholds Islam) and *Ummat al-Daʿwah* (a nation to be invited to Islam).

Scholars like al-Rāzī, al-Qaffāl, and al-Qāsim ibn Muḥammad Abū al-Ḥasan al-Qaffāl al-Shāshī (d. 1010) were more in tune with Islam's teachings and sources, as well as with the true concept of universalism, than are many contemporary leaders of Islamic movements, who ignore or are ignorant of Islam's universality and thus restrict it to their circumscribed geographical areas. Through the use of such labels as "East and West," they shut off a whole world of possibilities.

The absence of this universal dimension has inflicted untold intellectual damage on the Muslim mind. If Islamic movements had considered this missing dimension earlier, much puerile and uninformed thinking could have been averted. Meanwhile, secularists have been calling for universalism within the framework of the New World Order. This call, however, represents an abject surrender to the mentality of blind imitation and subordination, along with a readiness to submit to an all-out assimilation.

The more balanced Islamic universality will seek to invest in the recent fruits of human intelligence, including the information explosion and the more salubrious aspects of the evolving technology. Muslims must be a part of the steady movement toward globalism and the accompanying discussion so that they may discover the best way to implement it.

Modern technology is the product of a long historical process of development that human civilization has generated from ancient times as an expression of innate tendencies awaiting actualization. The universal disposition (and experience) in Islam has certainly provided an incentive for these innante tendencies' realization. This lies at the core of the Muslim contribution to human civilization.

With its historical credibility assured, Islamic universality has no fear of being overwhelmed by western centralism, since the latter is really no universalism at all. Rather, it is a centralism that cannot produce the state of integration necessary for uniting humanity equitably and organically.

Since the West has not extended the natural science's methodologies to their universal limits and philosophical ends, its crisis endures. Western civilization has released the genie of the natural sciences in a most spectacular manner, but has dealt with it only through limited, positivistic philosophies. Marxism tried to give western thought its philosophical ends; however, the scope of Marxism's crisis was larger than the solution it purported to offer. This is why it collapsed and why the crisis persisted on a much larger scale.

The West's present cultural order cannot move out of the maelstrom of its predicament. The capitalist West celebrated most joyfully when the Soviet Union collapsed and its death certificate was issued, for it saw the event as a triumph for its thought and methodology, forgetting that had it not been for the West's own original crisis, Marxism would never have emerged. It did not realize that any positivistic approach that tries to neutralize Allah is doomed to the same end. Nor did it recognize that the human dialectic, which is in harmony with the universe and the divine will, is bound to end any system that does not respond to its historical development. This is true regardless of whether the nature of that system is a theological order that ignores the laws of the universe, or a selective positivistic system that changes humanity into a cog in its production machine.

In view of the interaction between the various crises of the world, universal solutions need to be sought. Any one crisis is rarely caused by local or regional factors alone. Economic, ecological, strategic, political, and cultural interaction produced by the information explosion has transformed the particular cultural orders into constitutive parts that intersect to make a universal, global structure. Whether this intersecting is produced by the people's will or aspirations or by the implacable logic of dialectic interaction, which does not allow for any territory or people to be isolated from what is going on around them, does not matter.

CONCLUDING REMARKS

In his now famous "The Clash of Civilizations" article,[12] Samuel P. Huntington wrote about conflict among civilizations and postulated that the coming decades would witness the last stage in the emergence and development of conflict in the modern world. He also pointed out that some non-western nations, which were no more than targets for western imperial ambitions, have become a driving force alongside the West. In his projections, Huntington stated that the world of the future would be formed through the interaction of seven civilizations: Western, Confucian, Japanese, Islamic, Hindu, Greek Orthodox, and Latin American, with the possible participation of the African. In his sub-classification of Islamic civilization, he cited the Arab, Turkish, and Malay dimensions, thereby ignoring the Persian, Indian, and other nations that come under the banner of Islamic civilization. He divided western civilization into European and American, emphasizing the essential differences between all civilizations. Among these, he held religious differences to be most conducive to conflict. He also discussed several significant cultural phenomena worthy of study.

His omissions, however, betray a certain naïveté and lack of understanding inasfar as his view of Islam, its culture and civilization is concerned.

Sadly, this places Huntington in a conventional Orientalist context and deprives him of seeing those aspects of civilization and religion other than those adversarial and exotic elements that attract many Orientalists. One also feels that he read the historical map of some of these civilizations as though he were living in the sixteenth century. Not enough attention is given to the infinite possibilities for the good offered by modern (and future) information and other technology to humanity.

Huntington also fails to offer any deep analysis of economic and ecological factors or consider the significance of the Earth Summit, which was convened to discuss the common ecological problems facing our planet. He does not even consider the western paradigm's growing influence on the rest of the world. He simply (and unfairly) focuses on the conflict between Islam and the West, offering several pointers as to how the West can win the future battle against Islam and how to mobilize allies. Unfortunately, Huntington knows very little about Islam apart from the distorted image gleaned from Orientalist and media sources. Had these sources been treated with more critical reserve, this severely flawed analysis might have reached different conclusions. Huntington's projection may come true only if the world does not find the proper grounds for unity within the framework of an open civilization that stands as a pole of attraction, rather than as a monopoly, and whose values are broad and universally shared, instead of conditioned by commercial or racial interests.

The values of the Qur'an and Islam inspire people to do what is just and refrain from what is evil in order to pursue their innate goodness and capacity for good. They also allow people to enjoy that which is wholesome and pure and divert them from that which is bad and impure, while releasing them from idolatry's burdens and yokes. In this way, humanity becomes Allah's vicegerent on Earth, its blessed home, and all people are bound together by ties of fraternity and the vision of a common destiny.

Roger Garaudy, who studied Islam deeply and understood its characteristics, foresees a dialogue among civilizations, one that prepares the ground for universalism. In the introduction to his *Pour un dialogue des civilisations* (Dialogue of Civilizations),[13] he stresses that what was conveniently termed the "West" was actually born in Mesopotamia and ancient Egypt thousands of years ago. He criticizes the West for its ignorance of Islamic civilization's characteristics and properties in particular, and of other civilizations in general. In fact, he calls upon the West to discover for itself, as he did, the qualities of Islamic civilization. He candidly points out that his individual crisis before converting to Islam was (in microcosmic terms) akin to that of the

West and had largely been caused by it. It follows that discovering true Islam may serve as a prelude to solving the West's crises.

He also offers a vision (indeed a program) of a possible global cultural revolution, which he outlines as follows: Non-western civilizations should occupy a position in the curricula equal to that of western civilization at western universities and schools; philosophical thought should be reexamined, suggesting that theoretical and philosophical studies should not be underrated in comparison with scientific and technological studies; attention should be given to aesthetics as a science; and more attention should be paid to futuristic studies, with constant reference to universal history.

It may be germane here to recall that al-Shāfiʿī wrote his *Al-Ḥujjah* in Baghdad and read it to such Baghdad scholars as Aḥmad ibn Ḥanbal (d. 855), Ibrāhīm ibn Khālid Abū Thawr al-Kalbī (d. 854), and al-Ḥusayn ibn ʿAlī ibn Yazīd al-Karābisī (d. 862). When he went to Cairo, he reconsidered his jurisprudence in its entirety and revised his views, except for thirteen *masā'il* (issues in fiqh). In other words, he produced two different versions of his fiqh. Such was the experience of a scholar who lived for a mere fifty years!

The cultural difference between Baghdad and Cairo at that time could not have been as pronounced as those between, say, China and America today. Nevertheless, today's fiqh scholars endeavor to make Muslims live according to a cultural order based on jurisprudence formulated in the schools of the Hijaz or Kufah in the second Islamic century. The resulting constraints stem from their insufficient understanding of Islam's universality and its capacity to enfold various cultural orders within the framework of truly perennial values, rather than ones shaped by whim or prejudice.

Islam's universality is too profound and important a concept to be used as a mere slogan. It is a significant, far-reaching methodological entry that will cause us to review our heritage in its entirety, in a very critical, exacting, and painstaking way; to read that heritage methodologically and epistemologically; discern its paradigms; and reclassify and judge it in the light of the Qur'an and the Sunnah, and their methodologies, and as both are projected onto the real world.

This task calls for thousands of intelligent, resourceful, and diligent minds that are enlightened by the Qur'an's epistemological methodology and the Sunnah's applied methodology, to work at or alongside hundreds of institutions and universities. That attained, Muslims will find that many aspects of their inherited sciences will have to be replaced, rectified, or updated, and that this sound heritage can be built upon and extended to help them cope with present and future challenges.

Some will ask: "Why bother?" The simple answer will be: This is the Ummah's destiny and responsibility, its *raison d'être* and ennobling mission to humanity. Since Muhammad was the Seal [and last] of all Prophets, and since the Almighty has vowed not to chastise anyone until He has sent a Messenger (17:15), this Ummah has become responsible for humanity. Like the ancient Hebrew prophets, its scholars and intellectuals have been entrusted with delivering Allah's message to an unwary world. Conveying (and reinvigorating) this message is not an option, for Muslims must continually review the Islamic discourse and make it understandable to everyone. If they do not, the Ummah will be subject to what befalls a messenger who gives up his mission (see 7:175-77).

A man who "would have been elevated" by Allah's grace but instead "inclined to the earth and followed his own vain desires" may become a symbol of a nation that had received the signs of Allah but has departed from them – a nation that has, by its preference for worldly benefits and material comfort, degraded itself instead of striving to be the world's moral beacon and model.

Muslims would be well advised to be aware of the two divine laws of *istibdāl* (replacement of one people with another), as in: "If you turn back [from the path], He will substitute in your stead another people; then they would not be like you" (47:38) and *tidwāl* (turn-taking): "Such days [of varying fortunes] we give to people by turns" (3:140).

As the Qur'an recounts, the divine application of such laws has caused earlier nations to be replaced by the Ummah of Muhammad so that humanity would start to move toward universality. This began with the building of "the pivotal Ummah" and with the concept of "people" being replaced by the concept of a "world nation," and by a Messenger sent "as a mercy for all humanity." Along with this came the introduction of a system of legislation that was rational, broad, and tolerant enough to serve humanity in its various stages of development; direct divine chastisement was deferred until the Day of Judgment; and rule by Allah's direct intervention was replaced by the Qur'an's authority.

Instead of such miracles as sending manna from heaven and parting the Red Sea, which made an impression on humanity during a particular phase of its growing awareness, humanity was now placed at creation's center as a rational being who was to rely on the Qur'an, as well as Prophet Muhammad's Sunnah, to find its place and happiness within the universal order as His vicegerent. Hence, humanity's rediscovery of the Qur'an and its correspondence to the whole universe is imperative, for the Qur'an contains an epistemological methodology similar to the norms that control the universe and its movement.

Humanity is the pivot of this pattern, and its effort is the basis for application. Humanity is both the reader of the Qur'an and the reader of the universe. Thus, our understanding of the Qur'an's supreme authority and its human application is vital. In this sense, a *mujtahid* is rewarded (by God) twice if he/she is correct in his/her judgment, and once if he/she is mistaken. Once again within Islam, humanity is ennobled by the task of vicegerency, in the course of which each person finds integration and peace with his/her fellow human beings. This dimension of humanity's role on Earth can be ignored only at humanity's own expense.

NOTES

1. Ibn Khaldūn, *The Muqaddimah: An Introduction to History*, tr. Franz Rosenthal (London: Routledge and Kegan Paul, 1987).
2. Zakah: The obligatory sharing of wealth with the poor and the community at the annual rate of 2.5 percent of appropriated wealth above a certain minimum. It also refers to general charity, which is strongly encouraged by divine injunctions.
3. Ṭāhā J. al-ʿAlwānī, *Al-Azmah al-Fikriyyah at Muʿāṣirah: Tashkhīs wa Muqtaraḥāt ʿIlāj* [The Contemporary Intellectual Crisis: A Scrutiny of the Problem and Possible Solutions] (Herndon, VA., IIIT, 1989); *Iṣlāḥ al-Fikr al-Islāmī bayna al-Qudurāt wa al-ʿAqabāt: Waraqāt ʿAmal* [Reforming Islamic Intellectual Discourse: Capabilities and Obstacles: A Working Paper] (Herndon, VA: IIIT, 1991).
4. *Fiṭrah*: An innate, Allah-oriented nature with which every person is born.
5. Muhammad Asad (tr.), *The Message of the Qur'an* (Gibraltar: Dar al-Andalus, 1980).
6. Ibid.
7. Ibid.
8. Ibid.
9. The hijrah refers to the Prophet's migration from Makkah to Madinah in the twelfth year of his mission (622). This event marks the beginning of the Islamic calendar.
10. Asad, *The Message of the Qur'an*.
11. Ibid.
12. Samuel P. Huntington, "The Clash of Civilizations?" *Foreign Affairs* (Summer 1993): 22-49.
13. Paris: Denoël, 1977.

Authority: Divine or Qur'anic?

Any study of authority needs to consider the subject from a number of different perspectives, including an analysis of concepts and how they are formulated, as well as effects of these concepts at both the practical and the theoretical levels. This study does not claim to be the last word on the subject. Rather, its purpose is to open the door to further examination and inquiry, and to critically analyze the main concept and the network of concepts attached to and contingent upon it.

I shall not spend a great deal of time analyzing the lexical aspects of the concepts we are about to study, because terms and concepts are two different things. In a study of terminology, it might suffice to identify the lexical root and its particular meanings and then discuss the usages appropriate to a particular field, subject, or science. Thereafter, one might attempt to define the term in a way that gives a clear idea of its intended meaning. A concept, however, may be described as a term connected to a network of philosophical and cultural roots. Furthermore, regardless of the diversity of its roots, a concept will always correlate with the epistemological paradigm within which it functions. This assumption holds true in regard to Islamic concepts or those concepts that are key to understanding the Islamic order.

For example, an entire network of related concepts surround the Islamic concept of divine authority. Unless they are understood, both on their own and within the larger context of Islamic order itself, the concept of divine authority will remain unclear. This network includes the concepts of divinity, creation, worship, the world and the hereafter, the divine discourse, the lawful and the unlawful, the classification of texts as relative or unqualified or as general or specific, the religious laws of earlier communities, the unity

This article first appeared in the *American Journal of Islamic Social Sciences* 13, no. 4 (winter 1996): 536-50, and was translated by Yusuf DeLorenzo. It has been slightly edited.

of religion, and many others. Regardless of the nature or importance of these ancillary concepts, one cannot fully understand a concept without understanding its related concepts.

People sometimes arrive at mistaken notions of concepts when they attempt to understand them according only to their lexical meanings or usages. Over the past few decades, the concept of divine authority has been misunderstood in this way by several schools of thought within contemporary Islamic reform movements. This study seeks to clarify this concept and to rid it of the ambiguities and confusions that have grown up around it. I shall begin by indicating briefly a few points that are essential to understanding the discussion that is to follow.

Let us consider God's call to the Patriarch Ibrāhīm (Abraham):

> "Behold! I will make you a leader of people." Ibrāhīm asked: "And my offspring as well (will You make them imams too)?" Allah replied: "My covenant does not extend to those who are unjust." (2:124)

This is *imāmah*, a sort of leadership made possible by God: There is justice and injustice, as values that need to be acknowledged; there are those who are unjust (to themselves and to others) and those who are just; and those who outdo others in justice and good deeds. In this verse, leadership takes the form of a covenant between God and humanity – a covenant that may not be extended to those who are unjust or who draw close to injustice. The value of justice is highlighted here as the opposite of injustice, and is shown to be the second (after *tawḥīd*) of the higher purposes behind the missions of the prophets and those reformers who would later assume their place.

A second point to remember is that the idea of divinely appointed leadership, which is inherent in the concept of *imāmah*, naturally leads to the concept of election (*iṣṭifā'*): "Allah chooses messengers from among the angels as well as from among men" (22:75). This concept, moreover, is connected by means of certain characteristics to the process of the divine election of peoples and nations: "Behold! Allah chose Adam, Nūḥ (Noah), the family of Ibrahim, and the family of ʿImran over all of humanity" (3:33).

This divine election of individuals as prophets and messengers to peoples chosen to be the focus of their efforts, leadership, and guidance must be kept in mind throughout our discussion of divine authority.

Looking into the history of legal and political systems of ancient civilizations, we find that several of these were based on the idea of divine sovereignty or rule. For example, the Sumerians, Akkadians, and Babylonians had such systems. Among the most important peoples mentioned in any discussion of divine authority are the ancient Jews, known later as the Children of Israel. In fact, the form of divine authority understood by them was fairly well defined: revealed scripture, tablets inscribed by God with commandments they were required to follow, and prophets and messengers charged with communicating God's will to the people.

Among the most important elements in the Jewish understanding of divine authority were the notions that they were God's "chosen people" and that God ruled over them directly, chose His messengers from among them, and ordered them to enforce His rule and carry His teachings to the people. Perhaps no less important was the understanding that, as a result, they were the closest of all people to God, and so were "God's people," and that their land was thus a "sacred" or "holy" land. This concept of divine authority left clear imprints on every aspect of the Jews' lives, including their worldview, character as a people, and concepts of law, worship, life, and the universe.

The mission of Prophet Jesus may be seen as an attempt to correct many of the concepts that had influenced the Jews in their dealings or relationship with God, the universe, its prophets, and with itself and its neighbors:

> And I have come to confirm the truth of whatever there still remains of the Torah,[1] and to make lawful unto you some of the things that [aforetime] were forbidden to you. (3:50)

> Jesus, the son of Mary, said: "O Children of Israel! Behold, I am an apostle of God unto you, [sent] to confirm the truth of whatever there still remains of the Torah, and to give [you] the glad tiding of an apostle who shall come after me, whose name shall be Ahmad." (61:6)

> Think not that I have come to destroy the law or the prophets. I have not come to destroy, but to fulfill. For verily I say unto you: Until heaven and Earth pass, one jot or one tittle shall in no wise pass from the law, until all is fulfilled. (Matthew 5:17)

> And it is easier for Heaven and Earth to pass, than [for] one tittle of the law to fail. (Luke 16:17)

All of these verses clearly indicate that Jesus was sent to support the Torah, call people to its teachings, and, perhaps most importantly, explain to them how to implement those teachings in daily life. But Christian thought differed from Jewish thought on many matters, even if both traditions derived their concepts from the same source, perhaps due to Jesus's emphasis on reform in general, particularly on the rabbis' undue attention to the letter – rather than the spirit – of the scriptures. This was why he so often used parables in his attempt to help his people understand the Torah, which engaged both the hearts and minds of the believers.

In regard to divine sovereignty, however, the Christian understanding was based on the teachings of the Torah and the law derived therefrom. This is reflected in Jesus' reply to Pilate, when Pilate asked him:

> "Are you speaking to me? Do you not know that I have the power to either crucify or release you?" Jesus answered: "You have no power at all over me, except what has been given to you from above." (John 19:10-11)

The concept was further emphasized in Paul's letter to the Romans:

> For there is no power but that of God. The powers that be are ordained of God. (Romans 13:1)

In regard to the Qur'anic concept of divine authority, let us begin by considering the relevant verses:

> Not in my power is that which you so hastily demand. Rule rests with none but Allah. (6:57)
>
> For those who do not rule by what Allah has revealed, it is they who are truly iniquitous. (5:47)
>
> And on whatever you may differ, the ruling thereon rests with Allah. (42:10)
>
> But no, by your Lord, they are not truly believers unless they make you [O Prophet] a judge of all on that which they disagree and then find in their hearts no bar to accepting your decision and give themselves up to it in utter self-surrender. (4:65)

At the heart of Muhammad's mission was what Abraham specified in his prayer to God:

> O Lord! Raise up from the midst of our offspring a prophet from among themselves, who will convey to them Your messages, impart to them revelation and practical wisdom, and purify them. (2:129)

And then Allah answered:

> Allah bestowed a favor upon the believers when He raised up in their midst a prophet from among themselves to convey His messages to them, purify them, and impart to them the Book and practical wisdom – whereas before they were clearly lost in error. (3:164)

Prophet Muhammad was commanded to summarize his mission in the following terms:

> [Say, O Muhammad:] I have been commanded to worship the Lord of this city, He who has made it sacred, and unto whom all things belong. And I have been commanded to be of those who commit themselves to Him, and to recite the Qur'an to the world. (27:91)

When we consider the Prophet's life, we find that he acted as a leader, judge, ruler, advisor, and teacher. All of these roles were taken on as a part of his prophethood, rather than as the result of his having attained power. Given that his prophethood was instructional, nurturing, and purifying, he was not sent with the sword of domination or command.

At this point, we might do well to ponder how the Prophet ordered, on the night before he liberated Makkah, that bonfires be lit on all of the surrounding hills as a show of strength designed to quell any thoughts of resistance among the Makkans. On that night, Abū Sufyān, his long-time opponent, sought him out in the company of his uncle (ᶜAbbās) in order to announce his conversion and seek some gesture of honor. When Abū Sufyān saw the bonfires and realized how many followers the Prophet had, he said to ᶜAbbās: "Well, your nephew's kingdom has certainly grown vast!" ᶜAbbās replied: "This is prophethood, O Abū Sufyān, not kingship."

Clearly, ᶜAbbās understood the difference. To those around him, the Prophet emphasized repeatedly that he was not a potentate or a sultan. Once, for example, when a man began shaking with apprehension before him, he said: "Take it easy! I'm not a king. I'm only the son of a Qurayshi woman who used to eat dried meat [*qadīd*] (like you do)." In the same vein, the Prophet's prayer is well known: "O Allah! Let me live as a poor man and let me die as a poor man."

Thus, Muhammad's prophethood was predicated upon instruction, edification, recitation of the Qur'an and its teachings, and amelioration of the human condition. Under such circumstances, if he engaged in what seemed to be political matters, he did so out of instructional considerations. This is the difference between prophetic rule and all other forms of rule. Moreover, this was carried out after his death by his political successors, each of whom understood his fundamental role to include reciting the Qur'anic verses to the people, teaching them the meaning of its verses, instructing them how to apply the Qur'anic teachings (wisdom) in their daily life, and helping them to purify themselves. None of these aspects is related to the sort of authority derived solely from power.

In view of the foregoing, it is extremely difficult to propose that authority in Islam is a matter of power vested directly in God or wielded in His name, or in the name of the Shariᶜah, by the Prophet or his political successors. Rather, authority in Islam is bound irrevocably to education, edification, recitation, and purification; these, in turn, influence its exercise. It is interesting to consider the Prophet's words when he looked ahead to the Ummah's future: "*Khilāfah* will reign for 30 years. Thereafter, there will follow a period of gnashing monarchy." In other words, he differentiated between *khilāfah*, which followed the way of prophethood, and authority based on power and exercised under a certain name, slogan, or ideology.

In the Islamic understanding, then, there is prophethood and *khilāfah*, which follows in the way of prophethood. However, authority resides in the Qur'an, which is characterized by attributes not found in any of the earlier scriptures. For example, God guaranteed that its text will remain intact throughout history. In addition, it confirms all earlier scriptures and came as a guidance for all of humanity, its Shariᶜah is merciful and accommodating, and so much more. However, the important thing is that the Qur'an is to be understood and interpreted through a human reading, for its discourse is directed toward human beings. From this point, the entire matter of reading and interpretation comes into the picture, along with the idea of the "two readings" (reading of the texts in conjunction with a reading of the real-existential).[2]

Thus, whereas the concept of divine authority was understood by the earlier monotheistic traditions to involve God directly in human affairs, the Islamic understanding is that divine authority resides in His eternal message, the Qur'an, which is the Word of God:

> And upon you have We bestowed this reminder, so that you might make clear unto humanity all that has been revealed to them, so that they might take thought. (16:44)

> A Book We have revealed to you in order that you might bring forth all of humanity, by the permission of their Lord, out of the depths of darkness into the light, and onto the way that leads to the Almighty, the One to whom all praise is due. (14:1)

> We have revealed to you this Book to make everything clear, and to provide guidance, mercy, and glad tidings for all those who have committed themselves to Allah. (16:89)

Authority in Islam is the authority of the Qur'an; it is to be understood, and interpreted and then applied with wisdom by those who have committed themselves to it and to purifying themselves by means of it, each in accordance with their own cultural, geographical, economic, social, and historical circumstances.

As divine authority is vested in the Qur'an, Muslims are responsible for providing all of the guarantees demanded by the values shared by humanity in general, such as justice, truth, guardianship, and guidance. Moreover, this sort of authority is enhanced by many different dimensions, including the Shariʿah's universal and comprehensive nature and its basis in the texts of the Qur'an, which are open to all. Thus, the Qur'an may never become the exclusive domain of one group in the name of divine authority, owing solely to such people claiming to be the only ones capable of accessing and understanding it. Similarly, its authority is a liberating concept that empowers successive generations of Muslims to constantly renew their understanding of God's will for them and to order their affairs in a tractable manner:

> My mercy overspreads everything, and so I shall confer it on those who are conscious of Me and spend in charity, and who believe in Our messages – those who follow the Prophet, the unlettered one whom they find described in their Torah, and in the Injil; who will enjoin them to do what is right and forbid them to do what is wrong, and make lawful to them the good things in life and forbid them the bad things, and lift from them the burdens and the shackles that were upon them. (7:156-57)

In this Ummah, the one God intended to be the "middlemost" and whose message is intended to be the final message to humanity, the Qur'an is the final authority. Let me quote here from al-Shāṭibī:

> Thus, the Shariʿah [by which he means the Qur'an] is the absolute authority, over all, and over the Prophet, upon him be peace, and over all the believers. So the Book is the guide, and Revelation (*waḥy*) instructs in and clarifies that guidance, while all [members] of creation are the ones for whom that guidance is intended. So when the Prophet's heart and limbs, or his inner and outer being, were illumined by the light of the Truth, he became the Ummah's first and greatest guide, for Allah singled him out,

> to the exception of all others, to receive that clear light, having chosen him from among all of His creation. So Allah chose him, first of all, to receive the Revelation that lit up his inner and outer being, so that his character became, as it were, the Qur'an. This came about because the Prophet, upon him be peace, gave revelation authority over himself until his character was brought into accord with that revelation, into accord with the Qur'an. Thus, revelation was the authority and the standing speaker, while the Prophet, upon him be peace, submitted to that, answering its call, and standing by its authority. Then, if the matter was so, if the Shariᶜah was the authority over the Prophet, upon him be peace, or if the Qur'an was the authority, then all of humanity deserves to be subjects to the authority of the Qur'an.[3]

But, one may ask, how did so many contemporary Islamic movements acquire such mistaken understandings of divine authority? Why did they attempt, in its name, to vault into positions of political power and insist that Islam is based on this notion?

To begin with, the majority of these movements represent extensions of independence movements that began as attempted jihads against foreign colonialist powers. At the time, they brought everything under their power, including the entire intellectual and cultural heritage of the Ummah, to bear against the enemy by calling Muslims to the glory of the past. Even though very few of those movements actually accomplished what they set out to do, the colonialists left, new faces appeared, and national governments were established. At the time of their formation, however, the influence of western concepts was overwhelming, including ideas regarding nationalism, national governments, and the exercise of power. As a result, the new governments often bore little resemblance to the models of the Muslim past.

In such an atmosphere, Islamic movements began their internal struggles with the goal of achieving that for which so many of their predecessors in Algeria, Egypt, India, Iraq, and many other Islamic lands had given their lives. Moreover, the feeling among most participants was that the Ummah had fallen victim once again, but this time to its own people! Confronted with a state of dependency in economics, politics, thought, institutions, and even culture, the leaders of the Islamic movements turned again to the heritage of Islam in order to find the right sort of religious ideas and slogans with which to fire the masses' imaginations and oppose the ideologies and practices of their new rulers who, despite their Islamic names and the nominal Islamic trappings of their governments, differed little from their colonialist predecessors. Thus, the Islamists branded their opponents *jāhilī*, a designation for pre-Islamic pagans, and charged them with usurping the reins of power on the grounds that authority and sovereignty belonged only to God.

This is approximately what happened in Pakistan, where the Islamist leadership, especially Abū al-ʿAlā al-Mawdūdī, was quite vocal in its espousal of the dualist *jāhilī* versus divine authority equation. As a state formed in the name of Islam, and as a homeland for India's Muslim minority, the popular vision of Pakistan was that it would be an Islamic state. Therefore, it was only natural that when the debate over the form and legitimacy of its government began, the heavily loaded terms of *jāhilī* and *God's sovereignty* quickly gained wide circulation.

Looking at Egypt, we note that while its experience differed significantly from Pakistan's, there are many similarities between the two. For example, in both instances the Islamists were among the first to organize the populace against the colonialists. In Egypt, the Islamists played major roles in the ʿUrabī Pasha uprising, in the revolution of 1919, and in every resistance movement thereafter, including the attempt to rid the Suez Canal of its 70,000 British "protectors" and liberate Palestine. With all of these in mind, the Islamists fully expected their countrymen to recognize their rights and acknowledge their long and arduous struggle. So when the army officers moved to abolish the monarchy, it was the Islamists who undertook to quell the populace. At that time, it was well known that without the support and assistance of the Islamists (the Muslim Brotherhood), the revolution would never have succeeded. Even so, within a few short months the revolutionaries denounced their Islamist associates and broke their agreements with them. Yet in order to appease the masses and appeal to their Islamic loyalties, the revolutionaries were careful to pay lip service to Islam. However, they acted quickly to neutralize their former allies' influence by subjecting them to the worst sort of persecution.

From their prison cells, their places of secure detention, and their places of exile, the Islamists retaliated in the only way they knew: turning to Islam's cultural and intellectual heritage and pointing out to the masses how their new leadership had not only betrayed the Islamists, but also Islam itself and the Muslim masses. This message was conveyed in the studies and writings of several of the movement's most prominent thinkers, among them ʿAbd al-Qādir ʿAwdah, who wrote on legal and political systems, and Sayyid Quṭb, who used the emotive term *jāhilī* to refer to the revolutionary leadership. In addition, he cited Qur'anic verses that branded those who do not rule by the Shariʿah (as the ordered expression of Divine revelation) as unbelievers.[4]

In fact, Sayyid Quṭb dealt at length with the terms *jāhiliyyah* (pre-Islamic paganism) and *ḥākimiyyah* (authority). In his later works, his discussions of authority took on added importance due to his opinion that the people and parties that had come into power after independence throughout the Muslim world had wrongly assumed for themselves the right of authority that belonged to God alone. In Quṭb's opinion, no person had the right to claim legitimacy for his/her rule unless that rule was based on God's authority.[5] But he did not elaborate on the details of how a government based on God's authority would actually function, probably because his purpose was merely to bring it to the Ummah's attention and demonstrate that its rulers had failed to achieve their proclaimed post-independence goals.

Quṭb developed the concept of authority to a level of high sophistication. According to him, the creedal phrase "There is no god but God" included the meanings that God is the sole authority and that all power belongs to Him alone.[6] However, he did not differentiate between the meaning of Allah's authority as it pertained to the political sphere, for example, or to the sphere of the natural universe or to the legal sphere. Thus, both Quṭb and al-Mawdūdī attempted to show divine and human authority as being in opposition to each other. Just as al-Mawdūdī negated any role for either individuals or groups in the matter of authority, other than "hearing and obeying," Quṭb did the same for the reason that God is the sole authority.

Owing to the influence of these two thinkers and activists, the concept of divine authority came to be understood in Islamist circles in almost the same way it had been understood in the days of Moses: God would establish a state of His own, with His own laws and procedures that, having originated with the divine, are sacred and inseparable from belief and the details of the articles of faith. In such a system, there is no difference between what belongs to this world and to the Hereafter, and nothing to separate what is "civil" from what is "religious" or otherwise. This popular perception persisted, despite the attempts of others to explain, within the same general framework, the role of people involved in understanding and interpreting existing realities through ijtihad. In addition, many commentators and other people attempted to deal with such concepts as the state, government, and legitimacy by reading the Qur'an and the hadiths and studying history, and then transposing these contemporary meanings onto the texts of the Qur'an and Sunnah. As a result of such activity, they so distorted these concepts that a great deal of analysis and reconstruction will be required before any clear understanding can be achieved.

In order to clarify the concept of divine authority, it is necessary to consider a few fundamental matters. From their beginnings, the message and the discourse of Islam were universal: "We have not sent you [O Muhammad] otherwise than to humanity at large, to be a herald of good tidings and a warner" (34:28).

The message's attribute of universality means that it can appeal to everyone, whether Asians, Africans, Europeans, or Americans; answer their needs throughout history; and guide them to success in this world and the Hereafter. Even though Muslims may find themselves in a most difficult position, they should never attempt to transform Islam or its concepts into weapons or a means of overthrowing, because Islam, as the religion of God, is meant for humanity at large.

Furthermore, even though the Qur'an may have been revealed in Arabic, its meanings are universal and comprehensive. The Qur'an's relationship to the circumstances in which it was revealed, moreover, is of the nature of the relationship between the absolute and the relative, or of the unlimited to the limited. Finally, while its verses are limited, in a lexical sense, their meanings are unlimited and discernible through an understanding of its structural integrity and unique intellectual methodology.

As we move from these theological truths, insofar as they may be described as objective scientific postulates in support of Islam's eternal and universal message, we notice that several of its special characteristics are so self-evident that we never paid much attention to their methodological consequences. Among these are the concepts of prophethood's finality (*khatam al-nubūwah*), the principles of legal facilitation and mercy, and the Qur'an's absolute authority regardless of time or place.

Thus, while the Qur'anic discourse begins by addressing the simplest family unit: "We said: 'O Adam. Inhabit, you and your wife, the garden of Paradise" (2:35), then the extended family: "and warn your closest kinfolk" (26:214), then address the tribe: "O Children of Israel. Remember those blessings of Mine with which I favored you" (2:40) and "... verily it [the Qur'an] shall be a reminder to you and to your tribe" (43:44), and then an entity larger than just a single tribe: "... in order that you may warn the mother of all cities and those living around it" (42:7).

Thereafter, the discourse progresses to include those beyond the family and the tribe: "He has sent unto the unlettered people an apostle from among themselves" (62:2), in which the meaning of "unlettered people" is all those who had never received a revelation before. Consider what al-Shāfiʿī wrote in his *Risālah*: "He sent him (i.e., Allah sent the Prophet) at a time when people were divided into two categories."

One of these groups was the People of the Book, who had altered its laws, rejected belief in God, engaged in lying, and mixed falsehood with the truth that God had revealed to them. After that, Allah mentioned to His Prophet some of their unbelief, saying:

> "And indeed there are some among them who distort the scriptures with their tongues, so as to make you think that [what they say] is from the scriptures, when it is not from the scriptures; and who say: 'This is from Allah,' when it is not from Allah. Thus do they speak falsehoods about Allah, even when they know [otherwise]." (3:78)

> Woe unto those who write down with their own hands, [something they claim to be] divine scripture, and then say: "This is from Allah," in order to acquire a trifling gain thereby. Woe, then, unto them for what their hands have written, and woe unto them for all that they may have gained. (2:79)

> And the Jews say: "Ezra is Allah's son," while the Christians say: "The Christ is Allah's son." Such are the sayings that they utter with their mouths, following in spirit [those] assertions made in earlier times by people who denied the truth. (They deserve the imprecation) May Allah destroy them! How perverted are their minds. They have taken their rabbis and their monks – as well as the Christ, son of Mary – for their lords beside Allah. (9:30-31)

> Are you not aware of those who, having been granted their share of the divine scriptures, believe now in baseless mysteries and in the powers of evil, and maintain that those who deny the truth are more surely guided than those who believe? It is they whom Allah has rejected, and he whom Allah rejects shall find none to succor him. (4:51-52)

The other category was the group that rejected belief in Allah and created that which Allah did not allow. With their own hands, they raised stones and wood and images that pleased them, gave them names that they made up themselves, proclaimed them to be deities, and then worshipped them. When they found something that was more pleasing to them as an object of worship, they discarded what they had been worshipping, raised up the new objects of worship with their own hands, and began worshipping them! Those were the Arabs! A group of non-Arabs followed the same path, worshipping whatever they found pleasing, be it a whale, an animal, a star, fire, or whatever. God related to Muhammad one of the answers given by those who did not worship Him: "Behold, we found our forefathers agreed on what to believe – and, verily, it is in their footsteps that we find our guidance" (43:22). And He quoted them: "[And they say to each other:] Never abandon your deities, neither Wadd nor Suwā', nor Yaghūth, Yaʿūq, or Nasr" (71:23).[7]

The Prophet did not die until he extended the divine discourse beyond the family, the tribe, and the nation to encompass humanity and until the following verses were revealed:

> He sent His Prophet with guidance and the religion of truth, with the goal that He may cause it to prevail over all [false] religion. (9:33; 61:9)

> He sent His Prophet with guidance and the religion of truth, with the goal that He make it to prevail over every [false] religion. None can bear witness [to the truth] as Allah does. (48:28)

Thus, in a historical sense, the divine discourse was revealed gradually and within differing legislative circumstances, each of which had its own particular features. Likewise, each prophet faced his own special circumstances. This is why God gave each one of them a different legal system and way of life. As the Qur'an states: "Unto every one have We appointed from you a law and a way of life" (5:48).

This verse alerts us to the importance of comparing religious legal systems to our own, as these pertain to the differing circumstances of those who believe. Finally, when we come to the Qur'an and its universal message, we discover that its legal system is one of facilitation and mercy for humanity, one designed to bring all people together within the framework of shared values and concepts.

> Those who follow the Messenger, the unlettered Prophet whom they find described in their Torah, and in the Injil; the Prophet who will enjoin on them to do what is right and forbid them to do what is wrong, and make lawful for them the good things of life and forbid them the bad things, and lift from them the burdens and the shackles that were upon them. Those, then, who believe in Him, honor Him, assist Him, and follow the light bestowed through him – it is they that shall attain success. (7:157)

Therefore, it is very important that those of us within Islamic circles realize that we are face to face with a divine discourse that has progressed in stages until, at last, it is now directed toward humanity at large. Accordingly, it is no longer possible to understand the concept of divine authority as it was understood in previous religious traditions. The popular understanding of this concept by Muslims today has been colored by attempts to counter western concepts of authority, government, and legitimacy by taking Qur'anic concepts out of context and ignoring the Qur'an's structural integrity, universality, and the true significance of prophethood's finality.

Thus, in the concept of Qur'anic authority we may discern the responsibility of individuals to read and understand and then to interpret and apply. As for divine authority, however, the individual is no more than a recipient whose only responsibility is to adhere to whatever he/she has been given. The Qur'an's authority is like human authority in the sense that it functions through a human reading of the Qur'an and a subsequent human application of its teachings, regardless of the cultural, intellectual, or other circumstances forming the context of that reading and application.

If contemporary Islamic thought is able to correct its own mistakes, then, God willing, it will not remain dormant or be destined to revolve endlessly within the confines of its own history, unable to solve its own problems. Many of those problems are related to concepts of legislation, the meanings of power and society, the relationship of the revealed texts to changing social and historical circumstances, and to concepts of deference to traditional authority (*taqlīd*), renewal, and reform. If Muslims become serious about their responsibility to deal with these issues in the name of God, Who created and taught humanity by means of the pen that which it did not know, they will begin to contribute to the building of a new and better world, and thereby bring about the objectives of the truth for all of creation.

NOTES

1. See Muhammad Asad's explanation of the phrase *li mā bayna yadayhi* at note 3 in Qur'an 3:3. Muhammad Asad. *The Message of the Qur'an* (Gibraltar: Dār al-Andalus, 1984), 65-66.
2. See the author's "The Islamization of Knowledge: Yesterday and Today," *The American Journal of Islamic Social Sciences* 12, vol. 1 (spring 1995): 81-104.
3. Abū Isḥāq al-Shāṭibī, *Kitāb al-Iʿtiṣām*, 2:328.
4. See Qur'an 5:47.

5. See, in particular, Sayyid Quṭb's *Maʿālim fī al-Ṭarīq* and his *Muqawwimāt al-Mujtamaʿ al-Islāmī.*
6. By doing so, the further implication is that those who fail to give God His due in this matter are guilty of a form of *shirk*, which is clearly disbelief – and the worst sort of disbelief at that.
7. Imām al-Shāfiʿī, *Al-Risālah* (Cairo: Ḥalabī, 1940), 8.

Index

Abbasids, 200
Abū Ḥanīfah, 82, 100, 101, 104, 113, 115, 124, 125, 144, 172, 180, 200, 204, 213, 218, 225
accusation, 202, 203, 204, 207, 208, 210, 212, 217, 221, 223
Age of Enlightenment, 87
amānah, 6, 30, 72
Association of Muslim Scientists and Engineers (AMSE), 24
Association of Muslim Social Scientists (AMSS), 24
analogy, 88, 132, 138, 198
arts, 4, 15, 18, 19, 54, 55, 60
authority, ii, 3, 27, 31, 39, 43, 48, 73, 76, 88, 90, 91, 93, 107, 109, 115, 134, 169, 170, 176, 178, 200, 201, 202, 204, 206, 207, 208, 210, 217, 241, 243, 249, 254, 256, 258, 273, 278, 279, 280, 281, 282, 283, 285, 286, 287, 288, 289, 290, 293

behavioral sciences, 49, 58, 59
belief, 5, 6, 17, 22, 31, 32, 36, 51, 70, 76, 78, 80, 103, 124, 127, 162, 187, 192, 240, 244, 255, 256, 258, 259, 260, 273, 289, 291
bidʿah, 72, 80
building, ii, 14, 25, 30, 59, 88, 131, 134, 135, 148, 155, 156, 183, 190, 264, 278, 293

capitalism, 47, 135
capitalist, 55, 267, 274
cause and effect, 32, 34, 53, 54, 140, 259, 272
choice, 23, 115, 129, 132, 138, 139, 140, 141, 142, 143, 153, 166, 214, 216, 220, 262
Christianity, 60, 73, 87, 155, 190, 231, 263, 264
citizen(s), 77, 188, 189, 191, 224, 264
civilization, ii, 8, 9, 10, 13, 14, 15, 18, 19, 21, 22, 23, 24, 28, 29, 33, 34, 38, 39, 44, 45, 47, 53, 55, 58, 60, 65, 66, 67, 71, 72, 83, 89, 94, 117, 122, 124, 131, 134, 142, 147, 148, 155, 156, 188, 190, 191, 193, 194, 229, 232, 237, 238, 244, 245, 246, 260, 261, 262, 264, 265, 267, 269, 270, 274, 275, 276, 277
classification, 10, 19, 56, 275, 280
colonialism, 55, 265
commentary, 4, 81, 128, 169, 171, 186, 211, 225
communism, 47, 144
Companions, 39, 49, 51, 70, 76, 98, 99, 100, 101, 102, 103, 104, 111, 112, 118, 173, 175, 176, 178, 189, 197, 220, 222
confession, 197, 215, 216, 217, 218, 219, 220, 221, 222, 224
consensus, 102, 103, 111, 112, 121, 132, 134, 234
consultation, 4, 124, 239
contemporary thought, 10, 11, 19, 33, 36, 85
creativity, ii, 4, 11, 65, 68, 152, 190, 242, 255
cultural strategy, 15, 17
culture, i, 9, 10, 12, 13, 15, 19, 21, 22, 23, 24, 27, 33, 37, 39, 55, 67, 83, 86,

92, 114, 122, 125, 165, 168, 179, 187, 189, 193, 230, 239, 245, 266, 267, 269, 275, 287

decline, 10, 18, 22, 36, 56, 71, 93, 111, 112, 113, 114, 117, 119, 242, 243, 245, 266, 267
deduction, 4, 234, 244, 245
democracy, 4, 188, 189, 192, 193, 239
destiny, 23, 30, 78, 236, 259, 267, 276, 278
detention, 204, 205, 206, 207, 209, 288
deviation, 14, 52, 66, 72, 76, 243
dhimmī, 189
dialectical materialism, 31, 33
dignity, 8, 14, 109, 148, 224, 232, 258, 273
discourse, 27, 35, 37, 38, 136, 137, 163, 235, 241, 256, 257, 258, 260, 261, 262, 266, 272, 273, 278, 280, 285, 290, 292
door of ijtihad, 11, 82, 87, 88, 93, 108, 113, 120, 121, 122, 123, 124, 127, 128

education, ii, 4, 12, 14, 15, 17, 18, 19, 25, 50, 53, 54, 56, 59, 90, 125, 162, 178, 285
educational strategy, 19
elitism, 8
empiricism, 246
equality, 164, 165, 166, 167, 168, 169, 170, 171, 177, 178, 179, 182, 184, 193
ethics, ii, 7, 23, 69, 129, 131, 138, 139, 142, 143, 147, 151, 153, 245, 267
evidence, ii, 7, 16, 53, 58, 72, 73, 74, 75, 76, 77, 86, 99, 100, 101, 102, 103, 105, 121, 133, 134, 166, 169, 170, 182, 185, 197, 198, 202, 204, 205, 207, 208, 209, 210, 212, 213, 214, 215, 217, 219, 220, 221, 225, 233, 268
evil, 51, 75, 81, 89, 99, 131, 134, 137, 140, 141, 145, 148, 152, 153, 154, 156, 157, 163, 216, 218, 219, 231, 232, 241, 260, 276, 291
existence, 9, 21, 29, 31, 32, 34, 42, 45, 47, 51, 54, 56, 72, 73, 83, 124, 131, 141, 143, 148, 154, 173, 177, 196, 236, 246
experience, iii, 5, 22, 42, 50, 84, 94, 162, 172, 181, 182, 230, 231, 233, 246, 252, 270, 274, 277, 288

fables, 15
factionalism, 12, 254
faith, 22, 30, 31, 32, 34, 35, 36, 45, 47, 52, 72, 75, 111, 112, 146, 148, 163, 164, 171, 176, 194, 196, 207, 208, 211, 216, 257, 258, 266, 289
faqīh, 86, 87, 90, 110, 119, 147
fatalism, 78
fate, 23, 53, 117
fatwa(s), 40, 88, 99, 103, 104, 109, 110, 121, 123, 127, 133, 146, 147, 157, 218, 273
fiqh, 4, 52, 56, 65, 66, 79, 82, 86, 88, 89, 90, 92, 94, 108, 109, 110, 111, 112, 113, 114, 115, 116, 117, 118, 119, 120, 121, 122, 124, 125, 126, 127, 128, 129, 130, 131, 132, 133, 134, 136, 137, 147, 151, 152, 153, 156, 171, 172, 183, 229, 230, 232, 233, 234, 251, 263, 273, 277
fiṭrah (also see inherent nature), 6, 50, 58, 72, 241
follower, 99, 255
forgiveness, 217, 223
free will, 32, 53, 220, 260
freedom, i, 4, 12, 67, 106, 114, 122, 148, 189, 191, 192, 204, 205, 206, 211, 216, 262, 266, 268
fundamentalism, 269
fundamentalist(s), 27, 192, 270

gender equality, 164, 165, 167, 169, 171, 177, 178, 179, 184
guidance, ii, 6, 12, 23, 38, 45, 71, 72, 73, 147, 157, 236, 237, 253, 261, 265, 267, 281, 285, 286, 292

guilt, 52, 216, 217, 218, 219, 220

happiness, 139, 140, 148, 154, 155, 278
higher purposes, 6, 36, 39, 41, 84, 88, 93, 110, 210, 281
human life, 8, 30, 39, 44, 47
human nature, 6, 57, 58, 196
human rights, i, ii, 23, 191
humanities, 15, 19, 27, 29, 35, 49, 54, 56, 57, 59, 60, 69, 231, 240
humanity, i, 3, 4, 5, 6, 7, 8, 9, 14, 15, 16, 17, 19, 21, 22, 23, 28, 29, 30, 32, 33, 34, 35, 38, 43, 46, 47, 50, 53, 54, 55, 57, 58, 59, 70, 72, 74, 75, 81, 83, 86, 90, 91, 117, 122, 125, 131, 134, 135, 144, 146, 148, 152, 156, 157, 161, 165, 171, 177, 190, 205, 207, 223, 229, 232, 233, 235, 236, 237, 244, 245, 248, 250, 258, 259, 260, 261, 262, 264, 265, 266, 267, 268, 269, 271, 272, 273, 274, 275, 276, 278, 279, 281, 285, 286, 287, 290, 292, 293

Ibn Ḥanbal, 82, 100, 104
idolatry, 31, 40, 70, 73, 147, 164, 276
ignorance, 6, 24, 66, 71, 103, 107, 119, 141, 163, 166, 171, 255, 276
International Institute of Islamic Thought (IIIT), iii, 20, 24, 25, 47, 49, 57, 95, 96, 176, 194, 195, 239, 240, 246, 251, 252, 279
ijmāʿ,102, 103, 111, 112, 132, 215, 219, 234
imāmah, 281
īmān, 51, 52, 60
imprisonment, 206, 207, 215
inherent nature (also see *fiṭrah*), 50
innocence, 204, 205, 215, 222
innovation, 72, 80, 216
inquiry, 7, 26, 79, 115, 208, 246, 280
insight, 18, 99, 133, 271
intellectual activity, 6, 11, 122, 244
intellectual life, 9, 88, 173
intelligence, 5, 75, 152, 274
interest, 24, 34, 76, 98, 109, 115, 118, 139, 144, 145, 151, 157, 177, 201, 236, 260, 268, 273
intuition, 5, 246
Islamic Educational, Scientific, and Cultural Organization (ISESCO), 20
Islamic economics, 25, 130, 139, 140, 143, 146, 148, 156
Islamic knowledge, 18
Islamic legacy, 19, 55, 84, 239, 271
Islamic paradigm of knowledge, 4, 5, 6, 7, 26, 37
Islamic thought, 24, 49, 54, 57, 58, 85, 92, 144, 188, 194, 251, 293
Islamist(s), 27, 188, 193, 194, 287, 288, 289
Islamization of Knowledge, i, ii, 4, 21, 22, 23, 24, 26, 27, 28, 29, 30, 32, 33, 35, 36, 38, 42, 43, 44, 45, 46, 47, 56, 57, 58, 60, 83, 84, 95, 126, 248, 249, 250, 252, 271, 293

jabr, 78
jihad, 66, 67, 95, 142, 144, 175, 233
Judaism, 60, 190, 263, 264
jurisprudence, ii, 4, 65, 110, 122, 147, 181, 194, 243, 251, 257, 273, 277

khilāfah, 4, 6, 66, 82, 109, 232, 240, 242, 285
knowledge, i, 4, 5, 6, 7, 8, 9, 10, 11, 15, 16, 17, 18, 19, 21, 24, 26, 27, 28, 29, 30, 31, 33, 34, 35, 36, 37, 39, 42, 44, 45, 46, 50, 54, 55, 56, 57, 58, 59, 66, 68, 69, 71, 72, 74, 75, 76, 77, 83, 84, 85, 88, 89, 90, 94, 98, 99, 100, 102, 103, 104, 105, 106, 109, 116, 131, 132, 135, 136, 147, 153, 156, 170, 172, 180, 190, 194, 211, 229, 230, 231, 232, 237, 241, 247, 248, 250, 251, 254, 255, 258, 259, 261
kufr, 42, 74, 138

law, ii, 11, 31, 59, 68, 90, 105, 106, 118, 124, 127, 133, 134, 144, 153, 156,

168, 179, 189, 193, 203, 212, 213, 214, 215, 216, 220, 234, 241, 272, 282, 283, 292
liberalism, 35, 46, 267
logic, 29, 43, 46, 78, 166, 176, 188, 245, 246, 248, 249, 251, 270, 272, 275

madhhab, 77, 78, 86, 97, 101, 106, 110, 113, 114, 115, 116, 117, 119, 120, 123, 127
al-Mālik, 98, 125, 229
Marxism, 33, 47, 157, 191, 274, 275
Marxist(s), 14, 27, 146
mental slavery, 70
method, 14, 15, 28, 45, 71, 80, 125, 129, 133, 174, 182, 192, 214, 220, 238, 245
methodology, 5, 6, 7, 26, 33, 35, 36, 37, 38, 39, 40, 41, 42, 44, 46, 47, 49, 50, 57, 58, 59, 60, 65, 66, 70, 73, 83, 84, 85, 86, 88, 90, 94, 120, 130, 132, 134, 135, 138, 139, 147, 172, 173, 175, 176, 183, 188, 230, 237, 240, 241, 243, 247, 249, 250, 251, 257, 258, 259, 261, 262, 269, 271, 272, 275, 277, 279, 290
minhāj, 71, 72
modernism, 11, 46, 85
modernity, 34, 87, 130
monotheism, 269
mujtahid(ūn), 67, 68, 76, 84, 86, 90, 103, 111, 112, 113, 119, 121, 122, 123, 124, 125, 128, 132, 133, 137, 279
muqallid, 74, 86, 99, 100, 101, 102, 128
Muslim mind, 4, 14, 21, 22, 23, 28, 36, 37, 38, 41, 42, 52, 54, 56, 58, 65, 66, 67, 71, 72, 73, 77, 91, 93, 118, 119, 121, 123, 174, 175, 194, 229, 233, 240, 261, 262, 266, 273, 274
Muslim thought, iii, 13, 23
mysticism, 34, 35, 44
myth, 3, 157

nafs, 140, 141, 142, 143, 153, 154, 230
nationalism, 12, 188, 189, 192, 267, 273, 287
natural sciences, 29, 42, 43, 46, 59, 69, 176, 246, 249, 250, 252, 269, 271, 274
naturalization, 187, 188, 193
non-Muslims, 22, 32, 44, 71, 74, 76, 79, 189, 192, 194, 240, 265

obligations, 232
oneness, 7, 177, 232
Orientalists, 67, 79, 276
Ottoman Empire, 114, 116, 187, 262
Ottomans, 114, 115, 126, 138

pagan, 65, 165, 166, 168, 177, 178, 185, 188, 260, 264
paganism, 289
partisanship, 79, 114, 256
philosopher, 22, 117, 267
philosophy, i, 10, 15, 22, 28, 31, 37, 46, 53, 54, 60, 155, 191, 246, 250, 254, 268, 270, 273
politics, 54, 59, 69, 91, 125, 187, 219, 229, 232, 233, 234, 287
polytheism, 264
positivism, 3, 4, 34, 35, 42, 45, 46, 267
power, 5, 8, 13, 15, 27, 35, 51, 52, 78, 109, 113, 114, 135, 138, 191, 202, 206, 229, 231, 240, 245, 256, 260, 262, 264, 265, 269, 270, 272, 273, 283, 284, 285, 287, 288, 289, 293
predetermination, 32
privacy, 208, 209
progress, 3, 12, 33, 34, 42, 61, 70, 87, 117, 123, 171, 175, 184, 190, 194, 200, 231, 267, 273
prophethood, 39, 134, 258, 284, 285, 290, 293
punishment, 52, 199, 201, 204, 212, 213, 214, 216, 218, 220, 221, 222, 225
purification, 125, 131, 134, 156, 285

qadar, 51, 52
qadr, 23

rationalists, 88, 250
reading of the natural universe, 31, 32
reading of the real-existential, 33, 34, 35, 46, 285
real-existent, 32, 33, 34, 35, 38, 39, 40, 45, 46, 184, 285
real-existential, 32, 33, 34, 35, 38, 39, 40, 46, 184, 285
reason, i, 3, 5, 14, 15, 16, 21, 23, 25, 33, 43, 52, 53, 56, 66, 69, 72, 74, 75, 93, 94, 101, 103, 119, 121, 123, 141, 151, 155, 161, 165, 176, 180, 193, 202, 206, 207, 209, 211, 212, 216, 218, 219, 222, 231, 241, 249, 259, 289
reform, i, ii, 3, 26, 28, 41, 49, 51, 67, 70, 71, 72, 80, 113, 118, 124, 164, 235, 238, 240, 244, 251, 252, 254, 255, 266, 270, 273, 281, 283, 293
relativism, 152
religion, i, 3, 15, 17, 30, 32, 34, 43, 54, 73, 74, 84, 85, 91, 94, 99, 100, 109, 124, 126, 137, 153, 155, 167, 179, 180, 182, 189, 190, 192, 203, 215, 231, 236, 237, 263, 265, 267, 270, 276, 281, 290, 292
Renaissance, 87, 89, 117
responsibility, 6, 8, 24, 44, 57, 67, 79, 81, 97, 103, 105, 121, 122, 137, 149, 162, 167, 197, 198, 201, 206, 216, 223, 229, 237, 260, 266, 278, 293
revelation, 5, 7, 14, 15, 16, 21, 23, 29, 30, 32, 33, 34, 35, 38, 39, 40, 41, 42, 43, 45, 46, 47, 50, 52, 53, 59, 69, 73, 74, 75, 76, 94, 121, 137, 152, 155, 162, 163, 164, 166, 168, 175, 231, 232, 237, 243, 244, 246, 247, 258, 259, 272, 283, 287, 289, 291
revival, i, iii, 24, 80, 83, 87
rights, i, ii, 23, 89, 148, 170, 171, 180, 188, 189, 191, 197, 200, 201, 203, 205, 206, 210, 212, 214, 215, 217, 221, 223, 224, 233, 288
rūḥ, 141, 142, 143, 154

Ṣaḥābah (also see Companions), 51
scholar(s), i, ii, iii, 6, 11, 14, 18, 20, 24, 25, 27, 28, 29, 38, 46, 47, 55, 57, 58, 60, 66, 67, 68, 69, 72, 74, 76, 77, 78, 79, 81, 82, 84, 85, 88, 89, 90, 91, 92, 93, 94, 98, 99, 100, 101, 102, 103, 104, 105, 106, 107, 108, 109, 110, 111, 112, 113, 114, 116, 118, 119, 120, 121, 122, 123, 124, 125, 126, 129, 132, 133, 137, 138, 151, 152, 153, 154, 155, 156, 162, 165, 166, 169, 171, 172, 173, 174, 175, 176, 181, 183, 184, 185, 190, 194, 204, 206, 207, 209, 213, 217, 218, 219, 222, 229, 230, 232, 233, 234, 250, 251, 252, 254, 256, 271, 277, 278
scholarship, ii, 25, 27, 37, 46, 83, 84, 109, 116, 184, 194
science, 11, 15, 18, 23, 24, 27, 28, 33, 34, 35, 42, 43, 44, 75, 85, 105, 129, 133, 229, 230, 231, 233, 238, 246, 250, 251, 261, 269, 273, 274, 277, 280
scientific knowledge, 15, 16, 230, 261
scientific method, 33, 84, 182, 238, 262, 271
sectarianism, 25, 173, 177, 243
secularism, 3, 17, 87, 93, 122, 189, 192
secularist(s), 3, 27, 87, 93, 187, 188, 190, 192, 193, 194, 243, 270, 274
seen world, 16
self-awareness, 18
self-defense, 212
self-discovery, 26
senses, 5, 16, 21, 69, 72, 75, 232
shirk, 31, 73, 294
al-Shāfiʿī, 82, 95, 100, 104, 106, 125, 185, 200, 277, 291, 294
shūrā, 4, 23, 91, 124, 125, 232, 233, 239
six discourses, 29, 42
slavery, 70, 137, 138, 171, 264
social science(s), 15, 19, 23, 24, 27, 29, 35, 39, 43, 44, 46, 49, 54, 55, 56, 57, 58, 59, 60, 69, 88, 94, 126, 132, 133, 190, 229, 230, 231, 246, 271

socialism, 4, 135, 239
soul, 7, 12, 15, 58, 115, 140, 141, 148, 171, 242
speculation, 7, 46, 115, 151
spirit, 18, 75, 94, 98, 115, 129, 141, 177, 214, 233, 250, 255, 263, 283, 291
stagnation, 92, 110, 171, 237, 246, 262, 266
stewardship, 4, 29, 31, 34, 46
Successor Generation (also see Tābiʿūn), 98, 99, 109
Sunnah, 5, 12, 16, 19, 32, 35, 39, 40, 41, 58, 67, 70, 74, 78, 89, 100, 101, 103, 104, 106, 108, 111, 112, 117, 118, 119, 121, 126, 127, 132, 133, 134, 136, 147, 151, 152, 153, 168, 169, 170, 171, 172, 173, 174, 176, 177, 183, 184, 185, 189, 193, 198, 209, 210, 215, 216, 219, 220, 230, 234, 240, 242, 243, 244, 245, 248, 252, 253, 257, 271, 277, 278, 289
superstition, 3, 52, 54, 66
suspicion, 46, 202, 206, 208, 209, 219, 262

Tābiʿūn (also see Successor Generation), 51, 76, 98, 99, 100, 102, 104, 109
tafsīr, 4, 38, 126, 133, 251
tawakkul, 52
tawḥīd, 5, 7, 8, 29, 35, 36, 40, 65, 71, 72, 123, 131, 134, 139, 147, 148, 152, 154, 156, 237, 250, 264, 268, 269, 281
tazkiyah, 131, 134, 139, 147, 148, 152, 154, 155, 156
technology, 19, 24, 117, 149, 245, 266, 274, 276
testimony, ii, 70, 72, 102, 103, 119, 161, 162, 165, 166, 167, 168, 169, 172, 179, 180, 181, 182, 184, 185, 197, 203, 236
theologians, 52, 82, 105
theology, 34, 35, 36, 42, 53, 113, 123, 124, 268, 269, 270
thought, i, iii, 3, 5, 9, 10, 11, 13, 14, 18, 19, 21, 23, 24, 28, 32, 33, 34, 36, 42, 43, 44, 45, 49, 50, 51, 52, 54, 55, 56, 57, 58, 59, 60, 65, 66, 67, 71, 78, 79, 80, 83, 85, 86, 87, 88, 91, 92, 106, 110, 111, 112, 113, 114, 117, 118, 119, 120, 123, 125, 129, 130, 132, 134, 137, 139, 144, 146, 168, 187, 188, 189, 190, 191, 192, 193, 194, 200, 217, 225, 229, 230, 231, 233, 235, 236, 240, 245, 246, 248, 251, 252, 253, 255, 257, 258, 259, 262, 267, 268, 269, 270, 273, 274, 275, 277, 281, 282, 285, 287, 293
time, 3, 6, 7, 11, 12, 15, 18, 26, 27, 28, 34, 36, 38, 39, 40, 41, 42, 43, 44, 46, 49, 52, 53, 55, 58, 60, 66, 69, 76, 77, 81, 87, 88, 90, 92, 95, 104, 105, 108, 109, 110, 111, 112, 115, 117, 118, 119, 121, 123, 126, 128, 132, 134, 135, 136, 137, 138, 140, 142, 147, 149, 151, 152, 153, 161, 162, 164, 165, 168, 171, 172, 177, 182, 189, 191, 193, 194, 197, 198, 201, 207, 208, 215, 230, 231, 233, 241, 242, 243, 244, 246, 254, 258, 259, 260, 261, 262, 263, 264, 269, 271, 273, 277, 280, 284, 287, 288, 290, 291
tradition, 4, 18, 38, 65, 138, 168, 230, 249, 251, 257, 262
traditionalism, 85
traditionists, 88

ʿulamāʾ , 54, 76, 77, 78, 116, 126, 130, 171
Umayyads, 199
ʿumrān, 131, 134, 139, 147, 148, 152, 155, 156
unbelief, 42, 74, 216, 291
unicity, 5, 177
unity, 5, 8, 56, 65, 71, 124, 134, 187, 239, 243, 247, 252, 253, 259, 263, 266, 271, 273, 276, 280
universalism, 239, 262, 263, 264, 265, 272, 273, 274, 276
universe, 4, 5, 7, 14, 15, 16, 17, 28, 29, 30, 31, 32, 33, 34, 36, 43, 47, 49, 51,

53, 54, 55, 57, 58, 72, 74, 86, 117, 164, 175, 176, 177, 232, 236, 245, 246, 247, 248, 250, 256, 258, 259, 275, 279, 282, 289
unseen world, 16
utility, 6, 42, 139, 140, 141, 142, 143, 144, 148, 154, 155, 156

values, i, ii, 5, 6, 8, 15, 18, 19, 21, 23, 29, 32, 35, 39, 45, 46, 56, 57, 74, 83, 129, 130, 131, 134, 135, 138, 139, 140, 142, 143, 148, 170, 189, 229, 230, 232, 245, 262, 265, 267, 276, 277, 281, 286, 292
vicegerency, 4, 66, 177, 229, 232, 258, 279
vicegerent, 58, 72, 81, 85, 122, 146, 235, 236, 276, 279

waḥy, 12, 21, 74, 94, 232, 286
western thought, 9, 10, 14, 15, 19, 42, 59, 187, 191, 194, 230, 269, 274
worship, 4, 16, 32, 40, 46, 47, 73, 109, 125, 140, 145, 177, 197, 236, 240, 258, 280, 282, 284, 291, 292